LIZARDI AND THE BIRTH OF THE NOVEL IN SPANISH AMERICA

Florida A&M University, Tallahassee
Florida Atlantic University, Boca Raton
Florida Gulf Coast University, Ft. Myers
Florida International University, Miami
Florida State University, Tallahassee
University of Central Florida, Orlando
University of Florida, Gainesville
University of North Florida, Jacksonville
University of South Florida, Tampa
University of West Florida, Pensacola

Lizardi and the Birth of the Novel in Spanish America

Nancy Vogeley

University Press of Florida

Gainesville Tallahassee Tampa Boca Raton
Pensacola Orlando Miami Jacksonville Ft. Myers

06 05 04 03 02 01   6 5 4 3 2 1

Portions of chapter 1 were published as "Mexican Newspaper Culture on the Eve of Mexican Independence," *Ideologies and Literature* 4 Second Cycle (1982): 358–77. Used with permission.

Parts of chapter 7 appeared in "La figuración de la mujer: México en el momento de la Independencia," *Mujer y cultura en la Colonia hispanoamericana*, edited by Mabel Moraña and published by Biblioteca de América, Pittsburgh, 1996. Used with permission.

A version of chapter 8 appeared as "Questioning Authority: Lizardi's *Noches tristes y día alegre*" in *Dispositio* 15 (1990): 53–70. Used with permission.

Parts of chapter 9 were published as "A Latin American Enlightenment Version of the Picaresque: Lizardi's *Don Catrín de la Fachenda*," in *The Picaresque, A Symposium on the Rogue's Tale*, edited by Carmen Benito-Vessels and Michael Zappala and published by the University of Delaware, Newark, Delaware, 1994, 123–46. Used with permission.

Figures 1 and 2 and 5 through 16 are taken from materials owned by the Sutro Library (California State System) and are reproduced with the library's kind permission.

Library of Congress Cataloging-in-Publication Data
Vogeley, Nancy J.
Lizardi and the birth of the novel in Spanish America / Nancy Vogeley.
p. cm.
Includes bibliographical references and index.
ISBN 0-8130-2118-9 (cloth : alk. paper)
1. Fernández de Lizardi, José Joaquín, 1776–1827—Criticism and interpretation.
2. Fernández de Lizardi, José Joaquín, 1776–1827. Periquillo Sarniento. 3. Nationalism in literature. 4. Politics and literature—Mexico—History—19th century. I. Title.

PQ7297.F37 Z96 2001
863'.5—dc21   2001034782

The University Press of Florida is the scholarly publishing agency for the State University System of Florida, comprising Florida A&M University, Florida Atlantic University, Florida Gulf Coast University, Florida International University, Florida State University, University of Central Florida, University of Florida, University of North Florida, University of South Florida, and University of West Florida.

University Press of Florida
15 Northwest 15th Street
Gainesville, FL 32611–2079
http://www.upf.com

Wherever there are colonizers and colonized face to face, I see force, brutality, cruelty, sadism, conflict, and, in a parody of education, the hasty manufacture of a few thousand subordinate functionaries, "boys," artisans, office clerks, and interpreters necessary for the smooth operation of business.

They talk to me about progress, about "achievements," diseases cured, improved standards of living.

I am talking about societies drained of their essence, cultures trampled underfoot, institutions undermined, lands confiscated, religions smashed, magnificent artistic creations destroyed, extraordinary possibilities wiped out.

AIMÉ CÉSAIRE

¿Los reyes son puestos por Dios en la tierra?
[Are kings placed on earth by God?]
TITLE OF AN 1814 MEXICAN POLITICAL PAMPHLET

América, novela sin novelistas
[America, a novel without novelists]
LUIS ALBERTO SÁNCHEZ

Contents

Figures

Acknowledgments

In 1953, when Great Britain was announcing plans to pull out of Singapore, I remember asking my father the reason. "Because," he said, "she can no longer afford to defend and maintain her colonies." This was probably my first awareness of decolonization.

Since then, the present study of José Joaquín Fernández de Lizardi, his novels, and decolonization in the context of Spanish America has evolved. It is a pleasure to think back to how it began, the generous help of persons along the way, and where I traveled to pursue it. Its first form, my dissertation, dealt only with *El Periquillo Sarniento;* Jean Franco directed that study and I am grateful to her, as well as to Mary Pratt, Fernando Alegría, and Frederick Bowser, for helpful advice in defining the initial project. Later, two National Endowment for the Humanities (NEH) summer seminars, led by John Szwed and John Kronik, enriched my views of Lizardi's fiction.

I have worked long years to find primary materials in the various repositories of Mexican Independence materials: the Sutro Collection of the State of California (San Francisco), the Bancroft Library of the University of California (Berkeley), the University of Texas Library (Austin), the British Library (London), the Bodleian Library (Oxford), the Biblioteca Nacional (Mexico), the Archivo General de la Nación (Mexico), and the Archivo Histórico Nacional (Madrid). I want to thank the staffs of those libraries, particularly acknowledging the many kindnesses of the Sutro Library, where I often just dropped in and requested materials at the end of a long day. Gary Kurutz, formerly head of the Sutro and now director of special collections at the California State Library (Sacramento), facilitated the photography for the book's illustrations.

Gustavo Pérez Firmat graciously invited me to Duke University for the spring 1989 semester to teach a course, "Decolonizing Discourse," thus giving me an opportunity to extend the theoretical bases of my project with students there.

The University of San Francisco has helped me immensely over many years with library facilities, research and travel grants, sabbatical leaves, and computer and secretarial help. At the University Press of Florida, Susan Fernández, acquisitions editor, and Jacqueline Kinghorn Brown, project editor for my book, have made the publishing process a very happy experience.

The friendship and collegiality of many people have sustained me during the gestation and writing of this book. The following are only some of them: Rolena Adorno, John Brushwood, Hugh Dawson, Thalia Dorwick, Denise Gretz, the late James McKegney, Michael Mathes, María Rosa Palazón, Mary Pratt, Felipe Reyes Palacios, Martha Schaffer, Harold Sims, Doris Sommer, and Peggy Vota.

This book is lovingly dedicated to my parents.

Author's Note

Throughout the book, translations into English are my own except when I have indicated otherwise. In the instances where I refer to the Spanish original, I have kept the spelling and accent patterns so as to give a flavor of Mexican usage of Spanish in the early nineteenth century. Similarly, if I have used masculine pronoun forms, it is to reflect the fact that in the period gender distinctions were largely absorbed into the species language of "man" [*hombre*].

Introduction

Decolonizing Discourse

By 1820 Spain's 300-year rule in Mexico was finally nearing an end; in 1821 Agustín de Iturbide would proclaim independence. After a decade of fighting against Spain, but also among themselves, Mexicans would finally lay down their arms. However, in the war's last months, desperate to placate critics and stave off collapse of its empire, Madrid authorized reinstatement of the 1812 liberal constitution for all of Spain's territories.[1] Suddenly, one of the provisions, press freedom, allowed Mexican printers to publish the record that years of official history had silenced, the outrage that social controls had suppressed.

As part of that 1820 outpouring, an anonymous Mexican pamphleteer told what colonial life had been like, choosing to frame his criticism as a linguistic self-portrait. Publicly, he said, he kept silent, or inadvertently revealed his emotion in wordless sounds; privately, in the safety of his family, he expressed his suffering in a special "language of feeling" [*idioma de la sensibilidad*].[2]

> Neither the dark ignorance in which our oppressors buried us, nor the heavy weight of the harsh chains we dragged, nor the seemingly eternal stretch of 300 years of suffering, were sufficient to make our infamous slavery bearable. An education of toil amidst defeat and tears makes the hardest heart sensitive; it makes the most sluggish understanding active. We knew what our afflictions were; we felt the whole weight of our misfortune. But our lips did not dare . . . to articulate the least complaint so as not to irritate the fury of the

ministers of despotism, although many times against our will some sigh rent the air, borne of the pain tormenting us inside. We followed the slow step of oxen that were not ours, and the water of our sweat and our tears irrigated the earth. The mature fruit still did not quench the dropsical thirst of the avaricious landlords; and when we returned in the darkness of night to rest and recover our exhausted strength, surrounded by our family whose nakedness and misery wounded our heart deeply, when we ate the scarce food which was the only fruit of such excessive effort, we cried inconsolably and alone over the fatality of our situation.

In those moments, our imagination inflamed, we voiced the following words to our young children: See here, we said to them, the sad results of great labor: hunger, nakedness, deprivation, misery.[3]

Although many factors contributed at that moment to ending Mexico's war with Spain, press freedom, which permitted oppositional voices to "unmask the error"[4] of the powerful government gazette, was crucial in tipping the balance in favor of independence.[5]

The pamphlet is a useful point at which to begin my analysis of how colonialism and decolonization, large historical processes that are often thought of as abstractions, affected the individual colonial subject. As I studied the novel's first appearance in Spanish America early in the nineteenth century, in the midst of Mexico's revolt against Spain, I found the pamphlet's words to be the smoking gun that I was looking for—a suggestive personalization of colonial rule, one that equated it with linguistic interference and that took the process of decolonization from its macrocosmic dimensions and reduced it to the microcosm of an individual trying to speak. I thought it remarkable that the pamphleteer never once mentioned the metaphysical notions of "civilization" and "Christian salvation," which fascinated Spanish colonizers in the sixteenth century and continued to legitimize Spain's hold over American territories and peoples for centuries; instead, the writer was concerned with his own material, human needs.[6] He rewrote "family," an imperial metaphor that had been used to foster ties between the Spanish king and his two sets of sons (one on the Iberian peninsula and the other in his far-flung colonies) and narrativized it to imagine a new, American community.[7]

The pamphlet's focus on colonial consciousness, its testimony that "an education of toil" had made "the most sluggish understanding active," throws light on an old question: How is revolutionary consciousness acquired? The ways that the self discovers language, how it particularly may invent new language, is something much studied by philosophers, social psychologists, and revolutionary pedagogues.[8] In the Mexican case, the pamphlet's assertion that painful experience had taught colonials a language with which to name their suffering is valuable documentation for the purposes of my study that decolonization depends on creating one's own language. By that means one thinks afresh and perhaps also joins with like-minded others. Indeed, the pamphlet's description of the importance of thoughtful, inward groping for language so as to achieve what modern social analysts might call consciousness raising [*concientización*], reinforces what many believe—that the best consciousness raising is not instruction by enlightened outsiders, but individual experiential learning and introspection.

Economic realities appear to have been the stimulus for generating this Mexican generation's consciousness of its colonial status and linguistic impairment. The pamphleteer ignores Spain's supposed gifts to its colonies and remarks only on the "slavery" and "ignorance" the European system produced. He writes as one of the colony's workers, implying that the excruciating experience of labor to provide metropolitan wealth characterized all in Mexico. His narrative, while it personifies "them" and "us" in economic terms, nevertheless refrains from racial or other distinguishing representations of "them"; he places "the ministers of despotism" and "avaricious landlords" in the context of a 300–year-old system, thus displaying hesitancy in pinning the blame on any one individual such as the king. Indeed, the pamphleteer's broad, intellectualized vision and sorrowful, self-absorbed tone suggest the difficulties many would experience in the postcolonial period in directing resentments and hatreds at specific persons or groups.

Confession of the colonial's two linguistic selves—both oral but the private one the basis of a new, written critique of colonialism—contributes to the argument I develop that new habits of writing (and, concomitantly, reading) often accompany the decolonizing process. Writing the political pamphlet brings the individual's separated selves together; in a public mode previously denied to him, yet in language of his own making, he assumes the courage to represent himself and address others beyond his immediate family. Reading his words, fellow colonials would have recognized the honest voice and personality they associated with speech and family exchanges; his writing did not look like the varieties of print that had intimidated them, deceived them, and bored them in the past. Modern readers, too, absorb his testimony as if he were speaking to us. We are drawn into his experience, cry with him, and are made part of his family. Thus sentimentalized and politicized by the reading, we look around and recognize signs of "colonial" conditions everywhere. Muteness, emotional stuttering and other hesitancies of speech, ventriloquistic performance so that one speaks the words of others, even superficial glibness may all indicate the inhibiting pressures of other forms of colonialism.

What I call *decolonizing discourse* refers, then, not just to the words a colonial subject uses. Such language often makes explicit the oppressors' greed and foreign ownership of the tools of work and domestic labor. However, decolonizing discourse may also, if the speaker dares to say so, identify one of the most psychologically troubling aspects of colonial life—the individual's unnatural language usage. Colonials, we are told in the pamphlet, even if they had the words with which to speak honestly and feelingly of their subject condition, refrained from using these words in public. Terrorized, they were afraid that cries for justice would be counterproductive. Thus, equally important to decolonizing discourse are the circumstances that allow for the release of inner, private language into the public field, in this case, the conditions permitting the Mexican pamphleteer to appropriate the powerful medium of print, to break with silence and denounce as tyranny an institution Mexicans had been taught to think of as benevolent. Indeed, evidence that the linguistic freedom that decolonization brought was felt collectively is expressed in Mexico's Declaration of Independence (September 28, 1821): "The Mexican nation that for 300 years has neither enjoyed the exercise of its own will, or had the freedom of its voice [*ni libre el uso de la voz*] emerges today from the oppression under which it has lived" (Iturbide 262–63).

In this book I link "decolonizing discourse," a notion I have formulated to suggest a pattern of linguistic politics, and the birth of the novel in Spanish America, a historically specific belletristic phenomenon, because I believe each development sheds light on the other. When José Joaquín Fernández de Lizardi published *El Periquillo Sarniento* in Mexico

City in 1816, readers almost immediately recognized its European antecedents but they also remarked on its American originality; today the
novel, with its significant publication date, is almost universally acknowledged to be the first such work written in Spanish America.[9] Thus,
Lizardi's fiction symbolizes American rebellion, all the while within the
confines of an inherited language and the performance limitations of colonial censorship and civil unrest.

Literary historians have already studied the novel's tardy appearance in
the colonies. The delay, considering that the novel, a Spanish invention,
was exported and widely imitated in Europe in the seventeenth and eighteenth centuries, has suggested various explanations of why there was
not an American novel earlier; metropolitan fear of the genre's capacity to
arouse the colonial imagination and marvelous American realities that
robbed American writers and readers of the need for creating literary
fantasies are two of the most commonly cited.[10] Yet I ask different, although related questions—why the novel appeared in the final years of
Mexico's colonial history and how it authorized new language usage.
Possible answers to these questions are several: The form's ability to depict familiar speech permitted revolutionary expressiveness. Its dramatic
and satiric ranges gave voice to the colony's new diversity. Its imaginative
leap awakened Mexican readers to the numbing dullness of much colonial
language. Domestic portrayal of the Mexican Self broke with the images
colonials had been assigned. The new form's secularity, which competed
with and undermined habits of obedient religious reading, taught new
attitudes toward authority.

I have found that the novel's appearance at that moment challenges
Saussurean theoretical assumptions that *langue* easily becomes *parole*, that
a pre-existing community language satisfactorily provides the possibilities from which an individual chooses. Where and how Lizardi got the
language necessary for articulating a new identity is part of my inquiry.
How he activated perhaps already-existing alternative discourses, and
variations on key terms and metaphors of thought, for critical use by his
Mexican community, are questions I ask. How he used the novel at that
politically strategic moment will suggest not only the novel's potential for
decolonizing thought and expression, but also the reverse—decolonization's liberating effect on literary production. Rather than coincidence,
then, the simultaneity of the appearance of Spanish America's first novel

and a hemispherewide war for American independence, I argue, points to common causes and reciprocal influences.

However, a preliminary warning: If decolonizing discourse does not always indicate a fully confident self, or the first formulations of statehood, it at least suggests some critical distance from older colonizing rationale. If it does not always offer a new spirit of dignity and hope for the human condition, it at least confronts degradation and humiliation. If it does not automatically indicate a willingness to act and include a rationale for violence, it at least posits a mind no longer set, which is searching to resolve tension and bring about change. In a world of fear and lethargic tolerance of corruption, it teaches moral outrage.

Decolonization: A Review

Decolonization has been studied as a political, military, and economic phenomenon.[11] The view from above has often sought explanations for what is seen as the loss of power in failure and error, attributing, for example, the decline in the Roman empire to Rome's decay. Power has chronicled how, in the case of recent empires, they broke apart, and colonies in Africa, Asia, the Caribbean, and the Pacific gained sovereignty. Britain and France have provided most of the theories for the statecraft that undertook colonization and then decreed decolonization. Their histories have been analyzed to see how a ruler or a state mobilized individuals to undertake conquest of sometimes contiguous, but often distant territories, of how political and military projects, expansion of trade, and evangelism[12] were accomplished. In this way *colonialism* is often a synonym for *imperialism*,[13] and *decolonization* suggests a metropolitan decision to divest itself of colonial responsibilities.

Frantz Fanon, O. Mannoni, and Aimé Césaire, however, have focussed on the psychological aspects of colonialism. Their studies, written from the standpoint of victims of the French imperial system, have emphasized the racism and dehumanization that colonials suffer. Lately, North American and British critics in literature and cultural studies, sensitive to this point of view, have taken colonialism to mean not only the subjectification endured by the so-called Third World,[14] but also, extending the term nonliterally, the process by which any minority or marginalized group or individual is made to feel inferior. Accordingly, they have shown women, Jews, and African Americans in the United States,[15] or Gaelic speakers in Ireland, to be "colonials," trapped by the majority's language into believing they belong to a lower order of human beings, and hushed into subservience and silence.

This second group of scholars has also introduced the question of language deprivation. How does a colonized people, ground into submission and robbed of its original language (as the figure of Caliban has come to suggest),[16] begin to create an oppositional vocabulary? How do marginalized peoples, such as Basques and Catalans in the autonomous regions of Spain today, keep their languages alive when, although Madrid no longer forbids use of those languages as it did under the Franco regime, it now bombards the country's peripheral areas with its cultural and commercial artifacts, making *castellano* more attractive to their young? Liberation theologians have joined the debate over decolonization by showing the hold that idealistic, theological language has over a people forced to think with another's mental system. They have challenged the Roman Church's eschatological teaching that perfection is only achievable in some future life; and these theologians, among them many Americans, have affirmed the possibility of historical progress by redefining *salvation* as social justice here and now. Through such a challenge they have questioned the Church's authority in mediating "salvation" via its control of the language of salvation (Silva Gotay; Erskine).

Decolonization, therefore, has been used by persons sensitive to the power of language to refer to emancipation from languages formulated by others, particularly through discovery of the hidden assumptions of superiority and inferiority in those alien thought systems. This movement to a better world may also imply recovery of old tribal memories with the possibility of countering the language of the colonizer, incidentally retrieving useful knowledge of the colonized world which generations of indigenous peoples had built up in their language store. Some Anglo-American scholars (Said; Lawrence; Smith and Watson) have set out to identify imperializing language in the British literary canon; they claim their exposé of racism and land-grabbing is "decolonizing" literary practice. Similarly, a few Latin Americanists have seen "decolonization" in their critiques of modern poetry (Ruffinelli) and film (Solanas and Getino), finding that today's literature and media often replicate older forms of control. Latin American literary scholars and historians have looked for early attempts at decolonization in the contradictory discourses to imperialism that colonized peoples themselves produced; an important discovery of one such alternative "writing" has been the seventeenth-century book of drawings and Spanish gloss by the Peruvian Indian, Guaman Poma de Ayala.

Problems

Much of this theoretical discussion, possibly following a Marxist model of class divisions, reduces the players in the colonial drama to two groups (colonizer and colonized, the imperial Self and the native Other). Talk of "siting" suggests that geography will determine who belongs where.[17] Yet close study of the colonial history of Spanish America demonstrates that such division is difficult since many were then (and still are) simultaneously the Self and the Other; Spanish priests with long years of service in the Americas, criollos (Americans who, although born and resident in the New World, were racially and culturally European), American women married to Spaniards, and travelers between the two regions. Evidence that this complexity persisted into the postcolonial period is the fact that members of the domestic elite in Spanish America (but also in the former British, French, Portuguese, Dutch, and other empires), remaining in their homelands, have often perpetuated attitudes of colonial superiority toward their native peoples; national writers, frequently expatriates living in metropolitan centers, have sympathized with nationhood and written of colonial situations and locales yet also ambiguously used imperial tongues to tell their exotic stories to international readerships.[18] Some may call these wealthy ex-colonials and writers hypocritical, but I see their identity locked into literacy and class acculturation—the domain in which their "colonial discourse" operates is bookish territory, rather than real territory. I see the existence of these postcolonial categories, in which metropolitan and colonial identities are confused, as pointing to a decolonizing process in which there has often been no clear polarization to start with, and no neat historical dialectic of separation after official political independence.

   Colonial discourse, a phrase lately in use by literary critics, valuably shows language's instrumentality in the making of history; I use this ready-made concept as a point of departure for my book. Yet critics who use the term often sow confusion in equally labeling "colonial" the languages used by imperial institutions and majority interests, and those that subgroups or individuals have been assigned or have discovered on their own. However, the resulting ambiguity, although it contributes to methodological messiness, has the advantage of recognizing the extent to which the language of governance as the privileged set of naming terms encroaches on all thought. Hegemonic language seeps into the thought of the governed and particularly shapes their writing, the communicative form that aspires to contact with power.

Thus, my approach to "decolonizing discourse," in asking how newness was enabled and political independence was expedited by mental changes, focuses on the written word. I mainly consider only that writing produced in Mexico. Although there were Mexicans living and writing abroad whose ideas had a profound impact on the Independence movement (an important example, Fray Servando Teresa de Mier), I believe that by the first decades of the nineteenth century most of the writing (and particularly the reading) that qualifies as decolonizing was being done by the Mexican-born under colonial physical conditions. Although the orality of warfare, commerce and work, family and sexual relationships, and so on, characterized much language usage in the three centuries of colonial rule, I believe that the colonizing assumptions underlying the Conquest and subsequent continental takeover were contained in writing. Writing, with its origins in Peninsular thinking, is closest to colonialism's truths and deceits. Writing, with its superior political and religious values, perpetuated the colonial system and disciplined individuals, even those illiterates and persons relatively distant from administrative centers.

Instead of seeking examples of such writing just in "literature," which suggests the selectivity of the canon, I go to the broad body of "discourse."[19] Discourse, a looser category that suggests both oral and written expression yet also rubbish that has not yet been sorted out, allows me to consider archival material wherein linguistic wars were waged and evidence still remains of colonialism's variants and its opposition. In those records nonliterary items permeated with orality (such as sermons, letters, and legal testimony) and ephemera (such as newspapers and political pamphlets) throw light on the heterogeneous language of Lizardi's novels. Discourse analysis (Stubbs), employed by students of linguistics to look at orality's shifts in speakers, changes of code and registers, has been a useful tool in my study of fiction. Discourse theory (Macdonell) has taught me that alternative discourses usually start when users become aware of their new expressive needs.

The phrase *decolonizing discourse* suggests the twofold project of this book: a case study of one (frequently ignored) shattering moment in the history of a European empire, and a deconstructive analysis of the language of dominance. In the first instance, I want to go back beyond the decolonizing experience of the post–World War II nations to the nineteenth-century independence of Spain's American colonies. The Spanish empire, based largely on fifteenth- and sixteenth-century colonizing assumptions, permits a view of a theory of humanness, more grounded in legal speculation and theological certainty (because of Catholic notions of baptism, providential history, and the legal sanctions of natural law) than nineteenth-century political and economic versions of colonialism. The colonizations of the nineteenth century, although sometimes fortified by arguments of superior culture and race, did not attempt the indoctrination of native peoples that Spain did or reinforce control with institutions like the Inquisition to the degree that Spain did.

Even Spain's desire for American gold, it was said, was tied to that gold's usefulness in paying for the conversion of heathen peoples to the true faith (Gutiérrez chap. 3). One can disparage such ideology as a sophistry created after the fact of looting, but one then risks not taking the Spanish at their word and disregarding the power of language—particularly the abstractions and spiritual notions of religious language—in forming their mentality. Soon after the Conquest, Fray Bartolomé de Las Casas became "defender of the Indians" by contrasting the grimness of Spain's military and economic thrust with this theological, philosophical, and juridical thinking. At Independence, Americans who republished Las Casas's arguments in their desire to use the Spanish priest's denunciation of colonialism to complain of Spanish injustice and end colonial rule[20] nevertheless continued to validate this idealistic language in their appeal to religion's moral force. And as late as 1806–1807 Madrid used the rhetoric of faith to urge Americans to resist British occupation of Buenos Aires; Spanish officials said it was a Catholic defense against Protestants.

In introducing the second way in which I understand my study of decolonizing discourse, a rethinking of the languages of domination and submission, I recall the pamphleteer whose words began this chapter. No longer a languageless barbarian (as Europeans described the American), he expresses himself eloquently. This nineteenth-century subaltern not only speaks but he also writes, his literacy thus suggesting a variety of colonial nearer to the metropolitan mental world than may otherwise have been thought.[21] By now his European blood probably mixed with that of Indians and blacks, he combines traits of both the colonizer and the colonized. His description of farm work makes it seem that he, too, toils; certainly he shows solidarity with labor. So this colonial's identity, somewhere between the imperial Self and the native Other, points to a third category of colonial.

Additionally, the pamphleteer's emotion [*sensibilidad*], a sign of human-ness, challenges those who think of the colonized as so brutalized that their language amounts only to cursing.[22] Colonialism has often been described as hardening, coarsening, and depersonalizing its subjects; and I agree that hatred and anger may affect the language colonials return to their colonizers, use with one another, and even define themselves with. Yet the pamphleteer's choice of title for his essay, *the language of feeling*, raises several questions. Either his use of such language means he, the colonial, was never a brute (despite being treated like an animal, he re-tained complete human feelings and a basic expressiveness); or he appro-priated this refined language from his oppressors; or he evolved some independent capacity to synthesize emotional language from his subject condition.[23]

Indeed, *sensibilidad* as proof of their humanity was a principal talking point of the American delegates to the Cortes de Cádiz. In making their appeal for improved Spanish government to the short-lived liberal body in 1811, the delegates said some disputed Americans' rationality, but none could deny their capacity for feeling. Americans were so sensitive that they could no longer tolerate the pain of bad government; and this "feeling" defense of American human nature became a widely known le-gitimating reason for revolution.[24]

However, despite the pamphleteer's emotional words, one cannot con-clude that all colonials were sensitive, or that their emotion translated into the anger necessary for sparking insurgency. Therefore, I posit a range of responses to colonialism among colonial subjects, in addition to the obviously decolonizing modes of resistance and rebellion. Many colonials, as I have explored elsewhere,[25] were loyalists; Lizardi's novels, too, as I show, display this range and complexity of responses. In 1808, when Napoleon invaded Spain and news reached Mexico that the empire was threatened, many Mexicans publicly protested their loyalty. "Loyalty" was the identity they had been assigned; and they reached for that image in representing themselves as patriots in a flood of sympathetic poetry. Pride in their Mexicanness, which the poetry unleashed, might have disguised their growing self-awareness and hidden insurgent desires, which erupted two years later. However, it is possible that many also might have believed the idealism they professed; proof is that after Independence these faithful stubbornly remained loyal to Spain and the Catholic Church, becoming a reactionary force in national politics. Others converted their loyalty into Mexican patriotism, transferring their affection to another *patria*. Still others, liberals who celebrated Mexican Independence, although voting for anticlerical reforms, clung privately to their personal faith and agonized over their obligations to the Roman Church and pope. Indeed, Lizardi, observing this last remnant of colonialism in postcolonial Mexican society, wrote on his deathbed in 1827: "I leave my homeland independent of Spain and all other crowned heads of state, except Rome" (*Obras* 13: 1040).

"Loyalty" and "religious faith," then, were discursive holdovers from the colonial period, paralyzing the ability of many postcolonials to imagine other identities and forms of governance. "Colonialism" was another such notion, learned during Spain's occupation of Mexico, which remained attractive after Independence. In colonizing projects designed to develop unpopulated areas, national leaders recycled the same policies of land seizure that Mexico had complained of to Spain.

Indeed, the bipartite ideological division one expects in an independence war does not exist in the case of Mexico. The criollo class, the group that would provide domestic leadership later, was split in its loyalties on the eve of war. Criollo intellectuals and writers had been among the first to sing the praises of their birthplace and begin the process of retrieving knowledge of Mexico's indigenous past. Because criollos were shut out from the Mexican nobility, from the higher ecclesiastical and viceregal appointments, from business opportunities that Peninsulars largely controlled, and even from enterprises such as mining,[26] they became a disaffected middle class, thereby providing most of the insurgent leadership. But it is also true, as David Brading has said (*Orígenes del Nacionalismo* 40–42, 74–76, 97), that many criollos served in the royalist armies. Agustín de Iturbide and Antonio López de Santa Anna, national leaders in the decades after Independence, were criollos who first of all had been royalist officers.

Making the ideological framing of Mexican decolonization still more complex is the fact that the initial impetus for war against Spain was provided by two criollo priests, Miguel Hidalgo and José María Morelos —men who combined hatred of the *gachupines* with faithful belief. The Mexican independence movement, unlike that in other parts of Spanish America, was remarkably religious;[27] belief in the special patronage of the Virgen de Guadalupe motivated many insurgents and continued on as a vital national myth (Hamnett 13ff.). Thus, the either-or options of "insurrection or loyalty,"[28] the reduction of the independence movement to political and military alternatives—which characterize much discussion of the period's thought—are shown to be muddled in the Mexican experience of decolonization.

Homi Bhabha's description of colonial discourse[29] as often registering "sly civility" and "ambiguity" is helpful in suggesting other responses to subjugation besides outright hostility. His observation, which points not only to how the individual colonial subject might have coped but also, possibly, to the colonial's vacillating loyalties, supports my argument that, although there were necessarily many degrees of overt and covert resistance among the colonized so as to have prepared the way for Independence,[30] other colonial discourses were in use by the colonized at this moment when colonialism was supposed to be dying. *Resistance* may be too all-encompassing and strong a word to describe the various forces that brought about change;[31] in Mexico, because the independence movement was not initiated by the people but by the domestic elite and criollo classes, many patterns of dominance were preserved in working out the rupture. Thus, "colonial discourse" contrasts usefully with "counter-discourse" (Terdiman) and "minority discourse" (JanMohamed and Lloyd). In suggesting that subordinate responses took several forms, ranging from total identification with the colonizers to absolute repudiation of their power, the concept points to a blurring between the discourses used by colonizer and colonized—both during the colonial period and then later after Independence. One can explain the varieties as differences between "false" versus "true" consciousness. Yet this reductiveness falls into the same trap of thinking that one is either colonizer or colonized and begs the question of consciousness itself.

In considering the state of language in Mexico in the first decades of the nineteenth century, when domestic interests increasingly prevailed and local writers and printers took over the work of metropolitans or viceregal deputies, I begin with the question of the colony's linguistic self-consciousness. I ground my analysis in Louis Althusser's suggestion that consciousness is a function of "interpellation," a process whereby an individual accepts the labels dominant institutions have applied to him, so that he recognizes himself in the roles assigned to him, or not. I rely on Althusser's focus on the moment when groups begin to realize they use the same language differently. Old words are given new meanings; and, he says, the contest for words and how they are put together (discourse) is essentially the struggle between opposing ideologies. He sees competition between discourses as divisions along class lines, a conclusion that I want to test out in the case of the Mexican historical experience.[32]

Under Spanish colonial rule for three hundred years, the Mexican had acquired a sense of himself as a result of his inscription in the colonial text. Produced in the metropolis, yet also originating in the colonial world so as to convince the distant power that imperial demands were being met, writing reinforced daily, tangibly, the identities of both parties to the system. The mail system bound the empire together.[33] "Colonial discourse," both the message on paper and the circumstances surrounding the document's creation and delivery,[34] was importantly a performative act[35] involving writer and reader; both reaffirmed their identities each time they wrote and read. Yet the colonial writer, in missives designed for Spain, often substituted a portrait of colonialism's ideal operation for the real one; his own interpretation of events went to remote readers who might never know the truth.[36] Language stood for the action itself, and so the colonial learned that he might never need to act but instead get by with producing paper that satisfied a ruling elite. Suggesting that the colonial regularly flaunted metropolitan rules, there grew the phrase, *Obedezco pero no cumplo* [I obey {I say I will comply} but I will not carry out {the order}]. Nevertheless, at the same time he learned the hypocrisy of writing, the colonial also learned that the formalities of writing were powerful and had to be honored, however detached as signifiers they might have been from his circumstances. Writing—or reproducing over and over again what the hegemonic culture dictated—established its own reality; and some colonials were probably even duped by the language they produced, preferring its semblance of achievement and organization to the backwardness and injustice around them. For the colonial, reading was like the salute a subaltern gave his commander, or the sign of the cross with which a worshipper concluded his part of a common prayer.

The colonizing speech act, whether written or oral, had customarily been gestural and showy; and the colonized learned the advantages of looking and sounding the same way.[37] Literate colonials, in particular, imitated their colonizers, so thoroughly displaying compliance with dominant discourse that one gathers from reading the official literature that they especially had internalized colonizing language. The religious and political oratory they produced was pompous. Their poetry to celebrate a distant event such as the king's marriage, although it probably was only read by a small circle on the colonial site, was an attempt to transport there, through grand words, some courtliness. Licensed by the occasion, they produced set compositions. Any paper in circulation, any utterance that might be overheard, was monitored by snobbish taste, if not also the Inquisition. Even colonial legal appeals (in which self-representation might have suggested a simpler style) and works of satire (which derive from oppositional stirrings) generally reflect the attention to linguistic form of colonized peoples. Careful use of deferential proprieties and extravagant display of words show how completely upper-class colonials learned the lessons of hierarchy and dissimulation; their faithful imitation bespeaks hope of reward, if not also psychological bondage.

Evidence points, then, to the conclusion that colonialism denatured language as communication between individuals face to face, as spontaneous expression of thought and feeling, as honest recording of surrounding realities and the means for mastering them. Thus I ask how colonials came to their own use of language, how they ever made the jump from passive to active reading and writing. Given the special ideologizing that Mexicans were subject to, the intellectualized sense of a political order related to the mysteries of faith and the world of paper, I wonder in the pages of this book how even those who had gained some critical perspective on their colonial condition faced freedom with anything other than panic.[38]

Colonialism in Spanish America

In Spain's American colonies,[39] the Crown dictated tight control over the colonizing enterprise. The religious orders that carried out the missionary work, the military forces and administrative offices that accomplished pacification and governance, the commercial networks and tax houses—all these executed with appropriate actions and paperwork the Crown's centralist and monopolistic policies. The reporting effort was huge as layers of bureaucracy attempted to subject every reality to the categories laid out at home.

Upper-class colonials,[40] as I have indicated, were closest to this influence. Their privileges generally caused them to subscribe to its thought and zealously defend its forms. Whether European or American-born, these "whites," educated in Spanish, usually thought of themselves and their world in terms of their dependency. Down the social scale, Indians and mestizos (persons of mixed Indian and European blood), even if they continued to speak their native languages and retained some memory of the indigenous past, generally incorporated some colonial concepts into their thought if they were in contact with Europeans. Although the Crown had decreed their conversion and education in Castilian early in the colonial enterprise, most Indians in fact never learned Spanish.[41] The colonial elite, believing that the working classes were more submissive if they were ignorant of access to their communicative world, segregated the Indians (ostensibly for their protection) into separate living areas and refused to teach them Spanish (Heath 42–43). The religious orders mostly translated the catechism into the many Indian languages in order to secure the terms of control.

Anecdotal evidence of how colonial officials exploited Indian illiteracy and ignorance of Spanish—which draws on a common belief regarding colonial practices—is provided by an early nineteenth-century political pamphlet. In it a priest, who has married off his pregnant Indian maid, attempts to convince the irate Indian husband who discovers the deception that delivery of a child after four months of marriage is normal. He points to his breviary where he says the red letters tell what is natural law: "La moza del cura / que con pastor casare, / como está gorda y robusta / a los cuatro meses pare" [The priest's maid / who marries a shepherd, / because she is stout and robust / will deliver {a child} in four months].[42]

When the husband protests that he cannot read, the priest replies "Pues, mejor" [So much the better].

Blacks present a problem for correlating linguistic acculturation and adherence to governing values. Imported into the New World to work on the plantations, they variously lived in primitive conditions in barracks or, if they were domestic servants, in the great houses with white families. Accordingly, they retained their African tongues or they learned the Spanish of their masters. During the colonial period, Spanish-speaking blacks, Indians who aspired to become like whites and learn Spanish (*ladinos*)—or indeed translators of any kind—were judged impudent, disruptive of social boundaries, and dangerous (Heath 43; Aguirre Beltrán 157–58).

Why was it, then, that Indians and blacks, knowing Spanish, were thought to be subversive, whereas instruction in Spanish linguistic rituals was generally understood to be essential to whites' loyalty? The answer, I believe, has to do with the kind of education in superiority reserved for a white elite. The white colonial's more frequent literacy and advanced education, involving philosophical, theological, and legal study, bound him to the majority discourse's way of thinking more compellingly. Basic oral skills only guaranteed partial immersion in the majority's language; but ideological education could ensnare white leadership in such a way that dissociation from that colonialist discourse was more wrenching.

In studying Lizardi's novels as "decolonizing discourse," I focus on this literate colonial class. I draw on the work of present-day African writers whose attention to language in the process of ideological change is more than just academic. Ngugi wa Thiong'O, for example, in his book, *Decolonising the Mind: The Politics of Language in African Literature*, dramatically renounces the colonial language; he writes: "This book . . . is my farewell to English as a vehicle for any of my writings. From now on it is Gikiyu and Kiswahili all the way" (xiv). Ngugi's decision is an example of what Michel Pêcheux might call "disidentification," a move to be undertaken when the individual or collective consciousness understands that separateness is necessary. "Counteridentification," a less radical move that does not require a complete rupture, may seem to provide some alternative to "identification"; but it still depends on the hegemonic discourse for its contradictory structure.

Ngugi's preference for Gikiyu and Kiswahili is predicated on his judgment that these languages, still vital in the oral tradition, can be the basis for new forms of communication in postcolonial Africa. He believes that the experience of oppressed peoples, seeking their own voice after Independence, can be handled only with the expressivity these peoples originally created for themselves. And even though Ngugi intends to use the novel—a form he calls bourgeois and European (chap. 3)—to communicate with his African readers, he gives examples of how he will employ not only African languages, but also metaphors and narrative techniques from the oral tradition, in designing a new novel for them.

By 1810, however, restive Americans, who were searching for a means to criticize home conditions and plan for reform or independence, generally had no choice as to which language they would use. By then Spanish (or Castilian) was the only signifying system most upper-class colonials knew. At issue was not whether one used Spanish but how within the structure of the Spanish discourse system old ideas could be modified or destroyed and new ones created. These Americans from the upper and middle classes were struggling with transforming the rhetoric that had enslaved native peoples and blacks at the time of the Conquest, the legal and theological concepts that still bound colonial subjects to Spain. In declaring war on Spain, Mexicans had to justify their criminality, as well as begin to provide an intellectual frame for nationhood.

Frantz Fanon has written that "decolonization is always a violent phenomenon. . . .[it] is quite simply the replacing of a certain 'species' of men by another 'species' of men" (*Wretched of the Earth* 35). His description of decolonization suggests no process, no period of transition—a kind of tabula rasa when "from the very first day, the minimum demands of the colonized" are met. Yet nineteenth-century Spanish American history teaches that revolution was anything but definitive there. Newness and originality did not automatically emerge with the postcolonial age. Indeed, Leopoldo Zea says that mental colonization still characterizes the Latin American.

Zea's work is central to my thinking about decolonization. From my point of view, his most useful statement is that originality, a basically European idea, may not be essential. Zea concentrates instead on the notion of "humanity"—both the subhumanity of the colonized peoples, which the Conquest insisted upon, and the inhumanity of the colonizers, which Independence rhetoric proclaimed. To get beyond feelings of inferiority and hatred, Latin Americans must, Zea argues, see themselves and their supposed masters in new human terms. In this way, Latin Americans will not only free themselves, but also those peoples whose imperialistic states still inhumanly bully the weak.

Zea's plan for decolonization may sound utopian. Yet it is in the nature of decolonization that the colonizing myth is challenged—that what passes for civilization, moral superiority, natural mastery, and just war is questioned. Decolonization, Aimé Césaire believes, calls for the eradication of what he terms a "pseudo-humanism," a belief that only Europeans adhere to religious and national ideals, a myth that is really just their excuse to oppress others. Having learned to feel superior in imperial dealings with nonwhites abroad, having justified cruelty in the name of high principle, many European powers treat their own citizens and their neighbors inhumanly. Indeed, Césaire traces Hitler's crimes to Germany's colonial past (14–15). As defined by Zea and Césaire, then, decolonization implies a liberation of more profound change than use of the word by national apologists or freedom fighters commonly suggests.

One troubled colonial of Lizardi's day wrote: "[H]umanity is a pure phantasm of virtue, if we conceive of it independently of charity and separate from that spirit of religion which sacralizes all human actions in homage to the Supreme Being."[43] Thus, decolonization for this American suggested the difficulties of secularization. Although his predicament reflects a nineteenth-century clash between religion and humanism, it also reveals the universal difficulty of dissociation from ideological language —especially if that language contains worthy notions one does not want to leave behind. This colonial's suspicion that "humanity" may only be a language "phantasm" registers some developing consciousness of language's shifting nature and its connection with idealism. In this case, his fear that the love for others the word *humanity* describes may die if it is made a purely secular concept typifies a colonial's confusion in progressing toward postcolonial status.

Today, when colonial history and colonialism's versions have equally vigorous advocates and detractors, the study of decolonization is pertinent. Colonization for many good-hearted people still evokes nostalgic visions of glory and beneficent giving. If colonial "service" is couched in such noble terms as "self-sacrifice," "loyalty to king" (or any other national symbol), "winning souls for Christ" (or any other metaphysical ambition), even "humanitarian love and aid," these phrases—good in themselves—call forth a positive view of colonialism. Many in the former imperial power and the neocolonial state still view decolonization as an unnecessary separation from a larger world community, regression to a backward state, and frustrated altruism. Yet Césaire's words, which preface this book, record the experience of the colonized and contradict this appealing discourse.

Development studies have, I believe, begged the question of decolonization. Nationalism and its new epistemology are discussed without attention to those moments when Independence is declared and won.[44] Formerly colonized societies are described as "postcolonial" without sufficient inquiry into the nature of their transitions. Michael Hechter's term, "internal colonialism," lately favored to describe a nation-state's suppression of its minority groups, is often used, forgetting historical analysis.[45] Anne McClintock and Ella Shohat have both argued that the term *postcolonial* is, to quote McClintock, "prematurely celebratory" (87) and a "bogus universal" (92); and I agree that unless decolonization is studied more fully so as to identify colonial language's inhibiting influences and unsettled questions, McClintock and Shohat will continue to be correct.

Spanish America's First Novel

Discussion of "the novel" in Spanish America involves questions that may not be as obvious in the genre's history in the United States. Spanish colonization of the New World was characterized by a much more hierarchical class structure. In Catholic America, "art" was surrounded by an aura that Protestant America's puritanism and democracy did not allow.[46] The Spanish viceregal administration and the Catholic Church prescribed culture for the Spanish-speaking elite. Church architecture, statuary and music, aristocratic costume and display, and Baroque speechmaking to impress the indigenous population were all part of the colonizing strategy for art (Maravall). Consequently, although the birth of the novel in Spanish America somewhat parallels its emergence in British America (see Davidson *Novel*, for the latter), the "novel" is, and is not, the same literary form in the two areas. In both Americas, however, the novel's appearance and growth are linked to the phenomenon of the printing industry and its invention of a domestic book designed for a literate class that was increasingly becoming receptive to such a new commodity. In both Americas the rise of the novel coincides with political independence, suggesting the book's function as a "voice."

With these reservations, I call "novels" the four works Lizardi wrote between 1816 and 1819. Generations of readers and critics have viewed them as such. Yet, while using the label, I also question the transfer of a European form to the colonial world. Lizardi's wish to have his works considered according to this European definition of prestigious writing meant he both wanted his work to be valued as such yet he also felt his "art" should not be kept aloof from common readers but somehow enter their everyday lives.

In the history of Lizardi's principal novel, *El Periquillo Sarniento*, I see a valuable example of how reader response to a national icon indexes decolonization; in fluctuating attitudes toward this voice and the book's "art" one can measure what successive generations thought was Mexican, and therefore what appeared to separate the nation from Europe. I start with what is perhaps a logical perception—the colonial censor saw the *Periquillo* as a Spanish book, in line with Peninsular precedents. In 1816 José Mariano Beristáin de Souza wrote that Lizardi "has in progress the *Vida de Periquito Sarniento* [sic] which, according to what I have seen of it, bears resemblance to that of *Guzmán de Alfarache*" (Beristáin de Souza 2: 191).

Little else is known of the initial acceptance of the *Periquillo* (for a survey, see Reyes "El 'Periquillo Sarniento' y la crítica mexicana" *Obras* 4: 169–78). Some readers seem to have been offended by the fact that Lizardi drew their attention to nonstandard language. One critic facetiously said that Lizardi performed an imperial service by adding new words to the Spanish lexicon. Writing several years after the novel's publication, he reminded Lizardi that the Spanish Constitution of 1820 obliged lay writers to educate the public: "First I charge my readers, and especially those who may be friends of the Pensador Mejicano, with giving him proper thanks in the name of all those devoted to the *patria*, because he continues in the praiseworthy and antique project of enriching the impoverished Castilian idiom with some words which have not come to the notice of the Spanish Academy . . . and the same goes for the important grammatical innovations he has begun to introduce." However, the critic reported favorable opinions that seemed to be widespread—Lizardi showed "not only talent and liveliness, not only an ease of composition, not only grace and fluidity in style, but also what is the most commendable, a great fund of morality and honesty." Yet his writing lacked "correctness and good taste," which could be remedied if Lizardi started reading classical works and got rid of Quevedo and Torres Villarroel and his "mania of writing on all manner of affairs and occurrences."[47] In fact, interest in the *Periquillo* appears to have been so great that in 1825 Lizardi published a second edition.[48]

Throughout the nineteenth century, national readers and literary critics generally celebrated Lizardi's affinity with the Mexican people and the novel's nationalistic message. Ignacio M. Altamirano lyricized: "'The Pensador' is an apostle of the people, and for that reason they love him tenderly and they venerate his memory, like the memory of a dear friend. . . . He suffered a great deal, he ate the bread of the people watered with the tears of misery. He went to his grave, obscure and poor, but with the holy aureole of the martyrs of liberty and progress" (42). Altamirano's conversion of Lizardi into a secular saint and a popular hero shows the myth-making of Porfirio Díaz's regime.[49] Oligarchical interests exalted "the people" even as the class sold off the peoples' land and resources to foreigners.

In the first decades of the twentieth century attitudes changed. Alfonso Reyes, member of the influential Ateneo de la Juventud (Atheneum of the Youth) and an important arbiter of literary taste, began the process of reconsidering the *Periquillo*'s "art": "The *romance of the Periquillo* . . . is loved without being read—much less enjoyed. But the common people, always complicated, think that they enjoy it. The popularity of Lizardi (as a novelist, one understands) is the popularity of [his] name" (*Obras* 4: 171).[50] Reyes thus eliminated the novel from the list of books Mexicans read, instead situating it at a point well below high culture, in the life of "common people." However, this passage from the world of print into the orality of Mexico's masses is contradicted by the evidence of the many editions of the *Periquillo* throughout the nineteenth century and the first decade of the twentieth century—1816, 1825, 1830–31, 1842 (two printings), 1865, 1884 (two printings), 1896, 1897, 1903, 1908, and 1909; some percentage of the literate class was reading the novel.[51]

Reyes here reveals the dilemma Lizardi's "popularity" presented to educated Mexicans both in his period and in Lizardi's day. How could a book whose democratic language made it so accessible to so many levels of readers satisfy the aesthetic criteria for complexity most educated critics admired? How could the story, which was specific to Mexico and laden with lower-class realities,[52] enter a *Weltliteratur*? Their solution, to say that the work was popular but did not qualify as "art," began the processes of denigrating Lizardi but also of making of art a politically pure, elitist category.

Carlos González Peña, like Reyes a member of the Ateneo, also began to discredit Lizardi's reputation. Collaborating in a project to trace the history of Mexican literature in the one hundred years since Independence, he said Lizardi was important only because he introduced the novel to Mexico: "Four generations have kept silent about or disguised the truth, and the truth must be told: the *Pensador* was a bad novelist who does not deserve the destiny of immortality for his intrinsic value, for his literary representation in our art. His importance is only historic; he has been a precursor and a rebel. He brought with him to the field of letters a new genre" ("El Pensador Mexicano" 74–75).

Mariano Azuela conceded the *mexicanismo* of Lizardi's work. Yet he found it tedious to read and technically crude, like village art. Azuela claimed the readers of his day had become more refined in their literary tastes than Lizardi's original readers "of rudimentary intelligence, supine ignorance, and infantile ingenuousness" (3: 571–83). He thought that his readers could recognize Lizardi's work as a historical statement but they could no longer respect it as a novel.

Azuela, Reyes, and González Peña must be seen to have been affected by the Mexican Revolution of 1910. Its success in transforming Mexican society would have required that the earlier independence war seem ineffective by comparison. The more developed realism of the novel of the Mexican Revolution, with its explicit message of class conflict, needed to render the earlier novel stylistically unaccomplished and thematically insignificant if the myth of progress was to be believed.

Agustín Yáñez revived interest in the *Periquillo*, calling the character of Periquillo "a national type" in much the same way that Martín Fierro has been thought to express Argentineness. Yáñez interpreted the Mexican as a *pelado*, a victim of social forces beyond his control (the term *pelado* suggests someone plucked or skinned). His reactive personality, Yáñez said in his introduction to *El Pensador Mexicano*, was to be found at all levels of

Mexican society and thus was characteristic of the Mexican (vii–x, xix–xxvii).

However, despite Yáñez's effort to reinstate the *Periquillo* as a national book, what Reyes said about the *Periquillo* may be true today; its title frequently invoked, it is not usually read. Excerpted in school texts, it entertains juveniles. Adults, apart from a few historians who turn to it for documentation of the period, seldom know much more about the work than the fact of its existence. Perhaps the bulk of the critical studies that have been done on the *Periquillo*, by insisting on a literal historical view of the novel, have been responsible for the sense that Mexicans do not have to read the book because they already know what it says. If Mexicanness is now an established commodity, they can jump over the novel's historical complexity, fitting the book into a present-day political scheme.

Lately, however, several scholars have reexamined the text. Noël Salomon has pointed to the criollo representativeness of Lizardi's picaresque hero, and thus the novel's deeper structural message. Jean Franco sees in the *Periquillo* an attempt, through print, to control the colony's diversity at that explosive moment. Focusing on the novel's language, on its plain style which moderates the high and low styles in the novel, she sees Lizardi's effort at social control, at a prescription of correctness. Lizardi, she believes, was an ideologue serving the emerging bureaucratic-administrative class ("Heterogeneidad" 17).

I believe that the novel's language shifts are important to Lizardi's intent. But instead of social control in the *Periquillo*'s recording of alternative discourses and invention of a plain authorial voice, I read Lizardi's decolonizing motives. Taking into account the absolutism of colonial government pronouncements, the thunderous way in which they were delivered, the baffling obscurity of their language, I understand the book's publication and its plain style as a reproach of earlier colonial discourses and, therefore, a subversion of colonial power. Drawing on the *Diario de México* in my first chapter, I argue that, to a great extent, Lizardi was inspired to write his multivoiced novel by the example of an emerging newspaper debate and pamphletry exchange.

My debt to these and other scholars is huge. Luis González Obregón has provided much of the basic information about Lizardi and his period. Paul Radin, James McKegney, and Jefferson Rea Spell have also contributed significantly to a knowledge of Lizardi's life and world. Over the last decades a team at the Universidad Nacional Autónoma de México has worked to locate and publish all his writing. In this project, Jacobo Chencinsky, Luis Mario Schneider, Ubaldo Vargas Martínez, Irma Isabel Fernández Arias, Columba Camelia Galván Gaytán, María Esther Guzmán Gutiérrez, Mariana O. Castañeda, Felipe Reyes Palacios—and most especially María Rosa Palazón Mayoral—have labored heroically.

In studying Lizardi's four novels, I want to examine these imaginative experiments as contributions to decolonization. I explore how Lizardi attempted in each to bring competing discourses together, thereby formalizing the existence of some of the feared or encroaching forms and permitting their interaction as character and plot development. In the *Periquillo* he questions patriarchy. In *La Quijotita*, a novel for women, he confronts women's natures, thereby inquiring what the nature of any subordinate (that is, a colonial) may be. In *Noches tristes* he tests the language of faith, which the Church and official culture taught with didactic books such as the catechism, against the evidence of suffering and uncertainty. And in *Don Catrín* he takes the vocabulary of the Enlightenment and speculates on its consequences for Mexico.

Because the first of these novels, the *Periquillo*, is the innovative book, I devote proportionally more space to its analysis. However, I aim at understanding how, in all of the novels, monarchical ideas of government were (and were not) laid to rest, religious definitions were (and were not) increasingly transformed by a secular society, and aristocratic, military codes of honor were (and were not) absorbed by commercial values. I want to show how the domestic novel, with its stories and pictures of the Mexican Self, broke with previous colonial writing and reading practices. In this manner, I suggest, Lizardi's texts began a decolonizing process in Mexico and the rest of Spanish America, analogous to the work of soldiers and politicians.

Extending Bakhtin

While my study of Lizardi's novels points to ways in which that literary mode aided Mexican Independence, I do not mean to imply that the novel is always revolutionary or that there is a tight, theoretical paradigm by which all writing and reading, coincidental with decolonization, might be measured. For too long, I think, approaches that have stressed the novel's form have imperialistically inferred that the novel must be the same in all times and places. As a consequence, non-European developments, occurring at different intervals and in response to other social circumstances, are often ignored because their forms do not match the Western prototype or their appearance cannot be linked to a European time frame. My study of the appearance of the novel in Spanish America rests, instead, on Mikhail Bakhtin's discourse approach to the novel, thus deemphasizing form and suggesting the genre's diversity. Yet I also believe that Bakhtin's view of the novel as competing voices needs to be measured by a view that the novel is performance as well. "Voices" do not sound freely where there is a history of colonial oppression, censorship, and a set literary tradition that is built on the production of stupefying verbiage, thus forbidding deviance. The "social heteroglossia" and "dialogization," which Bakhtin asserts are the "basic distinguishing feature of the stylistics of the novel" (263), are only possible in circumstances where the novel can be published at all; and even then maybe this feature only appears to operate. If one understands that in all societies individuals are subjected to group pressures, if one knows language to be a social invention that directs thought (Bakhtin himself, for example, recognized the importance of the family in shaping the self, 137), one then understands that it is illusory to read "freedom" into Bakhtin's definition of the novel.

My study of decolonization in the novelistic context is intended, at one level, to add to general discussion of the genre and appreciation of its specific history in Spanish America. The view I hold of narrative as discourse downplays linkage with earlier European fiction, instead emphasizing that Lizardi's works were "books," linguistic packages with ties to American usage, whose publication and reception were an American breakthrough performance.[53] Yet, at another level, in seeing decolonization as individual self-determination, I want to show the extent to which writing and reading imply a psychological, even spiritual journey inward via linguistic probing toward self-discovery. The kind of linguistic decolonization that I am speaking of, then, is basic not only to the cultural and political ways in which decolonization has been thought to function[54] but also, as is increasingly being recognized, to the deeply human and personal.

1

Background

1

Lizardi and Print Culture

When the *Diario de México*, an alternative to the official gazette, began daily publication in Mexico City in 1805, colonial habits of writing and reading changed. Unlike the official *gaceta*, which delivered pronouncements by means of one authoritative voice, editors and readers together wrote for the *Diario*'s pages, resulting in a mixture of voices.[1] The commercial form introduced new topics. In reporting that, although censorship was still the rule in Mexico, restraints on printed matter were loosening in other parts of the world, it opened up the notion of a free press. Some feared this freedom, however; and one writer (October 21, 1811) reassured readers that, even though a free press unleashes powerful forces, experience quickly teaches it to moderate its passionate attacks:

> Confused with what I had read and heard about freedom of the press, both *pro* and *con*, and seeing the first effects of it in the newspapers and pamphlets which have arrived from Cádiz and Havana, of watching them jab and parry without exception . . . and without leaving any puppet headless, I believe it can be compared to a bull which comes out furiously from the pen where he has been held. . . . He butts blindly at whatever is in front of him; he runs, attacks, knocks over or hits in vain. But after two turns around the plaza, he is tired and plants himself in the middle. And, although they call to him from afar, he does not move from his spot without measuring the charge well; and those who fight him respect him and do not approach him as they did at the beginning. (José Diéguez)

When press freedom was finally granted in Nueva España on October 5,

1812, Mexican response was like the mad charge of a bull into the arena. Stored-up emotions exploded as reformers and revolutionaries alike published new newspapers. Print shops printed manifestos, pamphlets, and tracts; they reprinted government documents that had not previously been available. Worried, the viceroy revoked the freedom on December 5, saying that the liberal Cortes de Cádiz, which had decreed such freedom as part of a new constitution, did not have the power to do so since they were only a rump government while Spain was at war with Napoleon. Yet an unusual arrangement would characterize Mexican print production between that date and May 4, 1814, when Fernando VII returned to Spain and abolished the Cortes; throughout that period, although colonial writers were subject to severe restrictions, the colony received uncensored, liberal material from Spain (Neal).

Lizardi's Life

Lizardi made his first print appearance in 1808 as the author of some incidental poetry, and he soon participated in the exchanges in the *Diario de México.*[2] But on October 12, 1812, taking advantage of the relaxed restrictions, he launched his own weekly newspaper, *El Pensador Mexicano,* in which he commented, as he would continue to do for the rest of his life, on Mexican politics, morals, and culture. Editorship meant that he largely authored every issue; and the title gave him the pseudonym he sometimes used later (Lizardi never hid behind "Anonymous" but always signed his work with "El Pensador Mexicano" or his own name). Until December 7, when he was arrested for an issue of *El Pensador Mexicano* in which he asked the viceroy to revoke the permission given to military courts to bring insurgent priests to trial, Lizardi used his newspaper to discuss Mexico's problems, usually in the context of Spanish colonialism. Even during the six months he was in prison, he enjoyed great success.

Lizardi was born in Mexico City on November 15, 1776. Although, as a note on his baptismal record states, he was of Spanish blood, the family was poor. When Lizardi's father became physician at the Real Colegio of Tepotzotlán in 1780, the family moved to that center of Jesuit seminary education near Mexico City, where Lizardi learned to read and write. When he was six, he was sent back to the capital to study with one of the six Latin teachers who operated schools there (Rangel 47). In 1793 he entered the Colegio de San Ildefonso, but it seems he never completed his studies for the *bachillerato*. In 1798 he finished a year-long course in rhetoric, which included logic, physics, and metaphysics; at the same time he enrolled in a *"curso temporal de Artes"* [short course of arts].[3] Luis González Obregón in his biography of Lizardi records the extensive reading Lizardi did in the only public libraries in Mexico City at that time (in the cathedral and at the university), as well as in books borrowed from friends (*Lizardi* 4). Lizardi himself said of his education: "If I cite laws, canons and councils, if until today I have the satisfaction of having sustained my opinions, it is because knowledge is not isolated in the walls of colleges but [is found] PROBLEMATICALLY in books; and I have never let them out of my hands."[4] Lizardi's contemporaries criticized this scattered reading and lack of a formal education; they accused him of unsystematic and undisciplined thought.

In 1798 Lizardi left the university and returned to Tepotzotlán, probably because of his father's death. What little information there is suggests that their relationship had been troubled. A 1786 document reveals that Lizardi's mother had died and that his father was remarrying (Spell, "New Light"). In 1794, Lizardi's father denounced his son to the Inquisition for owning a deck of cards that, in telling fortunes, also suggested off-color humor (Spell "New Light"; González Obregón, *Novelistas* 159–78).

The period between 1798 and 1808 is a mystery (Vogeley "Inquisition"). He married in 1805 or 1806. Paul Radin has discovered that in 1810 Lizardi had his own printing press and suggests that he earned his living as a maverick cut off from conventional publishing.[5] What is probable is that, because of Lizardi's father's death and the son's lack of resources, he also drifted during that time, learning about the demimonde he detailed later in his picaresque stories. González Obregón writes, without citing his source, that friends frequently saw Lizardi in Tepotzotlán (*Lizardi* 18–19). And González Obregón, to be followed by Jefferson Rea Spell, also places Lizardi in a small town along the south coast near Acapulco, and in Taxco.[6] In Taxco, in 1810, Lizardi seems to have been acting as *subdelegado* for the Spanish government; and official documents record an incident when Lizardi turned over arms and ammunition to insurgents. He justified his action later to the viceroy, saying that he had done so to protect the townspeople from possible violence. However, colonial authorities did not believe him and Lizardi was imprisoned for several months in early 1811.[7] Lizardi himself never clarified this period in his life; and, when later he sought compensation for his service during the Independence war from the Mexican government, friends and enemies argued as to his loyalties.

Lizardi continued to publish *El Pensador Mexicano* under censorship until 1814. Publication of the second series had resumed on September 2, 1813, while Lizardi was again in prison; and, in the prospectus for the semiweekly paper, he sarcastically called attention to the review he knew the paper would undergo:

> I won't deny the utility of freedom of the press. But because it was suspended by the government, I won't be the first to shout for it [to come back]; there must be reasons [for the revocation] that it is not for us to examine. Besides, because it is not my intent to trespass beyond the limits of justice and prudence, such freedom is indifferent to me since I don't need it (in regard to what I write being censurable). But if that were the case, so much the better for my personal safety since prior censorship exempts me from responsibility." (*Obras* 3: 162)

In these years, Lizardi also wrote political pamphlets. Of the nine published in 1812, seven are either dialogues or they rely heavily on conversation. One is a *respuesta* [answer] to another writer, thus its format, too, suggests differing voices. In 1813, of the eleven pamphlets published, only one is a dialogue per se. One responds to another writer. The remaining pamphlets indicate by their titles ("Proclamation," "Proposals," "Recipe," "Warning," "Reflection," "Importunings") an increasingly univocal and assertive Pensador.

In volumes 2 (1813) and 3 (1814) of *El Pensador Mexicano* Lizardi continued his imaginative experiments with fables and fictional personae. A critic claims to have seen one number of a newspaper Lizardi wrote for children, *El Correo de los Niños*, dated 1813.[8] His first known work of theater, *Auto mariano*, has also been thought to have been written in 1813. In 1815 he wrote and published three other newspapers, *Alacena de Frioleras*, *Caxoncitos de la Alacena*, and two numbers of *Las Sombras de Heráclito y Demócrito*. All three, although described as newspapers, employ poetry and dramatic invention; and the last makes use of the satirical fictional form, the dialogues of the dead, which political satire reinvigorated in the seventeenth and eighteenth centuries.[9]

Valuable for understanding Lizardi's use of literary techniques and figurative language at this time is an 1824 tract ("Pronóstico político del Pensador Mexicano, y esplicación de otro igual que escribió el año de 1814" [Political forecast by the Mexican Thinker, and explanation of another similar one which he wrote in 1814] reprinted in *Obras* 12:661–67). In the tract he reprints a poem he wrote earlier and explains that its references to a Lion are meant to suggest Spain, a Toad (France), a Fish (England), an Alligator (America), a Dolphin (the first born of the king of France), an Eagle (the imperial ambitions of Napoleon although later an American symbol), and "the queen of birds, the Mexican Eagle." It is not clear why, ten years later, Lizardi felt the need to explain this 1814 allegory. But the confession does reveal that, at the same time Lizardi was planning his first novel, he used fiction for purposes of political disguise.

Between 1816 and 1820, when censorship was finally lifted, Lizardi wrote four novels—two long and two relatively short. Although the first three volumes of *El Periquillo Sarniento* were published in 1816, the fourth, dealing with slavery, was suppressed by orders of the viceroy; to satisfy those subscribers who would not receive this last volume, Lizardi published a collection of verse fables, *Fábulas*, in 1817. In 1818 he published *La Quijotita y su prima* and *Noches tristes*. In 1819 his two-volume collection of miscellany, *Ratos entretenidos*, came out, combining some of his poetry and essays with works by contemporaries; the *Día alegre* ending to *Noches tristes* was also published in this collection. His last novel, *Don Catrín de la Fachenda*, was probably written at this time, too, although it was not published until 1832.

From 1820 until his death in 1827, Lizardi was an important social critic in the new media of journalism and pamphletry. (He wrote almost three hundred pamphlets during his lifetime.) In addition to the newspapers he published (*El Conductor Eléctrico*, 1820; *El Amigo de la Paz y de la Patria*, 1822; *El payaso de los Periódicos*, 1823; *El Hermano de Perico que Cantaba la Victoria*, 1823; *Conversaciones del Payo y el Sacristán*, 1824–25; and *Correo Semanario de México*, 1826–27), he also produced some almanacs and plays. Several times his religious and political loyalties were called into question;[10] in March 1821, Lizardi was jailed for a few days for writing in a pamphlet, "Chamorro y Dominiquín," that Mexico should be independent of Spain (independence when first formulated under Agustín de Iturbide preserved the fiction of Spanish loyalty). And from February 22, 1822, until December 1823, Lizardi was excommunicated for apparently supporting Freemasonry, a ban that severely isolated him and caused him to consider moving to the United States.

Newspapers

In the years before war broke out in 1810, *language* was a code word by which Mexican men and women discussed their awareness of their country's colonial condition. Letters in the *Diario de México*, from readers in the capital and in the provinces, used the topic as a shorthand for the politically sensitive debate. Generally recognized to be an instrument of empire, *language* in the historical context of Greece and Rome suggested contemporary concerns. Typical was the discussion surrounding the inscription to be placed on the Seminario de Minería, a much-vaunted building just built in Mexico City, in whose construction Spain claimed to be sharing its culture and technology with the colony. Readers argued whether the writing should be in Greek, Latin, Castilian, or an Indian language; why one should be chosen (to communicate with as many in the population as possible, to let travelers to Mexico know the function of the building, to record for posterity the memory of the benefactor); and if Roman or Arabic numerals should be used. The general sense seems to have been that a country's signs should be written in the language of that country and that Latin was inappropriate in Mexico.[11] Yet it is equally true that some readers believed still in the universality of Latin.[12] However, one correspondent wrote that Latin was unsuited for the inscription on the Seminario, since that language was not used for instruction there, but Castilian for the same reason was unsuited to the Mexican university. In using words like "dissonance" and "incongruity," he conveyed his feeling that labels were wrongly matched for the many language groups in the colony. The wrangle told that these divergent views regarding language expressed deeper ideological divisions.[13]

Mexican use of *castellano* drew the most discussion. One loyalist reproached his countrymen for their "bad pronunciation," suggesting they might be deviating in other ways from Spanish rules.[14] Other loyalists invoked *patria*, a union based on the language, religion, and customs New Spain shared with Spain, to insist that Mexicans observe orthographic rules that reproduced Castilian habits of pronunciation.[15] Another reader, seemingly caught between Mexican sympathies and obedience to Spanish authority, argued that, if Mexicans spoke the way Spanish was written, they should not be ridiculed as *agachupinados*;[16] he noted that Mexicans customarily said "cabayo" instead of "caballo," "licensia" instead of "licencia," and he urged that "viva voz" [speech] instruct these speakers. However, other colonials, in whose writings one can read a separatist consciousness, argued that because Mexico's linguistic development had been different—*seseo* pronunciation and distinctive lexical forms had evolved—the written system should be changed to reflect the different oral usage ("Isn't the written word the image of the spoken word?").[17]

"Style" also connoted politics. One of the editors of the *Diario*, Carlos María de Bustamante, told of a history written by Chimalpaín in Nahuatl or *mexicano* at the time of the Conquest; in claiming that its Indian style rivalled the Spanish style of the court chronicler, Antonio de Solís, Bustamante suggested the equal worth of that indigenous history.[18] Yet whether they were advocates of Mexican Spanish or of Latin and Peninsular Spanish, all seemed to agree that certain norms, which could be thought to unify the society, should prevail. These literate members of the elite class preferred educated speech to the rusticity of the *payo* [provincial]. And a strong sense existed that Mexicans appreciated what one newspaper writer described as *buen tono* [naturalness or nonbookishness]; this phrase, newly coined because, the writer said, *castellano* did not yet have a word to describe the notion, referred to that expression characteristic of good conversation, one that might replace the convoluted *culternanista* style of writing, and the affected speech of the "*petimetre*" [dandy].[19]

A riddle, published in the December 3, 1805, issue of the *Diario*, sheds light on the colony's fascination with language. If three men, each speaking a different language, could somehow communicate with one another by means of one written system, what might that system be? The answers, published in the January 22–23, 1806, issues, show the range of colonial thought—they include Egyptian hieroglyphs, music, mathematical signs, Chinese characters (understood to be Chinese and Japanese), and Peruvian knotted cords. An American sign language on the list points to an appreciation of pre-Columbian civilizations.

In their arbitration of the language issue, newspapers were becoming an important instrument of an emerging Mexican culture. Newspapers were thought to convey knowledge; but they were also expected to be the means by which members of a confusing and disparate speech culture might be won to a new kind of reading.[20] Reading was increasingly understood not just as training in literacy that children or unschooled Indians might require but also as a means by which adult colonials might become accustomed to liking and trusting the printed word and claiming it as their own. The task of spreading Enlightenment ideas was considered more difficult where there was false knowledge, rather than complete ignorance.[21] And so the newspaper, because it dealt with topics at hand, was favored by many and even thought of as eventually replacing the book, which did not address the problems of everyday life in America.[22] (Biographies and histories, however, were an exception, since their vivid pictures of life involved readers in the books' content.) The newspaper opened up a discourse space for colonials in which readers actively learned to correct and counter official language.

A measure of the newspaper's range is the fact that the 1805 subscription list for the *Diario de México* gives 507 names in the capital and 177 in the provinces (Wold; Vogeley "Newspaper"). In addition, there is evidence that many passed their copies on and that in the provinces a lone subscriber, the parish priest, took it as his obligation to spread the news of what he read.[23] In fact, Lizardi records that his novels circulated in much the same way as these early newspapers; when he announced publication of *La Quijotita* in 1818, he warned subscribers that they should take good care of their weekly chapters and, if they lent them, should ensure the borrowers would preserve them, since "not everyone knows how to treat a piece of paper." Lizardi says he knows that many were left with a dirty or incomplete *Periquillo*. His instructions are surprising; one would think that, as a general practice, colonials would respect paper as a symbol of power, yet those Lizardi was familiar with clearly did not. They needed to be taught how to care for a book, thereby suggesting that these readers not only were unaccustomed to owning such a commodity but also that Lizardi's first book circulated with less than iconic value.

Although other newspapers were published in the colony later, the *Diario de México* was probably the most important in lasting the longest and imposing its format (short, entertaining, useful selections) on others. The *Diario* (1805–1814) published discussions of cultural, literary, moral, and scientific concern, as well as local news and commentary; its four pages also reprinted material from other papers in places like Cádiz, Ha-

vana, the Bahamas, and Buenos Aires. It was the work of three editors who frequently wrote essays for its pages: Carlos María de Bustamante, Jacobo de Villaurrutia, and Juan María Wenceslao Barquera.

After 1810, provincial presses, and portable presses that traveled with the insurgents, began to turn out openly political papers: *El Despertador Americano, El Ilustrador Nacional, El Semanario Patriótico Americano,* and *El Correo Americano del Sur.* They provided insurgent news that generally was picked up in the capital's newspapers. For example, on January 14, 1811, *El Mentor Mexicano,* a week-old newspaper dedicated to "popular enlightenment," published an article on Hidalgo's uprising. Between 1811 and 1814 Mexico City responded to the insurgency challenge with several new newspapers: *El Verdadero Ilustrador Mexicano,* founded in 1812 by José Mariano Beristáin to counter its homonym paper; *El Pensador Mexicano,* in which Lizardi, if not sympathetic to the insurgents, took many of their same arguments;[24] and *El Museo Mexicano,* begun on July 1, 1812, and also edited by Bustamante, which attributed the turbulence of the time to collective ignorance and sought to subordinate politics in a broad program of Enlightenment education. In Guadalajara, Francisco Severo Maldonado, who had been editor of Hidalgo's paper, *El Despertador Americano,* changed overnight to royalist sympathies and began to publish *El Telégrafo de Guadalajara,* a series (May 27, 1811– February 15, 1813) in which he set out the rationale for that point of view (Hamill "Rector to the Rescue"). *Noticioso General,* whose first issue was July 24, 1815, was semi-autonomous, although it mainly served as an official organ. These various papers represented many views, even bordering on antimonarchical sentiment. For example, after Fernando VII returned to the throne, censorship somehow permitted the printing of a fictitious dialogue mocking Fernando's scorn of modern ideas such as popular sovereignty. The king is imagined to have said: "I want to do away with those metaphysical concepts which have caused such fatigue in the imagination of modern philosophers" (*El Redactor Mexicano,* no. 7, fall 1814).

At this critical moment, then, newspapers gave colonials the opportunity to hint at, or in some cases voice openly, their concerns. One reads of the country's growing ideological division in a letter to the editor of the *Diario* in December 1809; there "contradiction" presages the war in which Mexicans not only would fight Spaniards but also one another:

Contradiction supposes almost always a certain plethora of ideas and a certain facility of expression, which only are found among civilized peoples who are more alive and impatient than those less-cultured. The latter are slower and more stubborn in judging, and also more devoted to the truth once it is known because it takes possession of them without any contradiction; while in the more civilized nations, society is very active and the spirit of contradiction is almost a corollary or consequence of the need to speak and to speak a great deal. Thus it is seen: with the need to always speak, to write, without repeating the same thing one has heard or read, the most expeditious means is to contradict all the time. On the contrary it would be necessary to adopt a profound silence most of the time, or plagiarize (an unpardonable crime these days) or endure a dull tolerance for what others have said or written. And at what cost? At the cost of not admitting any spirit of contradiction? ("Q")

However, the writer muses that "imitation," a code word for docile colonial reproduction of Spanish norms, can have public benefits. He says that a spirit of contradiction grows out of self-love, a dangerous concept at that time; and thus he seems to abjure the new climate of doubt and diversity. Nevertheless, he soon changes tack again and concludes that imitation and credulity are signs of a backward nation and that contradiction is good because it furthers development toward a civil society in which differences are acknowledged and respected. A sign that this colonial is beginning to tolerate ambiguity is his admiring discussion of France, a country symbolic of fashion and innovation that had always refused to imitate; yet he cautions that French taste must also be feared.

Imitation is the subject of another *Diario* article (February 2, 1809) in which "F. Adan Cajazul" calls imitation dangerous when agents of knowledge are themselves only superficially acquainted with the external signs of that knowledge. "Cajazul" describes nuns and priests who fumble when they recite prayers because they do not really know the Latin they are saying and only mouth the forms obediently. His criticism, seemingly intended to argue that Latin is dead, paints a foolish picture of these Church men and women.

Newspapers, then, took their distinctiveness from analysis and disputation. Their language was alive, not only in shunning Latin and generally preferring the vernacular, but also in permitting a light familiar tone, which offended some yet entertained others. Newspapers allowed colonials to challenge received wisdom—and the authoritative language with which it was presented—in a way that books seemingly did not permit. Books, associated with ancient history, did not interest colonials in the same way that the newspapers' discussion of current topics did. Books were part of the "theater" of a lawyer's office, in the words of one colonial writer, designed to impress a visitor with the owner's position.[25] Books, another complained, did not provide a knowledge of American plants (suggesting that imported science was not applicable to Mexican realities).[26] And, in an allegorical exchange attributed to "Mr. Klopstock" (March 1809), "Arts" and "Letters" argue which is more useful. "Letters" finally seems to win, yet doubts have been raised that books may be the best path to truth. In fact, the visual arts may be more useful for teaching public morality:

> Arts: The appearance of a book warehouse, can it perchance afford the enthusiast delicious pleasures? There are to be found works covered with dust, which pretended to the honor of immortality and are now sad tracings . . . of the futile efforts at human understanding. . . . [T]hey would not find buyers if they were not adorned with engravings. On the other hand, what is more common than a book? It costs so little that everyone can buy it; it entertains the lazy man and presents ideas that are often false to the reader who, on his own reflection, would more surely arrive at the truth. . . .

> Letters: The advantage that we have of directing the spirit and the heart of man . . . of making him fond of his obligations and of guiding him unceasingly toward happiness . . . is the only one of which we have the right to be proud. We grant with pleasure that Arts can also make virtue attractive; but we dare to assert . . . that its means are insufficient to extend its dominion. By its very nature it seems that beauty, rather than utility, is the object of its production . . . and it is incapable of producing that mixture of ideas and sensations that must be stirred in the heart of man so that he may know virtue.

Truth, which scholasticism had taught was the sum of universal, rational propositions, the product of the exercise of men's minds, was now being redefined. In the *Diario* (October 23, 1806) in an article entitled "La

Mentira" [Lying], "Juan Reforma" stressed the need for practical, immediate truths and credible exponents, if society were to be held together:

Effectively, this astonishing edifice of republics is sustained by the reciprocal veracity of their peoples. . . . The child believes the parent, a wife her husband, the King his vassal, the servant his master, and depending on the veracity of their words, some trust in others; mutually they bring about happiness for one another. Let's take away truth from this climate and good faith, individual and common security will disappear. . . . The world would be the setting for disorder and with this whole of beauty and harmony shattered into parts, men would be similar to beasts since, not having their needs satisfied by reciprocal contracts and good faith, they would appeal to force, and the weakest would be the victim of the strongest. . . . What is a man, that because of his lies, he has lost the right of being believed? He is an object of derision and scorn. . . .

The topic suggests that Mexicans, mistrusting the spokesmen for the colonial truths they had been taught, were beginning to wonder how reliable those truths were.

Newspapers had to respond to this desire for truth telling because the performance rules characterizing colonial discourse were being altered. "Tellability," as Mary Pratt terms it in her study of literature as a speech act (136–47), now dictated the newspapers' subject matter. A concept derived from oral exchanges, where participants are more frequently equal and situational demands advance one topic over another, "tellability" was influencing newspaper content. Newspaper writers, producing for fellow colonials, felt obliged to address immediate concerns. Newspaper language, so as to contrast with the empty words of earlier colonial discourse, took on the character of speech; so as to earn credibility it suggested the *Diario* writers' presence around a table, their conversation and debate. Truth, then, as defined by "Juan Reforma," only emerged with social interaction, under conditions of "reciprocal veracity."

Cafes, flourishing in Mexico at this time, provided another opportunity for the development of new discourses. These public meeting places, reserved for members of the upper and criollo classes (since the poor would have gone to their own bodegas, *pulquerías*, or *vinaterías*), were the setting for amicable controversy and the testing out of ideas. The alameda (promenade) and the theater were other valuable sites for exchanges among compatriots.[27]

If "colonial discourse" had previously been characterized by ritual displays of authority and obedience and by the use of prescribed language for communication with distant officialdom, now "decolonizing discourse" was issuing from spontaneous oral exchanges among speakers who shared interests. Decolonizing discourse was also growing out of a sense of responsibility on the part of an educated elite, a recognition of the need to Mexicanize Enlightenment science and transmit its lessons to a lay audience. Questions previously limited to professional groups such as theologians, philosophers, doctors, and lawyers were available to non-specialists; and these persons, in turn, felt the obligation to pass this new knowledge on to even more ignorant persons. They especially were expected to communicate lessons in urbanity, civility and citizenship. A *Diario* writer describes this filtering-down process:

> Although the rude, coarse people of the population may not read the dailies and the rest of the public papers (perhaps they are even ignorant of their existence), the useful instructions that the papers can communicate pass without their knowing it into their ken by means of enlightened persons. Thus, knowledge is diffused little by little; and the ignorant leave behind many errors which are injurious to them and which make society ugly, perhaps even dishonoring Religion. (Unsigned, "Sobre los bayles nocturnos con motivo de la muerte de los parvulos," January 13, 1806)

Although the Enlightenment in Europe also entailed a certain deprofessionalization of intellectual activity, a pragmatization of truth, and vulgarization, the Mexican process was different because colonial language policies still prevailed and the many Indian and African languages complicated the question of what language to use as a lingua franca. In the city of Mexico, statistics show that, in the first decade of the nineteenth century, in each one hundred persons there were two Europeans, forty-nine Spaniards, six mulattoes, twenty-four Indians, and nineteen of other castes (mixed races).[28] These racial categories possibly indicate class affiliation and thus, literacy and language usage. Although the number of Spaniards seems high, many might have placed themselves in that prestigious category because they identified with that European culture and could pass as such. In the countryside the percentage of nonwhites would have been much greater. Indeed, four-fifths of Mexico's total population was Indian or of mixed race. With such a population imbalance, then, the most important task of enlightened leaders, it was thought, was development of a civic consciousness; the upper classes were to be taught social responsibility, and the lower classes civilized behavior.

However, not all Mexicans were enthusiastic about the new cafe culture. In the February 27, 1810, issue of the *Diario*, "El tocayo de Clarita," later a critic of Lizardi's, ridiculed these popularizing philosophers and their forum:

Happy a thousand fold the present century in which . . . great men have appeared in wisdom and politics! Oh you who live in the dense fog of ignorance! Come and enjoy the enlightened epoch of which you never had the least idea. Come quickly to listen to sublime doctrines which so many other Senecas of the new stripe spill out; how many are the erudite professors of the cafes. . . . You will hear talk of deeds of love and honor, of physics, of metaphysics, of theology, morality, orthography, and geography; also of -neutics and astronomy, of maxims, rules, projects, feuds, observations, calculations, sad happenings, happy happenings, toads, snakes, scorpions, and. . . .

His attack provoked an immediate defense:

In the cafes a public gathers and even if learning is not cultivated, our Spanish language is polished and enriched. One's reasoning faculty is exercised while one develops one's ideas. These social gatherings . . . should . . . be encouraged so that satire, criticism, history, even philanthropy and politics . . . may form now and then the opportune concept of morality in the population. . . . [T]ocayo, get to know these social gatherings and you will read what isn't written in the tomes of your effete eloquence. The very Roman senate, the areopagus of Athens itself, to the surprise of its great rhetorical artists, many times had to admire the products of the natural ingenuity of low slaves. In the courts of Europe, where in the promenade areas both sexes meet socially and reason together, many women are to be found who astonish the old men and the erudite;

and the latter are delighted when they see the grace and energy with which a woman develops the ideas which come to her. (March 5, "El Cafetero padrastro de Clarita L.F.E.")

"Cafetero" argues that women are often excellent speakers because of "their mode of reasoning, their development of conceits, and their skill of knowing how to speak energetically"; he defends the inherent worth of women and slaves. His argument, that language skills are developed and polished in the cafes and that in the verbal exchange thoughtful faculties are trained and the criticism necessary for a country's moral growth is learned, suggests that any deficiencies lesser peoples may have can be remedied by these means. Reference to the Greek areopagus and the Roman senate evokes the disputatious origins and rhetorical underpinnings of knowledge; and "Cafetero" may even have been suggesting that, in the same way that earlier cultures produced their appropriate forms, Mexicans could invent theirs. "Tocayo," however, only saw the disorder brought on by unworthy pretenders to "sublime doctrines."

If cafe conversation was simultaneously reviled and held up as the key to Mexican civil development, the new language of courtesy also had its critics and its defenders. "R. el culti-locuente" satirized affected Mexican speech (June 11–12, 1806, *Diario*) in his article "Falsa cultura" [False culture]:

Farewell nephew. Proceed in peace to the grand city of Mexico, where the resolution of your litigation is awaiting you. The Enlightenment and culture have their proper abode there; learn enlightenment there and endeavor not to be taken for a rustic in the gatherings you attend.

In order to accomplish this you must forget all our familiar salutations, substituting the civilized ones such as "I kiss your hand," "I am at your service," "I await your command" and, although it may not be exactly pertinent, "I am delighted that you are enjoying it" since you must suppose that health is being spoken of.

With young ladies always have at hand the words *madame* and *obsequious*, beauty, and some other opportune comparisons with Venus, which will be where you will have greatest success. Use "Sir," even though you are dealing with a freight hauler, and give a thousand expressions of rank to those who accept the greeting without deserving it. Inquire of married men about their *Mistress* for they won't understand consort, wife or woman.

In style you will be cultured and Latin-speaking; and [if you don't follow these rules] you will show that you don't have the least idea of good taste.

If one sector of the Mexican population memorized set phrases (as their colonial education had taught), another sector could see that Mexico City's pretense of teaching progress and culture through snippets of language was foolish and dishonest.

Imported language brought uncertainty. Some thought, for example, that French refinements taught duplicity. "Anonymous" ("Conversacion," *Diario*, September 29, 1806) complained that at a dinner party in Paris, "About the same man, at the same dinner table, one says to the right he is an eagle and to the left he is a duck." In Paris, words counted for so little that "dress [spoke] more than the person."

Debates as to which language communicated best with the illiterate masses suggest that the Mexican elite understood the desirability of increasing exchanges among compatriots. Yet the fact that some realized that the Indian and mixed-caste population would not be reached through words shows their frustration that one language might unite the colony. In the *Diario* one reads that illiterate and non–Spanish speaking peoples only understood the symbolism of masques, parades, the Mass, and so on; architecture, too, was recognized to be a sign system, which did not depend on literacy and could transmit a message of power.[29] Dress was discussed as a wordless advertisement of rank.[30] The language of the *silbido* [whistle], used by illiterates and criminals, also interested *Diario* readers,[31] perhaps because this propertied sector of the population realized that uncontrolled forms of communication threatened their wealth and safety. Records of political satire, which have survived in Inquisition archives, show that educated, Spanish-speaking colonials heard this oral world and may have tried to manipulate it, disguising their identity and criticism of colonial conditions in "anonymous" poems and songs, which could then be heard and broadcast by the masses.[32]

It is clear, therefore, from this review of newspaper discussion that colonials were widely self-conscious as to language's role in Mexican society. Normally of theoretical interest only to philosophers and rhetoricians, language was regularly discussed, from every conceivable angle, in the new media and forums. Thus one asks why, if large numbers of Mexicans at this moment understood the shaping power of words, the arbitrary nature of the linguistic sign, and the important role of language in social relationships, cultural decolonization did not take place coincidentally with political emancipation?

The Book, Political Pamphletry, and "Truth"

Irving A. Leonard has studied how, despite tight restrictions Spanish policies were thought to have imposed, many books were licensed to enter the colonies throughout the 300–year administration. Contradicting general belief, Leonard shows that legislation controlling imaginative literature was designed to protect Indian peoples, thought to be weak and in need of protection. However, nothing was said about their white masters (*Books of the Brave* 81); and indeed, there is evidence that almost the whole run of the first edition of *Don Quijote* (1605) was sold in the colonies, where wealth permitted the purchase of this expensive item.

In 1800 books remained a precious commodity in Spanish America, coveted by the elite and those who aspired to that status. Newspapers criticized books yet books seem still to have been valued for their contents as well as for their leather bindings. Not only did private libraries contain the new secular literature that was being produced in the cultural centers of Europe as the Enlightenment spread its message (for example, licensed members of the boards of censors had access to new books that might be controversial [Pérez Marchand, Longhurst]), but also many such books were for sale in Mexico.[33] And, if a work was judged to be unfit (as was Edward Gibbon's *Decline and Fall of the Roman Empire* "for containing doctrines which were erroneous, heretical, impious, and injurious to the Catholic religion"), the *Diario*'s notice of such censure had the consequence of publicizing the book.[34] However, many books entered the colony clandestinely, brought back by Mexicans traveling abroad or imported by sailors and corrupt merchants in the port cities.

One measure of the extent of the legal book business in the colony at this time is a lengthy list of all the bookstores and convent and school libraries, prepared for the Inquisition in 1802. In order to recall the works of a dangerous author, officials went to fourteen bookstores and twenty-six schools and convents in Mexico City, as well as to establishments in Puebla, Valladolid (Morelia), Mérida, Durango, Guadalajara, Oaxaca, Querétaro, Veracruz, Campeche, Jalapa, Guanajuato, Zacatecas, Celaya, San Miguel el Grande, San Luis Potosí, Chihuahua, Tlaxcala, and Orizaba.[35]

The holdings of one such bookstore, which was also a print shop, have survived in fairly intact form as the Abadiano collection in the Sutro Library (San Francisco); the range of materials to be found there is a valuable index to the kinds of books available to Mexican readers in the first decades of the nineteenth century (see also Wold chap. 9).[36] The Abadiano family inherited the library and warehouse of Alejandro Valdés, an important printer in Mexico City in the first decades of the nineteenth century. Valdés published volumes 1–3 of the first edition of *El Periquillo Sarniento*, volumes 1–2 of Lizardi's *Ratos entretenidos*, which included *Noches tristes y día alegre*, volume 2 of *La Quijotita*, the first edition of *Don Catrín*, and many of Lizardi's political pamphlets.

The collection's secular imprints, from the period prior to Mexican Independence in 1821, are mostly Spanish (principally Madrid, but also Barcelona, Sevilla, Gerona, Medina del Campo, Cádiz, Valencia, Alcalá, Palma, Salamanca, and Zaragoza). Thus, the long list of publishing centers there indicates that the fragmentation of Spanish cultural integrity had begun even before Napoleon's troops entered the Peninsula. Although Madrid continued to exercise a print monopoly, granting printing permissions until the end of its imperial rule, its hold on Peninsular and colonial production can be seen to have been declining. The books printed in Mexico to be found in the Abadiano collection are mainly Lizardi's works and religious materials from the sixteenth through the nineteenth centuries. In the late eighteenth and early nineteenth centuries, Mexican printing houses were important businesses, both printing government and Church materials and the new newspapers and political literature, and selling imported books.

The subject matter of the collection's eighteenth- and nineteenth-century books reflects an awareness of new fields of investigation, such as the natural and social sciences; it also reveals a desire to transform theory into practice and to simplify abstruse knowledge. There are still many religious books (now mostly in Spanish rather than in Latin); but the collection also contains many works of secular literature—histories, military manuals, biographies, books on philosophy, the arts, and the sciences, cultural studies from comparative and evolutionary points of view, political essays, moral and erudite miscellanies, dictionaries, new editions of classical works, and so on. The imaginative character of many of these works, as well as the varieties of prose fiction, drama, and poetry, reflect Neoclassic expectations for reading, that is, that truth be illustrated by the imagination, that utility be enhanced by sweetness and beauty. Some of the Abadiano's authors were Spanish (Padre Benito Feijóo, Padre José Francisco de Isla, Tomás de Iriarte, Ramón de la Cruz, Vicente García de la Huerta, Diego de Torres Villarroel, and the exiled Spanish Jesuit Lorenzo Hervás y Panduro). However, many were also French, Italian, English, and Portuguese, and I discuss later the translated nature of these latter works.

Colonial Mexicans came to their understanding of the importance of language through their own experience. Yet Spanish consciousness of the topic, which many of the above-mentioned books set out, helped to authorize its discussion. Feijóo's essays, particularly his "Paralelo de las lenguas castellana y francesa" [Parallel between the Castilian and French Languages], provided Mexicans with an exemplary discussion of language's political implications, as Frenchifying fashion swept the Spanish court. Both national languages, modern versions of an imperial tongue, Feijóo wrote, were equal; and, therefore, the supposed superiority of one was only a political myth. Loan words, traded in a free climate of "commerce" (*Teatro* 1:223), usefully extended a country's language; yet to borrow, when one's language already possessed a way to say the same thing, was shown to be the mark of a conquered nation (225).

José Cadalso in his *Cartas marruecas* [Letters from Morocco, 1789] worried that a new international state made up of Europe's nobility ("different in idiom, dress and religion," 70) was diminishing national culture in Spain; consigned to the homeland were the backward poor whose speech was the only preserve of national tradition. In his *Exequias de la lengua castellana* [Exequies for the Castilian Language, 1782], Juan Pablo Forner feared the death of Spanish because of upper-class decadence and excessive imitation of foreign expression. He traced national literary style to a preexisting oral fount, in which each group of people expressed itself uniquely: "Each nation, each people has its own particular character. Writing accommodates itself to this character the way water does to a glass" (58).

Yet the most popular Spanish book of all in Mexico was Isla's *Fray Gerundio* (1758). In it the Jesuit author parodied the tradition of religious oratory in Spain, which *culteranista* excesses had emptied of meaning. Fray Gerundio's pompous sermons were reproduced and then corrected and ridiculed by more theologically trained, or more sensible, listeners. A novel built around varieties of language, the work attacked those representatives of the Church who perpetuated institutional power through obfuscating language. In the Abadiano collection, there are copies of the 1787, 1813, and 1820 Spanish editions of the work, as well as an 1820 collection of documents related to *Fray Gerundio*. And, to prove further the impact the book had on Mexicans, an 1820 political pamphlet, written by A. A. A. to defend the monarchy and the Spanish constitution, introduces Fray Gerundio into Mexican political discourse. The pamphlet's title, "Viaje de Fr. Gerundio a la Nueva España" [Fray Gerundio's Journey to New Spain], brings the orator, who cares only for language style and repeats uncritically the ideas he hears, to Mexico, his proper home.

Other Spanish Jesuits, writing some of their works in exile in Italy, also influenced Mexican attitudes toward language at this time. The comparative study by Lorenzo Hervás y Panduro, *Catálogo de las lenguas* [Catalogue of languages, 1800], helped Mexicans appreciate their distinctive language; the list of American Indian languages, compiled as a result of Jesuit missionary efforts, included Mexican Indian forms. In another work, *Historia de la vida del hombre* [History of man's development, 1794], Hervás explored alternative medical and botanical classifying systems (such as those of Linnaeus and the Chinese herbalists); and his study had the effect of legitimating diversity in understanding knowledge. Yet in comparing the eloquence of the Greek and Roman metaphysicians and the rhetoric of contemporary philosophers, he attacked the latters' methodology as bad language practice: "Even in the briefest discourse thoughts about objects which are physical and metaphysical, natural and theological, civil and moral, simple and allegorical, without any dialectical, rhetorical or verbal connection, are heaped up and confused. The philosophical style consists of vomiting up tumultuously thoughts of all kinds with a concision of words" (3: chap. 1, 67). A book by another Spanish Jesuit, Juan Andrés, *Origen, progresos y estado actual de toda la literatura* [Origin, progress and present state of all literature, 1784–1787], also influenced Mexican thinking about language. Andrés's broad synchronic and diachronic approach to language and literature taught Mexicans important lessons, one of which was the way the figurative language of poetry had arisen.

"Poetry" was the subject of a cluster of articles in the *Diario*, in which writers used the topic to explore connections between political and religious language. "Poetry" framed their discussions of metaphor and formulaic language, of men's access to truth through language. These writers noted that, as vernacular literatures gained legitimacy in the eighteenth century, modern poets such as Milton and Camoens sought inspiration in earlier sacred and classical languages, which had attempted to name and revere deities. The *Diario* writers said these modern poets, through their mythological stories of gods and use of epic language, were increasingly calling into question these first formulations of faith. One writer distrusted the religious value of their modern myths.[37] However, his doubts were contradicted by a traditionalist who argued that all poetry was divinely inspired: "Holy Scripture offers sublime models of poetry and eloquence, whose beauty and force exceed what even the most enlightened experts may admire in this genre. Thus it is that a divine religion, teaching its eternal truths, accommodated itself to men's way of thinking so as to move their souls. And the truth is that it is a great honor for us that this daughter of the heavens has deigned to make use of our language."[38]

Another unidentified author, however, did not believe that poetic language was sacrosanct. In a series called "Historia antigua" [Ancient History], which ran from March through May 1809, he traced the figurative language of poetry and fables to the awe with which early peoples attempted to speak of their kings and gods. He described first the Egyptians and Assyrians, who invented hieroglyphs and allegories; but, he said, these expressions soon confused the idolaters who borrowed from these peoples. Error grew up because persons who take for their own use languages invented by others' experiences are often insensible to those languages' distinctions. For example, in that early Mediterranean world, hyperbole began to be understood literally:

The first time that the people wanted to establish a cult, that is, the first time they attempted to give to the divinity exterior signs of respect and love, they could not do anything else but avail them-

selves of those [signs] with which they demonstrated these sentiments to their [political] leaders. Consequently, the acts of homage,
which they offered to their [political] leaders, they offered also to
their gods. . . .

In fact, the cult created for gods not having been invented until
after the homages rendered to [political] leaders, one could not
speak of a king whose memory was dear unless one had spoken of a
god. The signs of love, of respect and recognition, titles, names,
everything was common; and on account of this everything was
confused very quickly. Gods came to be men and men came to be
gods. Perhaps this is the origin of fables which, on the one hand,
made gods rule on earth, giving them our passions and our virtues,
our vices, and, on the other hand, situated sovereigns in the heavens,
entrusting them with the government of the universe.

The passage demonstrates how, through research into ancient languages
and the origins of poetry, colonials were learning how religious belief had
evolved and how they might separate allegiance to a king from respect for
the divine.

The same *Diario* writer then discussed how Greeks and Romans borrowed Eastern linguistic habits.[39] These newer peoples took literally the
"poetic fictions" from the East's impoverished languages and passed these
marvelous traditions on uncritically (one surmises by way of the Christian
language of faith). Some "two or three men" knew the truth, but for most
"an invented error [was] more sacred than the very truth." The "people
and the average literate (who almost always is 'the people' in the eyes of
learned men)" were taken in by "the shell of mythology" because "it was
shiny and varied." However, the writer said that those who knew the error
of language refrained from criticizing traditional belief because "it would
have been dangerous to doubt" and "the explanations of these wise allegories hung on too sublime speculations."

In using "mythology" to suggest how a conspiracy of silence on the
part of linguistically educated persons worked historically, the author
implied there were other times when only a few men knew that "truth"
was really "invented error." And appropriately for Mexico's condition, he
argued that the peoples' credulity based on ignorance particularly produced benefits for an emerging culture: "In these assemblies [the Pana-

thenaic Games] in Greece heroic actions, marvels, fables were the subject. Everything that was seen, everything that was heard, increased valor, led to heroism and made useful notions last. Curiosity had all the attractiveness that the beginnings of knowledge provide, and credulity was great because ignorance made it all possible. . . . These peoples who only a little before hardly knew [one another] began to look at themselves as one and the same nation, and to scorn all others." Educated readers of the *Diario* might have flattered themselves that they were among the instructed. They might have been convinced that, in a developing Mexico, some men could live without the mysteries of belief but that "public virtue" would be enhanced if the masses did not know the truth. However, they might also have learned how the metropolis had manipulated their colonial ignorance.

Interest in figurative language is only one manifestation of a general Mexican awareness of language's history. The humanism of the eighteenth century, which foreign books spread in Mexico, also stimulated this interest. Hugh Blair's *Lecciones sobre la retórica y las bellas letras* [Lectures on Rhetoric and Belles Lettres], popular in Mexico, showed the new vernacular literature's capabilities; José Luis Munárriz's 1798 translation of Blair's work (second edition 1804) enriched it for Hispanic readers by long passages devoted to Spain's literary development.[40] But also old books were read anew; for example, new editions of the *Retórica eclesiástica* [Ecclesiastical Rhetoric] by the sixteenth-century Spaniard Luis de Granada, in which he advised religious educators on their employ of persuasive techniques, made colonials aware of how authoritative voices manipulated their audiences.

However, colonials also seem to have come to a consciousness of language's importance through their perception that European books did not match American life. There is a great deal of evidence that many Mexicans suspected that another's language limited their thought, that imperial shifts prevented them from creating their own truer expressions of solemnity, honor, and reverence. For example, a rather uniform condemnation of proverbs, "*evangelios chiquitos*" [tiny gospels], is to be found in various sources,[41] suggesting not just a learned culture's scorn of orality but also a reluctance to trust fixed phraseology. Perhaps all experience was not equal, or the maxim's original thought lay buried under spurious language.

In the many "dictionaries" of the day, key words were defined in colonial, that is, politically relevant, terms. "Burlesque" or "political" dictionaries presented new thoughts on *patria, patriotas,* and *independencia.* Essays, such as some of Lizardi's political pamphlets, redefined set language; for example, in an 1812 title, "He is not a gentlemen because of birth, but he who knows how to be one," Lizardi corrected the meaning of *señor* [lord]. *El pueblo* [the people] was another term that required redefinition. In the 1821 pamphlet, "The tribune of the masses, or the writer of the down and out. Dialogue between the Tribune and the Masses," the anonymous writer contrasted *el vulgo* (an ignorant group, composed of many penniless, yet pretentious, aristocrats and clerics) with *la plebe* (men whose labor was useful such as artisans, miners, and farmers) and *el populacho* (the idle, the beggars, who made no contribution to society).[42] *Señor* and *pueblo* were two key words that Mexicans needed to rethink in establishing an independent, republican future.

The conflict surrounding "truth"—who knew it, who proclaimed it, by what means it was made known, what "error" it opposed—is nowhere better visible than in the titles of some of Mexico's political pamphlets. An absolutist stance is revealed in "The imperious voice of truth and political disillusionments regarding common concerns" (1810). Religious truth is buttressed by experience in "The plain truth to the insurgents of New Spain, seduced by the Free Mason agents of Napoleon, the truth of the Catholic religion and experience" (1812). "Truth" is variously asserted in: "True patriotism" (1809), "The naked truth" (1811), "The true liberty, happiness and independence of nations" (1813). And in 1820, when the Spanish constitution was again in effect and a measure of press freedom existed in the colony, titles claiming to state the truth proliferated: "Truth triumphs over deceit" and "Error confounded and truth demonstrated." "Truth" was shown to come from hitherto silenced voices in "Truth. The account of the Indian woman" (1820) and "Drunkards and children usually reveal truth" (1820). "Truth," or truth telling, was often expressed as *desengaño* [disillusionment, disenchantment, or denunciation of the lies others told so as to reveal the real truth]. Emanating from both loyalists and insurgents, truth had to be dispersed, as in "The plain truth to the Indians making them see how much they owe the Spaniards" (1810), "The ridicule and plain truth about the insurgents" (1811), and "Things are made so clear that even the blind see them" (1812). In 1820 critics of a free press, who said that the many who were rushing their thoughts into print were ignorant, were overruled by the sentiment expressed in one pamphlet's title, "Truth although it may embitter is many times the precious object of a free press."

Colonial readers understood truth's competing claims. For most, however, "truth" was experiential knowledge, an American perspective, full linguistic rendering of new political realities. Woman was often made to be both the source of truth and its transmitter. For example, in an 1820 pamphlet, "La Malinche of the Constitution," the writer assumes the voice of the Indian mistress of Hernán Cortés, interpreter for the invading Spaniards and mother of the first mestizo.[43] Now made to symbolize Mexico's dual European and Indian identity, she maternally shows an interest in her Indian and mestizo descendants by translating the freedoms and protections the Spanish Constitution afforded them into their Mexican language. This printing of an Indian tongue in the context of a political pamphlet was probably prepared for priests to read to their Indian parishioners; and its bilingual format shows that not only were national speech varieties increasingly being written down but that also (as in the remainder of the pamphlet) Spanish legalese was being translated into another, more understandable level of Spanish. An excerpt from the Spanish introduction follows:

Indians of this World, whose natural idiom is Mexican—you only understand of Spanish the usual words of your miserable commerce—do you know what Constitution means? You do not know nor will you ever know if it is not explained to you in your language. Listen, then, to what it is advisable that you know, while things are being established and experience is gradually teaching [these things] to you. Know that you are already free of the harshness of the overseers on the *haciendas.*

La Malinche appeared again in an unsigned 1821 pamphlet, "The Informed Malinche who came with the Trigarantine army. Dialogue between a lady and an Indian." Here La Malinche, who is made to speak in rustic Spanish, brings news of Guerrero's troops. She also teaches the señora the meaning of the Mexican names *Tenochtitlan, Anahuac, Montesuma,* and *México,* and the upper-class woman concludes approvingly with respect to her Indian language lesson: "in nothing of what you have

told me do I find anything repugnant, but on the contrary, much natural-
ness and verisimilitude."

Finally, in considering the colony's awareness of its special linguistic
character and the artifacts by which communication among Mexicans was
accomplished, I want to recall those translated books that came into
Mexico from Europe. Many of the Spanish books in the Abadiano collection, for sale in Mexico, were translations of works published originally in
French, English, Italian, German, and so on.[44] To emphasize their sev-
eral-times-removed linguistic status, I cite some titles whose translation
histories are particularly revealing. *Reflexiones sobre la naturaleza, ó consi-
deraciones de las obras de Dios en el órden natural: escritas en aleman para todos
los dias del año* [Reflections on nature, or Considerations on the works of
God in the natural order, written in German for every day of the year],
a German work by H. S. S. Sturm (Madrid, 1803), was translated first
into French and then into Spanish. Henry Fielding's *Tom Jones* (Madrid,
1796) was translated first into French and then into Spanish. Another,
*Viages de Enrique Wanton a las tierras incognitas australes, y al pais de los
monos . . .* [Voyages of Henry Wanton to the Unknown Western Lands,
and the Country of the Apes] (Madrid, 1778), came via Italian into Spanish (although its Spanish translator claimed the work, an adaptation of
Jonathan Swift's *Gulliver's Travels*, was written originally in English).
Still another, *Zumbas* [Jests] (Madrid, 1790–1799) by José and Santiago de
Santos Capuano, satirized translation when it claimed to be translated
"from Spanish into Castilian." In introductions to these books, Spanish
translators often carefully explained how they translated the work, particularly when the book was from Protestant England or liberal France; as
Juan de Escoiquiz wrote in his preface to the edition of the *Obras selectas
de Eduardo Young* [Selected Works of Edward Young] (Madrid, 1804), he
felt free to suppress anything he thought worthy of censure. Munárriz's
preface to Blair's *Rhetoric*, which explains how he "translated" the work, is
twenty-eight pages long. Thus, Mexican readers were exposed to the fact
that "translation" often meant that not only did one set of words replace
another, but dangerous ideas disappeared.

In the eighteenth century Spanish authors were increasingly "translating" ancient works, not only taking their words to the vernacular but also
chopping them up for modern compendia, simplifying their language,
and converting their ideas into dialogues for school instruction. Spanish

authors, because politics and economics made Spain a second-rate power, often recast the work of other countries' scientists and philosophers so that Spanish readers, if they wanted to read contemporary literature, were forced to consume these pallid works. Yet in Mexico these new books, which suggested a departure from old-fashioned Spanish thought, were attractive. A colonial author explains why in the *Diario de México:* "in all epochs [since the Conquest] Mexico has been a faithful sunflower to the Metropolis." He lists Spanish architectural styles, literary tastes, and painting modes, which set taste in the colony, to complain of Spain's "reigning . . . governing . . . and commanding."[45] Therefore, the eighteenth-century retrieval of Spanish classics, such as *El Cid* and Siglo de Oro writers (in separate editions or part of the multivolume *Parnaso español*), seems to have had limited appeal in the colony. Similarly, editions of Alonso de Ercilla's *La Araucana*, El Inca Garcilaso de la Vega's *Comentarios reales de los Incas*, and histories of the Conquest of Mexico by Antonio de Solís and Bernal Díaz de Castillo seem to have generated less enthusiasm in Mexico because their stories reinforced the lesson of Spanish power.

"Books," then, were an important topic used at this moment of decolonization to permit Mexican discussion of cultural imperialism. Many distrusted books, yet they remained powerful symbols of European civilization; and, for those desirous of repudiating Spanish culture and embracing non-Spanish bookish developments, they permitted access to prestigious Enlightenment thought. Mexican ambiguity with respect to books seems to be proof of a growing consciousness of the double bind colonials found themselves in. Caught between old and new, they found fault with Spanish production yet they also seem to have been wary of the new taste for French and English culture. Lizardi's novels, visibly drawing on Spanish narrative forms but also recognizing the freshness of French and English ideas, apparently tried to avoid the linguistic trap represented by translated books. Their Mexican stories told of contemporary realities in straightforward, often colloquial language, thus attempting to bring the colony's Spanish language into line with modern developments and lived exigencies.

2

Lizardi and the Satiric Novel

Julio Cortázar's complaint, made in 1966, that Spanish America lacks a "real literary tradition, where literature reflects the evolution of language" (Harss and Dohmann, 234), restates the dilemma Lizardi faced 150 years earlier in creating the first Spanish American novel. Although Cortázar is referring to the preferences that educated Argentineans showed for translated foreign books throughout the nineteenth and twentieth centuries, his insight helps explain, I believe, Lizardi's problem at the moment of Independence: How could the colonial author find among the range of literary discourses in Spanish a suitable one to use for the decolonizing novel he envisioned? How could Lizardi make the writing and reading of "literature" relevant to everyday American language practices?

Cortázar and other writers of "the new Spanish American novel"[1] have subsumed under *style* concerns over the bookish language they have inherited, and their deconstructive and reconstructive efforts to rework it so as to address national and hemispheric concerns. Cortázar writes in *Rayuela* [Hopscotch] that it is necessary "to declare war on language turned whore" (452), meaning that a literary language, resulting from the unnatural embrace of other languages' ideas and stories, has grown up in Spanish America, separate from the region's spoken languages. Literature, he says, has not enabled real American thought; instead it has perpetuated a taste for fancy language that covers over ugly truths and makes the area dependent still on foreign culture. *Style*, therefore, a term that often suggests personal idiosyncratic usage and a self-indulgent circle of writer and readers, connotes for Cortázar a new kind of anti-writing that attempts to democratize literary writing and make its language useful in solving American problems. In the same way, the frequent appearance of stylistic varieties and direct authorial discussions of "style" in the pages of Lizardi's novels signals the critical function of his texts and their language.

In 1816 Lizardi, a criollo writer who wanted to create a novel for a Mexican readership, needed to redefine the colonial speech act, that is, the activity by which a colonial participated in the processes of writing or reading, speaking or listening, all the while using an imposed language code and conforming to authoritative performance expectations. Resident in Nueva España, Lizardi observed the frequent gap between *palabras* [words] and *obras* [deeds]. He saw that over the centuries of colonial rule, words, rhetoric, and paper had acquired their own reality. He witnessed the fact that the Mexican elite often cooperated with Spanish cultural tyranny out of self-interest, but also perhaps because they were trapped by its powerful language. "The people," on the other hand, knew that de facto practice was different (that is, worse, base, corrupt) from the obedient reports or terminologically skewed interpretations of the colonial world that were sent back to Spain. The "people"'s language, spoken at home, every day, to sort out economic, political, and material concerns, was newly gaining some de facto credibility as public discourse. Therefore, Lizardi concluded, a new kind of literature might be made to bring together the several official languages and the many varieties of Mexican speech, so as to dramatize the colony's linguistic concerns.

Earlier Mexican writers such as Sor Juana Inés de la Cruz and Carlos Sigüenza y Góngora had also produced literature for Mexican readers. Yet the readership for their work, often a response to patronage, was limited to a small section of the court. In contrast, Lizardi had to sell his new mix of learned and popular topics and languages to large numbers of colonials, who were only recently won to reading by the newspapers and political tracts of the day. These numbers would have been extended by the habitués of the cafes, who recognized in Lizardi's text resonances of their oral exchanges. He might also have drawn some readers from among the pious who consumed the readily available sermons, prayers, saints' lives, and so on; and these would have looked for moral benefit in reading Lizardi's novel. Another group might have come from the elite class, familiar with the diversionary literature from the Continent and England; these persons, probably, would have compared Lizardi's work with these prestigious antecedents, approving of similarities and disapproving of differences. Some, undoubtedly, were new readers, like women, whose expectations for the written word were often critical in some ways and uncritical in others.[2]

Before Lizardi could even worry about how these various categories of readers might receive his innovative text, he had to sell the book. The commodity value of an entertaining book is indirectly revealed in a discussion of scarce coinage in the March 24–29, 1810, issues of the *Diario de México*. Because cacao beans were commonly being used as money in Mexico, Central America, and the Caribbean, the Indians who then consumed these much-handled beans in the form of chocolate were getting sick. At the material level, then, the shortage of legal tender, the nakedness of many of the poor (who lacked even clothing to cover themselves),[3] and the stringencies many were suffering in a hungry region (where the countryside was destroyed by war and where trade was interrupted) made many question the purchase of a luxury item such as a book —let alone one written by an ordinary, upstart Mexican.

Luxury is the subject of a series of articles appearing in the *Diario* in April 1809, in which art is viewed as a luxury a country or an individual wishing to be strong must dispense with ("When man opens the door to new needs he gives evidence of weakness"). The author, identified as a Frenchman writing from Paris, appears to have been criticizing the tastes of a decadent aristocracy; and many Mexican readers must have sympathized with his condemnation of that class and its "art" (superfluous goods such as jewels, and pastimes that uselessly stimulated the senses). However, in late April 1807, an anonymous writer argued that a developing state must protect the arts; in his example of Alexander and that emperor's patronage of Homer, he suggested a view of "art" as a civilizing force and appeared to be criticizing Spain for neglecting art's educational role in Mexico.

The book Lizardi would create—and here I take as one invention Lizardi's four novels—emerged then as "art," but also as a commercial venture, paralleling Mexican newspapers and political pamphletry. These new print modes of the first decades of the nineteenth century had proven that paper could be claimed to state domestic concerns; they prepared the colony for a new style of writing and a different use of the European novel. Lizardi's tie to this ephemeral literature is underscored by the fact that his novels were soon taken back into that medium; rather than circulating just as books, they appear to have been widely talked about and their imagined characters made real. Evidence is an 1820 political pamphlet in which Lizardi's characters appear: "Who is this apparition (I asked D. Ingenuo). He's the Guard of this area. And the mangy lackey? His name is Periquillo and he's the brother of Catrin, and both are brothers of a girl whose name is Quijotita, and she is in . . . the Hospital of Cayo-Puto (I said admiringly). But hardly had I offered this, when Lackey and Catrin, asking me at the same time and in a menacing tone, what business do you have with Quijotita? . . . since the Quijotita and we are children of the Pensador Mexicano and of the land in which he philosophizes."[4]

The writer seems to have read the unpublished *Don Catrín;* and he also appears to have counted on his readers' familiarity with the work, thereby suggesting that, despite the censors' disapproval, the manuscript had been passed around a private network. It is true that the *Periquillo* was published in installments so that it looked like periodical literature. But Lizardi's other novels seem to have been published as wholes or in large chunks as volumes. In any case, Lizardi's novels did not remain aloof from Mexican culture as bookish artifacts following their publication but instead were absorbed into the lively discourse world of Mexican print. In fact, in the 1820s Lizardi as a correspondent with other pamphleteers and letter writers himself became a kind of literary persona, perhaps because he chattily talked about himself in his writing.[5]

Lizardi's experiment with the novel form can be seen to have been encouraged by several official literary contests, or calls for literary production, in the first decade of the nineteenth century. The first appeal, for poetry, was designed to commemorate the placing in the capital of an equestrian statue of Carlos IV, according to the design of the sculptor, Manuel Tolsá; two hundred poets responded and a volume of the work of "las musas mexicanas" was published by José Mariano Beristáin de Souza in 1804. This outpouring celebrated the artistic presence of the king in the colony; and although the literary forms were suitably imperial, the opportunity released feelings of civic pride. Local consciousness—and the realization of artistic abilities—grew still more when, in the last days of July 1808, news reached Nueva España that on May 2 the Madrid populace had risen against Napoleon's troops; unasked, Mexican poets sympathetically protested the colony's loyalty to Fernando VII.[6] Again, the response, eighty-nine poems by thirty-four identifiable authors, was published in a forty-six-page "book." On September 7, 1809, the *Diario* announced a contest, which interests in Cádiz had arranged, soliciting artistic expressions of patriotic feelings in Spain and the colonies. Also in that issue a letter by a Cuban, Josef de Arango y Castillo, was published, proof of the wide circulation of news. He argued that a separate category be created for American writers:

> I will not say . . . that America, far from the academies, wrapped still in the rough swaddling clothes of Nature, although robust, poor in ingenuity [which must be] cultivated, is capable of undertaking the grandiose, singular and difficult theme proposed. Nor will I say that it is necessary to send out a special call to Spanish Americans on the most important occasions, because the indissoluble fraternity which unites us excludes even the suggestion of distinctions. But because enthusiasm can compensate for genius and because distance can also make fruitless the efforts of those of our compatriots whose creations probably arrive here after the prizes are decided, I think that it is fitting this time that a special convocation [be held] for Americans.

This invitation to write, while seemingly a boon for Americans, nevertheless furthered the impression that Peninsular writers were superior; and immediately, a letter in the September 14 issue of the *Diario* criticized Arango. The author of the letter cited a study by Beristáin de Souza that Nueva España had had more than 4,000 writers since the Conquest and voiced particular pride in Bernardo de Balbuena's *Grandeza mexicana*. Still another request, not unlike the commissions of patrons in former times, publicly called for "an American tragedy." The two-page announcement is unsigned and undated but internal information suggests it belongs to the period.[7]

> A Spaniard, who has been traveling for eight years now throughout the Americas without any special bias, and who admires the antiquities of this hemisphere which are unknown to Europeans, is anxious to see a *national* tragedy which is well written. He offers to the

author of the most perfect [one] (either in prose or verse) 100 *pesos.* Present the work in the bookstore of Arizpe, Monterilla Street, before San Fernando Day, in honor of our Prince whose fealty we swore to in the Cortes. The jury will be composed of three persons of known intelligence. The pieces should be delivered with the same insignia that the binding has with the name of the author; and it is requested that this come in Indianized language, serving as a sample [and demonstrating] there is no shortage of plots suitable to the case [such as those] Clavigero narrates [in his]. (*Ancient History of Mexico,*)

The writer then proposes as worthy of literary elaboration by Americans the story of a Tlaxcaltecan general, taken prisoner by Moctezuma. The Tlaxcaltecan had fought heroically for the Aztecs and when he asked to be sacrificed in a gladiatorial struggle, Moctezuma sorrowfully witnessed his death. The announcement then concludes: "When Americans want to sing of their own, they will find in Clavigero many passages similar to this one. And they will find them in Garcilaso, Ercilla and manuscripts. I, an enthusiast, will be happy to read their work and publish it." This invitation to explore Mexico's history would surely have been an incentive to Mexican writers. Demonstrating the viability of the printing industry, "writers," "printers," and "readers" were beginning to be social categories in the newspaper and pamphletry discourse of the period.[8]

The "novel" was also an identifiable, newsworthy category in the *Diario*'s pages. Although the general sense of the novel was critical, the fact that the literary form was featured, even disparagingly, shows its increasing prominence. Interestingly, the novel was often mentioned in connection with attempts to tell the story of Mexico's Indian past. Sadagier, a writer in the April 25, 1808, issue of the *Diario*, criticized a plot taken from the *Ancient History of Mexico* by Francisco Javier Clavijero, a Jesuit historian who in that work admiringly chronicled Mexico's pre-Columbian heroic history. Sadagier called the story "a ridiculous novel," "a falsehood like those which are usually heaped around the ancient history of Mexico." He seems to have objected to the literary category out of his belief that the novel presented an invented reality, whereas history recounted what had truly happened. In a few days (May 12–20), however, the *Diario* published a counterargument; "J. J. Z." said that it was illogical to scorn the genre when theater, which was generally approved of, often invented a story that might have happened so as to demonstrate a moral "truth." "J. J. Z." thereby defended the novel's capacity to tell of Mexico's Indian past.

In the May 31 and June 1 issues of the *Diario* still another correspondent, "El Desengañado," ironically named all those Spanish writers of the Conquest whose works would have to be destroyed if Sadagier's criticism of less-than-accurate historians were to be acted on; he imagined a great book burning: "Goodbye Cortez, Bernal Diaz, Herrera, Torquemada, Acosta, Clavijero, and so many others, who had the audacity to invent, in some cases, temples, cities, palaces, markets, arts, commerce, agriculture and a heap of other things, as they tell us, of those Mexicans—and, in other cases, the weakness of trusting in fabulous narratives because they gave us as real things that weren't, like wind-mills as giants and herds of sheep as armies." Here the writer's reference to the illusions of the *Quijote* reveals his suspicion that some of the detail provided by the colonial historians he names might also have been marvelous inventions. He goes on, playfully accusing Clavijero: "Come here, inventor of frauds. . . . So the population of that great Mexico, the vain show of its Emperor, and everything that you tell, is no more than a tissue of lies? So the policy and customs of Mexicans were no more or less than those of the Apaches in our times?" Should Mexicans rely more on paper accounts of the past (which spoke of the glories of Indian civilization) or on the degraded Indian realities they saw around them (which seemed to give the lie to those accounts)? Might the novel not be a more truthful way of getting at knowledge of the conquest of Mexico than the Spanish accounts labeled "histories"?

Because the colony was caught at this moment between several cultures whose attitudes toward art conflicted, it viewed the novel ambivalently. French neoclassic aesthetics generally frowned on the genre, causing authors to label their narratives *histories, letters, dreams* or *reveries, lives* or *confessions* to avoid the pejorative *novels* or *romances*. French writers, therefore, and those Spanish authors influenced by French taste tended to hide the novelesque form of their works behind such labels.

But loyalists in the colony used the term openly and wrote proudly of the novel's origins in Spain. The writer of one *Diario* article described *Don Quijote* admiringly and compared Cervantes' hero with Avellaneda's inferior creation. In Cervantes' realistic account *Don Quijote*, he argued, is a believable person whose deeds, in his moments of sanity, might be profitably imitated:

> Don Quixote, according to the notion that Cervantes gives us, was a rather well-educated man who only erred in matters concerning chivalry, and this same education and sanity, which he demonstrated in all the rest of his actions, is what causes us greatest pity when we see his craziness in matters of chivalry. In Avellaneda, everything is the reverse because, far from showing Don Quixote to be a man, as I have said Cervantes painted him, he was a furious fool, to be feared; he had no discernment in anything, in short, he was a hopeless crazy man. ("El Doctor Pedro Recio, natural de Tirteoafuera," March 16–17, 1810)

In the quote, the reader understands, as well as a defense of the novel, colonial criticism of a story of an aristocratic education gone astray. Portrayal of such a character, who lacked judgment despite great learning, made *Don Quijote* a pertinent book in a period preoccupied with bookish education and its social benefits. Three recent biographies of Cervantes had also stimulated interest in his fiction.

The novel was discussed in connection with the theater's depiction of characters, particularly a comedy's, and the distance spectators were supposed to maintain from such comic characters. Was it legitimate for an artist to exercise his imagination, to exaggerate qualities in these characters, so as to improve on Nature? One article in the *Diario*, purportedly by G. E. Lessing ("Should the characters of a comedy be enhanced?" March 12–13, April 6–8, 1809) answered that it was. Giving the example of a miser, the writer argued that, although his vice was repellent, it was not sufficient to provoke laughter. Laughter was necessary to make his portrayal ridiculous and agreeable to watch so that spectators would both be interested in the theatrical reality and scorn avarice. Comedy was thought to require some separation of the self. The following speech from the *Diario*, supposedly by Molière, analyzes the risible experience: "In order to laugh at things in this world it is necessary in a certain sense to see it from the outside, and comedy removes us from it. . . . How many times does it happen that at the same time a part of us performs something with ardor and intent, another part of us laughs at it? And if one worries, still a third part is to be found which makes fun of the first two jointly" ("Diálogo entre Paracelso y Moliere por Mr. Fontenelle," April 11–12, 1808).

Lizardi, too, gave thought to laughter, concluding that the humor that usefully keeps a reader reading results from ridiculing high-born people, rather than low-born ones: "Perhaps we excuse the vices of plebeian persons, considering their lack of any rules of action and coarse breeding. In distinguished persons we don't find this excuse and it follows that their defects are more shocking to us. The brilliance of their birth, the fortune they achieve, the employment they obtain, only serve to make [their defects] more visible" (*Obras* 8: 22). Lizardi said it was funnier to see a count grasp a fork like a dagger to spear a piece of meat than if an Indian ate with his hands. Both lacked urbanity but the count's coarseness was more shocking and, thus, more ridiculous. Lizardi's sense of comedy here reflects his consciousness of class differences; involvement in the humor must depend on the spectators', or in this case the readers', ability to judge the extenuating circumstances of class.

A long article on the popularity of the novel in England appeared in the *Diario* on May 11, 1812. The reporting reveals the colony's interest in contemporary fashion; the thoughtful discussion of the Gothic novel reflects the problems Mexicans were having adjusting precepts of Enlightenment aesthetics to this new form of the genre. Verisimilitude was generally thought to be necessary to artistic representation so that men's reason might be convinced to accept moral truths. Therefore, any excessive affective appeal made for its own sake to the imagination, such as in the Gothic novel, abandoned concern for verisimilitude and was morally dangerous.

England is the country of novels, for it is the genre of literature which is most cultivated and read. Many men of talent have dedicated themselves to this genre, giving their country in this way a certain superiority in this respect. Richardson and Fielding have given us models, one, of the *sentimental* novel (or novel of tenderness), and the other, of the novel of social satire. The imitation produced by these two writers, and that of Sterne, has produced a kind of composition that we can call "the English mode." It consists of mixing the pathetic tone with the comic, the descriptive style and the dramatic and in the scrupulous care with which physical and moral truths are represented. The great number of women who have written novels have also contributed a great deal to the formation of this type of style. Of all the literary works, the novel is that in which women can most excel since love, which is their principal interest, is the passion they know the best.

The anonymous writer then describes the many novels which were produced in England every year, signed "By a Lady." He says: "It would be a mistake to believe that these novels are really written by a woman. Their author is probably some sad chap who uses this method to dispatch his work. Since women are the ones who read most of the novels, they always prefer those which it is said are written by persons of their sex."

However, he concedes that "Madame Radcliffe" has introduced a new genre in which "specters, ghosts, caverns, ruins of buildings, assassinations, burial grounds, etc." excited the imagination. This new kind of novel has "no moral purpose," and the *Diario* writer hopes that readers will return to "the good kind of novel." But he fears that the Gothic novel will not decline in popularity in England "since there is no other country in which there is such strong belief in goblins, ghosts and witchcraft." He concludes with some facts about the English novel that suggest both familiarity with the country and a critical view of English society and the novel: "It would be difficult to tell the number of novels which are published in England every year, although some say the number reaches 200. Almost all live a very short time, serving only as entertainment for the idle, mainly women." Effeminacy was feared in Mexico during this period of warfare; thus, the novel's associations with love and sentiment, and its connections with a female readership in England may have made Mexican colonials think twice about adopting the foreign taste.

Another long essay in the *Diario* (December 5, 1813, unsigned but noted as "translated") also linked the novel to England. Among the essay's startling statements, the writer lauds the novels of Richardson as superior to the poetry of Virgil. He praises the novelist and disparages epic poetry, saying that "epic poems are nothing other than novels in verse" and that "the *Aeneid* is nothing more than a bad novel, without any invention or design, written in magnificent verse. Its details, its descriptions and a certain poetic sublimity in its ideas, sweep the imagination away and elevate it so that the poverty of its characters and the awkward disposition of everything are disguised. They speak in an animated way to the poetic imagination, but they do not interest men's sensibilities and hearts." The writer prefers *Gil Blas de Santillana* to the *Lutrin* [Boileau], Richardson, Fielding, Marivaux, and the Abbé Prevost to Racine, Rousseau, and Crébillon. In the guise of rendering literary judgments, he defends his right as an amateur reader to represent his taste against "a handful of self-interested literati [who have] the audacity to dictate ridiculous laws and absurd judgments." In the context of the novel's discussion, then, one reads not only modern rejection of the classical past but also defiance of authority.

Several English novels seem to have been permitted in Nueva España in the first decades of the nineteenth century.[9] Inquisition records tell that *Tom Jones* and *Gulliver's Travels* were subjected to the censors' review in 1803; both were found to be generally free of moral error and were therefore available for distribution (Longhurst). The Abadiano collection has the Spanish translation of *Tom Jones* (Madrid, 1796) but lacks *Gulliver's Travels*. Again, the appearance of these and other translated novels in this collection suggests, rather than proves conclusively, their availability to Mexican readers in the first decades of the nineteenth century (although an inscription in an Abadiano copy of *Carlos Grandison* indicates that it was owned by Agustín Pomposo Fernández de San Salvador, a Mexican poet who published regularly in that period). Other English works in the collection are: Henry Fielding's *Historia de Amelia Booth* (Madrid, 1795–96), *Tom Jones* (Madrid, 1796); Samuel Richardson's *Pamela Andrews ó La virtud premiada* (Madrid, 1794–95), *Clara Harlowe* (Madrid, 1794), *Historia del caballero Carlos Grandison* (Madrid, 1798); and Sarah Fielding's *La Huerfanita inglesa ó historia de Carlota Summers* (Madrid, 1804). Many of these English novels came via French into Spanish. Indeed, Defoe's *Robinson Crusoe* is hardly recognizable; it appears as a work, originally by the German Joachim Heinrich Campe, written as a moral history in dialogue form, and then translated into Spanish by Iriarte.

French novels in the Abadiano collection include: François de Salignac de la Mothe Fénelon's *Aventuras de Telémaco* (Madrid, 1778, 1803); François Guillaume Ducray-Duminil's *Aleo ú la casita en los bosques* (Madrid, 1804); Isabelle de Bottens's *Carolina de Lichtfield* (Madrid, 1802); Gauthier de la Calprenede's *La Casandra* (Madrid, 1792–93, 1798); Jeanne Marie le Prince de Beaumont's *La nueva Clarisa* (Madrid, 1797) and her *Almacen de las señoritas adolescentes* (Madrid, 1804); J. J. Barthelemy's *Viage del joven Anacharsis á la Grecia* (Madrid, 1813); Bernardin de Saint-Pierre's *Pablo y*

Virginia (London, 1809); Alain René LeSage's *Gil Blas* (Madrid, 1800); and François René Chateaubriand's *Atala* (Valencia, 1813). *Pablo y Virginia* and *Atala* are the only of these novels to appear on a long list of books offered for sale by a Mexico City bookstore in 1822, thus establishing conclusively their availability to Mexican readers by that date.

Although Madame de Staël's *Corinne* (1807) does not appear in Spanish translation until 1818 (Madrid), the novel's great influence on European letters, and therefore on Mexican attitudes toward the novel, must be considered; a copy of the Spanish translation exists in the Abadiano collection. Ruth Wold in her excellent book on the *Diario de México* documents that the same author's *De la Littérature considérée dans ses rapports avec les institutions sociales* was listed in the paper's pages in 1809 as prohibited by the Inquisition; that book, too, is to be found among the Abadiano holdings. Public notice of the book in that manner may have served only to advertise it. (Censors rejected it, the *Diario* makes clear, because it was "written in a spirit of pure naturalism, and for containing heretical, impious, and antimonarchical propositions.")

The role of the Inquisition in prohibiting books at this time in Mexico still needs to be studied.[10] The Mexican board of censors apparently functioned independently from Spain; and those select readers at least would have had access to the books they later ordered prohibited, confiscated, or expurgated. It is not clear how close-lipped they were regarding their reading or what they might have done afterward with their dangerous books. Neither is it clear how, in the case of expurgations, a dictate to delete troublesome passages from a text, to skip from one word, which the censors indicated, to another where one could safely start reading again, really worked. Thus, whether de Staël's *De la Littérature* was read in the colony, or the extent to which its ideas might have been disseminated to writers like Lizardi, can only be conjectured.

However, a feature of Madame de Staël's *De la Littérature* and *Corinne* that may have caught Mexican readers' attention is her outright discussion of the various European languages' capacities for expression. In *Corinne* her characters say that Italian excels in the musicality of its poetry but that its prose style is like "a piece of assemblage, entirely foreign to the Italian soul; it is a material, mechanical work in which the imagination never enters" (2: 9). Love as practiced in Italy bears no resemblance at all to its portrayal by poets; consequently, as the Italian Corinne complains, "our literature expresses little of our character and our customs" (2: 33). Spain, the Englishman remarks, saw the glories of its tragic theater at the same time it shone politically but, he suggests, its power and its literature are now in decline (2: 41). That this literary conversation could be made part of a novel's story line is an instructive example of the novel's non-mimetic purpose in the period. That a Spanish prose writer could thereby learn of the difficulties of using what he thought was an expressive language is also significant. Although it is clear that the Spanish translation of *Corinne* would not have been available to Lizardi as he wrote the *Periquillo*, I believe that he might have been familiar with Madame de Staël's fiction innovations and ideas about language and literature via the intellectual climate of his time.

Among the Abadiano collection of translated works from German is the already mentioned Campe's *El nuevo Robinson* (Madrid, 1798, 1820); from the Italian, *Viajes de Enrique Wanton, a las tierras incognitas australes y al país de las monas* (Madrid, 1778, authored by Count Zaccharia Seriman); and also from the Italian, *Cartas de Isabela Sofía de Valliere* (Valencia, 1805).

The appearance of the classical work by Heliodorus, *Historia ethiopica de los amores de Theagenes y Chariclea* (Madrid, 1787), also casts light on Mexico's understanding of the novel and its development. In the prologue the anonymous editor describes the book as a "pleasant fable or Ethopian novel" and its author as "a model for all writers of novels that have followed him; it can be said with as much truth that all have borrowed from him as it is said that all poets have borrowed from Homer." The editor claims to be drawing his discussion from Pedro Daniel Huet's *Origen de las novelas* [Origin of the novel]. But by associating the genre with a fictitious form already existing in the classical world, he takes the novel away from those who claimed it had grown out of history writing and thus attempts to save the genre from invidious comparisons with history.

This editor also points out, as do translators of many of the other novels cited, the stylistic difficulties of bringing a work from another language into Spanish. The translator of *Carolina de Lichtfield*, for example, found the abrupt, rapid pace of the original dialogue foreign to Spanish; he perceived the simple narrative passages to be too declamatory and too full of rhetorical flourishes for the Spanish taste. Even the means of conceiving of thought ["de concebir los pensamientos"] he thought was strange when rendered into Spanish. And he concluded: "I have not found any work of ours [from the Spanish literary tradition] that could serve as a model, unless I used some remnants of comedies."

Still another editor of a foreign work, José Luis Munárriz, who translated and rewrote huge portions of Hugo Blair's *Lecciones sobre la retórica y las bellas letras* (1783, 1804), brought to Mexican readers notice of the Spanish language's differences from other European languages. He complained of the lack in the Spanish literary tradition of good translations of the classical authors because, he said, the Church had impeded such work. And he criticized Spain's canonical writers, saying their excessive displays of elegance had blocked the development there of natural expression. Munárriz was particularly severe in his criticism of epic poets writing in Spanish, saying that "none of our poets has achieved a perfect understanding of the epic" (4: 156). The denunciation of this category of writer (Munárriz especially singled out Ercilla for embellishing accounts of American history) attacks the poets' language but also, incidentally, the honesty and fairness with which they portrayed combatants. Thus, Munárriz's focus on the Spanish epic poet, who imperialistically wrote colonial history and represented Americans, can be seen to foreshadow concerns of the nineteenth-century domestic novelist.

The history of the novel in Spanish America, therefore, to return to Cortázar's discussion of its stylistic problems, implies issues of language choice. Because so many translated novels formed the taste for the genre in Spain and Spanish America, readers there learned to expect a disjuncture between literary language and oral expression. Because there were no good literary precedents in Spanish for expressing the new stories, translators created artificial, awkward prose that readers began to value as "literary." Because the novel's origins were still disputed (some believed it originated in the classical world, others that it grew out of history writing and the epic poem, laden with imperial politics, still others that it had more recent antecedents in Cervantes' work and other European developments), colonials were perplexed as to its rules.

The consequences of these historical facts are staggering: The emotional side of men's lives, which novels have been thought to illuminate, were generally shaped by authors foreign to the Hispanic cultural experience. The moral lessons the European novel supposedly dramatized, with the expectation that the surrounding culture would reinforce its message, were thus ignored or fell into oblivion amid the overwhelming corruption of the colonial Spanish American world. The dogmatism, intellectualism, and formalism, which underlay vernacular Spanish as an inheritance of the religious and political discourse from which it descended and into which foreign ideas were channeled, silently operated to block new thought in the Independence and postcolonial periods. Questions of novelistic "style," therefore, are basic to understanding Mexico's first attempt at self-expression and self-representation.

The Design of the Periquillo

Lizardi's decision to write a novel based on the character named Periquillo Sarniento is revealed in a letter to the *Diario* dated February 14, 1812. Several considerations might have led him to this endeavor. The literary competitions and surges of the first decade in Mexico must have made him realize the possibilities for utilizing domestic themes and given him some license to create the work. Next was economic necessity. As scholars have pointed out, in 1816 press censorship had so severely limited journalistic production that Lizardi, in order to earn a living, was forced to try another form of writing that censors would approve and the new circle of newspaper readers would buy (Spell, "Life," "Genesis"; Radin "Bibliography: First Period"). He probably dismissed the idea of writing poetry, the most admired literary genre of the time, because his poetry had earlier been criticized.[11] Poetry belonged in the colony to the elite *Arcadia*, a group of poets who imitated the European pastoral mode and sentimental style; and Lizardi expediently cashed in on their prestige later when he printed some poems by their leader, Fr. Manuel Navarrete, along with his own poems in his *Ratos entretenidos* (1819). However, Lizardi's verse fables were successful; and it is likely that the personification by which he dramatized debate in them, as well as in his journalism and political pamphlets, gave him reason to think he could experiment with longer fiction.

In the prospectus Lizardi published for his first novel in December 1815, he announced that the *obrita* would be published in installments, two chapters a week (one on Tuesday and one on Friday), beginning in February 1816. It has been estimated that the first edition consisted of five hundred copies (Lizardi, *Obras* 8: xl). However, as I have shown, references to the book in political pamphlets suggest that the book circulated in ways beyond what this figure may indicate. Lizardi called for subscribers and apologized for the cost of four pesos per volume for city residents, and four pesos four reales for those living beyond. He defended the price, saying "it cannot be less, given the exorbitant costs and problems which writers face in this kingdom, and the little demand there is for works of this nature, whether because of a lack of curious persons of taste or because of the grievous circumstances of the time." Reports later said that the book soon sold for two and three times more than its original value.[12]

Lizardi seems conscious of the fact that he was writing a novel yet that he somehow had to disguise the fact. In the text Lizardi's mouthpiece, Pedro Sarniento, says: "What I would wish, my children, would be that you didn't read my life as one reads a novel" (235). He cautions: "The story you have heard, dear children, has nothing fabulous in it; everything is certain, everything is natural, everything happened to me, and much of it (or perhaps more) has happened, happens and can happen to whoever lives (as I did) the life of a libertine" (403). And in a statement that seems to reflect colonial attitudes, Pedro disparages novels: "it was never advisable that I read *Soledades de la vida*, the novels of Zayas, *Guerras civiles de Granada*, *La historia de Carlo Magno y doce pares*, nor other foolishness of this sort which, far from forming the spirit, conspires to corrupt [it] in children, or dispose their heart to lust, or fill their heads with fables, adventures and ridiculous yarns" (27). But, although Lizardi's narrator avoided using the term *novel* to describe the book the reader had in his hand, Lizardi did not hesitate to use it in his *apología*. There he answered the critic Terán: "Speaking of style he says that I am the first who has created a novel in the style of the rabble. Now, in my novel . . ." (*Obras* 8: 21).

Lizardi may have been reluctant to claim his work was a novel because he then would have had to align himself with French, English, or Spanish developments. He would have had to argue with some of his critics that his story was truthful. He was on much safer ground if he declared that his Mexican story had happened and his readers should accept it as fact. He also seems to have been convinced that the novel was less a form or foreign historical tradition and more a mode—particularly a satiric one.

Satire, a form of moral literature, permitted the safe depiction of unpleasant realities. Colonial readers would have felt comfortable with its literary conventions, and its ironic humor and frequent language play would have created a suitable distance from troublesome truths. Satire, with its suggestion of multiple realities (actual and corrected, targeted and diversionary), suited Lizardi's need for literary realism and moral vision, yet also discretion. However, if satire posited moral guidelines, it also gave expression to deviance. Its audiences, both polite and vulgar, might have been attracted to it for different reasons. If some of its seamy spirit had earlier manifestations in the denunciations the Inquisition encouraged among morally superior individuals so as to root out disorder, some of its appeal also grew out of low enjoyment of a neighbor's discomfort and the titillating spectacle of viciousness and burlesque. Satire was a respectable written tradition with origins in western Europe, producing theater, poetry, essays and, of course, the novel. But the mode also had a long oral and manuscript history in the colony, which was related to subversion of colonial authority. In addition to being a literary concept, *satire* was a police term used to describe imaginative works that released licentiousness and spread a demeaned picture of officialdom.[13]

Therefore, Lizardi, I believe, came to write a satiric novel through his recognition of its appropriateness for combining the many discourses around him—Spanish and Mexican, official and unofficial, corrupt and moral, decadent and vital, written and oral, learned and popular, idealistic and material, to name only a few. His sense of the novel conforms to Bakhtin's definition of it as "a diversity of social speech types . . . and a diversity of individual voices, artistically organized" (262). His novel's form reflects the period's suspicion that, not only was Latin losing power as a medium of authoritative expression, but also that Peninsular Spanish usage was being eclipsed by Enlightenment innovations in thought and writing and by peculiarly Mexican expressions. Lizardi's solution—to bring the various languages together realistically (and sometimes parodically) in a text—had several consequences: it subjected the dogmatism and frequent hollowness of the official modes to critical review yet it also problematized the relationship of thought to language. His colonial vision of layers of reality, conveyed through the various languages of satire, opened up all sorts of questions with respect to language, only one of which was what his choice for a framing idiom might seem to promise politically.

Lizardi's fiction has often been discussed in terms of the conventions of the European picaresque.[14] The colonial censor, when he reviewed the

Periquillo, may have determined this picaresque expectation for the novel when he declared that the book bore a resemblance to *Guzmán de Alfarache*. However, even though in the novel Lizardi makes the *pícaro* a symbol of a person whose conduct is detestable, he never discusses his work according to that bookish tradition or seeks comparison with Spanish Siglo de Oro models such as the *Lazarillo*, *El buscón*, or *Guzmán de Alfarache*. Instead, his preference for classifying his work seems to be indicated by his choice of a quote from a work by Diego Torres Villarroel to introduce the *Periquillo:* "Let no one say this is his portrait, but remember there are many devils who resemble one another." The quote, while humorously claiming that the author intended no attack on specific individuals, invokes the presence of the eighteenth-century moralist Torres Villarroel, whose satire of Spanish university life Lizardi might have thought resembled his own critique of Mexico. Here and throughout the novel Lizardi demonstrates no consciousness of reproducing a book pattern (the picaresque); his preoccupation is rather with earlier satiric authors and a style of writing.

The question of satire (and its danger of libel) occupied him at length in several articles (August 3, 23, 25, 29, November 1, 1815) in the *Alacena de Frioleras*, a newspaper he was publishing at the same time he was writing the *Periquillo*. There, he traced satire's origins to Greece and Rome with authors like Juvenal and Horace and then said that each enlightened nation respectively had its satirists. And he importantly linked the colony to Spain's satiric tradition: "we have first-rate satirists in Spain, such as Quevedo, Cervantes, Villegas, Torres, Santos, Iriarte, Feijoo, Gil Blas (or the author of this novel), Amato and many others who have deserved the appreciation of the wise" (*Obras* 4: 106).

In the discussion of satire in the *Alacena* essays Lizardi articulated the question of his originality versus his role as a copyist in his depiction of everyday realities. Could he be thought of as inventing, or was his task merely that of a writer who said what everybody else knew? Similarly, indicating his defensiveness that his personal motivation for writing satire could be subject to criticism, he said his satire sprang from "a noble soul"; he was not malicious in wishing to injure specific individuals but simply concerned with eradicating the vice itself. This distinction is a standard disclaimer in most moral and religious preaching, but certainly Lizardi, as a colonial author, had to rehearse it to ward off critics. Satirists, who often exaggerated their victims' vices so as to provoke laughter, were vulnerable to charges that they were seeking vengeance.[15]

The picaresque is generally absent from literary discussions in the *Diario;* and one can only assume that works which today are regarded as picaresque were regarded then as satiric. The anti-aristocratic message of the *Quijote,* the counterdiscourse to the romances of chivalry that this novel and the picaresque forms offered, seem only to have been in the process of being understood. The satiric mode and the novel (particularly as it was being defined in England) were only just coming together.[16]

However, the fact that Lizardi realized the American function of his first novel is evident in an announcement he made of the second edition of the *Periquillo* in *La Aguila Mexicana,* January 12, 1825: "I am very far from believing that I have written a masterful work, exempt from defects (it has many that I know of) and it probably has others that I have not noticed. But it also has an undeniable particularity and it is that of being the only romance-type work proper to the country, which has been written in its class by an American in 300 years. Perhaps to this fact alone the affection is owing which everyone knows about." Without explaining why no American attempted to write a novel before him, he shows he understands his "romance-type work" is singularly filling a gap.

In the prospectus for the *Periquillo,* Lizardi emphasizes the work's identity as a book. He says his book is different from those works whose titles promised much more than their texts delivered. Many authors of old, he claims, like the charlatans in medicine who baptized their useless drugs with important-sounding names so as to dupe the populace, put labels on their works, "offering in them nothing less than all knowledge and the key to the arcane [mysteries] of God and Nature." He chastises many from among "our writers," presumably American as well as European authors writing during the period of colonial occupation, who venerated this custom and continued this language usage that confused the ignorant and made the wise laugh. By contrast, Lizardi's book title is plain: *Vida de Periquillo Sarniento, escrita por él para sus hijos, y publicada para los que la quieran leer, por D. J. F. de L., autor del periódico titulado El Pensador mexicano* [Life of Periquillo Sarniento, written by him for his children, and published for those who wish to read it, by D. J. F. de L., author of the newspaper titled The Mexican Thinker]. That he was very much aware of the risks involved in changing to a new style is revealed in a seemingly flip remark that if he did not promise much, he did not have to deliver much; but he also confessed his fear that the title, which advertised the work, might be seen as "too common and low" and that he would suffer financially.

In setting his own work alongside earlier prestigious books of wisdom, Lizardi subtly borrowed some of their fame while still satirizing them. Later, in 1819, in a defense of the *Periquillo*, although he disclaimed his attempt to do so ("I don't try to compare my work with that of the great Cervantes; what I am doing is making use of his *Quijote* to defend my *Periquillo*") (*Obras* 8:23), his invocation of the Spaniard's work shows that he did indeed intend some comparison with the *Quijote*. He also used Cervantes' book to defend himself against the charge that his characters spoke in too low a manner:

> But I . . . take the *Quijote* of Cervantes, the masterwork in the category of romances, and I do not see any rare action, anything extraordinary, anything prodigious. All the events are more than vulgar and common such as could have happened to a crazy man of the circumstances of Don Alonso Quijada. At the same time I notice that each one of the characters of the fable speaks like those of his class, that is, vulgarly and commonly. Until today I was under the understanding that one of the charms of this style of composition was correcting customs, ridiculing them and painting them as they are, according to the country where one writes. But Mr. *Ranet* has just delivered me from this gross error since "finding . . . people in books acting the way we see them and speaking the way we hear them, our curiosity is not excited and we stop feeling any interest" (*Obras* 8:20).

And, in 1820, in a claim one can read as bragging, he said that his novel was being called "el *Quijote* de la América" (*Obras* 10: 242).

Yet if Lizardi tried to draw off some of the European book's prestige, he also made it clear that his American book was different. He argued that many of his readers needed some explanation of European books' meaning: "Today many people need a commentary to understand the *Quijote*, *Gil Blas* and many other works such as these in which they only find entertainment." Lizardi's readers read his work, perhaps because his style was simple and he stated the story's moral clearly, or because his colonial readers could not afford to buy the *Quijote:* "Many poor persons (or not so poor persons) who buy the *Pensador* don't have the *Quijote* or have ever read it; for that reason and because they see the truth of what I have said, I will tell them a little story" (*Obras* 3: 171). Experience with publishing his own newspaper, observations of the success and failure of rival newspapers, together with the criticism his early poetry engendered, would have taught Lizardi to expect a mixed reaction to his novel;[17] he soon learned that it caused hostility and incomprehension as well as enjoyment. One critic (Manuel Terán, the *Ranet* of Lizardi's *apología*) charged that the cast of characters in the *Periquillo* was unrelievedly low, that Lizardi included no picture of high society in his book, such as the portrait of "an ambassador, a prince, a cardinal, a sovereign." Lizardi answered: "How could there be if in this land this class of persons doesn't exist?" (*Obras* 8:23).[18] The critic reveals himself to be an educated colonial whose failure to understand Lizardi's book reflects his traditional expectation that reading expose the reader to a prettier, better (that is, socially higher) world. Blinded by a colonial discourse that offered no points of contact with his life, he misread the focus of Lizardi's book.

There is evidence that Lizardi perceived this colonial blindness and that one of the tasks of his novel was to eradicate it; his assertion that American readers needed a commentary so they could interpret the story suggests unsophisticated readers who read literally. Yet what is more probable is that many colonials were skilled in interpreting oral discourse and reading between the lines of other kinds of texts (judging by the in-jokes of many of the political pamphlets of the day). But faced with a book or another authoritative pronouncement, they reverted to being obedient colonial subjects who seldom questioned the discursive package, never expecting it to touch an area they might be familiar with.

Colonial education placed great emphasis on memorizing, on learning by mastering the words of the lessons.[19] Students in their university philosophy classes, Lizardi says, recited aloud Latin syllogisms, often stupidly garbling the words; yet they counted on the power of these words to baffle and impress, when they used them in conversation with the less educated and the illiterate. Lizardi describes in the *Periquillo* the singsong way in which Periquillo's teacher used to read aloud to the students, and he admonishes: "he who reads ought to know how to distinguish the various styles in which the book is written" (19).[20] Lizardi here is emphasizing to his own readers that to understand the meaning of words they must be sensitive to "style." He continues: "The orations of Cicero are not to be read like the annals of Tacitus, nor the panegyric of Pliny like the comedies of Moreto" (19).

What does Lizardi mean by differentiating between "styles"? At one level he simply implies his readers must gauge the general tone of the piece, whether the author intended to entertain, teach, and so forth. He is criticizing the colonial education system for failing to teach children and adults how to understand and use words properly. At another level he is signalling to his readers the complexity of the distance they must keep from his own comic work. Should they laugh or cry at his portrayal of familiar surroundings?

I believe that Lizardi, in wanting his readers to adopt a critical perspective on the book, was urging a broader critical attitude toward language usage in the colony. His presentation in the *Periquillo* of an assortment of speech styles—from the pedantic jargon of doctors and lawyers, to the low codes of beggars and thieves and the broken Spanish of Indian speakers, to the clear, plain style of the authorial voice with which he corrected and explicated the first two—should have, in the first instance, removed Lizardi's readers from the text by laughter, horror, or moral indignation, and joined them to it sympathetically in the last. This plain style, which often functions as a kind of translating device to make meaning clear, is described by the narrator somewhat apologetically at the novel's end: "He wrote his life in a style neither base nor high-flown; he avoided sounding learned; he used a homely, common style, that which we use every day and with which we understand each other most easily" (463).

Terán, whose criticism of the *Periquillo* seems to have been the most thoughtful of the day, apparently perceived these three levels of language. He wrote of the book: "Its style passes from a very average simplicity to lowness and with excessive frequency to the grossness of the tavern" (*Obras* 8:21). Then he lumped these three into one category when he complained: "We look for a variety in the locution of the *Periquillo* which derives in romances from the diversity of characters; but the action [of Lizardi's book] is so uniform it is like the flow of a sewer, which lulls us as it is released from the 'Prologue, Dedicatory and Notice to the Readers' until the last page of the third volume." In his response Lizardi confronted Terán with the contradictions: "How can a thing be the same in everything and yet different in its three parts?"

Terán's inability to put the parts of his reading experience together suggests several clues for understanding the importance of the reading dimension in Lizardi's decolonizing plan for his novels. First, the fact that Terán labeled as literarily inappropriate any level of language from a plain style on down to the gutter forms he scorned reveals, I believe, his previous exposure to books; his expectation for a high style prevented him from noticing the jargon of the doctors and lawyers (which Lizardi marked as funny), from accepting Lizardi's plain style as a viable literary form, and from seeing any merit in the recording of substandard speech. Second, because Terán was unaccustomed to valuing what Noe Jitrik terms the deferred stage of the reading process (69–71), he misread Lizardi's words. According to Jitrik, this reflective period, after the initial literal and suggestive moments, is essential to critical reading. Terán, seemingly, saw the parts of Lizardi's novel but was uncomfortable with using any part of his colonial experiential knowledge to alter his expectations for a book. His paralysis, I argue, has to do with the performance aspects of colonial discourse.

Terán, like other colonials, had learned that the consumption of the book—reading—was part of the colonial ritual of learning and professing obedience. As children colonials learned from the *cartilla* and the *catón* to repeat syllables and then the catechism lessons (Gonzalbo and Tanck de Estrada in *Historia de la lectura*); they never questioned the words on the page. Their exposure to the written language was only meant to be a socializing and a catechizing tool. Yet, at the moment of decolonization, colonials give evidence of having been aware of the mesmerizing power of the book. Various articles in the *Diario* counselled that one *not* read merely for diversion or for news gathering but that one read purposefully and freely, choosing one's books and newspapers, reflecting on what one read by making comparisons, summarizing in one's own words what one read: "We ought not read if it does not help us to think." Adult readers, and particularly those wanting to write, were permitted to read according to their own plan; but children had to proceed methodically. Finally, all imaginative wanderings had to be subjected to reason.[21]

Influenced by these considerations, Lizardi, I believe, wrote his first novel as a kind of primer, wanting to teach adult Mexicans to recognize differences between various styles of language in print, as well as many kinds of orality. Seeing words via reading, perhaps words they had only heard before and perhaps stigmatized as "Mexican" and incorrect, colonials were being asked to think about their colonized language. Thus, I believe, Lizardi intended the experience of reading his book to be part of the decolonizing process whereby colonials learned to match their inherited Spanish language with its standards for literacy, correctness, and stylistic elegance against everyday Mexican communicative needs.

2

El Periquillo Sarniento

The Discourses

3

The Family

Sons and Fathers

In titling his first novel *El Periquillo Sarniento* [The Itching Parrot], Lizardi likened his criollo protagonist to a bird whose mindless sounds imitate human language. Readers first of all meet Pedro Sarmiento, who is soon rebaptized by his bullying classmates. In their mouths, "Pedro" becomes "perico," a parakeet or small parrot, a mocking reference to the bird's plumage because Sarmiento once wore an odd combination of green and yellow clothing; "periquillo" with its diminutive suffix further ridicules him. "Sarniento" debases his respectable Spanish surname, "Sarmiento," taunting the boy with a reminder of the filthy affliction, *sarna* [mange, scabies] he once had.[1]

The novel's title, then, signals that naming and parroting language are keys to Lizardi's portrayal of colonial identity.[2] Because colonial controls had dictated his unthinking obedience, because the books he read seldom pertained to his life, because his world lacked incentives for thinking and creating, the American had become skilled at imitation. Intimidated by tradition and power, he silenced any original thoughts he might have had and only repeated the sounds his master taught him. His language usage, like the parrot's squawking, had become merely an awkward performance.

Periquillo's naming, made part of the story early in the novel, is only one of many language-related fictional structures that make readers conscious of language's important role in Lizardi's text. The seemingly inoffensive custom of giving nicknames, Lizardi tells his readers in a digression, reproduced the vilification and humiliation of much language usage in the colony. Over centuries Mexicans had learned habits of abuse by their Spanish overlords, and so they turned the ugly, destructive language (the only one they knew) against one another. Indeed, Lizardi thought that the Mexican taste for familiar joking really disguised the anger and self-hatred they had learned as colonials. The nickname stays with the youth and, like the colonial's sentence of inferiority, seems to cause his fall to a life of crime. Warning of language's power to injure men and determine events, Lizardi editorializes in the novel that the "Laws of Castile" and Jesus Christ (the colony's two official sources of legal and moral guidelines) condemn cruel language.[3]

However, the *Periquillo*'s satiric title promised both tragedy and comedy. Readers might have recognized in the animal reference some hint of Lizardi's earlier fables; in those seemingly light stories parrot and monkey often appeared. Still, in one of his essays, Lizardi used an animal metaphor for darker purposes to essentialize colonial dependency: "Spain is the ape of France, and America the ape of Spain" (*Obras* 3: 259).[4] In the eighteenth and early nineteenth centuries, Spain was under the cultural control of France; consequently Mexico, Lizardi complained, was twice removed from any source of originality or authenticity. The Mexican hero of the *Periquillo*'s title might have appeared to implicate Mexican readers, yet the title's playfulness (with its roots in school humor) also permitted them to think that the fiction was not realistic and they were not being attacked. Based on a Spanish name, the title might have seemed to Mexican readers to parody the similarly composed titles of Spanish chivalric novels, thus leading them to conclude, as it did the censor, that Lizardi's work belonged to a European book tradition and that they could enter and leave it at will.

Yet, on reflection, the title's resonances of a talking bird confronted colonials with other, nonliterary questions. Man as an *ente discursivo* [speech-making entity], set off from beasts by his ability to use language for rational thought, was a common definition in classical theological and philosophical circles. New studies such as Rousseau's *On the Origin of Language* (1749) distinguished the human species by means of this quality. Eighteenth-century debates universalized "man," yet also remarked on racial and cultural differences, setting the American primitive off from the civilized European. Bringing this European discussion home, the *Diario de México* told of a child who was being exhibited as a freak in

Mexico City. The boy, the son of an Indian father and a black mother, supposedly was covered with scales, had horns, had run away from his parents for long intervals to the mountains, wore no clothes, walked on all fours, and lacked language. The writer stressed the importance of language to the civilized state and described a European boy who, after being reared among wolves, eventually acquired human language.[5]

Lizardi's echo of a bird in the novel's title, then, hints at the way in which, after three hundred years of colonial rule, colonial nature was being reconsidered. An animal that imitates sound or gesticulates with no capacity for willed behavior or thought suggested earlier bestial images of Indian Americans, which sixteenth-century legal debates had variously promoted and challenged. In Lizardi's novel dealing with contemporary realities, however, the criollo now analyzes his own identity. The beholder is no longer a European, whose view often relegated the American to the category of the Other, but instead a Mexican who observes himself and his fellows.

In several essays in *El Pensador Mexicano* Lizardi discussed "the American character." Americans were no different than other national groups, he asserted. Yet they did display a special docility and disposition to "imitation." The upper classes were excessively concerned with foreign fashion, slavishly copying it; and the lower classes, often illiterate and ignorant of the dominant language, relied on their eyes to tell them what was wanted and reproduce it (however, Lizardi admired their natural talent for arts, crafts, and the trades). Labels such as "fool," "automaton," "machine," and "ape," by which others described the American character, troubled Lizardi. Did these attributes really define the colonial character? Could ignorance, because colonials were denied a proper education, explain their lack of language and apparent lack of thought? It could not be concluded, he said, that because Americans had been badly educated in the past, they were necessarily smart. Yet he pointed out that the barometer to measure their talent had not yet been invented (*Obras* 3: 257).

Thus, in this first Spanish American novel in which an American author seized the publishing opportunity to make inherited words real for his fellow Americans, in which Otherness was appropriated and the American Self was represented, language—the medium whereby colonials were judged to be rational beings and to possess the capacity to originate thought—assumes a vital role. The topic undoubtedly grew out of the newspapers of the period, where, as I have shown, "language" functioned to permit political discussion. What is also likely, however, is that Lizardi, increasingly observant of the novel's ability to mirror society, and in so doing to record a range of Mexican discourses, understood its potential for representing more accurately and fully than colonial texts perhaps had done before the linguistic uniqueness of the Mexican Self. He understood not only that dialects, registers of formality and informality, speech varieties, and so on could be realistically reproduced in the novel's pages, but also that the metaphors by which colonials lived could be dramatized in such a way that readers could judge whether they were wise or foolish, moral or immoral, advantageous to Mexico or harmful—thus helping Mexicans to consider decolonization.

Sonship

Colonials were defined by their sonship. If, throughout the colonial period, political and religious representatives had explained their identity in terms of filial dependence, if their obligations were construed as obedience and gratitude to a wise father, then dissociation logically began with rethinking this metaphor. Decolonization meant examining this model of familial harmony, and recasting or rejecting it.

First of all, then, Lizardi's generation of colonials needed to stop acting like parrots. Whether Mexico assumed a more important role in the empire according to the analogy with a youth's growth toward maturity (autonomy), or whether the colony broke with Spain, which suggested a son's rebellion (independence), Mexico's leaders had to examine the language by which the colony thought of its Self. Conquest rhetoric was hard to argue against. When the emotionally satisfying notion of the king as father (and membership in the empire as belonging to a family) combined with the seeming givenness and rightness of natural law (so that Mexico's place in the world order was rationally explained), personal and impersonal metaphors of thought appeared to coincide.

By 1816, however, the War of Independence was setting son against father and brother against brother. From the point of view of the son, therefore, the paternalistic metaphor was destabilized. The person of the king, as the image of God on earth, had been enhanced by divine associations, requiring that he be both obeyed and loved.[6] "Patriotism" meant loyalty to this fatherly figure, despite the fact that by the eighteenth and early nineteenth centuries Spain was a state with its own raison d'être and the military obligation to a monarch that conquistadores had earlier felt no longer compelled the dedication of the Mexican aristocracy. Peninsular Spaniards and American Spaniards were supposed to be brothers; yet Mexicans saw no official encouragement of brotherly love between the two. One's inheritance was thought to be the common language, religion, legal code, and even racial nature that Spaniards on both sides of the Atlantic were told they shared. However, increasingly Americans were coming to understand that they were not equal to their Spanish brothers and that they were being denied their share of the father's wealth.

Lizardi, in an essay published in 1812, conceded the legal fiction: "We, the natives of Spain and America, are one by descent, religion, vassalage and social intercourse." Then he corrected it with this historical fact: "Until this epoch in the world, singular and fortunate in the Indies, we were called Spaniards by name; and we were Spaniards but we did not enjoy equal privileges. However much the kings protected us like children, however much the wise and just Spaniards defended us like brothers, others were not lacking who wanted to place us at the level of beasts. Precisely here is the origin of the so often mentioned antipathy, the cause of the denial of employment and the beginning of discord" (*Obras* 3: 70). This analysis was intended to explain Mexico's recent revolt; and, although it absolved the king and other well-meaning Spaniards from participation in American oppression, it pinpointed the lie of paternalistic language.

In this essay from *El Pensador Mexicano*, Lizardi anticipates his examination of colonial sonship in the *Periquillo*. He separates the monarchy from the idea of divine endorsement by treating it merely as a human institution whose functionaries in the machinery of empire do not at all act consistently with a parent's benevolence. Kingly protections are seen to be more the result of a particular king's personality than any immanence of God the Father. And, reflecting a new maturity, Lizardi shows the extent to which the son perceives that colonialism harms the adult. Departing from the premise that Spain is *la madre patria* (a term that mixes mother and fatherland but shifts attention from the male king to a female nation), Lizardi observes that she is an unnatural mother who robs her children of their mineral wealth, taxes them outrageously, and prolongs their dependency by prohibiting industry from developing there: "The mother country, directed by the indiscretion of her governments, made us unhappy without herself gaining in fortune. She believed that gold and silver were the true wealth, not just signs pointing to it; instead wealth lies in the free industry of peoples. As soon as the Americas were discovered, nothing else was thought of but extracting . . . from them the quantities they could of these precious metals" (*Obras* 3: 67). The result of enormous quantities of minerals and money flowing into Spain is that hard work and industry, the real sources of wealth, are discouraged there. And Lizardi concludes with the image of a mother taking food away from her children and giving it to foreigners, the businessmen who come into the colonies and "make a fortune without conquering" and the bankers in other European countries who eventually own Spanish gold. Spain and America, he says, have both become skeletons.

Periquillo's dilemma is the criollo's. Connected by birth to titled families in Spain, he identifies with privilege. Yet he himself has no fortune; and scornful attitudes toward work, which the landed class hold, do not permit him to learn any craft or skill by which he might support himself honestly. Noble status forces him to be "depraved, shiftless and a drifter" (29). Lacking a protector, he attempts to milk advantage from the moment; he sponges on relatives, lives by deceit and exploitation (his kind usually never marries), and finally ends up committing serious crimes.

Periquillo's experience as a son, free of a father's rules, suggests the colony's disobedience. In the colonial lexicon disobedience would have meant deliberately turning away from authority and truth. Catholic teaching countenanced the unbelief of gentiles and the ignorance of pagans, both of whom had never come into contact with Christianity, but not the rebellion of apostates or heretics who had been exposed to the lessons of the true faith and reason. Heretics were particularly characterized by their freedom of conscience and spirit of tolerance. The great heresiarchs, Mohammed, Luther, Calvin, and the impious French, Lizardi wrote in an essay in *El Pensador Mexicano*, attacked both thrones and altars in Europe in the name of freedom; their refusal to submit to authority was viewed as both a civil and a religious crime.[7] Therefore, Americans, in avoiding the label of "heretics" and discharging guilt for their revolutionary "disobedience," had to establish the extent to which they had been instructed by their Christian father and the terms according to which they had moved away from his teachings.

Pedro, unlike his Siglo de Oro *pícaro* counterparts who were often orphans, has a father who attempts to set his son on the right road. However, the son's departure from his father's counsel, rather than defiance of authority, is an easy slide because he has been taught false values and he listens to misguided friends. He does not challenge his father out of deeply held, opposing views. He is not by nature wicked or perverse (although Lizardi makes sure his readers understand that he has ordinary urges and passions, which require constant restraint and supervision by elders). Instead Periquillo absorbs the stupidity of the criollo class around him; because his earlier moral formation has been haphazard (he has been alternately exposed to doting women and harsh discipline), his own nature is weak and his temperament is fickle. His start down the wrong path suggests the criollo class's ignorance of the substance behind the forms it imitates and its consequent lack of any thought-through ethical system of its own to guide it.

Periquillo's educational choices are obvious dead ends. They are the only ones available to colonial youths whose family names require that they go to Latin school. As Periquillo successively enrolls in the *colegio*, the university, and then enters the seminary (to a large extent because his mother believes that a priest adds luster to a family), Lizardi shows the inadequacy of these colonial institutions. The colony already had too many doctors, lawyers, and clergymen; and, anyway, these occupations did not really help colonial society in the ways it needed. Because colonial youths only had these alternatives for their future, many were forced into them against their will; the results were, as Lizardi says editorially in the *Periquillo*, "hack lawyers, assassin doctors and corrupt churchmen" (31). In rejecting these colonial possibilities for his life, then, Pedro shows some wisdom.

In Lizardi's critical view of parent figures (his mother and father, but also Indian wet nurses and maids, teachers, and school systems), one reads an increasingly impatient view of adulthood and authority, and a growing consciousness that colonials were not to blame for their faults and inadequacies. For example, Lizardi's fiction proposes the possibility of "effeminate men" and "over-bearing women" (34) who harmed their children—in the one case superiors who failed to exercise proper leadership and in the other case inferiors who willfully refused to accept their subordinate role. Teachers were guilty of leading the young into error if they taught them only superficial things such as rules and terminology. In describing Periquillo's philosophy classes at Mexico City's Colegio de San Ildefonso (which seems to be based on the author's own experiences there), Lizardi suggests that there was no sure system to guide the faculty at that late moment in the colonial regime and that, therefore, teachers took what they judged best from Aristotle and what seemed most probable from modern scientists and philosophers, inventing a mishmash of words and ideas to teach to their students. In a ridiculing tone that censors might have read as wishing that old-fashioned orthodoxy might return, Periquillo says: "we were true eclectics and we didn't adhere capriciously to any opinion or defer to any system simply because we were inclined toward its author" (38). The statement shows a growing realization that a youth might question his father, that he might look for truthful "systems" beyond personal attachment to representatives of "truth."

Pedro's father is well meaning in his desires for his son's future. But he is poor, and this and the lack of family connections help damn the boy. Similarly, the father's weakness in acceding to his wife's pleas that her son not become an ordinary craftsman or tradesman ensures his uselessness. Once his parents die and Periquillo squanders his slight inheritance in lavish living, he drifts. His situation reproduced the quandary of many criollo youths whose poverty or lack of protection (that is, family or patron) forced them into a solitary life of survival. But his dilemma also illustrates the larger problem posed by Mexican independence from Spain. If the colony cut its ties with the European country that had given it birth and protected it, it ventured into the world alone and vulnerable.

The rhetoric of paternalism was chiefly a Spanish product. However, the scientific theories of the French naturalists, such as Buffon and de Pauw, which were known in the colony at that time, also helped Mexicans to think of theirs as a young world. Comparisons of the more developed forms of life in Europe with the seemingly more primitive forms in America (see Gerbi), while damaging to America's sense of itself as civilized, opened up the notion of organic growth. This modern reasoning enabled Americans to think that their youthful condition was not permanent and, by analogy with species development in the animal and plant worlds, they might graduate to equality with the father.

Periquillo emerges at the book's end as a respectable father, restored to his identity as Pedro Sarmiento. However, in the bulk of the story (which describes his adventures), the text's stylistic deviation from standard literary Spanish traces the youth's debauchery in Mexican taverns, gambling dens, flophouses, jails, and then exile. Substandard language, which Mexicans heard around them but which had not yet found its way into the pages of a book, conveys an impression of the wandering son's confusion and error. A new realism, tolerated in satiric literature, deviates from literary good taste and reproduces the character's transgression. A light tone, at odds with the gravity of the wrongs described, intensifies the sense of youthful flippancy and challenge to authority.

Confronting the criminal codes and scarcely Spanish languages of Mexico's lower social classes (the poor and racially different, where delinquency was usually thought to occur), Mexican readers must have been shocked. However, these low forms, readers learn, are the speakers' own invention; and they satisfactorily permit full communication among members of that speech community. When, then, readers also learn in the novel that many of these persons (speakers of broken Spanish, and sometimes even of Indian languages) are often honest, and many of the rich (whose speech is closest to Peninsular linguistic usage) are frequently corrupt, Lizardi raises a fundamental question with respect to a benefit Spain was supposed to have brought to the colony. The Spanish language, colonial educators had taught, was inherently superior for leading the mind and soul to a knowledge of God and goodness. Correct language performance (that is, adherence to Peninsular norms) correlated with virtue. Yet as Pedro finds goodness among Mexico's illiterate lower classes, where incorrect speech was understood to be a sign of these classes' natural evil, the novel asks whether colonial theories of language and moral education might have been wrong and Mexicans might develop communicative forms based on these classes' uniqueness. The novel suggests that Mexicans should not be arguing whether Castilian or Mexican Spanish was better but rather how, at all levels of colonial society, Mexico might end dishonest, degraded language habits and initiate an honest, mutually respectful discourse.

Lizardi never says that Mexicans should abandon their use of Spanish. Instead he shows how colonized language is at the root of Mexico's social phobias and pathologies. Schoolboy nicknames are only one example of the harm cruel language can do. Fearful, secretive language is another inheritance from the colonial Inquisition.[8] Excessively familiar forms of address (*tú* rather than the formal *usted*) are still another Mexican custom, traceable to conditions of colonial servitude, which show a diminished self-image and confusion as to who among Mexicans deserves respect. When, as in the following exchange, Periquillo asks for a friend in jail in exaggeratedly grand language, Lizardi ridicules Mexican ignorance of what language to use:

"You, who are you looking for?"

I said to him Don Januario Carpeña (for thus my companion was named). Everybody laughed merrily when I answered, and the leader of the gamblers said to me: "Perhaps you are looking for Long John the Cheat, the one you came here with before?

I could not deny this and he said, "Friend, he's neither gentleman nor lady; if anything at all he's Don Straw-Mat or Don Stripped-to-the-Hide, like the rest of us." (49–50)

The satire conveys Lizardi's concern that many colonial problems derived from long years of being gagged and forced to imitate magisterial sounds.

A consciousness of language, then, is at the heart of Lizardi's story of sonship. Hollow courtesy and nonsensical jargon stand for colonials' mindless repetition of the father's language. Wit, which is often a function of Lizardi's juxtaposition of phoniness and honesty, enacts the colony's taste for elegant euphemism yet also its desire for truth. The caustic words with which Mexicans insult one another in the book carry the bitterness of the civil war. Its ugly tone reflects the daily military violence, civilian terror, official secrecy, and accusations by opposing forces.

Spain's presence in Mexico, no longer benign as proponents of colonialism had made believe, was increasingly a military occupation with greater displays of force (Archer). In 1815–16 the *Gaceta del Gobierno de México* was filled with news of fighting in Mexico between "rebels" and royalists; the newspaper also told of war throughout Spanish America and Europe, thus imprinting the language of conflict on the Mexican consciousness. In the colony one was either victimizer or victimized. Toughness and harshness (that is, manly attributes) were valued; and, in fact, an

1815 report to the king says that Mexico had more men than women.[9] Hostility characterized all interaction; emotion was expressed guardedly; and language, rather than a tool for negotiation or defense, seemed to be counterproductive as frankness elicited even greater repression.

Needing to break into this mood of hatred and fear, Lizardi chose the satiric novel. He recognized its appropriateness, yet he also understood its power to devastate the persons and the institutions he was describing so that future reconciliation might be difficult. As Padre Blanchard wrote in his 1797 *Ecole des Moeurs* (a book Lizardi gave evidence of being familiar with in an essay in *El Pensador Mexicano*), "one is ashamed of esteeming at some future time persons one has made fun of" (3: 190). Much depended, therefore, on Lizardi's choice of an "artistic" form such as the novel, and his use of a temperate tone in the story's framing language.

Satire allowed criticism of colonial realities yet also proposals for moral improvement. Its tradition of comic entertainment relieved Lizardi of some burden of seriousness. Its imaginative history gave him license to contrast idealism (Spanish notions of imperialism) and materiality (Mexican experience of imperialism's realities). Its dramatic range allowed him to repeat voices that had been ignored or silenced. By claiming veracity in showing the hero's progress along the way stations toward improvement, Lizardi could publish a national self-portrait that official documents probably would have avoided.

The genre's length and breadth gave Lizardi an opportunity to explore sonhood, although still seeming to affirm the need for patriarchy. His novel's conclusion, in which the rehabilitated Periquillo repeats his instructive tale of waywardness to his children/readers, affirms the wisdom of the family structure and the father's essential goodness. Lizardi, therefore, does not show that he is free of colonialism's governing metaphors; instead he finds solutions within them. Like other colonials, Lizardi mainly thought of religious faith, political loyalties, and familial duties according to relationships of dependency. Order depended on conforming to natural law and assuming one's proper place in the social hierarchy. The novel, therefore, reveals the difficulty of freeing oneself from learned language. However, the *Periquillo*'s fiction seems to say that Mexico could also grow from adolescence to maturity and equality with other adult nations. In dramatizing sonship, therefore, Lizardi helped his readers to think about decolonization.

In the first years of the nineteenth century, Mexican loyalists, and at first many insurgents too, thought of patriotism as allegiance to, and love for, the Spanish king; the latter only wished to oust a viceroy whom they perceived as corrupt and return the colony to good government. Many Indians in rural areas fused native and European beliefs in making the king's figure a messianic, charismatic leader (Van Young "Quetzalcóatl"); they had been taught that they were especially protected by his fatherly love. Some of this same faith in his person seems also to have inspired Carlos María de Bustamante in his 1817 plea for reform to the newly restored monarch. Entitled "The Mexican Indian or Advice to the King Fernando VII for the Pacification of North America [América Septentrional]," the document shows the colonial habit of appealing to the Madrid government personally, as if one kind soul read all colonial reports. It is not clear to what extent letter-writing etiquette promoted this fiction of a king's oversight of colonial affairs; but it is true that many among Mexico's elite pinned their hopes for good government in the colony on Fernando's return to the throne. In pleading his case, Bustamante couched his arguments in references to the king's person; he made it clear that earlier monarchs had shown compassion for America's indigenous peoples, and he appealed to Fernando to remember the suffering he had personally endured while jailed in France in order to imagine the Indians' oppression.

The king was a much-manipulated symbol. Medieval scholasticism, which had emphasized governance as a personal relationship between the king and his vassals, was resurrected by the regalists in the late eighteenth century to buttress support for the Crown. In an effort to reduce the pope's control over Spanish affairs, parts of the *real patronato* were transferred back to the Spanish king, thus channeling American reports to the pope through his person (Stoetzer, *Scholastic Roots* 73). The notion of his personal power justified Carlos III in his expulsion of Jesuits from all Spanish territories in 1767; later, liberals at the Cortes de Cádiz invoked the king's authority to substantiate Fernando's claims to the Spanish throne (MacLachlan). And, in various documents sent back to Spain between 1805 and 1810 to argue that Mexico was the monarch's most beloved possession and that the colony deserved the special support of that "idolized" person in bringing about reform, Manuel Abad y Queipo, bishop in Puebla and later archbishop of Mexico, drew on the language of father and son. But Abad, born in Spain yet sympathetic to Mexico, turned the rhetoric around and asserted that the "love" (that is, money) Mexicans had shown for their sovereign over the years now required the king's gratitude (91, 157).

Viceregal policies in the colony depended on the fiction that the viceroy personified the king. Public ceremonies evoked the king's presence through the display of his portrait; statues made his power physical; coins circulated his image (Marin *Portrait*). However, for persons who would never see the king, who would never dress as he did or look as he did and who would only experience grandeur through symbols, the patriarchal language of government often suggested orphanhood or bastardized status.

When the old order was overthrown throughout Europe, colonials were told that these attacks on established monarchies were family feuds and interpersonal hatreds. Napoleon was referred to in the *Diario de México* as a usurper, one who had wrongfully interfered in a dynasty's orderly pattern of inheritance. It was reported how he had taken the crown from the pope's hands and placed it on his own head.[10] However, when Napoleon invaded Spain, Mexican opinion, which up until that time had admired his military triumphs, particularly over Protestant England, changed.[11] France's actions were then described as Napoleon's arrogance, his motives as a tyrant's egotism, which held his subjects forcibly rather than in the traditional bonds of *vasallaje*.[12] France became the example of a formerly Catholic state torn apart by irreligion, where personal ambition and private interests and passions had destroyed the selfless love characteristic of family unity.[13]

In the history of the Spanish empire, there had been earlier complications, if not breaks, in the traditional relationship between vassal and king. Lizardi argues in *El Pensador Mexicano* that ministers such as the Conde Duque de Olivares and Manuel Godoy had interfered with it (*Obras* 3: 57). Colonial experience of inept viceroys and the abuses of long-distance administration had proven that these bonds were not sacred. Furthermore, belief that the royal family was a model of love and sociability was particularly shaken by events during the reign of Carlos IV. Late in 1807 the prince Fernando VII was charged with patricide; and although he was later declared innocent and the blame thrown on others, a wedge was driven between father and son in the public's mind. In March 1808, due to French pressure, Carlos IV abdicated in favor of his son. This family dispute and the extent to which it shaped the government were publicized in an official document circulating in Mexico in 1809; in it, colonials read Fernando's appeal to his father for love and understanding of how Godoy had deceived the queen and usurped what was rightfully Fernando's place and power (by now Fernando was imprisoned in France). Godoy, the prince said, had insinuated himself into the royal family through marriage, and he complained that his rival maligned him and treated him like a child (49). Republished in the colony to foment hatred of France and rally support for Fernando, these revelations of court politics helped weaken the monarchy in Mexican opinion.[14]

However, Mexico's faith in a patriarchally ordered universe was profoundly shaken when Miguel Hidalgo's insurgency began on September 15, 1810. When José María Morelos joined Hidalgo, officials called the priests' independent thought and incitement of the Indian population a betrayal of their fatherly responsibilities. The priests were described as a Satanic force bent on destroying religion and the government.[15] They were accused of ingratitude to various father figures and of selfishness, thus personalizing their crime and denigrating their motives. When, finally, they were excommunicated, their severe punishment reflected the extent to which political treason was understood as subversive of all paternalistic systems of order.

The archbishop of Mexico, in an edict the *Diario* reprinted, censured Hidalgo and invoked the Church's teachings on submission and obedience. He began by saying that Hidalgo was wrong in interpreting Christ's admonition to "Render unto Caesar what is Caesar's" as advice to Christians to distinguish between religious and secular demands; instead, the archbishop said, Mexicans should continue in their obligations to a foreign empire: "The response of our Holy Mother the Church has been at all times: Obey, pay."

He then rejected Hidalgo's description of the rebellion as an Indian "reconquest"; only Spaniards, it seems, had the right to "conquer" and "reconquer." Spain had lawfully conquered the Americas three hundred years before and Spain was justly, at that moment, reconquering Spanish territory from Napoleonic forces and fighting to hold its American colonies. The archbishop thus attempted to prevent Hidalgo from seizing control of the language of domination: "He [Hidalgo] errs in fact, and his project of reconquering America for the Indians not only is anti-Catholic, but chimerical, extravagant, ridiculous and highly prejudicial to the author who proposes it . . . for hardly is there today any nation in the world which has not found itself possessed by conquest and consequently should not be alarmed at the Sovereign or Republic which governs it."[16] In his bald recognition of imperial land grabbing, the archbishop revealed patriarchy's loss of idealism.

Lizardi may have sympathized with the insurgents; certainly he shared many of their grievances. But it is also true that he feared rupture in an order thought to foster mutual obligations. He believed that *desunión* would only hurt Mexico still more. Americans, he said, already suffered from a lack of social cohesion:

> On account of being disunited they have been poor; on account of being disunited commerce has been for them a mystery; on account of being disunited many times they have been vile flatterers; on account of being disunited they have perished from hunger having wealth in their own home; on account of being disunited they have been, in short, and will continue to be, slaves of ignorance and of the tyranny of passion. Because the man who is not joined to a rich man always will be poor and he who does not join with a wise man will always be ignorant. (*Obras* 3: 272)

Lizardi's diagnosis of Mexico's problem as *desunión*, and the solution he recommends as individuals coming together, show the cast of his colonial thinking. His images of "rich man" and "poor man" suggest that Lizardi was recommending political decisions, based literally on personal relationships. However, his language suggests a more profound understanding of the importance of human bonds than fictional personification may indicate. At the time of this writing (1813) the evidence of Lizardi's political writing and what is known of his personal beliefs make it seem that Lizardi decried civil war and did not want separation from Spain (Fritz). Although he recognized the frequent evil of colonial authorities and the injustice of the colonial system, he feared abandonment by a powerful protector. Lizardi knew that then anarchy would ensue and Mexico would be vulnerable to invasion by other European nations. Although this essay from *El Pensador Mexicano* can be read either as an argument for imperial or national union, his insistence that America was weak and disunited suggests he did not yet think that independence was preferable.

Lizardi's ambivalence can be seen to be the result of his formation in the ideology of paternalism. A metaphor originally designed to draw Americans into union with a distant ruler and his already pacified subjects, paternalism was a figure of speech that worked well on several levels simultaneously. The family has moral and psychological as well as political and economic resonances; and Lizardi, under the influence of this mode of thought, gives evidence that he reasoned easily from an understanding of family as a biological unit to an idea of it as a collective entity. He writes in the *Periquillo:* "If I am not mistaken, the reason for parity is the same in a kingdom as in a people; and if from a people the comparison descends to an individual, the same effects are to be observed proceeding from the same causes. Let's hypothesize about two boys under our absolute direction: one is called Poor and the other Rich. Let's educate the latter in the midst of abundance, the former in necessity" (338). Here Lizardi's logic is another instance of his understanding that patterns of individual behavior were mixed with those of a corporate body.

Colonials could point to specific issues in which abstractions were concretized in the lives of individuals, in which family considerations at one level were connected to consequences at another level. One such issue was celibacy, which kept the colony's many nuns and priests from marrying and thus contributing to the country's productivity. Another, explainable in family terms, was vagrancy, which resulted to a large extent from a father's failure to find honest work and which, in turn, prevented family units from forming and nourishing the young.[17] Still another social problem with individual roots was the selfishness characteristic of many wealthy Americans who, despite their professed love of *patria*, ignored the poverty of their compatriots. A fictitious Frenchman speaks for Lizardi in *El Pensador Mexicano:*

> Americans hold themselves to be very fond of their *patria; but* they are very unloving with their fellow countrymen. There you will not see a rich American helping or succoring a poor man, even though they may be relatives. Nationhood in common does not influence at all the hearts of those egotists; you will not see there but a thousand unhappy persons, defeated not only by their countrymen but by

their well-off relatives, and you will see that the latter prefer foreign-ers to their own when it comes to offering employment in some shop, *hacienda*, etc. . . . The greatest vice that I noted in them was the disunion amongst themselves, which is the cause [of the fact] that they neither help one another nor civilize one another nor instruct one another. The American who has money is for no one else but himself. (*Obras* 3: 271–72)

It is true that Lizardi perceived the problems of the colonial system as basically economic.[18] But his solution still depended on a belief in the personal virtues of selfless love and loyalty, which the family and paternal-istic structures seemed to foster.

A son's relationship to his father—or an inferior's relationship to an older, wiser, propertied person—is a theme repeated throughout the *Periquillo*. The fiction stands for colonial rule, but also the male network cre-ated by lineage and patronage. The frame of the novel, a warning by the writer/father to his readers/sons not to repeat his follies, seems to convey the father's point of view.[19] Yet the narrative voice that predominates is that of the rebellious son. The latter disregards the good advice of various father figures and instead follows the bad counsel of false friends and evil masters. Some of the characters are the stock types of the picaresque novel (such as Doctor Purgante), but others are uniquely Mexican—tradesmen, a barber, a scribe, beggars, gamblers, and prisoners.

When Periquillo starts on the road of life, he meets the kindly Anto-nio, who treats him like a son and relates his own story of sonship. When his father died, some, who seemed to be fatherly, deceived him. One, the executor of his father's estate, robbed him; the other, a *marqués*, pre-tended to be his patron so as to seduce Antonio's wife. However, Antonio also benefitted from several good surrogate fathers; one gave him em-ployment and made him his heir.

Periquillo then comes under the fatherly protection of a military man whom he accompanies to the Philippines: "I came to love and respect the colonel like my father, and he grew to correspond my affection with a similar love" (323). Next his benefactor is a wise Chinese man who helps the youth along the road to self-discovery. However, Periquillo willfully remains incorrigible, scorning all authority; and, on his return to Mexico, he joins a band of highway robbers (this last situation comes as close as Lizardi dared to describing the robbing and murdering *gavillas*, many of whom had turned insurgent after the start of the Independence War).²⁰ Witnessing a friend's hanging for these crimes, he decides to abandon his sinful ways. And then he meets another Father: "I am 33 years old and I have had a sinful and wasted life. Nevertheless, it is not too late; I still have time to truly be converted and change my conduct. If the lengthy span of my wasted years saddens me, it consoles me to know that the Great Father of families is very liberal and kind, and He rewards the one who enters his vineyard to work in the morning as well as the one who enters in the evening. That said, let's change our ways" (415).

Finally, Pedro Sarmiento, adult and responsible, becomes an employer and patron to others. He marries Antonio's daughter, thus cementing his tie to Antonio: "I was your favorite, someone who asked you for help; today I am your friend and, if you wish, I will be your son and we will form one family" (445). When later his father-in-law is old and sick, he cares for him. He repays his social debts by befriending persons whom he had wronged. He rescues a man from debtors' prison, restoring him to his wife and family. He saves a misanthrope by discovering that the man's love has been requited and that he can still marry into the family of the girl he had loved. The trust he places in the bookkeeper who works for him on the *hacienda* is validated when the bookkeeper learns the inheritance unjustly denied him according to the laws of primogeniture will now pass to him. Pedro's own position is owing to the kindness of still another fatherly figure, who left him his property. Pedro's obligations at the end are to manage the old man's estate and educate the children he now has.

Lizardi's fictional resolution of conflict and his description of the domesticity and tranquility his hero enjoyed in his last days sound suspiciously like an affirmation of the colonial status quo in Pedro's assumption of the role of a gentleman farmer [*hacendado*]. Given Lizardi's insistence that an individual assume economic responsibility through useful endeavors, preferably a mechanical skill, his character's reluctance to take a job and earn money through his own initiative is curious. The character still wishfully shows the myth of depending on a fatherly figure whose wealth one inherits and only needs to administer. And when Pedro refuses to become involved with the workings of society (he declines a job as judge) Lizardi suggests through his character's attitudes his own belief that colonial society is corrupt and personal virtue is only possible if one remains apart from it.

The nature of the self relative to the rest of society can be seen to be undergoing changes at this moment in history. Secularizing ideas were beginning to define man economically in terms of his utility to other men, rather than theologically, or even politically, in his relationship with God and king. Lizardi's novel, as well as the outright discussion of the struggle in essays in *El Pensador Mexicano*, reveal that the conflict in his mind was far from resolved. The coded word for handling this topic of the secularly defined self was *egoísmo* [selfishness, self-interest]. The *pícaro* embodied this total disregard for the opinion of others, assuming no social obligations, and indeed exploiting others in living only for himself. Lizardi addresses such a selfish person in *El Pensador Mexicano* in words that show the extent to which he believed identity to be predicated on hierarchical relationships and virtue to be tied to social usefulness: "you won't be good as a husband, the father of a family, a friend, king or vassal, or as a judge or subject, or anything" (295). He continues: "[Egoism] is the art of making a man the center of everything which surrounds him, or more clearly, it is the quintessence of self-love, according to which man always endeavors to make all creatures serve him and benefit him at any cost, without his ever caring to be useful to anybody else for the only reason of doing good. So, for this reason, the perfect egotist has in himself his *patria*, his law, religion, relatives, friends and the complete realization of his delights without recognizing any other honor than his interest, nor any other society than the satisfaction of self."

Yet in the novel Lizardi questions whether self-love [*amor propio*] is necessarily an evil by showing how a desire to maintain reputation helped Periquillo live up to the good opinion the *coronel* had of him: "Since the principal residents of Manila saw the way the colonel treated me, the confidence he had in me and the affection he showed toward me, all those who valued his friendship held me in special favor and esteemed me more than a simple assistant. And the same affection that I won among decent people was a brake which restrained me from not doing anything that could be talked about in that city. It is certain that well-ordered self love is not a vice but a principle of virtue" (343).

The *Periquillo*, in the tensions of its dramatic structures and the differing voices of its characters, shows that Lizardi was wrestling with changes in Christian and colonial definitions of the individual and society. New demands, such as deciding the role of the self, were not as simple as he had made them in the earlier essays of *El Pensador Mexicano*. His novelistic meditation on the responsibilities of fathers and sons, therefore, problematizes the growth of the individual and collective selves.

Slavery

Selfishness was the sin of the Mexican insurgents. It was also the sin of their sympathizers, who accused the father of his failures and advocated independence. It was a sin of omission, if not commission, in which colonials, like Napoleon, refused to accept their designated slave status, according to Aristotelian teaching that natural law dictated one's social station (Hanke; Stoetzer *Scholastic Roots* 61–63). Instead Americans placed their own needs ahead of the needs of others and took, through violent means, a place equal to their supposed moral superiors. Early nineteenth-century Americans rehearsed the sixteenth-century debate of Las Casas and Juan Ginés de Sepúlveda, which had studied American Indian nature, and not only concluded that their identity was no longer exclusively Indian (and thus inferior), but that slavery, that is, the ownership of one man by another on the grounds that the first was worth less, was philosophically groundless.[21]

Lizardi confronts the intellectual debate in a dialogue at the beginning of volume 4 of the novel when, in a discussion between Pedro and a black man, he explores the issue of slavery. Censors in the colony immediately suppressed this last portion of the novel; and it did not appear in print until the third edition (1830–31) when the complete novel was published. The censors wrote that traffic in slaves had been authorized by the king and that, therefore, Lizardi's criticism was "very repetitious, inopportune, prejudicial under the circumstances, and unpolitical for going against trade permitted by the king."[22] It seems, however, that handwritten synopses of this portion of the novel circulated at least its story line (Moore "Un manuscrito inédito").

Newspaper advertisements in the *Noticioso General* tell that slavery was still an open, legal practice in Mexico City in 1816, despite the fact that Hidalgo and Morelos had make the abolition of slavery one of their demands (Bueno). American delegates to the Cortes de Cádiz were sensitive to the issue and debated it with their Peninsular counterparts, since racism and labels of inferiority damned all colonials; their mixed blood was often an excuse for their being denied the legal status their Spanish brothers enjoyed.[23] Thus the dialectical play of Lizardi's voices suggests not only discussions of slavery but also of colonial selfhood. Coming at the beginning of the last book, the dialogue can be read as the climax of the novel's back-and-forth thoughtfulness (345–50).

The black is a worthy debater. Described as a businessman who magnanimously spared the life of an Englishman who had challenged him to a duel in Manila, he advocates a hierarchical structure of government, the sine qua non of any society whether civilized or barbaric. But he condemns those among the rich and powerful who abuse their superior position; their rank, he maintains, is only the necessary condition of men living together in an orderly society and results from an accident of Nature or Fortune. Pedro speaks first and affirms all men's essential equality:

> Mister, it is certain that all men descend from a first cause, from a created beginning, called Adam or whatever you wish. It is equally certain that, according to this natural beginning, we are all intimately linked by a certain relationship or undeniable connection so that the emperor of Germany, although he may not want [to acknowledge] it, is a relative of the vilest thief, and the king of France of the basest ragpicker in my land, however much they may be ignorant of the fact or believe it. Thus it is that all men are related to one another since the blood of our progenitor circulates in all of us. So, it is self interest, as you say, or foolishness to scorn a black just because he is black, an act of cruelty to buy and sell him and undisguised tyranny to mistreat him.

Pedro then utters a fear shared by many colonials. If we all are equal, he asks, "who would obey? Who would give the laws? Who would contain the perverse person with the threat of punishment? And who would protect the individual security of the citizen? Everything would be confused, the voices of equality and liberty would be synonymous with anarchy and the release of all passion" (348).

He continues: "no one would recognize himself as subject to any religion, submissive to any government or dependent on any law." Here religion is equated with obedience, submission, and discipline, forgetting earlier theological notions of the soul's salvation. The state, too, whether a kingdom or a republic, is thought of in terms of dominance and submission: "seeing from the beginning that such a state of brutal liberty was too harmful to him, man subjected himself willingly and not by force; he admitted religions and governments, he swore [to obey] their laws and he bowed his head to [accept] the yoke of kings or the leaders of republics. From this submission dictated by a well-ordered egoism are born the differences of superior and inferior that we notice in all the classes of the State" (348–49)

The phrase "a well-ordered egoism" can escape detection in the long speech. But it shows the extent to which the colony was rethinking the principles of its governance; perhaps self-interest was useful in declaring Mexican independence. Pedro concludes that, given this class structure, black slavery is justified because of the money that has been exchanged (strange logic that suggests, however, that the business of slavery, in which some token is received for the value of human life, is some advancement over the unpaid exploitation of human labor, which characterized Spanish use of Indians).

Then the black—urbane, well-traveled, and familiar with the organization of many societies—corrects Pedro. He shows that belief in a black man's inferiority runs counter to principles of reason, humanity, and moral virtue; he discounts any religious or secular rationale for slavery: "I now dispense with [any discussion] as to whether any particular religions admit it or if any commerce, ambition, vanity or despotism sustains it" (345). Thus he invalidates any justification for slavery based on authority or the notion of preordained law.

He returns to Pedro's assumption of men's basic equality deriving from their common humanity. He, too, understands the need for a hierarchical society, according to Pedro's two arguments, which can be seen to have their foundations in contemporary thought. If submission is necessary to "the economic order of the world" so as to avoid the chaos and anarchy that would result if everyone thought himself equal to his neighbor, the logic is based on utilitarianism. Similarly, the other argument, reflecting a new anthropological sense, seems to derive from recent travelers' reports of different societies (349–50), which report that all societies, whether civilized or primitive, have formed some notion of rank to escape the brutish state. In both instances men submit willingly to domination out of self-interest.

The black man does not develop the topic of slavery. Instead he continues on to analyze the personal qualities that inequality breeds. He reproduces a uniquely colonial criticism of lesser officials, safe in the protection of higher authorities and cruel in their treatment of those beneath them. This contact with power is the only one most colonials would have known. Their historical experience of corruption by colonial officials, the exploitation of their native wealth, would have taught them all they knew about the supposed benefits of submission.

Superiors, the black says, should be gentle and generous; they should be lovable if they want love. But they have abused their position. Both grandees and the rich—a distinction that shows Mexicans' increasing awareness of a dying nobility and a growing merchant class—are usually proud and haughty, thus turning the hearts of their subordinates cold:

> It is an abominable thing to deal with a superior who at all times has his neck proudly erect, grumbling a few words, shielding his eyes and wrinkling up his nostrils like a bulldog. This, far from being a virtue, is a vice; it is not gravity, but foolishness. No one purchases more cheaply the hearts of men than superiors, and the less it costs them, the greater is their feeling of superiority. A gentle glance, a soft response, courteous treatment, costs little and is worth a great deal in capturing the will; but, unfortunately, affability is hardly known among grandees. They use it, true; but they only use it when they have need of it, not with those who really need it. (348–50)

The black's—and Lizardi's—only recourse in trying to change this abuse was to identify it, to shift the language terms according to which it was accepted. Consequently, the black's point—that *seriedad* [seriousness] should not deteriorate into *altivez* [haughtiness] and that *afabilidad* [affability], so prized as a mark of courtesy by the upper classes, should be extended to those most in need of it, the servants to these classes—conveys colonial sensitivity to the language of subordination. Similarly, the black's emphasis on love and sentiment, on the ties that join a wife to her husband and a servant to his master, recalls the basic, interpersonal bonds of a social contract.

In the prologue to the *Periquillo* Lizardi despaired that an American author could export his work and that the message of his book would reach the attention of readers in Spain (2). Lacking the protection of a noble patron, Lizardi had to depend on colonials to buy and read his book. He underscored his Mexican readers' common birth, their perceived low condition in the eyes of Europeans, in writing that many probably would be "plebes, Indians, mulattoes, blacks, vicious persons, fools and nuisances" (4); and he linked them to the great sinners of history. Consequently, his rebuke of lesser officialdom in defining the reciprocal responsibilities of a social contract must be read literally, as intended to bring about attitude changes in his probable readers, members of the ruling classes in the colony, rather than in the Madrid government.

Salvador Bueno has called the *Periquillo* "the first anti-slavery novel in America" (138). Bernabé Godoy has identified the chapter in which the black speaks as one of the most affecting of the book and the point at which French liberal thought is most daringly seen (28–30). John Pawlowski also remarks on the chapter, stating that "Lizardi's presentation of the Negro lacks the ring of authenticity which characterizes the mulatto, Indian, rustic, and other types populating his novels" ("Novels" 114). Godoy's reaction to the sentimentality of the scene contrasts with Pawlowski's note that emotion is lacking; however, the fact that both single out the chapter proves its power. The contradiction in their responses may be accounted for by the difference in Lizardi's technique at this point. Disembodied voices isolate what is the clearest statement yet of Lizardi's principal preoccupation in the novel; up until this time, colonialism was only suggested as Periquillo's and the interpolated stories enacted the father/son relationship. Pawlowski apparently responds to this tonal change, whereas Godoy is sensitive to the cry of oppression, intellectually uttered. The fact that Lizardi forsakes his customary humor in this chapter also upsets the reader's expectations.

I have no wish to detract from the book's critique of slavery. Yet I want to underscore the relevance of the philosophical discussion to questions of colonialism and despotism. Lizardi wrote in *El Pensador Mexicano:* "people accustomed over a long period of time to suffer in silence the harsh chains of despotism begin to think slavery is natural, in terms that, like ingrates and fools, they resent the hand of the very benefactor which is trying to untie them from the fatal cart of oppression and tyranny" (*Obras* 3: 176). The despotism referred to here is the tyranny of the Inquisition, which had been abolished at the time of the publication of the article (September 30, 1813) but which some pious people thought needed to be reinstated. Lizardi, in contrast, lamented the childish morality representatives of the Church and its political instrument, the Inquisition, imposed on the poor and the ignorant.

In the *Periquillo* Lizardi shows a greedy provincial priest who sells spiritual favors; and even though his bad example is partially offset by the decency of another priest, Lizardi makes his point that ecclesiastical abuses were common in Nueva España. Also in the novel, a long discussion of the *mayorazgo* system [primogeniture inheritance] simultaneously signifies colonial relationships. When an older son inherits all goods and properties, thus excluding the younger, wealth is concentrated in the hands of a few. Lizardi makes it clear (vol. 2, chap. 8) that this European custom injures the state and that, although monarchs have tried to end the practice, it persists. Although Lizardi does not explicitly tie this discussion to the political family, it is clear that official rhetoric, which had taught that *españoles peninsulares* and *españoles americanos* were brothers, would have allowed Lizardi's readers to interpret the discussions of *mayorazgo* inheritance as a commentary on their dispossessed state. Therefore, one concludes that bonds based on exploitation rather than on charity and mutual feelings of gratitude often hold men in a kind of tyranny, which Lizardi recognizes variously as slavery, political oppression, economic legislation, and the manipulation of ignorance and fear by religious authorities.

4

Law and Utopia

Most of the *Periquillo's* fiction elaborates a personal system of paternalism in Mexico. However, the novel takes another turn when Periquillo leaves Mexico to go to the Philippines. On his way home from that other Spanish colony he is shipwrecked on an island whose society, based on impersonal law, allows Lizardi to theorize about government and social organization. The three chapters in which Lizardi digresses to describe this ideal world represent an even longer excursus if one sees them as part of a grouping with previous episodes (Periquillo's sorry try as judge in Tixtla, a discussion of Spanish law, his voyage to the Philippines, debates he has with foreigners—a black, an Englishman, and a Spaniard), and then a later segment when Periquillo returns to Mexico, accompanied by the brother of the Chinese ruler of the island. Together these parts make up book 4 of the third edition (when this portion of the novel was finally published), the volume ending with Periquillo's expulsion from the house of the wealthy *chino*. Thus, the imaginative creation of an alternative, non-Mexican world, a well-ordered, harmonious society built on principles of government other than those of Mexico, is set apart from the realism of the larger Mexican story.[1]

Law

The book is characterized by Periquillo's good fortune, and the transition is signalled by a change in the hero's name: "If the boys at school, instead of giving me the defiling nickname Periquillo Sarniento, had named me

Periquillo the Jumper, surely I would say they prophesied my adventures, because I jumped from one destiny to another and from one adverse lot to another favorable one so quickly" (314). Yet the apparent focus on character disguises an important shift. In the fanciful Utopia, Lizardi escalates the narrative to the level of ideas and projects a social construct which then casts its shadow back onto the rest of the text. Taking his readers to strange places, Lizardi asks them to suspend their suspicion of difference, rooted to a great extent in their Catholic fear of other religions and their colonial obsessiveness with the Spanish model of civilization. Introducing the notion that other peoples, whom he treats sympathetically in the text, might hold different views of social organization and progress, he relativizes "civilization" and suggests that European views of Others as inferiors might be wrong. Juxtaposing the Oriental society and the Mexican, he contrasts the two but he also posits commonalities basic to all cultures; for example, he asks why it is universally the case that residents of a country feel a sentimental attachment to their birthplace. Free of the references to a country with a known history, Lizardi could appear to be playing intellectually. Yet the fantasy, while it seemed to overlook Mexican realities, such as food shortages, civil war, immorality, and ignorance,[2] in fact challenged the Mexican status quo.

A literary Utopia's existence, confined to the text, is nonthreatening; as a "play in space" it is only discourse limited to the reading experience (Marin *Utópicas*). Earlier, in an essay in *El Pensador Mexicano* (1814) that anticipates the novel's Utopia, Lizardi "played" imaginatively by creating an island that suggested Mexico. His fiction-making reproduced the hard facts of Mexico's past and present predicaments, but the paper's fragility also hinted at evanescence and possible rearrangement. The essay is a patently fictitious letter to Lizardi from a writer on the island of Ricamea, somewhere in the Americas, where the population resembles Mexico's in its Catholicism and racial mix. Half-savage Indians predominate; and although they are considered "rude by nature, idiots, superstitious and cowardly," their countrymen rely on them for their manual labor. There are also blacks, mulattoes, and mixtures of these races, as well as a third *casta* (racial category) made up of Europeans and Indians whose children are called criollos.[3] The fictitious writer pins the source of hostility over the years to racial inequities and then he describes the present war between criollos and Europeans: "It has arisen in my lifetime, provoked by [the criollos], and it is still continuing despite the fact that under the previous government all these residents, because they were nationals, were declared citizens and equal in rights and representation to the rest of the individuals on the island" (*Obras* 3: 397–98). In this reference to contemporary Mexican realities, Lizardi says in his narrative voice that "the revolution began because of seduction or enthusiasm, now it continues out of vengeance and each side alleges a multitude of grievances." The blood of all races is being spilled, the country ruined; and in this weakened state, the writer fears, "the sword of a foreign power" may take it over.

Other Mexican realities, such as a legal pretense of equality and the colony's involvement with European politics, are apparent in the fiction. A young king, Annfredo II [Fernando] "of the illustrious house of Bornobes [Bourbon]" has just been deposed because of the dangers inherent in a monarchy; absolute power can become tyranny and a well-meaning ruler is often duped by someone he trusts. Instead the island has instituted a system in which a president checks the power of a "council or governing panel," composed of six nobles and six plebeian members (thus suggesting constitutional discussion going on throughout the Americas and Spain in those years). The president may be read as José Bonaparte, who, although called "el Padre de la Patria" and admired by some for his attempts at reform, was resented by many in Spain and the Americas because of his foreign birth. Lizardi makes his governor the symbol of enlightened rule, yet neither the "effort, disinterest and liberality" this fictitious ruler shows, nor the fact that Lizardi suggests dynastic legitimacy by marrying him to the former ruler's daughter (José was brother to Napoleon, married to someone the emperor had planned to marry) is enough to unite the island people.

Written before the restoration of Fernando VII to the throne in April 1814, the fiction shows Lizardi's thinking about what *patria* might mean. Patriotism could not be based on kinship with the king if the king was a foreigner. Its locus could not be the captive king, and only confusingly could it be the governing bodies set up in several Spanish cities, each of which claimed legitimacy. If European and American Spaniards had just witnessed a rupture in the royal line of succession, it follows that both populations began to question what held them together in a *patria* any longer.

Twice in the utopian fiction in *El Pensador Mexicano* Lizardi uses the phrase *un no sé qué* [I don't know what] to refer to the sentiment that binds one to *patria*—once when his Mexican letter-writer resolves to return home ("Seeing myself alone, rich and in a strange land, I determined to return to my *patria* because it has an I-don't-know-what that even its stones are beloved," *Obras* 3: 390), and again in his own voice in an essay entitled "Sobre el amor de la Patria" [On Love of Country], which immediately preceded the island fiction: "How is it that, in spite of everything [the ingratitude shown by one's *patria*] I feel in my heart an 'I don't know what' that inclines me with the sweetest violence to love the place where I was born and my compatriots with a certain predilection which I cannot shed?" (*Obras* 3: 379). Benito Feijóo, in an essay entitled "El no sé qué," had earlier used the phrase to consider the aesthetic experience of pleasure, and the individual's lack of words to explain it. Lizardi, who was probably familiar with the Spanish priest's essay, now takes this idea of groping for language so as to express a growing colonial awareness of local attachments and the difficulty of thinking about and articulating them.

The story of an island society in *El Pensador Mexicano* only suggests the possibility that there may be such a thing as a perfect world, a Utopia; Lizardi never details its design nor how to implement it. Instead the list of unsatisfactory conditions on the island, as well as a plea for advice on how to reconcile opposing factions, point to a sequel in which a satisfactory solution will appear. The correspondent says: "You are finally going to dream up a kingdom and make yourself king or minister in it; and thus you will give it your laws" (*Obras* 3: 398). Lizardi sets this plea in the context of the Utopian literary tradition, mentioning works by Plato, Aristotle, Thomas More, Saint Thomas Aquinas, Diego Felipe Albornoz, Diego de Saavedra Fajardo, José del Campillo y Cosío, "Foronda" (pseudonym of Juan Valentín Matías Fabbrini), and others (*Obras* 3: 399). However, these European works—philosophical treatises and counsel to kings, as well as specific recommendations for governance, such as Campillo's, which studies the Spanish enterprise in America—merely exist on paper; these ideal societies are the figments of men's imaginations and might, Lizardi suggests, come to nothing as the harmless ramblings of fools (such as the rules Don Quijote gave Sancho to govern his island). On the other hand, although Lizardi does not say so explicitly, these European drafts had real consequences in America as they determined conditions there.

Censorship forced Lizardi to discontinue publication of *El Pensador Mexicano* in April 1814. So the Utopia of the *Periquillo* probably contains his promised response. The prospectus for the novel reveals that by December 1815 Lizardi had conceived of the episode in which Periquillo travelled to distant lands and briefly enjoyed good fortune. In the intervening two years Napoleonic rule had ended, the Bourbon monarchy was restored, the Spanish Constitution was revoked, and the Cortes were suspended. In Mexico, at the Congress of Chilpancingo in 1813, Morelos had called for an end to obedience to the Spanish king and elimination of privileges for the clergy and the military. He had advocated racial equality and economic reforms, and these ideas formed the basis of the constitution of Apatzingán in 1814. However, revolutionary and reform hopes ended with Morelos's execution in 1815. One historian describes the turn in the war: "More and more the revolutionary cause became identified with rapine and personal ambition and the idealists began to abandon it in disgust. The rebel chiefs, scarcely distinguishable from bandits, built themselves impregnable strongholds in the high mountains, tyrannized over their adherents, and used for their own adornment the gold and silver, the jewels and expensive fabrics, which they stole from the *gachupines*" (Parkes 164). Indeed, this picture accords with Lizardi's description of *gavilla* life in the last episode of Periquillo's criminal career.

The ambiguous patriotism of the novel reproduces the confusion of this intervening period. Lizardi's notion of *patria*, rather than largely emotional as in *El Pensador Mexicano*, now goes beyond nostalgic love of place; instead the wise *coronel* says "the best *patria* is the one where one can work in a manly, honest way" (351). This statement should not be construed to mean that Lizardi urged an emotionless opportunism in choosing one's country, but rather that patriotism must allow for the fulfillment of one's manhood through self-satisfying, but also socially useful, work. Gratitude toward the social body that allows the individual to realize his talents through labor yet also contribute to the common good, the *coronel* says, will produce feelings of patriotism. However, a *pícaro* who does not work will always remain an outsider and he must not call the country ungrateful or its inhabitants unloving (as Periquillo has done) for denying him its benefits. Thus, the concept of birthplace or *patria*, which dominates the 1814 letter in *El Pensador Mexicano*, is replaced in the *Periquillo* by a class consciousness, in which the villains are no longer those born outside Mexico but those who refuse to work and contribute to society—both aristocrats and *pícaros* alike.

The Utopian digression begins aboard ship, where Periquillo, crossing the Pacific on his way back home, dreams of starting a new life in which he will even become viceroy of Mexico. He envisions investing the small amount of money he has earned in Manila in a commercial venture in Veracruz, marrying well, then getting a title and property. But he muses that a title based on his business assets sounds ridiculous (he will be called "el conde de la Muselina" [Count of Muslin])[4] and he decides instead to become a landowner. After several days of foolish self-deception in which he puts on the airs of a viceroy, a shipwreck interrupts his dream; and he is cast ashore.

It is not clear that the society and form of government on the island where he lands are ideal; however, they are meant to be a commentary on, and set of solutions to, Mexico's problems. The explanations that the *tután* or Oriental ruler gives of the workings of that society constantly contrast with, and criticize, "the customs of your *patria*." First, Lizardi confronts Mexico's problem of an unproductive nobility. Periquillo, who claims he is a nobleman and exempt from work, finds on the island that everyone works and one's station in life is determined by one's contribution to the common good. When the *tután* asks how one is made a nobleman in Mexico and what he is trained to do, Periquillo answers that honor comes from service one's ancestors rendered to the king and that the nobleman busies himself with either arms or letters. However, on the island these pursuits are foolish. There a citizen army makes the military occupation unnecessary; as a result the national treasury does not have this outlay and everyone's patriotism is encouraged. Letters, defined broadly as the activity of the learned professions, have practical value. Doctors, rather than memorizing Latin terms, experiment with herbal cures; they study nature and usefully function as surgeons, druggists, and practitioners. Lawyers are superfluous because the laws, which have been standardized for all, are made available to everyone everywhere on stone tablets. There are no theologians because their systematic thinking is thought to interfere with a person's direct knowledge of God; priests serve society concretely by performing manual labor. In Mexico,

Periquillo admits, many nobles, whose parents have taught them to scorn work, are not even self-supporting: "not all noble men are princes nor are all rich; rather many are poor, and so many, that because of their poverty they merge with the dross of the people" (361).

The language of work in this portion of the novel reproaches not only Mexico's unproductive nobility but also colonial economic notions; the concept of colonial territories as part of the *real patronato*, the theory of wealth as bullion from American mines, Spanish monopolistic control of the colonies represented as protection, even the sordid trade based on slavery—all these are thrown into sharp contrast as outmoded ideas of commerce. On the island benefits are only accorded those who work; and if one does not know how to be productive, the state will teach him a trade. So Periquillo is taught to work in the silk industry (this detail suggests Hidalgo's experiments with mulberry trees and silkworms to break the Spanish monopoly and make the Indians of his parish self-supporting).

Lizardi does not identify the economic system that will function best to recruit all members of society, utilize the resources of land and labor most effectively, and distribute the rewards. However, he reveals his authoritarian leanings; his concern is mainly with avoiding poverty rather than promoting individual happiness, just as his preoccupation with the law is to regulate crime rather than guarantee freedoms to the individual. The following exchange, nonetheless, shows Lizardi's awareness of the consideration of personal happiness:

"I can do no less," I said, "than praise the economy of your country. It is certain that if all the conditions which rule are as good and commendable as those you have revealed to me, your land must be the happiest, and here the imaginary ideas of Aristotle, Plato and others regarding the government of well-ordered republics must have been realized."

"I don't know if it is the happiest," the Chinese man said, "because I have not seen others, but to think that there are no crimes or criminals here, as I have heard it said there are throughout the world, is a mistake because the citizens here are men like everywhere else. What happens is that we attempt to avoid crime with laws and delinquents are punished severely." (374)

Work and law, key to Lizardi's Utopia, reveal, rather than any reliance on classical, medieval, or Renaissance sources, the impact on Mexico of the contemporary philosophies of liberalism and utilitarianism, which were being discussed in the press of the period. In an article in the *Diario de México* (1811), Carlos María de Bustamante quotes Jeremy Bentham: "It is well known . . . that public welfare should always be the objective of the legislator, and general usefulness the great principle of reason in all civil and criminal legislation."[5] A similar sentiment is expressed when the Asian ruler of Lizardi's island quotes from the work of Manuel de Lardizábal, *Discurso sobre las penas contrahido a las leyes criminales de España* [Discourse on Penalties, Contracted for the Criminal Laws of Spain] (Madrid, 1782):

" . . . the first and principal end of every society being the security of its citizens and the health of the republic, it follows as a necessary consequence that this is the first and general aim of penalties. The health of the republic is the supreme law.

" . . . besides this general aim there are other private [ones] subordinate to it, although equally necessary, without which the general one could not be accomplished. Such are the correction of the delinquent in order to make him better, if that may be possible, so that he does not harm society again; the ridicule and example so that those who have not sinned may abstain; the security of persons and the property of citizens; the indemnities or reparations for the harm caused to the social or to private persons." (378)

Lardizábal, a Mexican-born jurist, served in Spain as advisor to Carlos III in a projected reform of criminal legislation; and Lizardi draws extensively on his work in verbatim passages. Indeed, of the two chapters devoted to a description of island life, much the greater portion of the second shows Lizardi's reliance on Lardizábal's ideas in discussing the problems a secular society must confront in acknowledging evil and taking steps to control it.

Lardizábal's ideas about law show how far Spain and its colonies had come since the sixteenth century, when Francisco Suárez and Francisco de Vitoria emphasized law's internationalism. Lardizábal's statement that "the first and principal end of every society [is] the security of its citizens and the health of the republic" interprets *law* in a way that appears to favor local Mexican interests. Now laws domestically framed, rather than any long-distance relationship between king and vassal, will enable men to live in harmony with one another, restraining their passions as they fear laws' penalties.

Lizardi's preoccupation with crime and punishment reflects an awareness of the risk Mexicans were running for their crime of lèse majesté; it also shows the anguish Mexicans were experiencing at witnessing acts of retribution the Spanish justice system was carrying out on Mexican soil. In going beyond the rancorous attack on unproductive social classes, contained in the first chapter, Lizardi confronts the fact that enforcement of law's penalties was causing Mexicans to begin to feel fear for themselves and compassion for their compatriots' suffering, thus complicating their rational assent to the need for law. Significantly, it is a Spaniard, also a shipwrecked visitor on the island, who expresses the sympathy a judge and witnesses feel for the victim of a public execution: "it is a hard thing to be a judge and more so in these lands where, according to custom, they have to witness the supplications of the prisoners and have their tender souls tormented with the groans of the victims of justice. Humanity becomes resentful when it sees one of us given over to ferocious hangmen, who torment him without pity and many times deprive him of life adding ignominy to suffering" (375). However, the Spaniard protests that men cannot yield to their feelings but instead must insist on a system of penalties so as to reinforce a government of law. He describes what would happen if this pain were considered so abhorrent that penalties were abolished: "Neither the father would care for his child, nor would the latter have any respect for his father. Nor would the husband love his wife, nor would she be faithful to her husband. . . . [All] care and reciprocal gratitude in society would be destroyed; and then the strongest would be the executioner of the weakest and, because of this, he would satisfy his passion, taking what he could from him—his wife, his children, his liberty, and his life" (376). The Spaniard warns: "in this sad case the dikes of religion will be insufficient to contain the perverse man" (376). His conclusion, sadly arrived at, that human emotion must be suppressed in certain instances, suggests that Lizardi was struggling with the place of sentiment in forming a family or a nation.

Lizardi further reveals his ambivalence in the dialectic of the *tután*'s argument that public executions prevent crime; he is not sure of how a society calling itself civilized will mete out justice. On one hand, the cruel and public punishments of the island system would seem to deter crime; on the other, the sympathy Lizardi is encouraging brother to feel for brother in preserving the imperial system or forming a new independent nation is offended by witnessing state-inflicted suffering.

Public punishment of crimes was likened by one writer in the *Diario de México* to entertainment for the masses, such as bullfights and cockfights, walks along the alameda, and even the proliferating newspapers.[6] Previously, Inquisition *autos* had made available this kind of judicial instruction; and Lizardi also seemed to think the spectacle of the public execution of justice [*escarmiento*] was essential to his island Utopia. Yet in a long passage Lizardi traces the imagination of a sympathetic judge:

> "What affliction must this poor criminal be suffering!," he says to himself or to his friends, "what pain he feels when he sees that justice tears him from the arms of his loving wife, that he will never again kiss his young children nor enjoy the conversation of his best friends, but they will disown him once and for all, and he them for he will leave them forcibly! And in what condition does he leave them? Alas! His wife, a widow, poor, alone and defeated; his children, hapless, ill-cared-for orphans; and his friends, scandalized and perhaps repentant of the friendship they professed for him.
>
> "Will the reflection of human souls stop here? No, it extends yet to those miserable families. It follows them in thought; it finds them with the imagination; it penetrates the walls of their dwellings and, on seeing them submerged in gloom, insult and abandonment, that spirit can do no less than feel agitated by the deepest affliction, to such a degree that, if he could, he would grab the victim from the hands of his executioners and, thinking that he had done a good deed, he would restore him unpunished to the bosom of his adored family." (375)

The speech, filled with vicarious suffering, shows Lizardi's belief that in a civilized society, literature, which can imagine punishment, provides another kind of *escarmiento*, one with less painful consequences.

The discussion of the most effective and humane ways of punishment makes real a larger dilemma of the colony. In a state where numerous colonial regulations, such as sumptuary laws, were prejudicial in maintaining the power of a few, where many had not internalized the values behind the laws because colonial education had only cared about external signs of obedience, the law was not widely respected or adhered to. The poor were mostly blamed as society's criminals;[7] their lack of education condemned them.[8] Yet it was also recognized that the loss of native tradition at that level, as well as lax law enforcement and corruption among the wealthy, made it difficult to progress toward the rule of law;[9] "customs" [costumbres], unwritten laws but also extenuating circumstances to be considered in arriving at legal decrees, were increasingly regarded as important. Evidence that Mexicans were beginning to wonder about crime's causes and the remedies of law is contained in an article in the *Diario de México* in which the writer found an inverse relationship between the number of laws required by a society and an equitable distribution of wealth: "The state that favors with its laws an unjust distribution of wealth must extend its penal code, and expand its jails in proportion to the number of private palaces for, on the contrary, every state attentive to dividing patrimonies, to making the nutritive juices run through the branches, will have fewer crimes to punish."[10]

Michel Foucault has demonstrated how peasant criminality, resulting from the growth of capitalism, contributed to revolution in France (82–89). In Mexico, too, the lower social classes were newly visible as they provided the manpower for armies on both sides of the Independence war. However, the actions of this racially mixed sector of the population, both manipulated by military strategies and uncontrolled as banditry, were not attributable to the same economic development as in France, nor were the classes' militancy and violence the result of much class consciousness.[11] Lizardi's novel, which documents systemic corruption and widespread upper-class criminality,[12] treats Indians and *castas* neither as heroes nor villains but as part of a larger picture of colonial immorality.

The crimes the islanders punish most severely are murder and robbery. The first reflects the Mexican war; the second is significant because the protection of private property it suggests seems to say that the spirit of communism, so common in Enlightenment reform literature in the second half of the eighteenth century (Venturi *Utopia* 96), is absent from Lizardi's ideal society. However, it would be wrong to conclude that

Lizardi's concern with robbery meant he defended the rich and their wealth; as I have shown, Lizardi criticized the Mexican nobility's ill-gotten wealth, greed, and idleness. Yet, if Lizardi was anti-aristocratic, it cannot be concluded that he was a populist or an advocate of public ownership.[13] It can be argued, however, that Lizardi wanted everyone to enjoy the fruits of his labor and that, if his penalties for robbery were harsh (whipping, branding, or mutilation), he intended to indict not only the lazy and criminal poor, but also the metropolis, which stole the colony's wealth, and the nobility, whose unproductivity and exploitation were forms of robbery. In the *tután*'s admonition Lizardi emphasizes how important it was that each contribute: "The situation here is that no one eats our rice or the tasty meat of our cows and fish without earning it with the sweat of his brow" (360).

The Utopian city is a commercial center, suggesting the island's independent ability to supply its population's needs. Lizardi does not describe its physical layout, but he characterizes its organization by the external sign [*divisa*] each person wears to declare his occupation (373–74). Lizardi states that the code allows the government to control and eliminate idleness. A city with a developed commerce was thought to be easier to rule and to improve; one contributor to the *Diario de México* wrote: "A commercial city, which emerges from a well-formed government, is easier to establish and develop than those ancient cities in which there were imperfect, entangled laws, ridiculous customs and civil practices."[14] Another explored the importance of cities for the circulation of money: "Let's suppose that half of our population resides in the city where . . . consumption is much greater than in towns."[15] The article, which emphasizes the internal flow of money as city dwellers pay with cash and credit for what the countryside produces, suggests that a domestic economic system was (at least theoretically) in the making, different from the colonial one in which money ended up—and stagnated—in the king's coffers.

A series of articles on Paris and London in the *Diario* had made those cities models of urban life. Their parks, museums, libraries, paved streets, cleanliness, stimulus to the arts, and so on produced admiration and envy among Mexicans. Mexicans had been taught that they owed grateful thanks to Spain for the construction of their capital. Yet, reading of the progress other Europeans had made in building their cities and looking around at their world, Mexicans might have concluded that Spain had not favored them. The *Diario's* glowing reports of European capitals con- trasted with Mexico City's backwardness. The following dialogue from the *Diario* sets out typical Mexican self- reflection:

Pablo: "Mexico is the best city in the universe." Juan: "I agree with that insofar as the climate is concerned, its site and the proportions it has to accomplish what is necessary and useful for the conservation and comforts of life." Pablo: "And in everything. Is anything missing for it to be complete and perfect? Doesn't it have a lot of people, a lot of money, many good and magnificent buildings, much pomp and display, an abundance of all kind of provisions, foods of necessity, of pleasure and even of luxury, literature, printing presses, newspapers, foundations of all kinds, public establishments, and whatever is necessary and advisable?" Juan: "I respond with what a wise man said who was archdeacon of this Holy Church—and he was a *criollo*—that here there was a little of everything and nothing of what was neces- sary."[16]

Lizardi's vision of harmony and prosperity on the island condemns condi- tions in Mexico. Yet Lizardi appears to resent travelers' boasts of their countries and criticisms of Mexico; in the *Periquillo* the *tután* complains to the Englishman who has spoken too much about London: "you have made my head a map of London" (368). And the Spaniard asks Periquillo, who brags of his homeland: "How would it seem to you if I praised the wine of San Lúcar scorning the regional drink of your land, which is called *pulque*?" (368). Gratitude to the land and people providing nour- ishment, which Lizardi encourages so that social bonds might be strengthened, prevents him from disparaging his country through in- vidious comparison. For this reason then, as well as for the fact that censorship would have prevented him from publishing negative state- ments about the colony, his picture of an alternative city life is not a map but rather deliberately vague.

Rewriting Utopia

I have used the term *Utopia* to discuss this fanciful portion of the novel. Yet Lizardi never uses the term in the *Periquillo*, preferring instead "Jauja" to describe Periquillo's happy situation in Manila, on the island (named

Saucheofú), and in the company of the *chino*. He defines "Jauja" in a footnote:

An imaginary city that some, who have credited lying travelers, searched for fruitlessly in Spanish America; they were carried along by the magnificent descriptions and weighty praise that were made of their wealth, fertility and beauty. Today its name is only used as a synonym for the Garden of Delights in order to exaggerate the abundance of a city or country where the earth, without the need of cultivation, spontaneously produces everything necessary to man who does not have to work in order to be nourished there.[17]

The concept of Jauja, like Utopia, grew out of Europe's projection of its desires for wealth and social order onto America. In Spain's American colonies the experiments of the Jesuits in Paraguay and the *pueblos-hospitales* of Vasco de Quiroga in sixteenth-century Michoacán are only two of the most famous of the planned communities in which European theories dictated the life and work of American Indians. Jauja, in fact, named a region in Peru, fabled for its climate and the richness of its natural resources. Bookish idealism, then (but also European greed disguised on paper as economic theories and advantageous brokering arrangements), are the intellectual counterparts of invading armies.

Despite his earlier disclaimer that Utopian plans exist only on paper, Lizardi shows his understanding of how much American reality had been affected, and perverted by, the less noble of these Spanish projections. *Jauja*, rather than *Utopia*, underscores the base desires of men for easy gain. Jauja, while the term seems to reiterate Spanish dreams, nevertheless protests that, in actualizing those dreams, wealth was stripped from American lands and Americans were denied opportunities for honest labor. Jauja, unlike the literariness of Utopia, lived in the popular imagination; even today, for example, Mexican *corridos* sing of "La ciudad de Jauja" in order to indict injustices and comment on opportunities for work. Consequently, in preferring the term, Lizardi can be seen to have been tapping into Mexico's oral culture. In embracing a popularly used word that both repeated the notion of Spanish expectations but from an American viewpoint also criticized them, Lizardi was accomplishing several things. He was making the point that only changes in ownership of America's resources, paid American labor, and the reevaluation of work would solve Mexico's problems.[18] He was suggesting, by means of Periquillo's false sense of well-being as he pretends to be a nobleman and dishonestly uses the *chino*'s wealth, similarity with the colony's economy, which was artificially stimulated by the mining bonanza and the exploitation of black slaves and Indians.

Lizardi was also importantly calling into question the body of European literature generally referred to as Utopian. Already mentioned is his reference in *El Pensador Mexicano* to authors from that tradition—classical, Catholic, and Spanish. Lizardi's careful documentation there of his literary sources suggests his initial need to situate his imaginative construct in some legitimate listing. Jefferson Rea Spell's "The Intellectual Background of Lizardi as Reflected in *El Periquillo Sarniento*" remains one of the best studies of Lizardi's reading knowledge, as well as a guide to books other Mexican readers might have consulted. The range is surprisingly vast, including many contemporary works from Spanish but also other European literatures—French and even Scottish. However, Spell concludes that Lizardi may not have known directly the many authors he cited but instead relied on secondary sources such as *compendia*.

In any case, the range suggests that Lizardi and his generation were beginning to draw away from the sixteenth-century theological, military, historical, and poetic genres by which Spain had conquered American territories and imposed habits of thought. Instead, they were using eighteenth-century books, such as the studies of law done by Lardizábal, to construct the intellectual bases for their societies. Yet these newer books were not unproblematic and American use of them was probably not uncritical. For example, in addition to his *Discurso sobre las penas*, which has already been cited, Lardizábal wrote a forty-one-page introduction to an edition of the *Fuero Juzgo*, which was published under the auspices of the Royal Spanish Academy in Madrid in 1815. In that introduction, he traces the history of Spain's jurisprudence and the process of the legal code's translation from Latin to Spanish [*castellano*]. Another anonymous writer, in another twelve-page preface, further states that the academy's interest in the legal code is linguistic, to document early forms of the Spanish language; the academy does not intend the code's publication to be a comment on the late medieval code's legislative merit. However, in reading this emphasis on the language's antiquated tone (and the academy's disavowal of political meddling), it is hard not to think that the

Fuero's discussion of the monarchy and its relation to Church jurisdiction, despite the fact that it was published a year after Fernando's return to Spain and might have suggested a reaffirmation of monarchical supremacy, should not also be thought of as critical. The monarchy, like the code's language, was archaic, in need of updating in that enlightened age.

In the *Periquillo* Lizardi refers to sixteenth-century Spanish literature in the context of a discussion of arms and letters.[19] Criticizing military officials who only draw their reading from "their ordinances and Columbus" (329), Lizardi says that, in contrast, men like Alonso de Ercilla admirably combined military service to the king and the peaceful activity of writing poetry. Lizardi's literary allusion is intended to express exasperation with military privilege, which he will go on to criticize in *Don Catrín*. Nevertheless, this discussion of military restraint, in chapters prior to Periquillo's departure for Manila, when the *coronel* is lecturing on Spain's several legal codes (the Siete partidas, the Fuero Juzgo, and the Nueva Recopilación), and new theories of law by eighteenth-century jurists (Lardizábal, José Berni y Catalá, José Marcos Gutiérrez, and Félix Colón de Larreátegui), suggests that Lizardi recognized the importance of returning to Spain's sixteenth-century writers and writing practices so as to reconsider the colonizing assumptions still operative in Mexico three centuries later.

East versus West

Why Lizardi labeled the islanders "Chinese," however, raises several questions. Critics, while remarking on the Utopian interlude and noting its literary antecedents, have generally passed over the story's specific Pacific geography. However, the discovery by Edgar C. Knowlton Jr. of Filipinisms and almost word-for-word correspondences between Lizardi's text and a sixteenth-century work by Padre Juan González de Mendoza, *Historia de las cosas más notables, ritos y costumbres del gran Reino de la China* [History of the most notable things, rites and customs of the Great Kingdom of China] (1585),[20] suggests that somehow Lizardi was familiar with Mendoza's history and that he wanted to evoke that comparative study from the sixteenth century in the context of his contemporary story. It is true that many among Lizardi's readers would have traveled to Asia and would have felt that this extension of the novel was reasonable. Knowlton even suggests that Lizardi himself went to Manila and was thus familiar with routes there. Knowlton does not mention—and I believe the fact is pertinent—that the last ship in Spain's trade with Manila sailed from Acapulco in 1815, thus making Lizardi's novelistic inclusion of the Pacific interlude even truer to contemporary historical realities (Cárdenas de la Peña, F. S. Cruz). Mexico's economy, particularly its trade in luxury goods, was interrupted by the insurgents' seizure of Acapulco. I will not repeat Knowlton's arguments for Lizardi's source but instead accept that Knowlton is correct and move on to the implications of his amazing find of intertextuality between a colonial history and a large portion of Mexico's first novel.

Mendoza, a Spanish Augustinian who lived in Mexico for twelve years (1562–1574), returning there three times to preach in its principal cities (including fflacatecas and other Augustinian missionary settlements in northern Mexico), never went to China. Instead he talked to Spanish travelers who had been there and read Chinese books translated by Filipinos, thus producing a detailed account of Chinese and other Asian societies in the process of being discovered by Europeans. However, in the last fourth of his book, Mendoza also included the story of Spanish conquests in the Americas (with observations on the land and Indian peoples), updating his history for the second, 1586 edition with discoveries of unknown Indian nations in Nuevo México and reports of Chinese traders arriving in Acapulco the previous year. Thus, variously, he drew together recent Asian and American events. Mendoza praised China, but he also described Mexico enthusiastically, saying Mexico's wealth was only exceeded in the world by China's. His work, widely read throughout Europe in the sixteenth and seventeenth centuries,[21] was an early ethnographic study, textually joining Americans and Asians.[22]

One then begins to understand why Lizardi drew from Mendoza's work—part history, part travelogue, part ecclesiastical politics—not just his description of the Pacific island society but also Mendoza's critique of the rationale for European imperialism. In the sixteenth century Asia and America had both been fields of Spanish missionary activity. Both had called forth theological pronouncements as to their population's human nature. Because initial reports from China told of a developed religion, an organized and peaceful society, and a strong military that could not be easily overrun, the Vatican appeared to recognize its superior civilization and relaxed rules missionaries had earlier insisted on in the Americas, among other concessions accommodating the invariable-seeming Mass to Oriental custom. Americans, learning then of theology's specious reasoning and the Church's flexible classification of peoples, began to guess why they might have been defined as they were (childlike, naked savages, brutes, superstitious, etc.). Technologically backward and less well organized politically, and therefore more easily conquered, they had been assigned an identity that depended more on their conqueror's own measure of military success than on the potentially conquered population's essential nature.

Written some fifty years after the initial penetration of Spain into the Americas, Mendoza's book criticized the Spanish military and colonial policies that had imposed government by force and thwarted the spiritual goals of the ecclesiastics. By 1585 it was clear that Spanish government in the Americas and the Philippines, although firmly established, was being corrupted by military and administrative officials. By then it was apparent how theology had bent to the needs of politicians. Thus, by recalling to readers familiar with Mendoza's work the sixteenth-century thinking of Spanish conquest and Roman evangelization, Lizardi could suggest, if not the dishonesty of ideology in that early period and in his own day, at least the power of its language to fix European categories of the Other according to degrees of humanness.

Complicating my argument for the influence of Mendoza's work on the *Periquillo*, however, is the fact that I have found no mention of Mendoza in the corpus of Lizardi's writing or in other Mexican literature of the period. The Abadiano collection includes a copy of the 1596 Antwerp edition, in Spanish; but it hardly seems that this is the edition Lizardi would have read. It will require further research to find out how Lizardi knew of the work, and also to what extent his readers would have recognized in his novel resonances of Mendoza's history.

Anthony Pagden in *Spanish Imperialism and the Political Imagination* has importantly emphasized the contributions of the Italian political theorists Tommaso Campanella, Pietro Giannone, Paolo Mattia Doria, Gaetano Filangieri, and Antonio Genovesi to the fortunes of seventeenth- and eighteenth-century Spanish imperialism. Although references to these authors do not appear in the *Periquillo*, Lizardi, in the same section in which he discusses the conflict between arms and letters and mentions Columbus and Ercilla, does quote Alonso, king of Naples, in affirming the possibility that these occupations may coexist (329). Later, in *Correo Semanario de México*, a journal he published between 1826 and 1827, Lizardi tells the story of the popes. There, although he cites Pietro Bembo and Pico della Mirandola (*Obras* 6: 315), he omits several popes from his survey of the sixteenth, seventeenth, and eighteenth centuries and seems unfamiliar with the Italian authors whom Pagden mentions. However, whether Lizardi knew of a work such as Campanella's "Città del sole" (1602), perhaps through Campillo, Jesuit sources, or directly, is difficult to gauge; often colonial writers concealed their sources. As I demonstrate below, however, Lizardi was greatly concerned with the political philosophy of Niccolò Machiavelli.

Several conclusions, then, seem to emerge from Lizardi's preference for "Jauja," and the siting of his ideal society, constructed according to new attitudes toward work and law, in the Pacific. One is the fact that the popular term permits Lizardi and his generation of Mexicans to move away from a European bookish tradition so as to suggest the validity of American experiential knowledge. Another is the inference, resulting from the eighteenth-century economic and political theorists' emphases on work and law, that sixteenth-century colonizing assumptions had to be rewritten. Still another impression, deriving from Lizardi's suggestion that Mexico might begin to think of itself in terms of its own peoples and their languages, or in terms of the territory's Pacific connections rather than its European past, furthers the possibility of Mexican independence from Spain.

In this regard, the Abbé Guillaume Thomas Raynal's *L'Histoire philosophique et politique des établissements et du commerce des Européens dans les deux Indes* [A philosophical and political history of the settlements and trade of the Europeans in the east and west Indies](1770) is pertinent to Lizardi's consciousness of colonial governance and its formulations in European books. Lizardi referred to Raynal four times in works written between 1822 and 1826, once even quoting him extensively and giving evidence of having reflected on the philosophical underpinnings of Raynal's historical review.[23] In his book Raynal discusses European conquest and colonization, significantly also bringing America and Asia together. His view of European expansionism, emphasizing slavery and commerce rather than religious conversion,[24] draws, like González de Mendoza's text, a side-by-side picture of the particular attributes of the peoples and social arrangements of the two Indies.[25] Prohibited in Spain and Spain's colonies, Raynal's treatise on colonialism, masquerading as "history," nevertheless quickly became "one of the works best known in the whole Spanish world" (Spell, *Rousseau* 52).[26]

Thus, I believe it is possible to see in Lizardi's fictional depiction of the Chinese and their Utopian society a rethinking of the body of European literature that justified policies of colonialism and, incidentally, defined non-European lands and peoples. In reconsidering those books and their abstractions, Lizardi shows the American Self attempting to come to grips with labels of inferiority. Finding merit in a non-European, non-Christian, indeed nonreligious[27] civilization, Lizardi does not censure the Chinese as heretics, as Spanish colonial rhetoric would have done; instead his portrayal of difference seems to reflect American sympathies with Otherness. The Chinese government (a combination of Oriental despotism and civil service), the peoples' industriousness in commercial activity (now defined as self-sufficiency rather than extraction of another's wealth and slavery), recommend the society as advanced.

Therefore, Lizardi's Chinese are, I believe, more than a fanciful world dreamed up to contrast with Mexico. The novel's Asians suggest Mexico's own population. The fiction of Pedro Sarmiento's eight-year stay in Manila dramatizes Mexico's and the Philippines' common history. In Spain's language of government, both American and Filipino natives were "Indians" (Filipinos being called "island Indians" [*indios isleños*]).[28] Throughout the colonial period Mexicans and Filipinos had exchanged population. The Philippines were a dumping place for Mexican criminals (Periquillo was sentenced there for his crimes); and Filipinos, vaguely called *chinos*, came as laborers to Mexico, becoming merged in the Mexican imagination with the country's *indios*. José Toribio Medina in his study of the Inquisition in Mexico reproduces a document from Mexico City in 1769 (372–77) in which "Indians and Chinese" were together charged as idolaters. In the vocabulary of the *castas*, *chino* referred to any mixture of non-European blooded persons (Asian and Indian, for example, or African and Indian).

The *tután* is depicted in Lizardi's fiction as richly dressed in satin, velvet, gold, and diamonds. The fishermen of his island are poor, with barely enough food and clothing to be hospitable to Periquillo when he is shipwrecked. Lizardi does not elaborate this contrast; his intent, rather than to draw a perfect society, seems to be to decorate the *tután*'s person with signs of authority so that he may question Periquillo about customs in Mexico. Yet the double vision of wealth and poverty, of justice and injustice that the reader of Lizardi's text has, reflects not only confusion about what to think of that Asian society but also uncertainty with respect to the Mexican Self.

A letter in the *Diario de México*, in discussing Mexican images of the Chinese, voices this difficulty of choosing between assessments that others have formulated so as to judge a culture's worth. The writer says that, on the one hand, "our vulgar belief has thought it axiomatic that the Chinese are uncivilized and dull . . . and has produced the saying 'He's like a Chinese person,'" but on the other hand, "this error does not extend to the instructed." If many Mexicans believed the Chinese to be savage (reports told of how Captain Cook had been eaten by cannibals in the Pacific), others with superior knowledge would have known that Oriental cultural accomplishments were vast. Indeed, upper-class Mexicans knew of the excellence of Oriental production because they had acquired some of the cotton, silk, and porcelain goods that the Manila galleons had brought for shipment on to Spain.

Upper-class Mexicans also would have known through reading and travel that Europeans viewed the Orient, just as they might have viewed the Americas in the eighteenth century, with a mixture of respect and contempt. News of the Pacific, Persia, North Africa, and other Oriental cultures was increasingly entering Europe; Turkish diplomats were walking advertisements in European capitals of a high civilization. However, the Orient also symbolized despotic rule (Venturi "Oriental Despotism" 1963); and Rousseau called Orientals "voluptuous" (347). Borrowing these European views and adding them to their own experience of the Orient, Mexicans ended up with conflicting knowledge of another European Other.[29]

Lizardi's Asian fiction, therefore, rehearses the imaginative process whereby one draws near difference and tries to evaluate it. The task is made even more difficult if the difference is an aspect of one's Self, which one has been told to be ashamed of and which perhaps one still repudiates. In Mexico's case, like the Orient's, the Self did not declare its own essence but instead emerged as the thinking of others. Yet the novel's recall of European books dealing with colonization, from which a critical view could be extracted, shows American dissatisfaction with this thinking of others and the beginnings of a new inquiry into the Self. The novel's overriding sense that foreignness must be tolerated and even judged acceptable, which the Englishman and the Spaniard, Pedro's marooned companions on the island, convey, points to Mexico's approaching embrace of its own Indian nature. This literary exercise in identity formation would have been a valuable lesson for Mexico's criollos, concerned with retracing the steps of their own character assignment.

Francisco López Cámara tells that at the time of Mexico's break with Spain, the criollo "rejected by the European, subsumed into the Indian [identity, saw] himself as alienated, his [essence] diluted in a being that [was] not his own" (27). This criollo unease, caused in both cases by European denigration of his Americanness, might have been partially relieved by Lizardi's novelistic effort at finding merit in non-European cultures. Similarly, other literature of the period might be seen to have opened up these thoughts. Discussion in the *Diario de México* of Padre Francisco Clavijero's *Storia antica del Messico* (published in Italy in 1780–81 when the Jesuit was exiled from Mexico) told Mexicans of their Indian past. In his book Clavijero, attempting to refute de Pauw's thesis of American degeneracy, used Indian oral sources and the evidence of archaeological remains to authenticate and eulogize the high civilization of Aztec Mexico. Following is one of these *Diario* extracts from Clavijero's work:

love for the people where I was born, and love for the truth, have made me write an *apologia* for my countrymen, the Mexican Indians, whom I have tried to vindicate from the labels of barbarian and uncivil. . . . I have said that they used to live in well-formed houses of stone masonry that were even better laid out; they gardened excellently; they fashioned a fish in metal, casting its scales one in gold and another in silver, a marvel that even the best artificers in Asia and Europe were not familiar with as various of these pieces carried to the best cabinets of natural history on the old continent will testify to. . . . [T]hey knew the art of fortification, as fragments of the great wall of Tlaxcala, the majestic ruins of Xochicalco, the *plaza de armas* in Montalvan, near Oaxaca, situated on a hill, and the bulwarks of the palaces of Mictla will show. ("Y. J. A." "Arquitectura de Moctezuma," March 18–19, 1810)

Thus, inquiry into Mexico's pre-Columbian past was part of the criollo intellectual project of rewriting colonial views of Indian primitivism and savagery. Lizardi cited Clavijero in *El Pensador Mexicano* (*Obras* 3: 259); and his portrayal in the *Periquillo* of the accomplishments and social organization of the Chinese on his fictitious island, in its suggestions of cultural difference and tolerance, can be seen to relate to Clavijero's work and to the need of that generation of Mexicans to rethink the Mexican Self.

Authority of King or Law?

Periquillo's Utopia importantly poses the question of authority. It is a question Lizardi never clearly answers because the relationship between a ruler and his people in a society where laws, rather than respect and love for the person of the king, compel obedience, was a troubling problem for Nueva España in the years 1814–1816, when this portion of the novel was probably written. One way of coping with the lawlessness that a discredited monarchy helped cause is to be found in an essay published in a contemporary newspaper, *El Mentor Mexicano:*

No state can subsist without subordination and obedience. The greatest detriment to public tranquility is the state of anarchy; this is the ruin of empires and the beginning of all annihilation. The remedy for such a terrible evil is popular obedience.

The greatest happiness of peoples lies in the inviolable preservation of their rights, that is, life, honor and property; and for this reciprocal security, obedience is absolutely necessary. To the degree a people are happy, to the same degree they are dedicated to this virtue, allowing themselves to be governed by the hand of Providence which moves that of their rulers.

There are many impious philosophers who have preached obedience as contrary to natural law, as alien to rectitude and reason, and as opposed to the security of the state. But, in the first place, natural law teaches us a multitude of principles of superiority and dependency. Thus it is that in Nature force commands weakness, talent governs incapacity, knowledge directs inexperience, the least number yields to the greatest or to those who represent it; and above all, man reveres his maker and those who are his image on earth. . . .

[I]n no way can we say that these subordinations are contrary to natural law, although they repress liberty. Because liberty does not exclude subordination, nor subordination liberty.[30]

Obvious in this passage is the desire to reconcile two opposing views. On the one hand, tradition and orthodoxy relied on one sense of natural law to teach complacency with one's subordinate status; on the other hand, as this document suggests in referring to "many impious philosophers," many Enlightenment thinkers, whose liberal thought the writer seems familiar with, stressed another dimension of natural law, making the individual their starting point and emphasizing liberty as proper to man's natural state. "Liberty," which might then have suggested rebellion, is here subsumed into a rhetoric in which liberal and conservative beliefs are joined.

El Mentor Mexicano provides another example of this need to resolve conflict in asserting that "the sovereignty of the nation is not contradictory to the monarchy":

The limited notions of public law which generally exist in Spain, fruit of three centuries of the most shameful despotism, cause what for some is one of the most simple and intelligible principles to be an object of scandal. The sovereignty of a people (or let's say more properly) of the nation has seemed to many to be contradictory to a monarchy. This pernicious opinion, fomented by those who constantly refer to past abuses and because of their self interests enemies of all reform, has been found to be rooted in the good faith that many, ill-instructed in the subject, have that the rights of the people are opposed to the loyalty owing our king. It is advisable to dispel the fog around these ideas that malice has fed to ignorance, and understand the source of the question, examining the bases on which national sovereignty rests.

[Because] men are incapable of living without being governed, because of the violent shock between their opposing passions and interests, they submit to the dominion of one of their own, who assures them of their well-being, being charged with repressing the turbulent persons and of listening to the weakest through the medium of the law, in whose enforcement he must be zealous. From this one deduces that the power of the king is not his own but delegated or transmitted by the people whom he governs. The king is the perpetual representative of the nation. . . .

The nation with its king at its head is the sovereign. In order to exercise this sovereignty it delegates to magistrates the judicial part and to its removable representatives that of giving it laws. The execution of these and the glorious prerogative of ruling a free nation, of bringing forth good and, in exchange, receiving [the peoples'] veneration and love, is reserved for the monarch who, far from losing, gains a great deal if, instead of the forced obeisance of slaves, he receives voluntary homage from men in possession of their sacred rights.[31]

Although these articles, dated 1811, are an attempt to justify the Cortes's authority over the Spanish empire, they express the same spirit of trying to make two parts into a whole that I find in the *Periquillo*. Beyond the intellectual need of the time to modernize thought, to adapt notions of popular sovereignty to established beliefs in hierarchical structures, to envision a new entity, "the nation," that would be separate from either the king or the people, this reliance on old forms in expressing newness reveals the criollo dilemma of trying to merge two often-conflicting identities or sets of loyalties. The insistent desire to reconcile old and new discourse terms points to the difficulty of borrowing language for abstract thought.

The novel mainly affirms the value of education and the possibility of creating strong and effective father/son links; thus, it can be read as an optimistic statement that a patriarchal system based on love and personal attachment can be made to work. Such a faith, expressed in the greater portion of the novel, seems to be predicated on a belief in men's inherent goodness. Gratitude, not coercion, will produce the ties that bind. According to that reading, the Utopian portion appears to be based on a pessimistic view of nature that sees laws and a system of punishments as always necessary to regulate men's erring ways.

However, taken another way, what I have just described as Lizardi's optimism can be considered pessimism if one believes the dependency relationship of the monarchy to derive from men's weaknesses and inadequacies. If Lizardi had been truly optimistic, he would have espoused a government in which all men, equal in their capacity for reason, would govern themselves. In this case the Utopia is a positive statement, and the novel's essential contradiction may be seen to be the result of a hidden desire on Lizardi's part to leave behind the regressive colonial relationship based on paternalism and to progress in the Utopian portion to government by law—a desire he only dared express in the one atypical excursus describing Periquillo's good fortune.

I suspect that the ambiguity regarding the interpretation of the novel's parts existed even for the first readers of the *Periquillo*—those who received the work in the setting that produced it. The possibility for different readings, taken together with the novel's structural split, reflects a dilemma that many were struggling with in the colony and that resulted for most in some kind of political commitment, in choosing sides with the royalists or the insurgents. Lizardi, however, rather than promoting either cause, appears to have been politically indecisive at this point in writing a novel that could be understood to prove either philosophy.[32]

An unwritten assumption in this and other works deriving from Christian belief, as well as from classical and Bourbon political theory, is that the good ruler is wise and kind in not abusing the law, in not subverting it for his own ends. To do so would be tyranny; and, if Lizardi's novel, with the addition of the Utopian passage, is ambivalent with respect to paternal rule, it is very clear from Lizardi's emphasis on order that he condemns this disorder. Such evil action by a king or his ministers would be an example of the selfishness Lizardi despises.

Lizardi noticeably avoids developing the character of the *tután* in his fiction. What is the *tután*'s function with respect to the law in this state, suggestive of perfection? Does the *tután* have a hand in making the law? Is he accountable to it? The failure to answer these questions suggests that Lizardi was either unwilling or unable to define the limits of authority. Lizardi's Utopia, which draws a ruler and the law together, however, while imaginatively satirizing the despotism and harsh rule of the colonial administration, suggests several blueprints for change. Its legal design and order modernize colonial notions of "law" and powerfully condemn the devastating war that was sweeping away the pretense that "law" might be operating in the colony.

5

Education

At this decolonizing moment in Mexico reformers and revolutionaries agreed that change depended on redefining "education." Whether advocates of a renewed empire or an independent nation, Mexicans understood that "education," together with other constructs like the "father" and the "family," ensured the reproduction of colonial power. In this chapter I continue to explore how Lizardi's fictionalization of these and other key terms points to colonial sensitivity to language.

James Boyd White in an important study of language's reifying potential at critical historical points, *When Words Lose Their Meaning*, claims that social and political institutions derive life from language. He says that these institutions are not "practices set up on a permanent basis . . . [but] a constitutive fiction, a way of talking and acting that creates a public world" (11). Change occurs when these hidden meanings are understood and contested.

Colonials had been taught that "education," like "law," was preferable to force. In conquest rhetoric, "education" conveyed a range of meanings from lessons in Christian faith given to Indian Americans, to subjecting those Indians to the discipline of regular and hard work, to restricting their sexual habits. Later in the colonial period, upper-class colonials began to understand their American inferiority as their unequal access to Peninsular "education," that is, Castilian language and European knowledge. As they gained an awareness of American differences, they began to resent their obligatory conformity to the dominant culture's codes of conduct, the psychological habit they had acquired of self-denial. Although, by means of "education," some were prepared for the ecclesiastical, medical, or legal professions, others, excluded from power, began to suspect that this kind of "education" was only instruction in bafflement since these professionals seemed just to play with words and pontificate on nuances of meaning most cared little about.[1]

Although Enlightenment sensationalist philosophies taught that "education" depended on close observation of a correct model, in the colonial world "imitation" evoked flawed and corrupt teachers, thoughtless repetition of their behavior, and dissimulation. If Enlightenment theories of "education" presupposed child learners, Mexican critics of these theories understood the urgency of adult learning. However, in its emphasis on the diffusion of knowledge, the European Enlightenment began to extend colonialism's understanding of "education"; and in Mexico at Independence, a secularized sense of human reason suggested that criollos could use their own capacities to arrive at new knowledge and, in the formation of a new state, teach this useful knowledge to their lesser classes. Criollos learned from Enlightenment philosophers to take "reason" from its Christian meaning of a God-given faculty, to be used for knowing Him, and variously extend its meaning to signify (a) a social control mechanism, almost like a muscle, that monitored individual passion; (b) practical logic so that one moved backward and forward through mental effort to understand the causes and effects of historical forces and physical phenomena; and (c) a test to judge whether one could be admitted to an elite class whose members recognized one another's rational abilities to interpret data and arrive at a "consensus."[2]

"Education" had been training in loyalty to external bodies such as king and Spain; increasingly it was a socializing process in which all the members of a society participated as they became polite, dutiful, and loyal to *patria* (now redefined as Mexico). "Education" for the salvation of souls had promoted American dependency. Now, as the Enlightenment and other humanistic endeavors secularized society and separated morality from religion, it became clear that independence from the Church and its totalizing language could proceed along other lines.

The "family," both literally as a biological unit and metaphorically as the explanation for various social and political relationships, was newly assuming responsibility for "education."[3] Generally, although children were sent to schools or placed in the care of tutors to acquire the skills of reading and writing and study basic subjects, they were expected to learn morality and civility from contact with parents and other relatives. The ideal held that in the home fathers would teach sons, husbands wives, and that in the public sphere, rulers would provide a proper model for their subjects, landowners and householders for their workers, priests for believers, and so on. The flowering of the self's innate qualities, described by Rousseau in *Emile*, was generally an exception to the thought of both conservative and liberal colonials.[4]

The "family," with its person-to-person relationships, was thought to be uniquely structured to permit didactic display and observation. Newspapers contributed to this expectation by making parents conscious of their teaching role; for example, writers in the *Diario* stressed the importance of correct models of language, since imperfect transmission of a parent's fine Castilian accent would be lost—and, therefore, some legacy of power—if it were not passed on to the next generation.[5] Children, it was assumed, would docilely copy what they witnessed through their eyes and ears. "Imitation" was regularly featured in discussions of colonial education;[6] the topic implied the response of colonials to foreign rules and patterns, yet it also highlighted a suitable pedagogy for a multilingual, largely illiterate society. Showing someone how to do something, rather than telling him, eliminated the problem of which language to use and avoided the question of literacy.

As the biological family acquired more importance in Enlightenment secular thought, it personalized and domesticated the present's connection with the past, the individual's tie to authority. The link between father and son, Lizardi wrote in an essay in *El Pensador Mexicano*, was an important means by which "tradition" was passed from one generation to the next.[7] His focus on the term reflects the way colonials were rethinking a concept they increasingly suspected of rhetorical manipulation. Appearing frequently in the discourse of the period, "tradition," on the one hand, evoked practices of devotion and duty. It reminded colonials of Catholic teaching that tradition, time-honored repetition of the same words and practices, was an important access to Catholic truth; this truth was indisputable and invariable because it went back to, and was consistent with, natural law. Yet on the other hand, the word, although it could suggest reactionary politics, is often to be found in a context in which Mexicans complained that "tradition" begged questions and stifled discussion. Becoming aware of their own experiential uniqueness, many colonials thought "tradition" was inapplicable.[8]

When colonials read of revolutionary events in Europe, these disorders in Catholic countries such as France, Russia, Spain, and Germany were presented as challenges to "tradition"; Mexico's rebellion was also criminalized in this way. Thus, questions of whether tradition was good or bad were pressing. Arguing in favor of tradition was the fact that it was a kind of common-law code, which at least introduced some predictability into colonial life. And if colonials were beginning to distrust far-off kings and the preachings of remote historical periods, they often retained some measure of trust in near-at-hand paternal figures whose interest was thought to be more personal and whose knowledge was more immediate.

The role of books in the educational process, because books variously reinforced and interfered with person-to-person relationships, was debated in the *Diario*. As one letter writer (November 20, 1805) observed in a defense of books, books could alter, and were altering, the bonds authority traditionally depended on: "Before sowing the seed of good ideas, it is necessary to prepare the terrain of the imagination by teaching a love for reading, which is the only means of making it fertile. . . . I am of the opinion that this activity surely has more force than authority itself. The latter many times subjects slaves, but the former encourages devotees" ("Barueq"). Books, therefore, were a pleasing alternative to authoritative structures, which relied on harsh discipline to teach conformity to social order. Additionally, as another writer to the *Diario* wrote,[9] and Lizardi also observed,[10] books might have more of an impact on men's minds because they allowed words to linger longer and the slower, or more careful, reader could then ponder their meaning. Thus, colonials seem to have been aware that the reading experience promised a different kind of contact with authority—one that might even end the ancient pattern of dominance and submission, replacing it with an educational system in which learning about "ideas," rather than just memorizing words, might allow men to internalize the values of order and thus govern themselves.

The significance of the *Periquillo* lies in its portrayal of the decolonizing moment as the destruction of family unity and the interruption of the traditional educational process.[11] Lizardi tells that, at a personal level, there were families in Mexico who, once having had money and advantage, had fallen into such poverty that they could no longer support their children (*Obras* 3: 367–71). There were women whose husbands and fathers, rather than offering protection, were the cause of the women's immorality. At another level, many of the rich, who were supposed to confer charity, were selfishly ignoring their moral obligation to the poor and even dealing with the insurgents so as to continue to get their luxury goods. As I have shown, disillusionment with the king and his representatives was rampant.

The discourse of "education," formerly the property of the colonizers, now began to yield to colonials as they sought to rewrite not only that term's meaning but also that of its opposite, "ignorance." Increasingly one reads in the newspapers of the period and in Lizardi's novels of how the latter notion, historically applied to colonials, was being questioned.[12] "Ignorance" began to blame Indian rusticity and incivility, not on their condition of natural servitude, but instead on Spain's failure to provide schools and proper models. "Ignorance" began to connote the servility of the colonial elite, and the blindness and fanaticism the Inquisition had imposed on the colony, cutting it off from foreign thought and making reform impossible. It began to hint at colonial difficulty with reconciling the disparity between the morality Mexicans heard prescribed and the conduct they witnessed around them.

The *Periquillo*'s drama suggests how these governing terms were being rethought. If in the past colonials had been thought to be children, needy of protection, morally weak and dependent on the mother country for the basics of life, now, Lizardi's book says, they had reached adolescence and were ready to make use of their experience to begin a separate life. This rewriting of the biological metaphor also enabled Lizardi to contradict the myth that the dominant culture was the only access to wisdom and knowledge, its education the only means of deliverance from ignorance and damnation.

Empiricism

Studies such as Jefferson Rea Spell's "The Educational Views of Fernández de Lizardi" have recognized the importance of Enlightenment thought in the educational philosophy of Lizardi. Spell concludes, and I think rightly, that Lizardi was influenced in his educational concerns by

Enlightenment thinkers such as Rousseau and Fénelon. Although Rousseau's name never appears in the *Periquillo*, Lizardi does refer in the novel to Padre Jean-Baptiste Blanchard, a Jesuit priest who wrote *L'Ecole des Moeurs* (Lyons, 1782), a work in which many of the ideas from *Emile* are applied to a Christian educational model.[13] Yet analysis, which is limited to tracing Enlightenment sources in Lizardi's novel, concluding that it is "a novel whose underlying purpose was the reform of educational conditions" (Spell, "Educational Views" 274), does not go far enough in explaining the extent to which the topic of education interested Lizardi and his generation. Lizardi's story is much more than the exemplary dramatization of how an "ignorant midwife" and a "foolish and over-indulgent mother" (260) can ruin one young man, and thereby avoid the corruption of others. The book is an Enlightenment statement of faith that a newer and truer education—self-education—can enter into the chain of history, interrupt the eternally repeating relationship between father and son, and bring truth from error, good from evil.

Other kinds of education books had existed before. One thinks, in the Spanish tradition, of Don Juan Manuel's *El Conde Lucanor*; and, in the non-Spanish tradition, of Machiavelli's *The Prince* and Erasmus's *Discourse on the Education of a Christian Prince*. In the seventeenth and eighteenth centuries, Baltasar Gracián's writing, and Rousseau's *Emile* and Fénelon's *Télémaque*, instruct noble or, at least, economically comfortable youths. Although these works make an effort, in most cases, to reconcile Christian principles with the ethic of worldly success, they do not feature the negatives of human existence that characterize Lizardi's work. The Mexican tale of low-life degradation, and the message of colonial nastiness, are the objective correlatives of Lizardi's sense that something must be destroyed before rebuilding can occur. The fables of La Fontaine, Iriarte, and Samaniego, which like the *Periquillo* also aimed at educating the middle class, are not generally thought to possess this sense that a degenerate system must be swept away;[14] and it is precisely because these fables and myths avoided reference to specific social circumstances that their merit was questioned by colonial intellectuals concerned with providing a new secular moral literature.

The *Periquillo* is a bildungsroman in which emphasis on the negative—on the ugly realities the upper classes ignored and on the value of error—translates into the value of experience as the only proper education in the

colonial world. Lizardi's insistence that an individual rely on his own experience departs from conservative Enlightenment thought. Fénelon, for
example, reflects an older authoritarianism when in the *Télémaque* he has
Télémaque speak to Mentor, his guide on life's journey: "My dear Mentor, why have I refused to follow your counsels? Haven't I been unhappy
as a result of having wanted you to believe me in an age when one does not
have the vision to see the future, or any experience of the past, or any
moderation to manage the present? Oh! If we ever escape this tempest, I
will defer from myself as from my most dangerous enemy. It is you, Mentor, whom I will always believe" (Salignac de la Mothe-Fénelon 1: 20–21).
In a dream sequence in *El Pensador Mexicano*, a guide similarly escorts the
writer through Mexico City (*Obras* 3: 97–102). However, Lizardi's guide,
rather than Fénelon's old, wise Mentor, is Experience, thus suggesting
that an aspect of the self is responsible for one's choices. In the *Periquillo*
the model of the suffering *pícaro*, finally content in his self-earned knowledge, says that knowledge must derive from one's own unpleasant experience.

Empirical philosophy, predicated on the efficacy of trial and error, is a
particularly apt expression of the colony's experience with error; and I
think Lizardi points ironically to the philosophy when he describes the
grievous mistakes the incompetent Periquillo makes while treating sick-
ness, his only education having been Doctor Purgante's charlatanism:
"Not in vain have the laws of the Indies prohibited the exercise of empiricism with such energy" (*Periquillo* 415). I want to argue that this episode
concerning the practice of medicine, first his apprenticeship and then his
move to Tula where his imposture occurs, deserves greater attention than
has been recognized.[15] Although this part of the story has already been
singled out as important because, since Lizardi's father was a doctor, the
reference to medical and apothecary practices was thought to reflect the
author's family experience (Spell, "Mexican Society" 159), I believe that
in the original scheme of the divisions between the volumes, the episode,
occurring early on in volume 3 and continuing throughout three chapters, suggests pivotal importance in its placement and extension. Doctor
Purgante, rather than just a figure with autobiographical meaning or the
stock character of a picaresque novel, is the symbol of an elitist educational system that transmits a spotty knowledge of Latin phrases—language that does not at all serve to meet the human needs of the commu-

nity. His practice of medicine is a perfect example of how a field of knowledge, whose fancy jargon was usually what was applied in the colony, had no effect at all on whether a patient got well or died; the medical intervention might even hasten his death. If empiricism were really outlawed in the colony, as Periquillo says the "leyes de Indias" futilely tried to do (260), Doctor Purgante's patients would not have died as a result of his experiments based on trial and error. This line, although meant as a joke, gets at something real. Because Spain insisted on teaching traditional philosophy in the colonies and legislating against the introduction of new ideas such as empiricism, an American version of empiricism—trial and error as a result of ignorance and partial knowledge—was de facto emerging. In Periquillo's comic practice of medicine, then, Lizardi's point is that an empirical belief that knowledge is what one's senses reveal rather than what one is told was replacing the lessons of traditional education in the colony.

The *desengaño* [disillusionment, discovery of error] of Lizardi's novel is not the sordid statement of most Golden Age picaresque novels in which innocence, in contact with society's corruption, ends in disappointment and compromise. Instead the *desengaño* of the *Periquillo* results from matching the lessons of experience against the false values of institutional education. The book's framework of progress suggests that the criollo's succession of false steps produces a Fortunate Fall.

A. A. Parker's historical study of the picaresque, in which he sees the pattern growing out of the religious concerns of the sixteenth century,[16] raises important questions for my study of the *Periquillo*. Parker sees an "aristocratization" (121) of the development in the eighteenth century and then says that that "century could not present a significant literary treatment of delinquency" (133). An aristocratic concern for gentility and propriety, as well as a decline in the belief in heaven and hell, he claims, weakened the form by causing suffering to disappear from it (136–37). However, Lizardi's novel, although similar in many ways to the eighteenth-century *Gil Blas*, retains, I argue, much of the theological seriousness, and the ugliness and baseness usually connected with the lower classes, of the Spanish picaresque of an earlier date. Lizardi's tracing of the education of a *pícaro*—while certainly tied to a set of historical circumstances—shows he is still not free of a vision of human error. Whether it springs from a theological prejudice stemming from a belief in Original

Sin, or a psychological preference for experience over received knowledge, or a sense that the colonial world is characterized by greed and exploitation, Lizardi's vision makes suffering and evil necessary for growth toward goodness.[17]

Lizardi's concern with morality as a process brings him close to the Deists of his day, whose mechanistic explanations of the universe and ideas of God as a First Cause, even though they were judged heretical, appear to have been widely known in the colony.[18] At one point in the novel Lizardi states his belief that if some men suffer, their suffering is a consequence of their viciousness: "Let's understand that in this sad life, everyone suffers, but those who suffer most at all levels of society in the republics are disproportionately the evil ones—whether it is because of the natural order of things, or because of the punishment of Divine Providence" (403). Here, although Lizardi invokes the customary explanations that natural law reserves some men for suffering or that, alternatively, Divine Providence punishes them, his view of judgment posits cause and effect—something (he refuses to speculate as to what) causes suffering. The moralistic language expresses a colonial need to question disparities in men's tribulations; and although Lizardi here suggests justice in allotting misfortune, elsewhere (such as in *Noches tristes*) he seems less sure that the suffering he is witnessing in the colony is self-incurred or deserved.

There is no doubt that Lizardi believed that his hero's descent to hell began with the loss of the father. At the beginning of the second volume, he signals the transition to Periquillo's story after his father's death: "We are now entering the most disorderly period in my life. All my waywardness described up until now is fruit and frosted cake in comparison with the misdoings that follow" (96). And, when Periquillo enters the world of thieves, drunkards, and gamblers, he finds that the father is absent or unable to function there:

They are very vicious and lazy; they work in order not to die of hunger and perhaps [to get money for] their main vice, which almost always is drunkenness. . . .

"What shameful men!," I exclaimed. "And if they are married, what life must they impose on their poor wives, what a poor example they give to their children!"

"Reflect on it," Januario said to me. "Their wives go about almost naked; they are hungry and beaten. And their children run around with no clothes, lacking food and a proper education." (137)

The Mexican mining society, where representatives of law and justice cannot or do not exercise control, is fictionalized in Periquillo's orphanhood; separation from the Father also suggests theological notions of sin. Lizardi describes this abandonment, which some falsely think is paradise:

When one or two rich mines are discovered someplace, those people are said to be enjoying a bonanza; but that is precisely when things are worst. No sooner are the veins opened when everything becomes expensive, luxury is much greater, the population is filled with strangers, perhaps the most vicious, who corrupt the natives. In short, that encampment is changed into a scandalous theater for crime. Everywhere there is gaming, drunkenness, fights, injuries, robberies, killings and all kind of disorders. The most energetic efforts of justice are not sufficient to contain evil in all its root causes. Everyone knows that mining people are habitually vicious, easily incited, prideful, and wasted. (337)

In such a society all order breaks down. Skilled artisans leave their jobs to seek instant wealth in the mines. No one bothers to learn a trade, content to "*espulgar las tierras*" [pick the leavings from the land, to extract the fleas from it] and loaf. The result is an economy dependent on foreign suppliers. And when Periquillo is beginning to choose a career, his father excludes options other than law, medicine, or the clergy because, although he admits that other fields of knowledge [*ciencias*] exist, "I don't advise these because they are nonexistent in this country" (64).

In this hell of deprivation, depravity, and disorder, sins are graduated, recalling Dante's theological scheme. Periquillo witnesses sin and he also sins. Because Lizardi's construct of an ideal society on the Utopian island made charity and individual self-sacrifice for the common good social virtues, Periquillo commits his worst sin in one of his last escapades, when, participating in a ring of thieves posing as beggars, he abuses the charity of well-meaning persons and robs the truly poor. Any violation of the honorable relationship between two men, particularly as regards women, was also a serious departure from the fraternal ideal Lizardi described; therefore, Periquillo's service to the *chino* as *alcahuete* [pimp] is another of the socially harmful sins he commits. The novel's buildup of crimes ends in murder, which Periquillo is spared from committing; and the progression toward this sin of Cain dramatizes the contemporary moral dilemma of civil war.

I want to suggest now several ways that Lizardi, coming from this American hell (and probably even the criminal world that Periquillo's character hints at is autobiographical),[19] intended the novel as a guide to the way out. I have already pointed out how the simple title of Lizardi's novel, *Vida de Periquillo Sarniento*, condemned the extravagant titles of other books, whose pages did not provide the knowledge their authors promised. Books posed a major problem to Lizardi to explain their role in a renewed colonial education. Of the education a doctor needed to exercise his profession, he wrote, "the doctor's school and his best library are the bed of the patient rather than gold-embossed volumes, plentiful libraries and excessive luxury" (255). However, if Lizardi attacked all books, he undermined his own book's value. His solution, to define his novel as a new kind of book, in which words of counsel were coupled with words dramatizing what colonials saw, emerges in the following authorial comment in the *Periquillo:* "The good example touches (persuades) more than advice, suggestions, sermons and books. All of this is good but, finally, they are words which almost always the wind carries away. Doctrine which enters through the eye impresses itself better than that which enters through the ear. Dumb animals do not speak; nevertheless, they teach their young and even rational beings by means of their example. Such is the power of example" (113).

The statement affirms the didactic value of narrative example. It reaffirms the logic of a familiar story. Yet it also confirms an understanding of the changing role of words and of the visual dimension of print as larger numbers of colonials began to read.[20] In the transformation of Mexican society, personal and oral forms of communication (fatherly advice, priests' sermons, etc.) were being replaced by print, which required, Lizardi believed, new attentive modes. Readers now saw reproduced the words of authority figures they had only heard, or they were surprised by finding in the new literature heterodoxy, or unacknowledged facts of their Mexican existence. Colonials, therefore, had to blend old habits of reverence for the printed word and scorn for auditory information with their increasing recognition that some words were less important than sensory data from their surroundings. Colonials had to rely less on received language so as to look at the languageless or badly named world around them. They had to learn from a book like Lizardi's the lessons to be applied in their colonial world; in seeing persons who did not speak, or who only spoke imperfectly and brutishly, colonial readers had to supply with their own words the vision's moral lesson.

Lizardi thus contrasts his own "life of Pedro Sarmiento," whose dramatic narrative is meant to illustrate the moral message and thereby instruct doubly through the ear and the eye, with other moralistic books whose sermons only reach the ear:

> It is certain that moral books teach but only through the ear and that is why their lessons are easily forgotten. These [the life of Pedro Sarmiento] instruct through the ear and through the eye. They paint man as he is and they paint the ravages of vice and the rewards of virtue in events that happen everyday. When we read of these actions it appears to us that we are looking at them, we retain them in our memory; . . . we remember one character or another from the story when we see someone who resembles him and thus we cannot help but take advantage of the instruction which the anecdote afforded us. (463–64)

In using the metaphor of painting to talk about the power of illustrative anecdotes in reading, Lizardi shows his awareness of a book's visual and auditory dimensions. The novel, in the colonial context, will be a simulacrum of experience so that missteps are avoided as readers remember in the future what they have read and place it alongside what they have seen. By thus juxtaposing the actions and speech of his characters, and the actions and speech of real people, Lizardi wants his colonial readers to rethink the connection between reality and the words often represented as a natural part of that reality. His emphasis throughout the novel on Periquillo's story as deeds, therefore, rather than as words about deeds, suggests that he expected his experiment with moral teaching to elicit something akin to a visual response in the reader, a fresh reaction rather than one that is linguistically mediated.

After witnessing the events of a fictional life, colonial readers were asked to analyze the reasons for the imagined character's actions and the effects (rewards or punishment) that his choices brought. Reading should not be passive. Lizardi advised his reader not to stop with the shell of the facts [*la cáscara de los hechos*] but to continue "noticing the sad results of laziness, [social] uselessness, inconstancy and the rest of the vices that affected me; analyzing the wayward events of my life; looking into their causes; fearing their consequences and discarding the common errors that you see that I and others adopted; drinking in the solid maxims of the healthy, Christian morality that my reflections hold up to view" (235). Morality, therefore, was *not* obediently listening to others and following their rules, as earlier teachings might have insisted, but thinking for oneself. Reading could be viewed as an important first step toward the development among Mexicans of independent thinking. Instead of being disciplinary, reading was potentially revolutionary.

Print in Lizardi's day suggested divine revelation or, at the very least, the sanctions of power—what would be called today "the media." Yet Lizardi's view of the colonial "media" was such that one is reminded of Marshall McLuhan's not-so-dated question: "Is not the essence of education civil defence against media fall-out?" (246). In recognizing the role of the printed word in a revised system of education, Lizardi was paradoxically subverting the power of the book and strengthening it so as to use against the enemy (the governing culture) its own weapon.

He constantly lamented that books were not more widely available in the colony. In *El Pensador Mexicano* he proclaimed America's talent and capacity for learning to be the equal of other nations.' The lack of books and attendant institutions there had made it seem that Americans were less well endowed. What could Americans be *with* books, he asked (*Obras* 3: 268).

In his book, Lizardi set himself up as a new authority, whose wisdom would rival and surpass the ancients. Colonial readers might have believed his claim because of his indisputable right to tell a Mexican story and also because the novel's material focus reproduced the emphasis of the much admired new sciences, such as physics and natural history (even though in the novel Lizardi conventionally subordinated them to metaphysics [*Periquillo* 50]). The author's concern for morality, free of the salvational vocabulary of religion, fit with the new social consciousness; and Lizardi's view of how his book might contribute to this new moral education is contained in the following statement from *El Pensador Mex-*

icano, in which he finds a "book" in "man": "Man insofar as morality is concerned is the best book in the world (with the exception of that of sacred theology). His lessons are the most useful, however complicated they may seem, because knowing man we become familiar with ourselves; and thus only in this way can we learn of the difference that there is between us and God, the relations that exist among ourselves and other men, the happiness we are capable of in this life, the means of obtaining it and the method which is not the least of all, of bringing about peace with one another" (*Obras* 3: 164). An American author, therefore, was not deprived if he lacked books,[21] since self-study and observation of the world around him could provide him with the truths of human existence. Yet these lessons were most usefully passed on in the pages of a book in which the American author not only commented on human truths but also reconsidered the books in which they had been packaged before.

The Bible was routinely acknowledged to be the supreme statement of morality. However, after having invoked its special, sacred character, few secular writers in the colony quoted it much. Or, if they did, like Lizardi, their references were mainly to the wisdom literature of the Old Testament. The debate and politicization of language and textual questions, which the *Diario de México* records, did not extend to the Bible and the works of the Church fathers. Yet, as I show above, newspaper discussion of ancient civilizations did introduce to colonials the question of religion's accreted languages; it threw into question rhetorical and literary practices clearly coded up until that time as either sacred or profane.

Who owned truth, at what historical moment it entered men's consciousness, whether pagan authors prior to Christ's birth could know Christian moral truths and thus rival the Gospel writers, even whether men invented the Bible—these were questions that Lizardi posed in the essay reproduced below, which introduced the second volume of a collection of miscellany, *Ratos entretenidos*, published in 1819. The essay is by Rousseau from *Emile* (307ff),[22] although Lizardi reprinted it with no attribution. Whether Lizardi was influenced by its ideas in writing the *Periquillo* is unclear; but its discussion of the writer's authority is important for the light it sheds on Lizardi's awareness of himself as a secular author. In Lizardi's appropriation of this discussion of Plato and Socrates, and Gospel writers who told of Jesus Christ's life and death, one reads a daring consideration of the author's necessary virtue for knowing and stating truth. Christian truth, the author asserts, can issue from error and evil. Christ's life preceded the composition of the Gospel's text and gave rise to its truth; but Christian truths are also to be found in the work of pagan philosophers and contemporary impious philosophers. A writer need not have known Christ personally or have led an exemplary life in order to know what goodness and truth are.

TRUTH OF THE GOSPEL

If in this century there have been impious philosophers who have wanted to combat, although in vain, the luminous truths of Christian morality, there have also been others who, in the midst of corruption, could not resist confessing [these Christian truths]. Let's see what one of them says.

"The holiness of the Gospel speaks to my heart. Look at the books of the philosophers with all their pomp. How petty they are next to the Gospel! Is it possible to believe that a book so simple and yet at the same time so sublime is the work of men? Can it be that he whose story it presents is only a man himself? Is its tone that of an enthusiast or that of an ambitious sectarian? What sweetness and what purity in its customs! What expressive grace in its teachings! How elevated its maxims! What profound wisdom in its speeches! What presence of mind! How delicate and exact its responses! What control over passion! Where is the man, where is the sage who can work, suffer and die, without flinching or making a show? When Plato portrays the just man from his imagination, covered with all the opprobrium of crime and worthy of all the rewards of virtue, he is painting Jesus Christ detail for detail. The resemblance is so great that all the [Church] fathers have recognized it and it is impossible not to see it. . . . Socrates, dying without suffering and without ignominy, sustained his awareness until the end without any difficulty; and if this easy death had not brought honor to his life, one doubts if Socrates with all his talent was anything more than a sophist. It is said that he invented morality but others said that it had already been practiced before him and that, consequently, he did nothing more than articulate what others had done and put forth their examples as lessons. Aristides was a fair man before Socrates defined justice. Leonidas had [already] died for his *patria* when Socrates defined love of *patria* as an obligation. Sparta was sober before Socrates praised sobriety; and before he said what virtue was, Greece abounded in virtuous men. But Jesus Christ—where did he learn among men this pure and elevated morality of which only he has left behind an example and lessons? The death of Socrates as he philosophized tranquilly with his friends is the easiest death one could wish for; that of Jesus Christ expiring in torment, injured, insulted and cursed by the people, is the most horrible death that one could fear. Socrates, receiving the poisoned cup, blesses he who in tears presents it; Christ, in the midst of a frightful supplication, pleads for his executioners. Yes, yes, the life and death of Socrates are those of a wise man; and the life and death of Jesus are those of God.

"And shall we say that the story of the Gospel is invented on purpose? No, this is not the mode of inventing; and the deeds of Socrates, of which no one doubts, are less authentic than those of Jesus Christ. This would in substance elude the difficulty without destroying it. It is more difficult to conceive of the idea that many men got together to fabricate that book than that one man provided material for it. The Jewish authors would never have arrived at its tone or moral; and the Gospel has qualities of truth so large, so portentous, and in everything so inimitable, that its inventor would cause more admiration than its hero." (*Ratos* 2: 1–4)

The essay, here in its entirety, must be read in the larger context of Lizardi's relationship with his colonial readers. How could they accept his work when the official apparatus for censoring morally harmful material, which they had relied on in the past, was now under suspicion as a tool of Spanish imperialism? How could they trust his statement of wisdom and truth when the author was known personally by his readership and was arguably a flawed human being?

A measure of just how far Lizardi went in rethinking the colonial writer's role is a work, published in 1784, by the French Benedictine Nicolás Jamin—*Verdadero antídoto contra los malos libros de estos tiempos o Tratado de la Lectura Christiana* [True antidote against the evil books of these times or Treaty on Christian Reading]. Lizardi discusses another work by Jamin in the "Advertencia" [Notice] to the readers of the *Periquillo*, and several of Jamin's books are to be found in the Abadiano collection, thus arguing for the importance of this writer's influence in the development of Mexican writing and reading. In *Verdadero antídoto*, Jamin establishes reading guidelines for the new secular literature being published in Europe. He warns particularly about the seductions of the increasingly popular romances and says that reading their stories is not harmless but instead excites the spirit to sinful actions. To those who argue that good is to be found even in impious and blasphemous books he answers that we are all born with a propensity for evil and the imagination is wounded and weakened once the reader becomes familiar with these portraits of passion. Those who are concerned with public morality cannot justify the story of a libertine, he says; simply because the libertine commits one good deed one cannot infer that he is (or will be) a righteous man.

Clearly, Lizardi's idea of a book, although it builds on this same concern for individual reading and public morality, differs from Jamin's. Both understand that reading can influence behavior, but Lizardi appears to regard evil as a necessary ingredient in a realistic depiction of life, and literary realism as essential to bookish teaching of morality. Therefore, I see as basic to the design of the *Periquillo escarmiento* an attitude toward morality and education that, perhaps stemming from Lizardi's own contact with low life, as well as collective guilt over the colony's rebellion, justifies the inclusion of immoral material in teaching morality.

Escarmiento (the Spanish word meaning the infliction of an exemplary punishment, or teaching by experience) has rhyming echoes, I believe, in the book's title, *El Periquillo Sarniento*. Toward the end of Pedro's story of progress from immorality to morality, Lizardi has his repentant character muse: "And what better fruit can we gather from these painful experiences than the knowledge of humiliation to govern us in the future?" (414). The word and variations of it are to be found throughout the nearby chapter in which the legal system of penalties and restraints on the Utopian island is described; ideally, the Chinese ruler says, the vision of the humbled criminal and the knowledge of his suffering are constantly before the public so as to discourage any temptation to waywardness. The fictitious Spaniard quotes Lardizábal, that among the responsibilities of the state is "the warning and the example [*escarmiento*] so that those who haven't sinned abstain from doing so" (378). Consequently, this word with its dual vision of error and rectitude must be seen as central to Lizardi's sense of how a life gives rise to literature and how education must occur amid the immorality of the colony.

How morality might issue from immorality, truth from falsehood, were questions that troubled many colonial educators, as well as idealist theologians confronted by new empiricist notions. If education had been predicated on imitation, on the faithful copying of authoritative models, then this new version of a moral book, which Lizardi's novel represented, required that the learner/colonial subject think for himself so as to imitate selectively what he witnessed; this new discursive space represented a radical departure from old modes of teaching. After all, delinquency presented attractively in the form of a prestigious artifact might invite an impressionable youth to a life of irresponsible conduct. But presented with a humor that ridiculed the erring behavior—the essential distancing mechanism of *escarmiento*—delinquency could serve to deter such a youth.

Neoclassical aesthetics, as well as earlier Siglo de Oro practice, had tolerated the obvious untruths and unpleasantries of satire because the mode corrected social wrongs. In the discussions of artistic deformations of reality, which appeared in the *Diario de México*, Molière was frequently cited because his satiric humor was thought to instruct. Fables, although they were patently false, were justified because their lies were socially useful. Verisimilitude could be sacrificed if moral truth was at stake; "unrealism" was appropriate if it stirred the reader and convinced him of virtue. As Vivienne Mylne has pointed out in her study of the French eighteenth-century mimetic novel, critics today use the term *realism* anachronistically in considering literature of that period (2), since various representational modes were countenanced then if general "truths" were affirmed.

Lizardi, concerned with what mix of reality and unreality was appropriate for his colonial satiric work, so as to establish textual authority and guide his reader toward believing him, discussed his concept of art and his choice of novelistic material in his *apología* for the *Periquillo* (1819):

What causes most discomfort to this gentleman [his critic] is that the art which governs the whole work is that of sketching (according to him) repugnant portraits and low-life scenes . . . and that, to stick to reality, I have reduced myself to dealing with coarse people. My God! What innocence! Shouldn't this censor have noticed that when this happens, it is necessary, natural, conforming to the plan of the work and appropriate to the situation of the hero? A young, lazy, reckless libertine—with what people would he commonly deal and in what places would his adventures probably happen? Would it be proper and opportune to introduce him into conversation with the Fernandine fathers, to place him in prayer in the sacred schools or walking the stations of the cross in the convent of San Francisco? (*Obras* 8: 23)

This emphasis on writing about what is necessary and natural to the world of a *pícaro* flowed from Lizardi's desire to instruct, to convince readers of the reality of his fictional world but also to alienate them from it. The realism of the low-life scenes, therefore, must be seen to have been intended doubly to draw readers into the book's illusion of truthfulness, yet also to startle them by the recognition of actuality and to repel them by the scenes' ugliness. Yet as my discussion of the reception of the *Periquillo* has shown, despite the period's discussion of aesthetic distance, many contemporary readers were offended by Lizardi's "realism." Perhaps they suffered from the "social and historical catalepsy of the colonized" as Albert Memmi describes the psychological paralysis into which the colonized often retreat to survive (*Colonizer and the Colonized* 102). These readers' absorption into the mimesis of Lizardi's book was arguably the historical equivalent of "the annihilation of self," "assimilation," and "historical deadening" that Memmi from his later perspective observes that upper-class colonials are especially prone to. Taught that their colonial identity is subhuman and that their only hope for escape from this condition is imitation of their masters—yet consistently denied admittance into this closed circle—colonials, particularly at the level of the elite class, often sink into self-hatred, denial of the native realities around them, and muteness or thoughtless repetitions of the colonizers' words. Thus, the "realism" of Lizardi's book, as some of his readers use the term, may refer as much to their unquestioning handling of the book as to the text's mirroring.

The shocking inclusion in Lizardi's work of Mexican realities, taking into account the author's purpose of *escarmiento*, therefore, must be seen to have been a calculated attempt to break into this colonial impassivity, to use fictional representation of familiar characters and situations so that readers might say, not, "That's Mexico," but, "That shouldn't be Mexico." Unlike the overdrawn depictions of Molière's satire, however, Lizardi's treatment of Mexican realities does not seem exaggerated; his linguistic fidelity and familiar subject matter seem accurate. If readers encounter humor as a distancing mechanism in Lizardi's work, it appears to be a function of the narrative style and not a deformation of his Mexican world.

Realism continues to be the favorite literary mode for discussing the *Periquillo*.[23] Yet latter-day critics repeat the error of many of Lizardi's original readers, it seems to me, in understanding only one dimension of Lizardi's representational technique. In viewing the book according to nineteenth-century standards for *costumbrismo* and the realist novel, which posit a reader's absorption into the fiction as a result of mimetic technique, they misunderstand Lizardi's reasons for painting such "repugnant portraits." Too, contemporary critics of colonial discourse who worry about representation of the colonial subject would do well to appreciate how active Lizardi meant his readers to be at this moment of decolonization.[24] Lizardi's "realism" is predicated on the participatory role of the colonial reader whom he constantly addresses in his text and instructs in reading.

I return to my discussion of the *escarmiento* function for the *Periquillo*. To carry it out, Lizardi invented a technique that I call the "exposé." It consists of putting forth an accepted truth and then revealing it to be either a partial truth or else a complete falsehood. It is the technical counterpart of Lizardi's sense that something negative must be overcome, that the *corruptelas antiguas* [ancient corrupt customs] were so entrenched that any educational process must first end them. Its multiple manifestations in Lizardi's novel suggest that the deconstruction of colonial "truths" is a key element in the education he judged necessary for the colony, and that the exposé technique is an important aspect of his version of realism.

Like Cervantes, Lizardi parodied earlier books because he realized the powerful effect that reading had on personal and corporate morality. Like the *Quijote*, the *Periquillo* lists good and bad books (27). Yet instructions as to what to read are supplemented with advice throughout the novel about *how* to read and criticize the commonplaces of language. For example,

Lizardi's use of the exposé technique often means redefining words. As Periquillo starts on the road to perdition, Lizardi shows how colonial euphemisms often fostered immorality: "These devilish friends who led me astray, and who lead astray so many in this world, know the art of disguising vices with the names of virtues. They called dissipation liberality, gambling honest entertainment no matter how many savings were lost, lewdness courtliness, drunkenness pleasure, arrogance authority, shallowness dignity, rudeness frankness, coarse jests wit, stupidity prudence, hypocrisy virtue, provocation valor, cowardliness caution, loquacity eloquence, dullness humility, and simpleness simplicity" (423). Lizardi lists the Greek and Latin medical terms "that the foolish masses call dropsy, rabies, syphilis, pain in the side, gout and the other plain names they are accustomed to using" (256–57), implying that "the foolish masses" use language truly. Like the *diccionarios burlescos*, Lizardi's juxtaposition of two sets of words registers dissatisfaction with old meaning and points to a new community that is beginning to use language honestly. Yet the double vision also textualizes division and confusion.

The exposé technique holds up entrenched belief to experience. In a long chapter, Lizardi discusses beggary and the need for judicious charity in that society where there were many poor. A wise man lectures the naïve Periquillo on Mexico's many beggars:

> If you were to tell me that, although they may want to work, many cannot find a job, I would respond that, although there may be such cases on account of the lack of agriculture, business, shipping, industry, etc., there are not as many [of these persons] as may be supposed. . . . [L]et's take note of the many vagrants wandering in the streets and stretched out there, drunk, glued to the street corners, involved in tricks in the bars and taverns, women as well as men. Let's ask and we will find that many of them have a craft, and many, men and women, robustness and health sufficient to work. (312)

Here the meaning is mixed because, although Lizardi's voice appears to pin poverty to a Mexican character fault, he also slips in the possibility that colonial monopolistic practices were to blame for the lack of work.[25]

The exposé technique corrects social misperceptions. In the following example, Periquillo, who is learning to be a barber, meets an Indian and then a country woman, both of whom reprimand him for his stupidity in their broken language.

I, swollen up with pride as a result of this first effort, determined to try again with a poor Indian who came to be shaved for a penny. With a great deal of show, I draped him in cloth, made the apprentice bring a basin with hot water, tested the blades and gave such a display of filing and cutting with them that the unhappy fellow, unable to endure my rough hand, stood up saying, "Let me go, Christian, let me go" [Amoquale, quistiano amoquale]. Which was as if he were saying to me in Castilian, "Your method, sir, does not suit me, does not suit me."

Still not content with these unfortunate attempts, I dared to extract a molar from an old woman who entered the shop, out of her mind on account of sharp pain.

In fine, as soon as I cut sufficient flesh to feed the cat of the house, I made the bone fast with the proper instrument and gave her such a strong, badly placed yank that I broke her tooth, hurting her jaw terribly.

"Ay, Jesus!," the sad old woman exclaimed. "You took out my jaw, master of the devil."

"Don't speak, madam," I said to her, "because air will get in and it will corrupt the mandible."

"What malible or what devils!," the poor old woman said. "Ay Jesus. Ay, ay, ay." (224)

Lizardi's translation of Indian speech so that it is understood in the frame of a Spanish-language story thus corrects earlier colonial literature, which had ignored this Mexican voice. His text, in reproducing this cry of pain, points to the sounds of pre-language by which the mind articulates emotion; it legitimates experience despite the individual's lack of proper language. As Periquillo says elsewhere in the novel to a dialect-speaking friend: "You speak badly . . . but you tell the truth" (226).

The exposé technique also satirizes the obfuscating language of the powerful, who often flaunted the status symbols of scientific vocabulary.

Once, at a dinner party, Periquillo is invited to explain what a comet is. Instead of confessing his ignorance, he concocts a ridiculous speech, which a *vicario* promptly deflates by means of a reprimand but also by his own reasoned, informed discourse. Periquillo begins:

"Well, ladies and gentlemen, the comets (male or female, as some say) are stars which are larger than the rest. Because they are so big, they have a long, super-long tail. . . . "

"Super-long?," the vicar said.

And I, who didn't understand that he was marveling that I didn't even know how to speak Spanish, responded with great vanity:

"Yes, father, super-long. . . ."

I continued:

"These tails are of two colors, either white or reddish. If they are white, they announce peace or some happiness for a people; and if they are reddish, . . . they announce war or disaster. That's why *the* comet [he uses the feminine article which is grammatically incorrect] that the three Wise Men saw had a white tail, because it announced the birth of Our Lord and peace throughout the world. . . . This cannot be denied, for there is no *crèche* on Christmas Eve without its little comet with a white tail. The fact that we do not see them very often is because God has them there hidden away and he only allows them to come into our vision when they are going to announce the death of some king, the birth of some saint, or peace or war in some city. For that reason we don't see them every day because God does not perform miracles unnecessarily. The comet at this time has a white tail and, surely, it announces peace. . . .

. . . the vicar said, "the young sir, although he will excuse me, has not spoken one word correctly but rather a pack of lies. It is obvious that he has not studied a word of astronomy and, therefore, he is ignorant of what fixed stars are . . . planets . . . comets, constellations, digits, eclipses, etc. I am not an astronomer either, young friend, but I have a little bit of knowledge of these matters and, although it is very superficial, it is sufficient to know that you have less and that you have loosed a thousand barbarities. But what is worse is that you have spoken them with vanity, believing that you understand what you say and that it is as you understand it. . . . Be advised that comets are not stars, nor are they seen because of a miracle, nor do they announce war or peace, nor was the star which the kings from the East saw when the Saviour was born a comet. . . . I will explain briefly what a comet is. Listen. Comets are planets like all the rest, that is, the same as the Moon, Mercury, Venus, the Earth, Mars, Jupiter, Saturn and Herschel; these are spherical bodies (that is, perfectly round or, as we commonly say, balls). They are opaque; they do not have any light in themselves, the way the Earth has no light, since that which they reflect [Lizardi uses here the Spanish learned word *reflection*] or send us is sent to them by the Sun. (46–47)

The passage shows Lizardi's typical technique of counterposing rival discourse systems, in this case Periquillo's partial scientific knowledge, folk and pious beliefs, and the *vicario*'s fuller knowledge. The satire attacks pedantry, yet it also problematizes that linguistic crime, since any amateur who tried to use his new knowledge might be labeled a pedant in Mexican circles, where many were still ignorant. Lizardi's fiction teaches that Mexicans' education had to go beyond acquisition of specialized vocabulary, that display of erudition had to be more than vanity. Yet he acknowledges that learning about a new subject meant studying, first of all, its terminology; even Periquillo's education in gambling and thievery began with instruction in those vocabularies (127).

"Comets" was a topic with various meanings in the discourse of the day. Many pious and/or ignorant Mexicans believed that they were miraculous signs that the heavens had provided; and they explained the ongoing war accordingly. Others criticized this belief—not only the naïveté of the believers but the way in which politicians had manipulated the notion so as to sustain their interpretation of events. In the *Diario de México*, for example, one writer complained that the theater regularly dramatized Moctezuma's loss of his empire to Cortés with a stage "malign star."[26] His words suggest his anger that Spain continued to preach that such natural happenings were signs ratifying the Conquest. Another *Diario* correspondent rebuked *El Mentor Mexicano* for only teaching technical terms in its presentation of the subject: "read this astrological paper and you will not find anything else there of astrology but technical terms such as elliptical, orbit, perihelion, and whatever the wise Mentor had the talent to extract from the physical dictionary of Brisson." Periquillo's lesson in comets, therefore, would have suggested to readers these collateral meanings.

Lizardi's exposé technique relies on a strong authorial voice, by which no misunderstanding is possible, to teach irony:

> One day when I was traveling alone in the coach to a lunch I was invited to in Jamaica, I said to myself: "How mistaken my father was when he preached to me that I learn a skill or dedicate myself to working in something useful to subsist, because the person who didn't work wouldn't eat. That was maybe true in his time . . . when everyone used to work and men were ashamed of being useless and lazy. . . .
>
> "Thank God that this age was followed by the Golden Age and the enlightened century in which we live, in which we don't confuse the nobleman with the plebeian, nor the rich man with the poor man. Let the latter concern himself with work, the arts, sciences, agriculture and misery for we honor cities sufficiently with our coaches, galas and livery. . . ."
>
> Such were my crazy thoughts when I was becoming intoxicated with liberty and the opportunity I had of giving myself over to pleasure, without noticing that I wasn't rich or the money I was spending wasn't my own. (385)

The exposé technique, in its gradual unfolding of truth, imitates Periquillo's enlightenment. As the youth mistakenly trusts Januario, his schoolmate who is eventually hanged as a highway robber, he learns wariness in choosing friends. He is blind at first to his friend's evil, but the reader sees it. Januario has cursed him with the ugly name Periquillo Sarniento. While boys, Januario took advantage of Periquillo's vanity and impetuosity to deceive his "friend"; the narrating father provides the commentary: "Since part of me loved him and another part of me understood him to be an intriguing genius, I glossed over his evil intentions and let myself be led with no misgivings by his dictates" (58–59). Later Januario urged him to be a priest for the wrong reasons ("he told me many truths, but only partially," 81). Still later, orphaned and penniless, Periquillo is befriended by Januario, now a gambler who instructs him in the low ways of *léperos* [drifters]. Yet the dinner that Januario pays for symbolically provides no real sustenance since Periquillo vomits it up.

Periquillo begins to benefit from the lessons of experience when he can distinguish between true and false friends. He says of his good friend Antonio: "Don Antonio was not like, as you have seen, those friends who the only thing they know of friendship is what they mouth; he always confirmed with deeds what his words said" (203). Here the character's recognition that one must constantly compare what a friend says with what he does proves real maturity. He now has the discernment to criticize persons whom he has loved and the self-confidence to admit mistakes; he can overcome betrayal while still confessing a need for human relationships.

In the course of the *Periquillo*'s story, Lizardi retells the familiar fable of the crab. That animal, although he told his children to walk in a straight line, continued himself to walk crookedly; his example negated his words. If a new concept of education could be made to apply in Mexico, if error might be corrected in present models of behavior, Lizardi could then hope that reasonable sons might change their ways. Corruption would continue if the error were never acknowledged, if false values perpetuated its spread. Lizardi writes: "All of us, it is true, criticize, decry and ridicule the abuses of foreign nations at the same time that, either because we are ignorant of our own or, knowing them, we do not dare to get rid of them because we venerate them, conserve them out of respect for our elders who established them for us" (99). Lizardi's definition of education comes from a youth's perspective. It is based on a reconsideration of the absolute principles taught by imperial institutions and the blind respect and unthinking acceptance of tradition by subordinates. His redefinition of education insists that colonials compare what authority does with what its representatives say, weighing deeds against words.

6

Adolescence, Gratitude, and Whimsy

In the scholarship of psychohistory, the time during which adolescence entered the consciousness of Western thinkers is a subject of debate.[1] Frank Musgrove claims, "The adolescent was invented at the same time as the steam-engine. The principal architect of the latter was Watt in 1765, of the former Rousseau in 1762" (33). Musgrove argues that Rousseau, unlike previous thinkers such as Saint Augustine who understood the self in spiritual terms, began to see the self's development as a social process. *Emile*, for example, shows Rousseau's reevaluation of the passions that Christian moralists had previously condemned, associating them with "youth," "the most dangerous of all the ages of [man], . . . a torrid zone [that] is difficult to cross" (Blanchard 3: 252).

While reductive, Musgrove's historicizing identifies what I consider to be the importance of the eighteenth century in the emergence of the notion of "adolescence." Others, for example, the social historians John and Virginia Demos, have argued that adolescence was only recognized as a phenomenon in the United States at the end of the nineteenth century. They associate the concept with changes in economic conditions and freedom from farm work, which caused young boys and girls to be occupied with education until the work force could find jobs for them. Thus Demos and Demos connect it to the idea of leisure and assert that "adolescence was on the whole an American discovery" (632).

However, I think it is clear that Catholic notions of a youth's sexual awakening, which the catechism and pious books warned of, and political discussion, which in Spanish America was often framed in the biological language of infancy and adulthood, prepared Mexicans for understanding the idea of adolescence much earlier. In fact, at one point in *La Quijotita* (200), Lizardi specifically mentions "adolescence"; the narrator speaks: "I know that life is nothing but a journey towards death, a golden coach in which we travel. Time is the coachman . . . and infancy, adolescence and the other stages are each day's travel distance." In that novel Lizardi focusses on the period as a time of choice. As women leave girlhood, will they enter a convent or marry? By what standard can they choose a husband? When can they trust a father and obey him, and when must they instead defy him, relying on their own thinking? In a society that increasingly was abandoning Catholic values of chastity, obedience, and retreat from worldly pleasure, by what new logic could a woman join fashionable society? How could a woman recognize goodness in a man when old, Spanish customs of courtliness, with which she had some familiarity, were disappearing and new, French modes permitted him to hide behind other disguises?

The adolescent girl's concerns were similar to Periquillo's, although she remained economically dependent whereas he was forced into the world to earn a living and support a new family. Both adolescent stories, however, reproduced dilemmas of that Mexican generation.[2] What justification did the colony, a dependency of Spain, have in asserting its self-will and striking out against its parent, its historical protector and superior? What protection under Spanish legal codes did a rebellious inferior being have?

In the "Chamorro y Dominiquín" pamphlet, for which he was jailed in 1821 because of its open denunciation of colonialism, Lizardi also discusses adolescence, although he does not use the term in that political context. He traces traditional belief in three stages of man's development (infancy, manhood, and old age) and then, in elaborating the scheme, he ends up with four when, in addition to infancy and old age, he distinguishes between *joven* (when the youth is educated at home and taught in school, *lo eduquen y enseñen*) and *hombre consistente*[3] (when the now consenting adult takes responsibility for his own subsistence and even cares for others who depend on him) (*Obras* 11: 110). That Lizardi discriminates between the two developmental phases suggests his awareness of passive and active youth. That he defines the stages according to new legal and economic vocabularies shows that Christian explanations of the period were beginning to be replaced. That the pamphlet makes obvious what the novel could only hint at—the biological scheme has political implications and Mexico, having received Spain's benefits over three hundred years, no longer needs the parent's tutelage—proves the political import of the *Periquillo*'s story of adolescence. Lizardi says: "The laws of Nature with respect to morality are the same, proportionally, as those which govern the physical world" (110). Thus, the insurgents' version of history is made to seem inevitable; and Lizardi uses the very rhetoric against the parent to justify independence that Spain had used to keep Americans dependent.

However, it must be noted parenthetically that in the discourse of the period, *adolescence* was only used to characterize criollos and describe their role as fully functioning adults in a new Mexican "nation," which itself sought to be recognized as mature by world powers. Indians, the principal component of the population, were generally ignored when criollos spoke of this development. Indians were described as "men" by those few who sympathized with their plight and wanted to assert their human worth; the term was intended to oppose the language of the *Código de Indias*, which held that indigenes were minors in need of adult protection. As Carlos María Bustamante argued in his report to Fernando VII, *El indio mexicano* (1817), laws that claimed to protect Indians as childlike simultaneously denied them their rights and placed them in the care of self-interested tutors who only exploited their labor. Bustamante attacked "the absurd doctrine of Aristotle that certain men are born for slavery"; in America, he said, all lived the life of fish in the sea, where the largest ate the smallest. If the Indian was the lowest order of humans, it was because the Spaniard oppressed the white criollo, both took advantage of the mulatto and the black, and all exploited the Indian (34–35). Nature, Bustamante said, did not decree this hierarchy in which the Indian was infantilized; rather, it was a social system created by Spanish law. In Bustamante's document, Indians and criollos were together described as Americans. In most texts of this period, however, only criollos were individualized and permitted a human character that admitted the possibility of the self and its growth. Criollos reserved for themselves the maturational (and evolutionary) capabilities of adolescence.

In the *Periquillo* Pedro's father confronts his son with the economic implications of the body's development: "Pedro, you have already entered the period of youth without being aware of when or where you left childhood; tomorrow you will find yourself on the threshold of manhood or the age of consent without realizing your youth has passed. That is to say, today you are a boy and tomorrow you will be a man. You have in your father someone to direct you, to advise you and care for your subsistence; but tomorrow, when I am dead, you will have to guide and maintain yourself at the cost of your own labor and your own wits, or you will perish if you don't" (64). Adolescence here is equated with independence, with the death of one's father and assumption of economic responsibilities. Pedro soon learns that sexual features of adolescence, such as a beard (110), are only external signs of a youth's changing nature and society's expectations of him. Profoundly, there is now no one whom he can trust and whose money or advice he can rely on. He must learn himself how to judge the world around him and, importantly, how to choose his friends. "Friendship" in the novel's story marks this intermediate period when one leaves one's father and gains maturity so as to, in turn, become a father.

For colonials trained in the rhetoric of the empire as "family," independence signified the acquisition of new attitudes toward social relationships. Friends, persons outside the network of kinship yet members of an identifiable community with whom one randomly came in contact and with whom one established an emotional bond, had become newly important; and Lizardi's fictional depiction of friendship highlights the politicization of these changes as the monarchy threatened to give way to republican structures and Mexicans began to seek alliances with one another. The decline of the patronage system and the growing importance of free trade and competition, implied in the novel, also contributed to the need to recast personal loyalties. "Friendship," then, in America rewrote Europe's revolutionary language of fraternity.

First of all, therefore, in telling Periquillo's story after his father's death, Lizardi had to rethink traditional meanings of friendship. In an authorial discussion of the term in the *Periquillo*, he said that it could not be the colonial familiarity that derived from two people knowing one another's corruption—closeness based on common consent of vicious behavior (314ff.). Friendship had to be reenvisioned as an ideal in which virtues were mutually encouraged in the parties. Friendship should not be linked to hope of advantage or reward; Periquillo advised his children/ readers to distinguish between *amigos* and *amistades* (456)—the former, false intimates, and the latter, those persons who are faithful through prosperity and misfortune. According to Lizardi's paternalistic preferences, a true friend will be one who somehow combines the roles of father and brother. Antonio and the *coronel* are both; and Martín Pelayo, a friend from childhood who matures earlier than Januario and Periquillo, is fatherly in chiding the two: "Good God, Januario—are we always to be boys? Is this puerile humor never to end? It's necessary to differentiate between the ages of man; at some period the pranks of children are amusing and at other times the merriness of youth. But at our age it's necessary that the seriousness and solidity of men take over because barbers are already making money from us" (140). Later, when he is a priest, he tells Periquillo: "In the confessional I am your father, here [in a setting where both are equal] I am your brother; there I act at times as a judge, here I discharge the duties of friendship" (422).

Still, friendship without self-interest, that is, utility, posed a problem to that generation of colonials. To explore it, Lizardi arranged a dialogue between Periquillo and a businessman who tried to ingratiate himself with Periquillo so as to gain the protection of the *coronel* (Pedro's patron) when the ship on which they were traveling reached Manila (332–33). Pedro narrates his misfortunes, which the businessman listens to indifferently. Then, when Periquillo utters the platitude that all mortals suffer, expecting some human reaction of compassion from the man, he is surprised when the businessman says that such sentiment is old-fashioned convention and erroneous prejudice [*preocupación*]. The businessman, who voices the doctrines of self-interest, greed, and materialism, denounces as "agreeable phantasms" [*fantasmas agradables*] teachings that we should participate in our neighbor's suffering as if he were our brother or a part of ourselves; he suggests that such beliefs are only pious words that few follow. Thus, although there is some mild irony here that may have been intended to warn Mexicans of capitalism's dangers, Lizardi succeeds in articulating the egoistic rationale behind the new commercial and utilitarian philosophies, which were increasingly attractive in Mexico. He problematizes the conflict between Christian teachings of charity and impersonal economic theories that, while promising to end Spanish mercantilism and open up Mexico to foreign trade, introduced new forms of exploitation and dehumanization.

The exchange between Periquillo and the businessman calls into question the role of feelings as Mexico progressed from colonial paternalistic relationships to new, economically conditioned social forms. Lizardi makes it clear that Periquillo feels affection [*cariño*] for the *coronel* and selflessly serves that master. In the same manner he shows the businessman to be coldly inhuman when the man calls Periquillo foolish for sympathetically feeling the pain of others. However, Lizardi, after having created this monster whose motive for friendship is only money-making advantage, comfortably lectures through his voice, the *coronel*, that for such an individual neither "the precepts of religion, nor the tight bonds of blood or society" matter—thereby suggesting that feelings derive from these traditional sources. Yet Lizardi less comfortably acknowledges that there are such men as "tolerable egoists" [*egoístas tolerables*] whose egoism is not harmful to society and who, although basically useless, once in a while serve society. Lizardi thus invents a category of selfishness, which shows he was speculating as to other causes of selfishness besides greed, and perhaps even wondering whether religion, blood, and society were sufficient restraints to moderate it. Lizardi never spells out in the novel the affective basis for friendship between persons of equal rank—their initial attraction to one another and their ongoing closeness.

Nevertheless, Juan María Wenceslao Barquera, discussing friendship in the *Diario de México* (July 17, 1806), was more explicit.[4] Friendship, he wrote, allowed man to use his human gift of language; without the fellowship of sincere friends who shared his joy and sorrow, this gift, "faithful interpreter of thought," which depended on communication, could not be fully esteemed. Friends were neither the companions of the miser, the partisans of the politician, the connections of the leisured man, the admirers of genius, the slaves of power, or the flatterers of the rich. Neither, Barquera argued, did friendship depend on sudden affection [*afición*]. This attraction was more proper to the feeling man felt for the fair sex and generally involved intemperate heat and disorder. "Friendship" called for a new examination of the self; and although some attempted to explain it in the Christian terms of pity and charity,[5] others saw it secularly as key to new social alliances.

It is generally thought that the adolescent, in looking beyond the self to seek friends, love another, and take on the responsibilities of a family, leaves behind self-centered goals. Lizardi's identification of "tolerable egoists" shows that this may not always be the case and that society must tolerate some drones who, although adult, persist in their selfish behavior. However, Lizardi describes how normally, as the individual grows, he learns to merge egoistic interests with those of the larger community. The process involves internalizing the voices one has heard so that an inner voice of conscience is formed, thus mediating between personal desires and society's rules. Lizardi anticipated Sigmund Freud, who also commented on this inner voice, suggesting that it was related to verbal memories—parents' commands or scoldings (Freud 19: 52–53). Later, parents' voices are replaced by those of other, public authorities, which impose new forms of discipline. Cicero (a source whom Lizardi quoted) also emphasized the power of the human voice in teaching morality; Cicero told his son to listen to the voice of a wise philosopher sounding in his ears.[6] However, Rousseau, in his definition of conscience in *Emile*, wrote of the difficulty of knowing, amid the clamor of different voices, which voice to listen to (289ff.). Rousseau's analysis of men's inner voices of "divine instinct" and sentiment as antecedent to their use of reason, when considered in the colonial context of conflicting opinion, might have suggested self-reliance, but also political and moral uncertainties.

Lizardi's emphasis on "voice" in the individual's formation is apparent in Periquillo's description of the way he heard first his father's voice, then those of well-meaning mentors and friends: "My father preached these truths [those proclaimed by all men who reflect deeply on them] from the time I was very young; and the colonel never stopped repeating these truths to me. I have read them in books and perhaps I have heard them from the pulpit—but so what? The world, my friends, my experience have also been constant teachers to remind me of these lessons over the course of my life, despite the ingratitude with which I have ignored their advice" (*Periquillo* 414). Periquillo listened instead to the voices of *malos maestros* and *malos amigos* [evil teachers and friends]. Yet these, although they led him astray, indirectly helped him by bringing about his *desengaño* (that is, his discovery of the deceit of their language and his awakening to a love of virtue). Cruel betrayal taught him that "bad teachers can communicate good lessons" (414). Consequently, Periquillo never curses these bad teachers; instead he remains grateful to them for having taught him valuable lessons. (One can read in this attitude that Lizardi refused to hate Spain but rather appreciated the negative lessons Spanish colonialism had taught.)

In *Don Catrín* Lizardi will have his character on the way to perdition silence the memory of the good "voices" (thereby suggesting some conscience might partially have been formed) and deliberately replace them with other "voices" of expediency and selfishness. But Periquillo's problem is the colonial's. As an adolescent, he was only then acquiring a sense of self (that is, self-confidence but also linguistic experience and self-reflexiveness) that would allow him to differentiate between good and bad voices. He had not yet learned to counter with his own language the voices of others.

The reference to Periquillo's new beard, repeated several times in the early part of the novel, suggests the adolescent's sexuality; the physical detail introduces into the story a consciousness of bodily urges and of social relations as regards women. The relationship between the sexes is seldom described in Lizardi's novel in terms of love. Indeed, even when his hero is married at the novel's end, the author avoids discussion of the emotional path that led him there. When Periquillo marries, the first time out of passion and self-interest, his ardor quickly cools and the marriage fails. The second time, when he marries Antonio's daughter, he is older than his young wife and the union is made to seem more like a bonding between Pedro and his mentor than a love match. As he crosses the Pacific and builds fantasies that he will acquire power in Mexico on his return, his wealth and success depend on his wife becoming a friend of the *virreina*. Thus love as a basis for marriage is absent; instead, Lizardi's fiction suggests marriage to be a political and economic arrangement for men's advantage.

Lizardi seems fearful of women, anxious particularly about their hold over men through marriage. Such an attitude may have several explanations. Lizardi as a result of his own wanderings may have had reason to know that a *pícaro*'s life usually meant involvement with loose women and that redemption by bourgeois society meant the end of that sexual freedom. He and others skirted the picaresque world only with difficulty and, finally, seemingly repudiated sexual pleasure when they married. However, the novel's suggestion of Periquillo's sexual nature may also represent Lizardi's effort to go beyond traditional Christian explanations of men's essentially lustful nature so as to explore the marital fidelity that an emerging Mexican middle class required.

Lizardi might also have understood that Mexico, according to the metaphor of the adolescent, was uncertain about the Mexican's emergence from a network of male protectionism into a world not only of freedom and parity with other males, but also of adjustment to life with a supposed inferior. I discuss this topic of men's and women's roles, especially in marriage, at greater length in the chapter devoted to *La Quijotita*. Periquillo's father weakly yields to his wife in sending his son to Latin school, rather than insisting that Periquillo learn a trade as he had judged best. The decision proves wrong; and Lizardi editorializes that, although men must love their wives, they must not allow women to dominate them. Generally, throughout the novel, men's knowledge is made to be symbolic of reason and self-restraint, superior to women's, which was thought to derive from passion and self-indulgence. Lizardi warns that man needs to guard against womanly ways, whether external to him in the form of a woman's temptation or influence, or within himself as feelings of tenderness. A man was *afeminado* [effeminate] if he acceded to women's wishes or spent time unduly in women's company.

After his father's death, Periquillo began his misadventures by listening uncritically to his friend Januario. Januario described the civilizing process in which Periquillo would learn to associate with women: "Come along with me. Grab the few pennies that you can from your father and trust me that not only will you have a good time you; will also become civilized because I see that you are a rustic Mexican and I want to lead you out of your provincial ways. Yes, I will take you to some houses of fine young ladies where I go for conversation; you will learn social skills, to dance, to talk with nice people. In addition to this, I will seat you in drawing-rooms so that you learn to get along with the ladies, because dealing with women educates one completely" (76). Januario's voice is generally not to be trusted. Yet it is obvious here that he articulates some accepted belief that a gentleman must learn to enter the polite world of women. However, Lizardi suggests that somehow he will have to remain at a skeptical distance from the modern French refinements of behavior, or the passion that the sex symbolized.

Dress, Lizardi says in the *Periquillo*, was a means by which woman often expressed dissatisfaction with her station and violated nature's laws by dominating her husband and assuming an identity beyond what she and her family had inherited. Reckless spending on dress, so as to appear to be of a higher social rank than one actually was, occurred often in Mexico; and Lizardi blamed women for the fact that husbands and fathers often spent beyond their economic means, thus ruining the family. Although this analysis accuses the upper classes for their luxurious consumption and reveals that class distinctions were becoming blurred, it makes women into scapegoats.

However, Lizardi also can be seen to have sympathized with women, or at least thought about their sexual vulnerability. He comments narratively that, if they erred, it was generally because they lacked a man's protection or they rebelliously refused to obey their natural masters: "I was acquainted with a great number of women and I knew that the reason most fell was because they did not agree to submitting to their fathers, husbands, masters or protectors" (408). He showed how single women could be victimized when he portrayed Periquillo, in his *pícaro* identity as *encargado de justicia* in a small town, seducing those women whose husbands he had contrived to send to prison. The episode dramatizes how any weak entity, even the colony if it should declare independence, might be preyed upon by stronger bodies.

Women's adultery drew together several concerns of Lizardi and his generation. In an aristocratic age, adultery was an insult to a man's *pundonor*; now it was understood to be a triumph of the woman over the man, an unnatural act perpetrated by an inferior against a superior so that the husband seemed more the victim of the wife than of her accomplice, another man. In a long and significant chapter (part 2, chap. 14)[7] Lizardi confronts the question of adultery; and the extensive discussion, grounded in references to old and new Spanish legal codes, suggests the importance of law in defining woman's (and the colonial's) identity and legal rights. "Adultery" is meant to be understood literally, an important issue whereby marriage and sexual relations might be discussed. But the topic also served Lizardi in opening up questions of social disorder and threats to paternalistic institutions.

The wise *coronel* is discussing a case in which a soldier murdered a man whom he suspected of adulterous relations with his wife. He sets out the strict penalties of the Fuero Juzgo and the Recopilación (Spanish legal codes); and then he shows how "the Enlightenment of the time" (324) modified the harshness of those older codes, even listing several instances in which the new laws might side with the adulterous woman. The emphasis on jurisprudence in settling such a dispute, the concern for who receives the woman's property if she is guilty, the possibility that woman herself might initiate legal action—all this points to a departure from aristocratic notions about women and marriage, as well as a new awareness of legal changes in Spain.

The discussion shows the importance of protecting the family unit, now for reasons of social utility instead of manly pride. Yet Lizardi's careful description of how far a prosecutor might go in charging the defendant is additional proof of adultery's usefulness in thinking about the implementation of Spanish law in Mexico. The woman's crime suggests the legal protections now more widely available to all inferior beings under the new codes, and the possible appropriation of Spanish legal language by colonials. Yet the preoccupation with adultery also externalizes fears particular to the Mexican upper classes—many Mexican businesses depended on the female partner's family connections, and adulterous behavior threatened those commercial interests.[8] Women's increasing economic activity, in the printing trade, for example, also made the former penalties of banishment to a convent or confiscation of dowry impractical (Arrom; Kicza).

The sexual uncertainties of Lizardi's story are apparent in the literature of the period. "La Coquetilla" wrote in the *Diario de México* (January 4, 1806), expressing a fear that men were losing their virility, that the period was succumbing to a standard in which there was no difference between the sexes:

Lately we are experiencing the fatal consequences of the feminization of men, of those beings who because of their sex and their inclinations were born to uphold legal codes and the rights of Religion, *patria*, the state, and of all humanity. Well, these very same ones are the ones who are destroying everything; and, not only are they completely useless to us women, but, what is worse, they are usurping our privileges, our attractiveness, our charms, and even our mode of coughing, laughing, walking and, . . . what shall I say . . . I fear, and with good reason, that in a few days our Sovereigns will have to recruit women in order to make up their armies and we women will be in war fatigues while these young gentlemen are checking their handsomeness in a mirror.

Lizardi's concern that men not take on womanly ways, expressed in the *Periquillo* six to nine years later, is perhaps even more acute. Manliness as militarism would have been valued still more then as war raged; womanly, or effete, behavior was associated with the noncombatant Mexican elite whose members were engaged in their narcissistic concerns. It is no accident that the *coronel,* a military man, exhorts Pedro to be a man: "You must dress decently avoiding any womanliness" (329); "Son, arms are not at odds with letters. Man is always a man wherever he finds himself and you must nourish your reason with erudition and study" (329); "the best assurance of good fortune for a man is his good behavior and the best *patria* one can have is the one in which he can dedicate himself to working in a manly way" (351).

Even love of country must be disciplined in a way suggestive of manly control. The *coronel* warns that there is often something "violent" in the love one has for the land in which one was born and that one must somehow be "philosophical" in disengaging from this local attachment ("the philosopher's homeland is the world," 352). However, one must be grateful for the start one's nurturing world provided because ingratitude was a social sin. Here Lizardi's counsel suggests that an international view and coolness are necessary to douse the emotion of civil war.

Lizardi, through his fictional invention Periquillo, thinks of himself as a child of Mexico, thus transferring to the colony the emotion previously felt for Spain and feminizing the land and its people with appropriate metaphors and symbols. In a dialogue with the *coronel,* Periquillo accuses Mexico of being a stepmother in showing her love for her children unequally (a figure of speech, as I have shown, he employed to indict Spain). However, the *coronel* says, this complaint reveals self-interest; rather, she deserves to be loved unselfishly, as one would love the mother who had given one life. Her geographical attractions, which previously had been religious centers of pilgrimage, could now be visited as tourist sites; Mexico City's buildings, which had been built in the latter years of the eighteenth century under the Conde de Revillagigedo, were new sources of pride. The maternal image of the Virgen de Guadalupe was becoming politicized, a symbol of Mexicanness;[9] and Lizardi has Periquillo appeal to her when he is shipwrecked.

Yet Lizardi seems confused by the feminine character he is imputing to Mexico.[10] He also seems to be caught up by changes in Mexico's attitudes toward marriage. In a society where clerical celibacy was a hard-fought issue (many argued that Mexico's depopulation and rural poverty could be blamed on the country's many religious, while others steadfastly supported that Church tradition), marriage was discussed less as a matter of love and sentiment than as a device by which the country would be assured of human resources in the future. In a society where many common-law unions produced numbers of abandoned children, marriage was seen matter-of-factly as introducing social responsibility.

This emphasis on reason and social benefits in the making of a marriage, while also characteristic of eighteenth-century European attitudes, reflects a general colonial fear that desires unleashed—whether sexual or political—might prove destructive. It may be that in a young country, anxious to emulate adult models, passion was dealt with uncertainly. It may also be that sexuality, dangerous to male bonding, was acceptable only when it was channeled in marriage.

Gratitude

In rethinking *patria*, Lizardi importantly redefined *gratitude*. The term, connoting a natural, voluntary association and hiding the historical fact that the conqueror had forced the arrangement, had been important in the litany of subordination colonials learned; like "obedience" and "loyalty," "gratitude" was a moral virtue few could quarrel with.[11] In Lizardi's picaresque story, Periquillo's education is a series of lessons in which the final one brings about his enlightenment—recognition that God's benevolence has saved him and he owes Him grateful thanks. When the band of thieves he has joined is attacked and most of the members killed, Periquillo escapes. In a long speech of repentance, he acknowledges that no merit of his own spared him, but that the merciful hand of God intervened. So his moral transformation is the result of his consciousness of dependency; acknowledgment of dependency takes the form of gratitude.

Periquillo's ingratitude for the moral code his father bequeathed to him is the beginning of his sin (94). When he meets his first good friend, Periquillo learns that gratitude should accompany the discharge of social obligations; to be ungrateful in the face of a benefactor's goodness is to act in a way inappropriate even for dumb animals (191). Working from the model of a good and just world, Lizardi constructs an educational process in which the individual awakens gradually to the goodness around him and then finds himself obliged to respond in kind. Whereas the gratefulness Lizardi's *pícaro* feels to God grows out of a sinner's absolute abjection, in the case of gratitude for men's goodness, Lizardi at least suggests selfish motives may operate to make a grateful person rationally aware that goodness may only be an expression of how the good man may himself like to be treated (191).

"Gratitude," originating in colonial paternalistic rhetoric, was taught by the Church, the political structure, and the family.[12] It was politicized in the contemporary paintings of the dying Fray Bartolomé de Las Casas, permitted to suck nourishment from the breasts of a young Indian woman while her Indian husband stood by—both grateful to the old man for his defense of their people.[13] At a personal level the teaching of gratitude interpreted maturation as recognition of the good lessons one's father provided, and conversion as the understanding of God's beneficence. At a corporate level it reinforced the loyalty subjects owed their king. Its invocation urged these subjects to higher standards of performance. But it also, as Lizardi wrote in *El Pensador Mexicano*, might be turned against the father to reproach him and his stand-ins (colonial governors) for their failure to comply with the moral laws binding them in the reciprocal arrangement. Their ingratitude was despotism, just as the individual's was license.

The term was susceptible to various interpretations. John Locke used it in his *Second Treatise of Government* in his discussion of paternal power to describe a child's honorable duty to his father. But Locke clearly established the difference between "political" and "paternal" and said that after a son's "nonage," gratitude did not mean a father had dominion over his son's property and actions (108–9). Lizardi does not mention Locke in the *Periquillo*, but the *Diario de México* cites the philosopher several times;[14] and it seems probable that Lizardi would have known of Locke's ideas about gratitude, which differed from traditional Catholic views. Invoking the term, Lizardi could be urging reconciliation between father and son. He could be accusing the Spanish king of ingratitude, in the face of Mexico's repeated gestures of filial devotion. Or he could also be suggesting the feelings of mutual obligation required of citizens in a new nation, thus envisioning new meanings for *patria* and *patriotismo*. Family structures, according to this model of dependency, would still function to bind Mexicans together.

Gratitude, strange in a modern political lexicon, was powerful in confronting Lizardi's colonial readers with the idealism of their social contract and the reality of the Mexican civil war. The binary possibilities of the term, which permitted discussion of *ingratitude*, posed questions of why Mexicans would attack their putative father and kill their brothers, why Christian, rational men would rebel against everything they had been taught and act in a way that animals refrain from. How might *ingratitude*, which described the Mexican condition, be converted into *gratitude* if goodness were not obvious there?

In a passage toward the end of the *Periquillo*, in a portion of the book that was not printed until 1830 after his death, Lizardi says the novel was being written in Mexico in 1813. He focusses on the "war [that] is the greatest of all the evils for any nation or kingdom"; and, he says, even more harmful are the emotions that accompany it ("anger, vengeance, and cruelty, inseparable from every war, [which] take hold in the citizens themselves, who arm to destroy one another," 452). At other points in the novel, Lizardi describes the social fabric, which had been rent by the insurgency. The obligations toward society, which Nature and religion placed on man (191), had given way to the expression of bloodthirsty feelings [*sanguinarios sentimientos*] (53). Mexicans, in their passion for revenge (52), had forgotten the restraints and ideals of charity, mercy, and pardon, which Christian doctrine taught. Lizardi identifies the two sides in the conflict ("the Spanish government . . . [and] the Americans who are trying to become independent of Spain"); and, although he questions which has right on its side (452), he generally avoids partisanship. However, a discussion of bloodthirstiness, positioned alongside a reference to the Spanish custom of bullfighting, which had been imported into Mexico and seemed barbaric to many Mexicans, provides a clue that Lizardi blamed Spain.

Gratitude rearticulated the question of human nature in the Americas. In a society beginning to detach itself from older religious explanations of the individual's role in collective life, it suggested that man's responsibility to his Maker might be less important than obligations to his fellows and opinions he might have of himself. The term's use served to reevaluate the constraints institutions imposed on the individual; *gratitude* as a more lenient stricture competed with the penalties of law. In the text of the *Periquillo* Lizardi includes references to "passions" and "urgings" [*inclinaciones*], which eighteenth-century philosophers such as Rousseau increasingly looked on favorably; however, Lizardi appears to stay within the bounds of Christian orthodoxy in his assumption that man's nature requires the discipline of education and reason to control those urges. His use of the term *gratitude*, therefore, is consistent with his preference for voluntary constraints, the individual's willing subordination to society's demands.

Building gratitude into his novel as a solution to conflict, Lizardi importantly posed the question of whether Mexicans, individually and collectively, were "fathers" or "sons." If they were the latter, they owed loyalty to and veneration of the father; their thanks for the father's benefits must take the form, not of words, but of dutiful fulfillment of obligations. But if they were the former, then the term was a reminder that authority not be abused. Still a third possibility existed, however, in Lizardi's making of "the land" and its "people" a new cathectic unit within which "gratitude" established other bonds.

Pleasure and Pain

Reflecting the strains of the generation's effort to break with the colonial past, yet also to preserve some wisdom from the past in moving on to an unknown future, the form of Lizardi's text is characterized by its ruptures. Showing the author's awareness that Mexican readers, acculturated to Spanish and other European literary modes, yet also sensitive to language changes in their Mexican world, required a new novel style, the *Periquillo* teaches its readers to adjust to a new reading pace. Readers are immediately conscious of the text's gaps, shifts, and interruptions. The mature Pedro frequently corrects the youthful Periquillo. Interpolated stories, such as Antonio's, duplicate the message of father/son relationships, but they also stray from the main story and slow down the action. Lizardi in his authorial voice summons his readers back to his story ("Returning to my progress in school," 22); he intervenes to sum up the moral of an episode; or he talks about subjects seemingly unrelated to the picaresque story, such as Roman burial habits and Church reforms by the Council of Trent.

The latter—the many erudite and moralistic digressions—have offended critics who consider them extraneous to the tale of adolescent waywardness. Mexican critics, with the exception of Agustín Yáñez, have generally been unanimous in finding the material structurally unjustifiable. And Spell's 1931 verdict that their didacticism intrudes unnecessarily into the lively picaresque tone has tended to prevail in the United States: "It is this persistent insertion of unrelated material which prevented Lizardi's work from approaching that of a master of fiction. The didactic portion—strongly suggestive of his pamphlets in both style and content—is too extensive, too unskillfully introduced, and too loosely and inartistically connected with the incidents of the main story to permit the whole to approach the proportion, the smoothness, or the finish of a work of art" (Spell, "Life" 31).

Critics who looked for a separation between art and instruction also disliked the digressions. In the 1942 Stylo edition of the *Periquillo* the moral and erudite digressions were printed in italics so that readers could omit them. Also in 1942, an English translation of the *Periquillo*, published as *The Itching Parrot*, prompted an interesting response to the shortened version. In charge of the project was Katherine Anne Porter, who, with the help of Ford Madox Ford and an editor from Doubleday, used Eugene Pressly's translation, cutting the "immense accumulation of political pamphlets and moral disquisitions" so that the picaresque novel might emerge (vii).[15] Lionel Trilling reviewed the translation and guessed how much the cuts had harmed the original text:

I found "The Itching Parrot" a bore. . . .

It is disquieting to be unable to respond to a book that has meant so much to so many people—so much, too, to such judges as Ford Madox Ford and Miss Porter. Perhaps I feel as I do because I have not read the same book as they read. Miss Porter's translation is a model of firm, simple prose in the manner of the eighteenth-century masters of realism; but she tells us that the allusive and obscene language of the original will not submit to translation. Perhaps in the verbal play of that incommunicable Spanish lies the power of mind which I feel so sadly absent from the translated book. Or perhaps that power of mind lies in the many moral and political tracts which have been cut out of this version. These, to a foreign public, would of course be dull, if comprehensible at all; yet I cannot help wondering whether their inclusion isn't just what endears the book to its native readers, who, it seems to me, might well be charmed by the exposition of serious matters in the setting of a picaresque novel's low actuality. (373–74)

Lizardi cautioned: "Be careful with my digressions because perhaps that is what should matter most to you" (252). In introductory words to his readers he said that his goal in the book was not to narrate his life but to instruct; and, conscious of his many digressions, he judged that they were not "too repetitious, disconnected or annoying" (7). He considered that he could have suppressed them; but then he wrote: "Periquillo, despite the economy which it represents, does not fail to corroborate its opinions with the doctrines of poets and pagan philosophers."

Here Lizardi suggests that, in the increasingly secular society he is writing for, truth is no longer perfect or self-evident; instead a truth is enhanced by the numbers and conditions of those who proclaim it. Lizardi says an irreligious person may be moved to change his ways by learning that pagan authors, as well as Church authorities, teach the same wisdom. Lizardi, therefore, needed to repeat the message according to both sources, not only because his less-sophisticated readers required it, but because no one authority was universally accepted anymore. Therefore, although the digressions, drawn from Church and pagan or secular authorities, are included ostensibly to underscore the serious dimension of the picaresque story, it is also true that the several voices, coming from different points of view, suggest doubting colonial readers who, if not convinced by one set of wise men, might be persuaded by another.

In an introduction to the *Periquillo* Lizardi quotes from the work of Nicolás Jamin, *Fruits de mes lectures* (Paris, 1775). Jamin, whose theories on writing and reading I mention above, attacked the Jansenists in several of his works; and, although he generally frowned on the secular writers whose impious books he described as "the destroyer of kingdoms" [*la polilla de los Reinos*], he apparently conceded the value of sensualist testimony in teaching morality (as the Jesuits also did). Lizardi quotes Jamin:

I have taken my reflections from the profane authors without omitting either the testimony of the poets, persuaded by the testimony of the latter. . . . although voluptuous as a rule, their testimony established the severity of customs in a stronger and more successful way than the philosophers. One suspects that only vanity has been the motive which has moved philosophers to establish austere maxims in the midst of a superstitious religion which flattered all passion. In fact, when I heard a voluptuous writer praising the purity of customs, it was evident that only the force of truth could have forced from his mouth such brilliant testimony. (7)

Lizardi continues on to argue that both the "voluptuous youth" and the "the old man inured to vice" will benefit if the wisdom of the Gospel and the Church is backed up by the advice of secular authorities "without perfect religion, solid virtue or the light of the Gospel" (the discussion recalls the *Ratos entretenidos* essay). Lizardi's use of the adjective *voluptuous* may be just a thoughtless repetition of Jamin's use of the word, but I believe it deserves a second look.

The word suggests an abandonment to sensual pleasure. "Volupia," the Roman goddess of pleasure, was fashionable in eighteenth-century France, as the age sought to rethink Europe's classical inheritance. Greuze depicted a young woman blowing a kiss as "La Voluptueuse" (Brookner 66). Rousseau describes Orientals as "voluptuous" (*Emile* 347). Diderot's *Encyclopédie* drew distinctions between "voluptuousness," "pleasure," and "delight," suggesting, in a mechanistic analogy, that voluptuous impressions were connected to a state of imbalance or inquietude where desire was awakened and pain issued from the deferral of pleasure. Voluptuousness depended on maintaining a delicate balance between "ennui" on the one hand and "chagrin" on the other.[16] Jamin, in his *Verdadero antídoto*, has a chapter on the dangers of reading "voluptuous or lascivious" books, fearing particularly the love stories of the new romances.

Jesuits and Jansenists were divided about the value of sensualist appeals to pleasure in teaching faithful lessons; yet that dispute, conducted largely in France, was balanced by the use that Counter-Reformation aesthetics had always made of the senses for religious teaching in Spain and Spanish territories. Jesuit educational methods, prevailing in Mexico, had taught the value of contemplation (with devices to stimulate interest and then prolong the gaze) and demonstration (with methods to illustrate religion and the new sciences).[17] Later, in my discussion of *Noches tristes*, I note how Lizardi found that the standard colonial catechism contradicted itself in describing *gozo* [joy], suggestive of sensory experience and pleasure, both as a vice and a virtue.

Therefore, Lizardi's early mention of "voluptuosity" in his novel recalls contemporary philosophical debates over the value of nonrational feeling, and it situates his colonial book in the midst of their theorizing. Recognizing that colonial readers were prone to boredom when faced with a text that spoke of authority, yet embarrassed by their cultural inferiority, Lizardi strove to create a fictional Mexico that interested them but did not mortify them, a satiric balance that afforded pleasure but not pain. Mexican readers (not only the less-instructed readers but also those among the colonized elite), unaccustomed to the severity of truth, needed the "voluptuousness" of "poets" (Jamin's language) to make them continue reading; one understands here not only concrete examples of vice and virtue but also savory details of wickedness. The poet's narrative, in which colonial readers traced with him his error (which seemed to characterize colonial experience), was more convincing, and thereby more rationally satisfying, than the philosopher's short, sententious pronouncements, which might have originated in austerity or vanity; this observation by Jamin would seem to have expressed the dissatisfaction of many colonials with metropolitan writing.

Too, involvement with familiar characters was more emotionally rewarding than the skepticism that cold rational argument required of readers. Lizardi's digressions would have provided sensual pleasure as their expansiveness assured colonials of the author's recognition of their sensory perception of their Mexican surroundings. Walter Ong has observed that digressions are often characteristic of oral language usage; and I believe that Lizardi's retention of this feature of orality was meant to recall the in situ performance of much colonial communication, the casual discursiveness family members and friends use in talking to one another. So, rather than tedious repetitions to be endured, the digressions offer the reader a gratifying sense of being thought special, of being given an assortment and a surfeit to savor. As Lizardi himself says in the novel, he needed various ways of making his excruciating realism acceptable: "to make the bitter pill more appetizing to swallow" (463).

A preference for variety in reading, for, as Lizardi phrased it in the "Prospecto" to the *Periquillo*, "a portion of heterogeneous news items with which reading is made less dreary," surely grew out of the colony's reading taste for newspapers and literary miscellanies (Radin "Some Newly Discovered Poems" 63). The quick switching from the author's mind and memory to paper, without affectation or pedantry, was a method more suited to "our natural whimsical taste" [*nuestra natural veleidad*], as Lizardi wrote in the *Periquillo* (11). An impression of variety also, Lizardi thought, resulted from the reader's alternating between something he knew and something he did not know. Returning again to the design for the *Periquillo* Lizardi sketches in the "Prospecto," one reads: "Sometimes it taught what one knew and other times one learned what one didn't know" (63). Indeed, he summed up his intent in a phrase that critics would do well to take into account in their assessment of the worth of the digressions: "it can be said that Periquillo tried rather to write an entertaining, critical, and moral miscellany than just his life, as the title says."

This concern for movement in the reading process is apparent in his analysis of the several stages he predicted his reader would experience. He envisioned contact with his book as "delicious ecstasy in the entertainment," an initial period when the reader enjoyed "the penetration of the satire," saw others satirized, and even applied the book's criticism to areas the author had not intended; but then at a later moment the reader might reflect on the serious message and realize he was implicated (463). Lizardi's division of the reading experience into parts—the moment with the book and then the reflective period afterward—suggests a simple division between the emotional involvement produced by a mimetic technique as well as the treatment of low life, and the rational distancing resulting from the book's idea structure. The morality of his book, therefore, depends on an interplay between sensual pleasure and rational rigor, if not pain.

The *Periquillo*, then, is not so much the story of Periquillo Sarniento as the tug between the differing realities that the different parts of the novel, the differing perspectives, represent. Periquillo Sarniento in his two selves as adolescent sinner and discursive father is too transparent an authorial voice to be believed as a free creature. The custom of reading *diálogos* as dramatized dialectic or *fábulas* as concealed criticism was too strong in the period for one reading mode to operate consistently throughout the text. The motivating energy in the book is not to be found in the hero but in the voice speaking through him, satirizing a corrupt reality through a juxtaposition of corrupt reality and the digressions in which reason, civilization, and advancements in learning, charity, and justice are portrayed.

The book's power of mind, which Trilling guessed was lost when the moral and erudite digressions were cut, depends on their retention. Not only does their subject matter balance the picaresque story but their simple, honest style contrasts with the pedantry, pomposity, and disguised corruption of the upper-class speakers, and the ignorance and more open criminality of the lower-class speakers. The digressions' language offers a model for real communication and instruction. The "homey, familiar style" of the framing digressions plainly mediates between levels of society, employing a form of principally oral language already used in the colony in nonofficial or informal (Lizardi uses the term *casero* or home) situations. Its easiness, with sometimes inelegant structure and substandard usage, but with the freshness of speech, brought upper-class readers to a recognition of the expressivity of this level of language and united them imaginatively for the period of the reading with the large numbers of illiterates whose distinctiveness Mexican thinkers were confronting. However, as I have shown, this speech style, in its reliance on middle and lower-class forms, struck many upper-class readers as reductive.

Richard M. Morse has identified an American pattern of language that he understands to be the result of an historical "plebeianizing" process. Beginning when many persons of low rank came to the New World, colonial language reflected the lack of restraints as all men mingled there on an equal basis. Morse writes: "Language in the Americas therefore exhibits two important characteristics which might be called the 'adaptive' and the 'mediative.' The former is evinced in accommodations to environment and to social leavening; in spite of new expressive tones and occasional picturesqueness, it represents an impoverishment of traditional linguistic resources. The latter reflects the need for mediation between the hinterland and the metropolis, between the freshly experienced and the historical or conventional and, by extension, between sense and intellect" ("Language" 535).

However, instead of what Morse calls "impoverishment," I see, as the years passed and Americans realized the need for a language more responsive to their realities, a healthy incentive to examine "mediation," thereby freshening traditional forms of thought and enriching American language. Rather than any loss of intellectual dimension, America's need to maintain ties with the metropolis suggests, as Morse says, American "mediation" in its progress toward decolonization points to colonials' appropriation of European systems of thought, their discard of dishonest or inapplicable ones, and their invention of new. It is in this way, therefore, that I understand Lizardi's novel to be operating. With its insertion of satiric, low, and plain styles into standard literary Spanish, the text integrates discursively the Spanish mental world and the Mexican physical world. It brings a Spanish discourse system into synchronization with American experience; it adjusts the domination of the past to the independence of the present. "Discourse," both in its Spanish and English meanings, suggests the distillation of experience through the rational faculty into some communicated form. In Periquillo's case, this mediation is conveyed in the summary of the *pícaro's* negative experiences, converted into a useful lesson to his children. In the novel, Lizardi attempts to show that if Mexico's various populations can communicate successfully with one another in the pages of a book, they can coexist successfully in real life.

Lizardi's exhaustive effort to subject raw reality to the resources of Mexican language (discourse) results in a constant authorial effort to repeat and refine meaning. Again, the contemporary critic Terán noticed this in his reading of the *Periquillo*, and he provides valuable information about how upper-class colonials at that time might have viewed this aspect of the text: "The mania of explaining enlarges annoyingly the points [of the story]. Each phrase determines the sense of the one which precedes it and traces it exactly to fix the meaning of the words. Diffuse and relaxed, [the style] seems as though it wants to persuade [us] that it is necessary to present the idea to us with a hundred different constructions, and [Lizardi] practically defines each word for us in the form of a dictionary. . . . One probably would say that this method is appropriate to a father who is instructing his children" (quoted in Reyes, *Obras* 4: 174).

This comment regarding the book's style and structure suggests not only Terán's perceptive reading of the text's repetitiveness but also his misreading in attributing such verbal restatement to childish speech. The literate classes who read Lizardi's book could believe that they needed to preserve their power by continuing to imitate Spanish forms of privileged language. It is this audience of thoughtless or tongue-tied speakers, however, and not children or the illiterate populace, whom the Mexican author is addressing with his variegated material drawn from many sources, his constant redefinition of common words and clichés of thought.

Lizardi's literary language is a model of decolonizing discourse in the digressions' clarity and the text's inclusiveness. His often coarse style, but also his insistent effort to explain jargon and expose double talk, show his defiance of colonial censors and his refusal to imitate the literary speech act of the past. His clarity was a reaction to old-fashioned Spanish Baroque taste, Inquisition rules, and obfuscation by powerful interests. Yet it was also the product of European, principally French Neoclassic aesthetic preferences, which suggested that artistic language be reformed in the interests of more effective communication; it resulted, too, from the arrival in Mexico of Enlightenment theories of the diffusion of new knowledge.

Lizardi's simple style, therefore, although designed to modernize colonial language, must be seen as an effort to repudiate the inherited Peninsular taste for linguistic virtuosity that so often disguised intellectual deficiency and blocked American thinking. In the following representative passage from the *Periquillo*, the series of parallelisms contrasts with, and indicts as elegant lies, the conceits of the Baroque picaresque storytellers: "Januario gave me a sign that I should shut my mouth, and the two of us laid down a billiard table, whose hard boards, the headache I had, the fear that those almost naked men inspired in me (men whom I naively judged to be thieves), the numbers of bedbugs in the blanket, the rats that ran over me, a rooster which crowed regularly, the snores of those who were sleeping, the farts of others who let them loose, and the pestiferous stink which resulted, caused me to spend a dog's night" (135). Here Lizardi's preference for common, even crude, vocabulary, which some may see as impoverishing the literary lexicon, really widens the language pool and is the linguistic equivalent of ridding colonial life of foreign enslavement.

Lizardi, like Andrés Bello, helped create a literary Americanism in the first decades of the nineteenth century. Lizardi's contribution, usually thought of in terms of adding a popular and social dimension to the literary range (Portuondo 105–7), served to introduce a democratized novel into Spanish America and open up the genre's possibilities for new thematic and stylistic expression. However, this linguistic and artistic innovation was only part of a larger moral project. The *Periquillo*'s realism in portraying Mexico's lower classes, the book's exposé of upper-class corruption and decadence, the careful clarity of its digressions—were all part of the appropriation of a moral stance by colonials. To justify the rupture with the father it was necessary to cloak colonial actions in the veil of education, to expose the immorality of the parent's past behavior so that continued domination by a defective model would not only seem outmoded but ethically unjustifiable. A new kind of moral literature, which included a portrait of immorality and in whose reading the rigors of self-criticism produced pain, was meant to help in this endeavor.

Fig. 1. Pedro de Valdivia *(falling from horse)*, the Spanish conqueror of Chile, is killed by the Araucanian Indians. From *La Araucana*, Canto 3, by Alonso de Ercilla (Madrid: Antonio de Sancha, 1776). Artist: Antonio Carnizero. Engraver: J. Joaquín Fabregat.

Fig. 2. Carlota, having recently found her parents, raises her arms in exultation as the king of England restores to her father *(far left)* his noble title and properties. Now she can marry as an equal Sir Thomas Bountiful *(second from left)*. From *La huerfanita inglesa ó Historia de Carlota Summers*, by Sarah Fielding. 2nd ed. (Madrid: Gomez Fuentenebro y Cia., 1804). Artist unknown.

¡O Alejo! Alejo creeme... entre nosotros es donde se halla la verdadera felicidad.

Fig. 3. "O Alejo! Alejo, believe me . . . between us is where true happiness is to be found." Clarita *(left, dressed as a boy)* and Alejo, in a pastoral scene. The sentiment of their innocent relationship—love based first on friendship, shared work, and mutual gratitude—contrasts with the hypocritical sociability of the city. Clarita's father and an old servant appear in the background. From *Alejo ú La casita en los bosques, Manuscrito encontrado junto á las orillas del rio Isera*, by François Guillaume Ducray-Duminil. (Barcelona: Imprenta de José Torner, 1821). Artist: Forner.

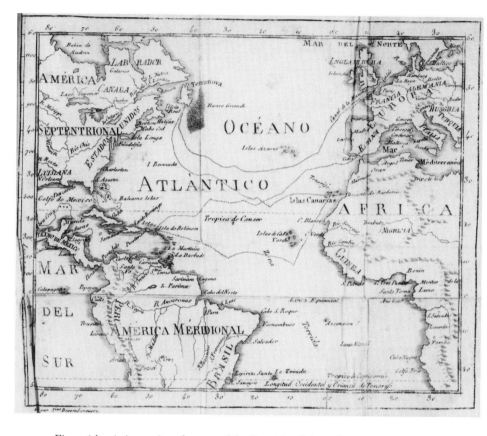

Fig. 4 (*above*). A map in volume 1 of the Spanish edition of Daniel Defoe's *Robinson Crusoe*. Iriarte says Defoe probably based his story on the report of a sixteenth-century writer who drew upon the experiences of a marooned Spaniard. From *El nuevo Robinson* (Madrid: n.p., 1820). Engraver: Josephine Decomberousse.

Fig. 5 (*right*). "Fifth Commandment of the Church: To Pay Tithes and First Fruits." Saint Severino exhorts the people to fulfill this precept. From *Catecismo por los Padres Ripalda y Astete* (Madrid: Imprenta de la Administracion del Real Arbitrio de Beneficencia, 1800). Artist unknown.

PAGAR DIEZMOS Y PRIMICIAS.

San Severino Obispo exhorta al pueblo á cumplir éste precepto.

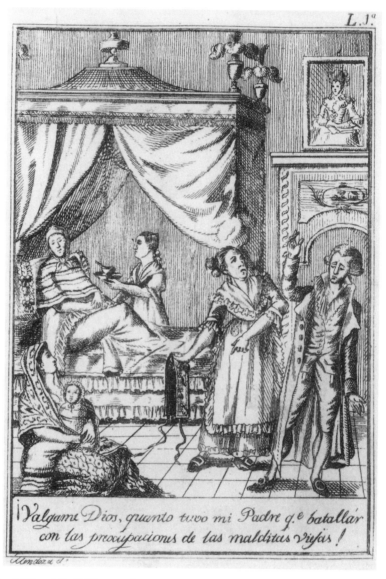

Fig. 6. "Good God! How my father had to battle against the prejudices of the cursed old ladies!" Pedro Sarmiento, just born, is held by a servant *(lower left)*. His mother, in bed, is ministered to by a family member, and a third woman holds a swaddling cloth with which she wants to bind the child. Pedro's father *(right)* attempts to counter the women's folk remedies. From *El Periquillo Sarniento,* by José Joaquín Fernández de Lizardi (Mexico City: Alejandro Valdés, 1816). Artist: Mendoza.

Fig. 7. "Take the pen from the inkwell, and all your blotters, and erase right now, before I go, this verse so perversely written." An educated clergyman *(left)* has entered Pedro's classroom and sees, under the image of the Immaculate Conception, a badly written verse. He angrily reprimands the teacher, who through improper puncuation has changed its meaning. From *El Periquillo Sarniento*, by José Joaquín Fernández de Lizardi. Artist: Mendoza.

Fig. 8. "My son following a trade? What would people say on seeing the son of Don Manuel Sarmiento learning to be a tailor, painter, silversmith, or other such thing?" says Pedro's mother as she and her husband discuss their son's future. From *El Periquillo Sarniento*, by José Joaquín Fernández de Lizardi. Artist: Mendoza.

Fig. 9. "Two other novices came and, presenting me with two leather buckets, said to me: 'Come, brother, and while it's time to go to choir, let's sweep the convent.'" Pedro (*center*) later describes his stay in the novitiate. From *El Periquillo Sarniento*, by José Joaquín Fernández de Lizardi. Artist: Mendoza.

Fig. 10. "The thing heated up in such a manner that in an instant we came to blows." Pedro, gambling in jail, is beaten by the other prisoners. From *El Periquillo Sarniento*, by José Joaquín Fernández de Lizardi. Artist: Mendoza.

Mendoza inv.   *Torreblanca f.*

La Quixotita y su Prima.

Fig. 11. Quixotita *(left)* and her cousin. From *La Quijotita y su prima, Historia muy cierta con apariencia de novela,* by El Pensador Mexicano (Lizardi) (Mexico City: Oficina de D. Mariano Ontiveros, 1818). Artist: Mendoza. Engraver: José Mariano Torreblanca.

Fig. 12. "Now let the woman, procuress and nurse to the dogs, leave, because if she doesn't I'll cut off her ears." Rodrigo and Matilde are seated as she, a good mother, breast feeds her baby. Pascual *(right)*, a farm foreman, threatens a hired nurse who has allowed her own baby to languish so as to feed two puppies, which he holds. From *La Quijotita y su prima*, by El Pensador Mexicano (Lizardi). Artist: Mendoza. Engraver: José Mariano Torreblanca.

Hallamos á Pomposita bañada en sangre, y á su madre privada.

L 3.

M za inv   Torreblanca

Fig. 13. "We found Pomposita bathed in blood and her mother senseless." Pomposita *(center)* lies in the arms of a servant. Eufrosina *(right)* is supported by another servant. The colonel, his wife, and the narrator stand at left. The accident is not serious. From *La Quijotita y su prima*, by El Pensador (Lizardi). Artist: Mendoza. Engraver: José Mariano Torreblanca.

Fig. 14. "Night One. Prison." Teófilo *(left)*, in jail with his jailer *(far right)* and another prisoner. From *Noches tristes y día alegre*, by José Joaquín Fernández de Lizardi (Mexico City: Oficina de D. Mariano Ontiveros, 1818). Artist unknown.

Dia alegre
y dignamente aprovechado

Fig. 15. "Happy Day, Worthily Utilized." As part of the tale's happy ending, Doro-
tea *(center)*, accompanied by Teófilo and her uncle, a priest, bestows the ownership
of an inn on a poor woman *(second from right)* who had shown her charity when she
was in need. From *Noches tristes y día alegre*, by José Joaquín Fernández de Lizardi.
Artist unknown.

Fig. 16. "The Famous Gentleman Don Catrín de la Fachènda." From an announcement for *Don Catrín de la Fachènda*, published as part of José Joaquín Fernández de Lizardi's pamphlet *Hemos dado en ser borricos y nos saldremos con ello* (Mexico City: published by the author, 1822). Artist: Mendoza. Engraver: José Mariano Torreblanca.

3

The Other Novels

7

La Quijotita y su prima

Colonial Nature

The dating of Lizardi's next two novels is a problem. Luis González Obregón calls *La Quijotita y su prima, Historia muy cierta con apariencias de novela* [Miss Quijotita and her cousin, A very certain story with the appearance of a novel] Lizardi's second novel (*Novelistas* 45, 78–83). Yet Jefferson Rea Spell believes *Noches tristes y día alegre* followed the *Periquillo* ("Life" 32). The dispute arises because both books were published in 1818 (in each case, only volume 1), and little else is known. Spell may have leaned toward his conclusion because in Lizardi's announcement for his *Fábulas* (October 8, 1817, *Noticioso General*), he states that he was writing *Noches tristes* and would soon publish it. *La Quijotita* was not announced in the *Gaceta del Gobierno* until July 23, 1818. Its second volume followed in 1819; but the complete edition, with the remaining two volumes, was not published until 1831–32.

However, I believe from internal evidence that *La Quijotita* followed the *Periquillo.* The patterns of their picaresque stories are similar; questions of colonial identity that each poses are related. Although both *La Quijotita* and *Noches tristes* share a concern for the catechism and the language of faith, *Noches tristes* appears to move away from Lizardi's initial fictional strategy of depicting a life. Yet I also think that the writing of the two books largely coincided.

In *La Quijotita* Lizardi continues his exploration of the proper education for colonial youth. But in this novel for women the picaresque adventures of the heroine necessarily undergo a change. The topic of education, which is how this novel is usually viewed (Jackson, Raymond), can be read in the girl's waywardness and disgraceful death. Yet she, unlike Pedro Sarmiento, cannot be rehabilitated. Woman cannot be redeemed, once she has fallen. So literature, newly capable of demonstrating the damage from error, must save her.

Beyond the entertainment and didacticism of the work, however, Lizardi confronts questions essential to colonial self-knowledge: the nature of women, their special character in Mexico, the unique knowledge they were thought to possess (faith, domestic management, folkways), their recent appearance in public such as in drawing rooms and cafe culture (although poor women had always been visible publicly), and their role in marriage and sentimental relationships. He says in the preface of the novel that he is writing for women but that "although it is dedicated to the fair sex, it will not be entirely useless to the other, on account of the close relationship between the two" (xxiii).[1]

Lizardi's focus on women particularly disguises his concern over the indigenous component of the Mexican racial and cultural mix [*mestizaje*], which the Indian-blooded mother in the Mexican family usually meant and which European culture represented as rustic backwardness to be overcome. Discussion of women's education in *La Quijotita* permitted Lizardi, I believe, to consider colonial assumptions of authority and obedience, the social order based on such a hierarchy, and biological destiny. Just as the discussion of slavery in the *Periquillo* concealed an examination of other colonial presumptions regarding dependency, so, too, the topic of "woman" in *La Quijotita* launched into Mexico's discourse world considerations of what this portion of the Self might be. In this respect, then, his book, while it apparently addresses issues specific to women, considers questions that go to the heart of colonial rule. Displaced onto "woman" are criollo concerns about what inferiority might mean—perhaps not because censorship would have frowned on such discussion but because Lizardi himself was struggling with verbalizing it.

The rise of the novel in Mexico, as I have shown, is a different phenomenon than its appearance elsewhere. If the novel in England and even British America has been tied to the emergence of a middle class, if the women of this class with new leisure for reading have been thought to dictate a taste for a form focussing on sentiment and private emotions (if not also sexual feelings),[2] then the evidence of Lizardi's four novels shows a somewhat different use of the genre. From Lizardi's preference for a man's story of ruination in two of these novels, of a man's religious doubts in a third, and a woman's fall (largely due to her father's error) in the fourth, it is clear that not only was Lizardi's novels' projected readership largely male but that these males preferred a public discourse in which women played an insignificant role in the more absorbing analysis of economic, political, and social problems. In *La Quijotita*, Lizardi avoided writing the sentimental kind of literature that articles in the *Diario de México* told him women readers in England wanted. He apparently had no fictional interest either in Mexican history, which several literary contests had proposed and which might have afforded the opportunity to tell personal stories of Indian and Spanish relationships (which could have been handled from the angle of love and might have been appealing to women). Indeed, Lizardi satirized "love" in *Don Catrín* in the union between that character and the woman who only cared for him so as to get his money. And he also disparaged love eight or nine years later, at a moment of press freedom, in a discussion of the catechism; there he called love the most powerful of the pleasures of the flesh—a *bicho* [cursed animal] that brought about the fall of David, Solomon, Samson, and other valiant men (*Obras* 6: 254).

Clearly, Lizardi's attitudes toward woman betray much of the phobia of the flesh associated with traditional Catholic teaching. However, arguably, his reluctance to depict "love" also reflects the inhibition of colonials who had only seen the term used in the contexts of love for king, country, or religion and who had not yet learned how to appropriate the sentiment for private expression. If one hears from the pulpit, or reads, with enough frequency, that the word is to be employed in combination with these objects, as in the pastoral letter the bishop of Puebla directed to his diocese ("Espíritu de acendrado amor a nuestro soberano" [Spirit of unblemished love for one's sovereign])[3] one has difficulty using it any other way.

Therefore, the unsentimental portrayal of women, and relationships between men and women, in *La Quijotita* poses several questions: Who were Lizardi's readers, intended and in fact? Given the topic of "woman," what latitude did Lizardi have to explore areas he could not explore with a man's story? Why did a Mexican male author, newly established in his role as a secular national writer, turn to writing a novel ostensibly for women soon after his first fictional experiment?

It seems that Lizardi was led to write *La Quijotita* by the example of French writers, such as Rousseau and Fénelon, whose treatises on the education of young men and women circulated in Mexico. He also saw in the bookstores and stalls evidence of women's appetite for literature in books such as the multivolume *Galería de mugeres fuertes* [Gallery of Strong Women], written by the French Jesuit Pierre Lemoyne and published in Spanish translation in Madrid in the 1790s; this provided a historical panorama of heroic women. In the Abadiano collection, indicating probable women readers, one finds *Las gracias de la niñez y placeres del amor maternal* [The Joys of Childhood and the Pleasures of Maternal Love], written by L. F. Jauffret and translated by Celedonio García Gutiérrez (Madrid, 1804), and reading miscellanies such as the *Almacén de las señoritas adolescentes, ó Dialogos de una sabia directora con sus nobles discípulas* [Treasures for Adolescent Young Ladies, or Dialogues between a Wise Director with Her Noble Disciples] (Madrid, 1804). Written in French by Madame le Prince de Beaumont and translated by Plácido Barco López, this latter work is a curious mixture of history and geography in which female voices even talk about the discovery of America and owning property there (vol. 2). Printed in Spain, works like the long poem by "El Filósofo Incógnito" dedicated to the queen, *La muger feliz, dependiente del mundo y de la fortuna* [The Happy Woman, Dependent on the World and Fortune] (Madrid, fourth edition 1804), and, by an anonymous author, *Memorias para la historia de la virtud, sacadas del Diario de una señorita* [Memoires for a History of Virtue, Taken from the Diary of a Young Woman] (Alcalá, 1792) are also present (the latter story is set in Italy and has English-named characters).

Finally, there was the religious literature targeted for women that generally was printed in Mexico, thereby suggesting its greater availability. Often written by women, this material points to female readers. For example, the Abadiano collection contains *Vida De la M. R. M. Sor Mariana Juana Nepomuceno, Fundadora y abadesa del monasterio de religiosas Capuchinas titulado Ntra. Sra. de Guadalupe y Santa Coleta* [Life of . . ., Founder and Abbess of the Monastery of Women Capuchines Called Our Lady of Guadalupe and Santa Coleta] (México, 1809) and, by María Francisco de Nava, *Sueño alégorico por la mexicana . . . dedicado a la religion, objeto amable de la antigua y nueva España* [Allegorical Reverie by the Mexican . . . dedicated to religion, beloved object of Old and New Spain] (México, 1809).

These shorter works, twenty-nine and eleven pages respectively, produced domestically and sold unbound, would have been cheaper than the foreign books.

Despite the fact that many English novels, translated into Spanish in Europe, came into the colony, the French novel seems to have been the preferred taste in Mexico. In the decade after independence, works like *Oscar y Amanda, ó los descendientes de la abadía* by Miss Regina-Maria Roche (translated by Carlos José Melcior, and published in Mexico by Galván in 1832) show a developing reliance on English production. However, it is not certain whether just women, or both women and men, read these novels.

Indeed, it is difficult to be precise about the extent of women's reading in Mexico at this moment. The first edition of *La Quijotita* has no list of subscribers for either volume 1 or 2. In the case of volume 1 of the first edition of the *Periquillo*, there is one woman's name listed (Doña Ignacia Flores) among the eighty-eight subscribers; and, of the fourteen persons outside Mexico City in Silao and Guanajuato, none is a woman. Of the eighty-seven subscribers for the second edition of the *Periquillo*, none is a woman. For the first edition of *Noches tristes* there were forty-three subscribers in Mexico City and forty-eight in Oaxaca (no woman in either list). One gathers a clearer view of women's role in reading and writing at that time from the evidence of journalism. Many women, in their own names and pseudonymously, wrote pamphlets and contributed letters and essays to the *Diario de México*.[4] Women-related topics fill its pages; for example, writers such as Juan Wenceslao Sánchez de la Barquera[5] increasingly recognized their participation in public discourse and appreciated their special needs. Articles appeared on the new Caesarean operation,[6] on midwives and child-rearing,[7] on the custom attributed to women of eating dirt.[8] The *Diario* in 1805 even printed a series of letters from a Miss Harrington in Bristol to a Miss Norwich in London on subjects such as courting.

Education of women appears to have surfaced in Mexico at this time because it was a European topic, thereby suggesting modernization and Mexico's merger into world culture. The fashion focussed attention on the shift of power from a court aristocracy (in whose culture women, their dress, and their treatment were important) to an emerging bourgeoisie.[9] However, if marriage and training of the young in obligations of citizenship were newly important ends for women's education in Europe (where some of the books used in American education were written), these values assumed a different character in Mexico. There lessons on one's social responsibilities, civility, and refinement, which book titles and newspaper articles designated for women, were complicated by colonialism's historic treatment of women; in the colony women (and Indians) often resisted modernizing change because, although they had been victimized by the male Conquest, they were especially brainwashed to be self-effacing and conservative by the Church.

The external signs of this new education (dress, manners, familiarity with classical authors and international topics), embraced by some, were recognized by others, however, to be only a new and different way by which the Mexican elite might continue to set itself off from the rest of the population and cultivate its parasitism. It must have been puzzling to Mexicans to understand how acquisition of curious facts such as the beauty secrets of Roman matrons,[10] which the new literature presented, was really going to uplift Mexican society. Bourgeois values, which were changing the cult of gallantry in European capitals and introducing new values in Mexico, were often ridiculed by old-fashioned Mexicans. As I discuss below with respect to *Don Catrín*, many retained retrograde attitudes of military honor and women's corollary role in that code of male identity; and they resented the changes brought by a commercial society such as England.

To complicate the Mexican condition still further, women at the upper levels of Mexican society had historically played an important role in cementing relations between Mexican and Peninsular businesses through marriage ties. Thus the cultural loyalties of the women of this important class, who lived in the capital and in the provinces, lay somewhere between the Spanish aristocracy and the new trading elite. At the middle level of Mexican society women frequently ran small businesses such as printing presses, dressmaking shops, and food stores like *chocolaterías* (Ladd, Kicza, Arrom). "Education of women," therefore, emerged as a different phenomenon in the Mexican context; and retention of the same European set of ideas in applying the concept to Mexico shows the extent to which the notion was liberating, yet also colonizing. Although its essentially French and English connections may have partially freed Mexican men from Spanish habits of thought in allowing them to see this other sex differently, it also shaped their attitudes toward women within the confines of "civilization" and "modernity."

Two Types of Women

The story of *La Quijotita* has routinely been thought of according to the contrasting plan laid down by Lizardi in the book's prologue. The wayward life of Pomposa (nicknamed "La Quijotita"), daughter of Dionisio and Eufrosina, is supposed to satirize the tragic consequences of an improper education and false values. Her cousin, Pudenciana, daughter of Rodrigo and Matilde, is intended to be the successful product of a good education; she is a model of feminine virtue. Histories of Spanish American literature note the book as an anomaly of feminist consciousness (Peña) yet usually pass over it quickly as a moral tract, hardly novelistic and eminently forgettable. Although Fernando Alegría finds value in the representativeness of the girl's life (22), he, like others, believes that the book's sermonizing is too overwhelming when set against the picaresque passages.

Quijotita's story does not really begin until chapter 20 of the thirty-nine-chapter book. In the meantime, while the two families are shown so as to explain the behavior of their respective daughters, Lizardi elaborates his views on two questions of interest to colonials. The first is authority and the second is women's nature—or, rather, the nature of any inferior, dependent being. The position of this interrelated discussion, strategically early in the book, in addition to conveying Lizardi's thesis that a subordinate's character is formed by the particular historical authority under which one lives, suggests that these predictions for family members are applicable to other social structures.

Lizardi proceeds characteristically, first redefining *authority* by means of the "exposé" technique (which I discuss in connection with the *Periquillo*), showing how one set of beliefs and language terms might contradict another. The voice of authority in the first twenty chapters is largely that of Rodrigo, a military man [*coronel*] whose Spanish-sounding name recalls the colony's Peninsular inheritance.[11] His speech, however, in constant lectures to his wife, daughter, and, when she will listen, his sister-in-law, recasts authority. For example, he states: "only in matters of faith must we be subjected to a belief in authority; but in human matters we are free to examine whether a thing is true or not, without looking at the person who said it. And when reason or experience persuade us that what they have told us is false, not only can we but we must scorn it, whoever the author of the lie is" (16). Although here he tells his wife to disregard her aunts' advice, not allowing deference to their age and family position to interfere with critically examining their counsel, his insistence that truth be tied to reason and experience can be read more profoundly. If truth can be separated from the rank and reputation of the person who proclaims it, if articles of faith can be detached from men's worldly knowledge, then the way is clear for Mexicans to take ideas from sources the Church labeled "heretical" and "impious." Although Lizardi, a few sentences later, adds that if such respectable figures as Cicero, St. Jerome, and Padre Blanchard corroborate the findings of reason and experience, so much the better, his point is unmistakable that authority must be questioned.

Matilde follows his speech with a solemn recital of her critical procedure for evaluating the words of authority figures. She is Lizardi's "ideal reader" (that is, colonial consumer of the written and spoken word), who is learning to discriminate between kinds of authority. But, lest her critical approach be read as skepticism, which could persuade readers to disregard advice, Lizardi is careful to have the *coronel* condemn such foolish persons. These few, he says, have a nature so perverse that education rarely changes them, and they must be separated from society (men to the army and women to a convent).

In the guise, therefore, of a husband's conversation with his wife, Lizardi sets out a plan for decolonizing authoritative thought. Lizardi's male model fulfills his obligations by instructing his wife; the educational paradigm is a familiar exchange where person-to-person dialogue allows for accountability and assimilation of the lesson. The husband does not browbeat his wife; instead his tone is kind and his words are clear, permitting full understanding. Matilde accepts her husband's ideas, Lizardi says, not because she loves him or respects him or fortuitously shares his beliefs, but because reason, experience, and a corrected version of authority (the repetition is beginning to read like a catechism) tells her that what he says is true.

With Matilde and her sister Eufrosina, Lizardi portrays two types of Mexican women of the day, and their differences point to complexities in ways Mexicans saw their national development. Matilde is the old-fashioned homebody, subordinate to her husband. She dresses modestly, cooks well and economically, cares for her child properly by breast-feeding her, and entertains herself by playing the piano. Apart from her husband, her only other sources of knowledge are the traditional oral forms family women have passed down to her; she apparently exercises some judiciousness in not listening either to the also oral forms of the Indian maids (although in this she is helped by her husband's caution). Eufrosina, in contrast, represents the new woman in Mexico.[12] She has learned the lessons of French civility requiring that men defer to women; from that source she concludes that women are superior to men. She dominates her husband, ignores domestic responsibilities, dresses provocatively, spends money liberally, and opens up her home as a salon so that private and public lives, familiar and formal distinctions, are confused. In spending time in public places she abandons her daughter to the inexpert care of Indian *pilmamas*, who mistreat the girl and fill her head with fantasies.

In drawing the two characters Lizardi does more, however, than give background for the two daughters' stories. Importantly, he raises the question of women's nature: Are women superior to men, as Eufrosina's attitude, representative of upper-class values, makes it seem many Mexicans were beginning to believe? Or are women inferior to men, as Spanish custom had always dictated and Christian orthodoxy taught? The *coronel* (Lizardi) seems to come down on the side of tradition: "According to natural law, civil law and divine law, speaking generally, she is always inferior to man" (27). Women's nature—to bear and care for children—requires that they be protected from the rigors of men's work. If women are not robust enough to tame a wild animal, risk bullets in warfare, or endure long study so as to learn the arcane ways of morality and politics, he concludes:

it is left to women to be the delight, the refuge, the greatest honest pleasure of men, the repository of their confidence, peacemaker in their upsets, magnet for their affections, balm for their spirits, reward for their efforts, the answer to their hopes and the ultimate consolation in their adversities and misfortunes. It is they who are, finally, the joy of men, advisors to the wise, a shelter for military leaders, the throne of kings, asylum for the just and the first altar of saints, since all of these are the roles of a mother at whose breasts and in whose arms wise men, kings, the just and the saints were reared. (28)

Yet women were entering the public sphere in Mexico in Lizardi's day. Upper-class women did not stay at home but were seen in salons, the promenade area, the theater, and cafes. Some women, from the upper as well as the Indian classes, had actively aided the insurgents; several had been sent to prison and Lizardi would later write of these heroines in his almanac of 1825.[13] Upper-class women increasingly were demanding treatment that accorded with the new mode. Eufrosina expresses this point of view:

> This business about a woman rising from her seat in order to receive or say good-bye to men, calling them "sir" or "your grace," using their first names and not their family names, and other things such as these are remnants from the past, outdated foolishness and provincial ways. No, sir: we women must always show that we are ladies and that we deserve the attentions of men, to whom we do a great favor permitting them to serve us and offer us gifts. If we civilized women, even with the superiority which cultured fashion concedes to us, still have to suffer the boorishness, impertinent advances, and scorn of men, what would happen if we humbled ourselves the way country women do? (26)

Eufrosina's words pose a problem because female docility and submissiveness could indeed be construed as the humble behavior typical of *payas* or rustic, lower-class women; for example, Eufrosina criticizes Matilde for appearing to be "an Indian woman from the country" (48). How was a woman supposed to assert her upper-class identity if she did not act haughtily? How did Mexicans, anxious to acquire status in the world's eyes yet historically disdainful of women, advance to modernity when one important mark of civilization was thought to be adoring treatment of women? As previously protected women were venturing out into public, they needed some public recognition of their social worth; for example, the wife of a lawyer wrote to the *Diario de México* that, like the *oydora* (wife of the judge) who received the benefits of her husband's title, she should be allowed to call herself *abogada* [wife of a lawyer] (February 18, 1806).

"The mode," which Eufrosina represents, was an important colonial preoccupation because accepting it or rejecting it called into question Mexican abilities to think critically, to choose which rule (old or new) to apply. Although Lizardi censures Eufrosina and says that her foolishness is finally the fault of her husband, who has indulged her and permitted her extravagances and rebellious thoughts, his portrayal concedes her some of the wittiest lines and the most pointed, if not intellectual, challenges to traditional arguments. Her women's network characterizes preachers of virtue as either old men left behind by the world who put down women and fashion, or "dirty old men" who hypocritically disparage what they covet the most. Although this interpretation is put into the mouth of a *chata* [snub-nosed, talkative woman] and is therefore meant to be read critically, Lizardi allows her to say it and does not disprove her vision. Eufrosina's character permits Lizardi to make the point that women's nature is determined and defined by men. If a woman is mistreated by her father, husband, brother, or lover, she is damned; but if a woman has been loved and treated humanely and wisely, she will be virtuous and happy. Many of the interpolated stories Lizardi adds to the basic plot of *La Quijotita* blame men who, pagan and supposedly Christian, have taken advantage of a woman's weakness to brutalize her and deny her the boons of a family structure, if not also basic respect. "Education," therefore, was a way of talking about the abuse of women and an ignorant populace.

If Lizardi believed women were biologically, and therefore legally, unequal to men, he also credited a religious belief that spiritually men and women were equal. However, he refused to acknowledge women's spiritual superiority, as some insisted on, even though he has the *coronel* say "women are naturally more compassionate, more sensitive and bound to their religion than men" and that "the holy Church honors them and distinguishes them calling them the devout sex" (34). Here Lizardi appears to be having trouble with the Church's contradictory teaching that if woman was responsible for man's fall, she was also, as represented in the Virgin Mary and in men's sacramental experience of marriage, an important means of grace. This confusion, coupled with the fact that the Mexican woman's sense of her religious faith owed much to historical syncretism and oral teaching, made her suspect in Lizardi's Enlightenment eyes. Women's knowledge—their folk remedies, use of thoughtless proverbs, irrational piety and backward superstitions, their obsession with expensive dress and the latest fashion—caused Lizardi to wonder about the sex's supposed special gift.

In thinking about women he especially shows his discomfiture in trying to find a cause-and-effect relationship between physical realities and the "spirit," which religious and secular thinkers had said women's makeup especially demonstrated.[14] For example, he ties the timidity frequent in women to their bodily weakness. Then, in a passage meant to show Lizardi's familiarity with the latest medical knowledge, he describes nymphomania, or uterine fury as it was commonly known, making it seem that all young women, on entering puberty, might be subject to these strange fits: "All doctors know that women at the time of puberty are subject to suffering a terrible illness which is called by the name of uterine fury, which is a period of delirium or frenzy which makes them commit, by word or deed, a thousand shameful excesses which are repugnant to every respectable, modest person" (35). Although the syndrome is used to illustrate the *coronel's* belief that the body's power to dominate the spirit is great (women's modesty conquers these moments of furious passion only with difficulty), the impression is that science has demonstrated her biological frailty and, therefore, her essentially sexual nature and her moral weakness.

The modern reader is shocked by the ease with which Lizardi attributes nymphomania to all females—and dismayed by its description in a medical dictionary Lizardi might have consulted. Written by Antonio Ballano and published in Madrid in 1805, a copy of the dictionary exists in the Abadiano collection. In it one reads that nymphomania is defined as little more than normal sexual awakening, which the reading of amorous novels and exposure to lustful songs could stimulate to excess. Often found in southern countries among women of ardent temperament, the condition—referred to variously as a disordered imagination and delirium—was said to be prevalent among reclusive women whose mothers had reared them severely. The dictionary suggests marriage to be the best remedy; and Lizardi's character, in discussing the subject, echoes this by saying that, although the science of medicine knows of a cure for this illness (the medical dictionary suggests hemlock), "our Catholic religion justly prohibits it and it is illicit, permitting instead that it be substituted for by legitimate matrimony."

Today's reader is both amused at Lizardi's (and the medical authority's) crude description of "uterine fury," yet horrified by another discovery of how female sicknesses and diseases often are relative to the historical age in which they are defined. Lizardi's discussion reflects not only an Enlightenment dilemma of how to label an aspect of women's nature, which earlier discourses (one thinks of men's poetry) had ignored. His awkward logic also suggests a real fear of Mexican women at all social levels, whose conduct had perhaps not yet been educated and refined according to male standards of control. His fear may also reveal self-hatred; *woman* may stand for some biological aspect of the male self that resisted being tamed by the spirit.

If marriage was the panacea the Church taught for channeling sexual energies, for structuring the "necessary dependency" of women, for accomplishing their education, the evidence of Mexican marriages showed that the institution was far from perfect. Instances abound in *La Quijotita* of young women whose pretty faces rather than their fortune caused their downfall. Once one of them attracted a wealthy suitor, his lust and a parent's greed quickly took her from a respectable household and forced her into prostitution. Or if the suitor did marry her, the physical infatuation soon became tyranny as the frequent inequality between their two social stations asserted itself. Contemporary Spanish writers such as Leandro Fernández de Moratín also wrote of these unequal marriages critically, and Goya satirized them visually. But the Mexican version suffered the additional complication of racial differences, which made the woman's place in marriage (because she was often Indian) even more precarious.[15] It is obvious, then, that marriage, once the property of the Church, was increasingly being rethought and secularized. In Mexico the woman's point of view was being discussed because her racial nature reflected the identity of many Mexicans and her inferior nature called up colonial attitudes of self.

The *coronel*'s speeches appear to put forward a traditional view of women. Reaffirming the essential dependency of women in the belief that if women err it is because they are ignorant, and that this ignorance is the fault of men, Lizardi seems to have retreated to an old-fashioned position. In the criticism of women (upper-class women) for their vanity and taste for luxury, one understands Catholic suspicion of the sex. As a priest approvingly says to the *coronel*: "your opinions seem to me to be as old and reliable as they are sure. They are like those [opinions] which because everybody knows them no one speaks them; but they are silenced so much, that many people are ignorant of them or they pretend not to know them" (66). Yet this Spanish discourse system was competing in the colony with a new Enlightenment language. So one can read Lizardi's position as critical of both these discourses, yet confused as to what role women might have in the evolving society (that is, what third discourse might establish their position).

In *La Quijotita*, as in the *Periquillo*, Lizardi shows that a colonial subject has no control over the language others use to determine his or her identity. He or she has no essence that resists others' valorization. The correcting authorial voice of *La Quijotita* calls attention to the way that language used to depict images of women arbitrarily reflects men's thinking; the attractive dress, for example, which makes a man notice a woman, becomes a liability once he marries her and has to pay the bills. Lizardi, using the same decolonizing procedure he used in the earlier novel, ranges two vocabularies against one another not only to defend women and show men's fickleness, but also to demonstrate the way the language of dominance determines general perceptions: "their seclusion is labeled hypochondria, their economy cheapness, their prudence dullness, their affection falsity, their fidelity lack of worth, their joyousness craziness, their attentions slight emotions, their devotion hypocrisy, their generosity a throw-away commodity and, in few words, in such a deplorable situation, everything they do to please, angers. Poor women!" (66). Lizardi quotes Sor Juana's warning that women must learn that men often use words to seduce them; such words mean nothing when later these men betray the women and sully their honor publicly.

At one level this linguistic self-consciousness in Lizardi's novel conveys an increasing colonial awareness (demonstrated also in the period's newspapers and the *Periquillo*), of how Mexican identity was created by others' language. But at another level, Lizardi's portrayal of how woman is victimized by language suggests his awareness of how necessary her reclassification was to the Mexican man's sense of himself. If decolonization meant that the colony had come of age, to use the metaphor of biological growth, the Mexican male needed to think about marriage and the family. To do so, the Mexican male had to redefine "love" (by which Spanish courtly poetry and English novels had explained relations between the sexes). He also had to reevaluate "sentiment" according to his experience of the Mexican woman (whose emotional range, Lizardi might have felt, extended only to religious practices, dangerous passion, and class responses of making the Mexican male feel inferior or superior). The Mexican woman, however, could help the Mexican male declare his independence from his Spanish parents (*la madre patria*) by encouraging him to take on family status and thereby demonstrate his maturity. She could aid the Mexican male by interrupting the colonizing cycle and educating Mexican youth.

Quijotita's Education

The choice of "la Quijotita" as Pomposa's nickname recalls Cervantes' *Quijote*.[16] One of the young men who familiarly surround Pomposa explains: "Don Quijote was a crazy person and Doña Pomposa is another fool. Don Quijote had very lucid moments when he talked beautifully, so long as he did not get to the subject of chivalry; and Doña Pomposa also has her moments when her conversation does not displease. But she becomes delirious when she touches on the topics of love and beauty" (166). Like Don Quijote, Quijotita ventures out into the world, a cardinal sin for women. Convinced of her great beauty and her special mission, "born to avenge her sex of the humiliation they suffer at the hands of men," she battles men. She enters combat confident that her beauty is all the weaponry she needs and she fears no one. And, like Don Quijote, she aspires to fame, if not honor; she trusts that her beauty will win it for her in the form of a husband's title.

Lizardi thus absolves Quijotita of any inborn perversity or natural problem such as nymphomania. Her waywardness as an adult is entirely the product of an undisciplined childhood. Left to her own devices and to the care of the maids who alternately spoil and ignore her, she learns nothing useful (Pudenciana has learned to read, write, do sums, sew, embroider, draw, play the piano, and fix watches). So that Pudenciana may not become like her cousin ("restless, idle, fun-loving, vain, conceited, and arrogant," 102), the *coronel* takes his daughter to the country; and after she is married off, the reader knows little about her.

The novel is clearly Quijotita's story. As a little girl she is caught smoking a cigar, thus frightening her mother when she takes sick and scandalizing her mother and her mother's friends. But the *coronel* defends the child, saying she has observed tobacco offered as a social amenity and has only imitated what she has seen—anyhow, he says, smoking is a household practice that is not necessarily bad. An important clue to her character is her speech. Because Quijotita does not spend her time reading, or when she reads she does so badly, her speech reveals her superficial knowledge and her muddled mind. The *coronel* explains:

> The whole cause of the ignorance and pedantry of Pomposa is her father's laziness and failure to take precautions.At first he did not care about whether she was educated and later he permitted her to read without making any distinctions among the books that he had bought in order to adorn his office. As a result the girl has picked a little here and a little there without the least discrimination. She has filled her head with a multitude of heterogeneous or unlike ideas, which she trots out when she wishes. And because she lacks a true knowledge of the matters she is talking about, as well as the true meanings of the terms with which she expresses herself, most times she utters tremendous absurdities. In truth it is a shame that she has not benefitted from their instruction because when she reasons in a balanced way one gathers that she is not foolish and she has read something. (102–3)

Lizardi's characterization of Quijotita's reading makes her seem less like a female in need of a man's protection and more like the colonial who chooses books because they decorate someone's office, acquires their vocabularies without understanding their meaning, and then interjects them indiscriminately into conversations. Quijotita is constantly held up to ridicule because of the discrepancy between her pompous-sounding speech and her ignorance; at a country wedding, for example, the fact that she does not know how to ride a horse contradicts her fine words and expensive saddle.

Indeed, an important difference in the two girls' educations is the way each has learned to read. In this Lizardi diverges from European Enlightenment writers, whose counsel to female readers (or to their parents) was concerned with protecting them from dangerous literature such as the novel. Instead of criticizing the novel, Lizardi, through his voice, the *coronel*, concentrates attention on the catechism and the way this book harmed colonial society by reducing complex theological questions into short, dogmatic statements of belief, and by giving the impression that learning was the memorization of words. The catechism was a book particularly associated with women's, children's, or Indians' education, thus suggesting colonial practice.

The *coronel* instructs his daughter at home, orally, making sure that she understands concepts such as the Holy Trinity by means of homely examples that suit her understanding. Pomposa, although she has learned to read in school [*amiga*] and has memorized the catechism, is ignorant of what the book's words mean. Reading in and of itself, Lizardi is saying by means of Pomposa's character, is not necessarily good; it can even hinder true learning if one thinks one knows a subject simply because one has mastered the words on a page. Yet Lizardi's criticism of the catechism is nuanced; rejection of moral absolutes and simple ways of teaching them was dangerous, as civil war and intellectual debate among meagerly endowed, self-interested Mexicans demonstrated. In an increasingly secular society, the catechism's religious education was important, not just for the individual soul's salvation, but also because of the social lessons and the restraint of the passions it was thought to teach. Lizardi's use of the novel, therefore, was meant to enrich the catechism, if not to substitute for it, in teaching colonials to consider the real meaning of a book's printed words.

Matilde, Rodrigo's other pupil, enacts the role of the adult learner. Of basic intelligence, she requires a reasoned, clear explanation; and she brings to her role in the dialogue trust in her husband the teacher and a desire for knowledge applicable to her sphere of activity. As the reader follows their exchanges and the novel's other dialogues (which, like the dialectical format of many of the political pamphlets of the day, sometimes set out irreconcilable differences), he or she learns to scrutinize the transmission of knowledge.

Pomposa is prone to superstition, not just to the patently false beliefs of the Indian women but also to the pieties of the *beatas* who encourage blind faith in such things as saints' miracles. One night she is awakened by a vision of the devil which, the *coronel* quickly proves, is only a shadow. But Pomposa and her mother, shaken, vow to begin a new life. Their conversion, because it has not been based on true religious principles, is mocked in Lizardi's description of their devotional practices. In their mechanical recitation of the *Padre nuestro*, for example, mother and daughter routinely interrupt the prayer with trivialities. They spend their days running from one church to another, commenting only that such and such a

church is beautifully decorated, the priest is divine, and they can successfully hear "eight Masses in an instant" (232). Pomposa even becomes a
hermit; and in Lizardi's version of Cervantes's book burning, Eufrosina
burns her daughter's pious books (although Eufrosina exercises this judgment, the reader understands some wisdom in putting an end to such
foolish piety).

The story then accelerates. Mother and daughter bankrupt Dionisio
and he leaves. They mourn but continue their extravagances. Pomposa
has many suitors but she scorns them all, hoping to find one with title and
money. When all but one have left, she allows him his way; and, pregnant,
she has an abortion. She flees in the face of her mother's anger; when her
mother claims her at the *coronel*'s house, his words suggest their future:
"Poor girl! She is going to become a prostitute at her mother's side and
she will live as a mercenary from her body" (265). Although Lizardi de-
picts woman's fall in the sexual terms that he avoided in the *Periquillo*'s
male picaresque story, he handles this portion of Pomposa's waywardness
quickly and delicately.

Mother and daughter spend the last of their money in a grand party,
with bountiful food, dancing, and gambling (an excuse for Lizardi to be-
moan this affliction, "more destructive than the most desolating war,"
that the Spanish revenue-collecting "agents of tyranny" have visited on
Mexico, 272). Dionisio returns with a long-lost inheritance; he dies.
Pomposa marries a Spaniard who claims, falsely, to be a *marqués* (Lizardi
complains that there are many such *gachupines* [hated Spaniards] in
Mexico, 285). He takes all her money. Pomposa and Eufrosina turn to
prostitution and alcohol. In a last scene before dying, Pomposa confesses
her erring ways and reveals that she and her mother were even imprisoned for robbery.

Pomposa's story of error and sin was surely meant as a warning to
young, inexperienced female readers. The depiction of a not-talked-
about, or only-whispered-about, world was meant to show them a life
they did not know just as, the *coronel* approvingly said, the theater made
his daughter aware of adultery. Yet the picaresque story was also intended
to be an inducement to read; it was the entertaining ingredient that new
readers required in the otherwise prescriptive work.

In his prologue to *La Quijotita*, the author reports that a female correspondent, "La Curiosa," requested that Lizardi produce a work for fe-

male readers that they could read and learn from for themselves. She complained that earlier authors, in producing books on women's education, either wrote for men or converted their instruction into a satire of the sex. She said that women were not accustomed to reading serious literature; therefore, it had to be appropriately entertaining so as to encourage them to read. Her request for lightness, for laughter, is, therefore, complicated. If Lizardi had to avoid humor at their expense, he also had to find entertainment in a satiric mode, which would draw his readers into his fictional world, yet at the same time distance them morally from it.

Lizardi's obvious literary models for *La Quijotita*, which Peninsular tastes can be seen to have developed and sanctioned, are the picaresque/ satiric mode and the *Quijote*. However, the book form, which I believe importantly underlies the narrative and silently guides readers' responses to this domestic experiment with print, is the catechism. Lizardi wants his novel to play against this kind of devotional literature, which is the type of writing most of his women readers would have been familiar with and which epitomized the blind acceptance of print by colonials of both sexes. In asking that colonial readers question this kind of authoritative book, he satirizes a *beata*'s blind faith: "I know that when a thing is set out in bold letters it has already passed by the eyes of the censors, who are very well-read. So when they give permission for something to be published, they must know that it is very certain and that there is no danger that everyone read it" (218). Lizardi wants his readers to take on themselves the task of judging a book, to accept or reject this form of authority they trusted unquestioningly (either because the Inquisition said they should, or because the subject matter excluded them from any critical perspective). Rethinking the catechism, then, a book that symbolized colonial obeisance before the text, can be seen to play a large part in the decolonizing design of the Spanish American novel.

Pascual

Woman, as I have shown, was increasingly audible and visible in Mexico's discourse world in the first decades of the nineteenth century. She was represented as the indigenous voice of truth (La Malinche and the *paya* who brought war news from the provinces). She was the mother responsible for educating new citizens, and the feminine personification of national struggle (the Virgen de Guadalupe). Men talked about women and their special needs in the new context of education and the family; and women were beginning to speak for themselves in previously male-dominated public areas.

La Quijotita's textual portrayal of Mexican woman—but also the novel's illustrations—were important ways in which Mexican readers saw this figure, which earlier colonial literature ignored, veiled, or beautified beyond recognition. The engraver for the first edition showed three kinds of Mexican women (one old-fashioned, one modern, and the third, seen from behind and barefoot, Indian).[17] Pomposa's décolletage is shockingly portrayed, and a child nestled at a woman's breast suggests breast-feeding. Three types of Mexican men (one traditionally Spanish, another dressed in the new French mode, and a third, a rustic) are also depicted (although in the scene in which Pascual appears only two of these types are shown). The rustic's Mexican garb—broad-brimmed hat, serape, boots and spurs—would have caused readers to confront their non-Spanish identity in this portrayal of class and race. One also finds among the pictures scenes of crimes.

Therefore, Lizardi's interest in women and the topics their role seemed to point to must be seen as related to his awareness of Mexico's class and racial distinctions. His fictional portrayal of woman and the Indian, which began in the *Periquillo*, effectively stops in *La Quijotita*; his last two novels focus largely on upper-class men. Women and Indians will only appear later in his theater pieces, almanacs, and political pamphlets (most particularly, "El indio y la india del pueblo de Actopán," 1820). After 1820, although other writers attempted to capture the peculiarities of Indian speech, Lizardi only used this language in occasional pamphlets. Therefore, I believe he did not attempt another long, imaginative exploration of this dimension of Mexican life because *La Quijotita*, in which he combined Indians and women into one grouping, apparently satisfied him.

The one instance in *La Quijotita* in which Lizardi attempts to reproduce Indian speech, by imitating its pronunciation and including its special vocabulary, occurs prominently in chapter 1. There, in a discussion of breast-feeding, one of Eufrosina's friends describes the practice as decidedly *not* one of "these things for persons of our class, but for poor women and ordinary people" (2). Matilde nurses her baby, although it drains her;

but Eufrosina sends hers to wet nurses. Then an episode begins in which Pascual, a *payo* and the manager of a ranch the *coronel* owns, enters to report a dispute in broken speech. He had grabbed two puppies from the breasts of a woman who had been told her milk was bad and so had used the puppies to suck her milk; her baby was languishing beside her because the *chichi* [wet nurse] she had hired for him was gone. Pascual indignantly recounts this injustice and then describes the woman's abundant physical attributes in barnyard terms: "if you saw her, my master, what a healthy color she has and she's fatter than a blooming capon. By my word, with those two huge teats, she would be worth a fortune as a milk cow" (4).

This fictive uncovering of woman's body, albeit in connection with a topic licensed by Enlightenment discourse, reveals an aspect of Lizardi's thought relative to Mexican women. Pascual's speech, intended as comedy early in the book, sets the tone of the novel; but it also joins women and the Indian classes in an imaginative union, which lasts throughout the reading. Lizardi sees biological functions in class terms, and the comment he puts in the mouth of Eufrosina's friend reproduces a typical view of both as useful only for work and breeding.

A woman giving suck is also seen in a contemporary political pamphlet of the period. Published in 1822, the pamphlet, "Ya no dá leche la vaca ¿qué tetas mamará el leon?" [The cow no longer gives milk, From what teats will the lion nurse?],[18] could not have provided Lizardi with inspiration for his breast-feeding imagery in *La Quijotita*. Still, this politicization of woman's body—and particularly the breasts' function of giving milk—was a standard part of the consciousness of America, which Spanish colonial allegory taught; one thinks of the representations of America as a female Indian nude. Thus, Lizardi's use of the image, and his readers' understanding of it, must be seen to reflect this linkage of woman, the land, and colonial exploitation. The pamphlet begins:

Mexico, this milk cow, so fat and so rich that from the beginning of the sixteenth century (1521) until 27 September 1821, has given generously and with astonishing prodigiousness to Spain and all of Europe. What am I saying? to the whole world—milk, *jocoque* [an Aztec word describing a food made of bitter milk], *coajade* [?], butter, cheese, curds, and a thousand other products or compounds that are made from that simple liquid. Tenoxtitlan, that sad, disgraced Indian mother of the most unfortunate sons who, over the long space of 300 years, by pinching and kicking have been violently, barbarously and cruelly torn from the sweet and tender lap of their dear, accursed mother so that the Spaniards and any other foreigners who have recently arrived could freely extract avariciously the delicious, nutritious and valuable juice of her mammary glands,* until satiating if that were possible the dropsical thirst of human greed. . . . (*the note refers to a "hieroglyph [with which in a pasquinade the Mexicans satirized the viceroy Lacroix] which represented America in the form of a large-teated Indian woman at whose feet her own children were lying, expressing in their languishing look the cruel hunger which was devouring their stomachs, and the foreigners, or fancy little Spaniards stuck right on her tits and sucking greedily.")

The semiscatological tone of the political pamphlet resembles Pascual's speech. Lizardi frequently engaged in humor in his novels and political pamphlets, but he generally refrained from ribaldry. Thus, the Pascual episode is a notable deviation from his customary wit and satire.

I, therefore, move to a discussion of what I think is an important subtext of La Quijotita.[19] I do not mean to detract from the book's literal message on women's education. But I think Lizardi wants his reflections on women's dependency, inferiority, carnality, and ignorance to further the discussion of colonialism, begun in the Periquillo. In the long speech by the coronel, Lizardi links class affiliation with tendencies to vice or virtue; and Pascual is cited as an example of a simple rustic, pure of heart, whose class members generally "are unfamiliar with the dissimulation, lying, vanity, and all of that which recommends them to all sensible people. It's true that they have never known the refinements, courtesies and other cajoleries of the cities; but, on the other hand, they possess many moral, Christian virtues with which they live happily in their station of life and which assure them eternal life. It is a shame that they are educated so badly and that they get so little instruction in their religion!" (115). However, the coronel is ambivalent in deciding whether education, which has been one of the supposed glories of Spanish colonialism, should be considered to have been good or bad. City dwellers are described in the passage as having been spoiled by the lessons of civilized society; rural peoples, less exposed to it, are better. Consequently, one reasons, either Indians—and women folk—are possessed of a superior nature and it is better to leave them uneducated, or colonial education needs to be examined for the harm it does.

Implicit in the discussion is the question of how Indians might have acquired Christian virtues without having had the benefits of Spanish religious instruction. It is possible that Lizardi is suggesting Fray Servando Teresa de Mier's recent, controversial theory that Spain did not bring Christianity to Mexico but that instead the indigenous population had miraculously received its own pre-Conquest message of Christian salvation through appearances there of the Virgen and Santo Tomás. This theory, which Mier preached in a sermon in 1794, stimulated great debate in Spain and Mexico. In 1797 Juan Bautista Muñoz, an important Spanish historian of the Indies, had published a critique of the Mexican's theory that contradicted established accounts of the Conquest of Mexico by Spanish historians. Mier answered Muñoz in two letters, and the Mexican José Miguel Guridi y Alcocer also refuted Muñoz's arguments in an "Apología" in 1820 (Lizardi's name appears on the subscription list).[20]

Lizardi's fictional double, a young man in need of the *coronel*'s instruction, voices a view of Mexico's Indians—one that prevailed among many of the colony's elite. Indians, he says, have a hereditary ignorance. Nature seems to have made them "grindingly poor, rough-mannered, lying, superstitious, suspicious and many drunkards and thieves" (115). But the *coronel* corrects this view, retorting that character is a consequence of "the climate, the customs, the laws and the religion where one is born." He links "character" to "tradition" (that is, socially determinative factors, rather than biology): "I understand by character that adherence to and enthusiasm with which each nation conserves the manners its elders taught it or which it successively accumulates during the course of time" (116).

The *coronel* then goes on to emphasize how "character" is formed by education and argues that a lack of education has produced these so-called Indian "qualities." The discussion, although it seems to recall early Spanish complaints that American nature was rude and required the intervention of Spain to refine it, instead can be seen to argue that nurture rather than nature has been important in causing these conditions. In an audacious speech by the *coronel*, Lizardi traces educational neglect in the colony to imperial policies. He describes the boons the Spanish kings wished for their colonial subjects; but, in telling of the schools that were supposed to be founded in outpost areas but never were, he shifts to the subjunctive mood to suggest that the kings' wishes were not carried out:

Our sovereigns, thoroughly imbued with this principle [the need for education in the governed areas], have wanted to carry out this divine precept. The repeated, pious orders that they have expedited over the years so that schools might be established in every town [para que se establezcan escuelas en todos los pueblos], the academies that have been founded in this and the other continent, the schools that have been begun under royal patronage, the prizes that they have wanted to provide to honor merit, etc., are unequivocal proofs that they have tried to stamp out shiftlessness and ignorance (and, therefore, misery and vice) from amongst their vassals. As Catholics the kings detested that iniquitous axiom of the false politician Machiavelli that said it was advisable for the metropolis to keep its colonies poor and stupid as if indigence and barbarism were more powerful in subjecting men to reason, rather than mediocrity, and doctrine or education [como si la indigencia y la barbarie fueran más poderosas para sujetar a los hombres a la razón, que no la mediocridad, y la doctrina o enseñanza]. (117)

If many colonials were poor and stupid because of educational deficiencies, the *coronel* concludes that blame must be placed on the priests and teachers responsible for their instruction. He asks why money is spent "on little parties, . . . soldiers' uniforms during Holy Week, theatrical works, duels, and other useless frivolities" (118).

In the quote, Lizardi attributes to Machiavelli a deliberate policy of colonial ignorance. Below, in discussing *Don Catrín*, I show how, in that book also, Lizardi invoked Machiavelli to identify a code of evil by which the colonies were managed. The point is here, however, that Lizardi, in addition to hypothesizing the laziness and perversity of minor colonial officials to explain educational inadequacies in Mexico, verbalizes the possibility of a consistent imperialism, which silently contradicted official pronouncements and operated to the detriment of the colonial population. This admission, for detecting the emergence of a decolonizing discourse, is enormous. Perhaps in the context of a work written for women, in which he was approaching taboo subjects, Lizardi felt free to voice such a damning thought.

This discussion of Spanish education, supposedly designed to save souls and eradicate barbarism, but which many Mexicans saw as a calculated attempt to impose discipline through ignorance and false knowledge, shows a decolonizing awareness of the historical record. Words (benevolent-seeming imperial legislation) are contrasted with deeds (the ugly realities of colonial ignorance, and lack of schools and intellectual incentives, but also the harmful labels that denigrated indigenous peoples by denying their educability). *La Quijotita*, therefore, in its consideration of colonial human nature extends the topic of education, begun in the *Periquillo*, to its logical conclusion.

8

Noches tristes y día alegre

The Catechism and the Language of Faith

The first edition (1818) of what is known today as *Noches tristes y día alegre y dignamente aprovechado* [Sad Nights and Happy Day Worthily Put to Use] contained only *Noches tristes* (one wonders if Lizardi considered its shorter, tragic story complete). In 1819 the longer text, with its *Día alegre* conclusion, appeared as volume 2 of Lizardi's collection of miscellany, *Ratos entretenidos.* The remarkable fact that a second edition was published after only one year is made even more extraordinary by Lizardi's reprinting, as part of the volume, of José Cadalso's *Noches lúgubres.* (The modern reader, who worries about copyright law, marvels at this appropriation of the Spanish writer's work.)[1]

Noches tristes represents Lizardi's effort to come to grips with religious discourse. This language was important to colonials because, from the moment of the Conquest, it functioned as a medium for teaching obedience to temporal and spiritual authority. More than just a linguistic register or a literary category, religious discourse was a set of attitudes toward language, a whole vocabulary and syntactical system that moved into one's mental frame and furnished its ideology; in this it differed from Saussurean notions of *langue* according to which the individual might freely borrow from that language pool. Its assumptions of belief, its prescriptions of faithful practice and morality, allowed no deviation. If one trusted in the absolute power of the Church and accepted its mediating role in the salvation of one's soul, one was then obliged to proceed in faith according to its terms.

Its suppositions and iteration mostly provided the only opportunity Americans had to exercise their minds beyond the mundane, according to a discipline different from the self's and society's material needs. The Church's sermons, edicts, celebration of the sacraments, and so on reinforced the language on a regular basis; and written materials such as catechisms, saints' lives, treatises on living and dying well, compilations of prayers and sermons, and the like guided adults and children by naming private urges and desires, formulating thought, and categorizing what the individual could only guess at. The priest was often the only contact many had with someone who knew a little Latin and was familiar with history, theology, and world events; consequently, intellectual life for many Mexicans was only possible within the confines of the Church. Censors, in reviewing foreign literature for distribution in Mexico, measured its morality against Church teachings.

In the latter years of Spain's colonial rule, the still vital Franciscan catechetical tradition of Fray Pedro de Gante, as well as the strong Jesuit emphasis on preaching, continued to make colonials aware that public utterances would be judged for their faithful consequences. Religious rhetorical handbooks, such as Fray Luis de Granada's *Retórica eclesiástica* (Spanish translation, 1770, and published in multiple editions in the last decades of the eighteenth century), set guidelines for speaking and listening, which in turn affected standards for secular writing and reading. Hugh Blair's rhetoric handbook, which had just been translated and was available in Mexico, was only beginning to set forth rhetoric in terms other than religious oratory.

Lizardi's choice of subject matter in *Noches tristes*, then, after writing two picaresque novels, extends their stories of delinquency to their political and philosophical logical ends—the colony's connection with Church authority and religion's hold over men's lives. The discussion was particularly pertinent since Church officials had just imposed a spiritual penalty, excommunication, on Mexicans for the political crime of insurrection; both the rebel priests and ordinary Mexicans were affected. If Church and civil authorities had appeared to work together in the past, if spiritual and political agendas had seemed to coincide and no one complained, now many Mexicans disagreed with the judgment of excommunication and resented the confusion between the two sources of authority. Ecclesiastical privilege had historically exempted the clergy from civil jurisdiction,[2] yet this privilege was called into account when the viceroy procured the censure of Hidalgo and Morelos. Some approved of the viceroy's actions but others thought the priests to be above men's laws and resented the cruel treatment they were suffering at the hands of civil authorities. Many Mexicans supported the priests even in their lawlessness and thought the priests were selfless in acting in behalf of their parishioners to correct injustice.

Excommunication of the priests was one thing; excommunication of their followers en masse was another. As one excommunicated insurgent wrote in a bitter letter to Morelos's newspaper, *Correo americano del sur,* good lay people were prevented from the sacraments of communion and marriage, thus forcing them into civil unions and illegal alliances which, he complained, contributed to widespread immorality, and the abandonment of wives and children. He concluded, carefully distinguishing between Church and state: "We insurgents are not heretics, we respect the Holy Church and its ministers, we agree on one faith" (164).

Thus, Lizardi's story of despair and faith, its troubling pairing of sincere questions and prescribed answers, addressed contemporary concerns. The book's words sounded pious, but the text's underlying structure can be seen to have been asking fundamental—decolonizing—questions about religion's absolute-sounding language and, by extension, the language of other sources of authority. Censors apparently gave permission for the book's publication because of Lizardi's misleading claims that it preached Catholic orthodoxy. Between 1814 and 1820, as I have shown, the Inquisition imposed strict controls on the publication and circulation of printed materials, as well as on all writing and speaking in the colony; and these were not lifted again until October 1820.[3] The last volume of the *Periquillo* was suppressed and only circulated clandestinely; just the first two volumes of *La Quijotita* were licensed to be published when the book was first written and probably only passed the censorship board by claiming to educate women; *Don Catrín* was never published during Lizardi's lifetime.

However, *Noches tristes* earned the censors' approval because the book seemed orthodox but also because Lizardi claimed that he was imitating a Spanish author: "Since I read the *Lugubrious Nights* of Colonel José Cadalso, I planned to write another *Sad Ones,* imitating it. And, in fact, I wrote it and now present it with the necessary license and approval. I do not flatter myself that I have achieved my intent; rather I know that just as it is impossible for rue to equal the palm in height . . . so it is impossible for my poor pen to equal the eloquence that one admires in each line of the works of the celebrated, modern writer" (113).⁴ By publishing his book together with Cadalso's, by describing his inspiration as a desire to imitate him, Lizardi apparently obeyed an eighteenth-century aesthetic that admired emulation of classical models.⁵ By invoking a Peninsular predecessor, whose other books were already known and permitted in the colony, the Mexican author could conceal his originality. Lizardi's imitating, self-deprecating pose was probably convincing because most colonials believed that one of their own could not attain to Spanish excellence.

Colonial literature has often been thought to be imitative, slavishly reproducing metropolitan patterns. As long as a territory remained a colony, governing tastes supposedly prevailed there, limiting the few domestic works licensed to be printed to those adaptations of European artistic modes.⁶ Looking back on that literary production, modern readers often scorn these works as inferior copies thoughtlessly repeating styles that had become outmoded in the metropolis.⁷

However, I want to argue that, for purposes of avoiding censorship and having one's effort published and read, this impression may have been encouraged by colonial writers.⁸ In both *Noches tristes* and *La Quijotita*, in which Lizardi claims to be imitating Peninsular models, one reads profound Mexican concerns. In Lizardi's careful statement at the beginning of *Noches tristes* that he is imitating Cadalso's style (113), one perceives a tactic to draw censors' attention to aesthetic questions of language and away from the book's content. Spell suggests (*Noches* xii–xiii) that Lizardi added his *Día alegre* ending to his novel because he read Cadalso's new conclusion.⁹ However, I believe Spell's theory only explains half the story. I think that Lizardi reprinted Cadalso's *Noches lúgubres* back to back with his own (adding Cadalso's new ending only after the book was printed) so as to direct attention away from his surreptitious questioning of religious language. The miscellany in which the novel appeared also included eight essays that touched on poverty, exploitation, colonial ignorance, and the history of Mexico City's cathedral (that is, the Church's presence in the colony). These essays might have offended the censors had they been read more closely.

That confessing imitation might have been a widely used ruse is

Cadalso's own claim, in seeking publication for his work in Madrid in 1789–90, that he was imitating the English style of Edward Young, whose influential work, *The Complaint, or Night Thoughts on Life, Death, and Immortality* (1742–47), was available in Spanish by way of a French translation. At one point in his *Cartas marruecas* Cadalso tells of the difficulties of publishing in Spain:

> The Spaniard who publishes his works today writes them with immense care and he trembles when the time arrives to publish them. That's why many men, whose compositions would be useful to the *patria*, hide them. . . . I have dealings with only a few people; but even from among my acquaintances I dare to aver that very valuable manuscripts on all manner of learned subjects could be brought forward. Today these manuscripts lie in a dusty grave when they have hardly emerged from the cradle. Of others I can also affirm that for every book chapter that has been published 99 others have been kept back."[10]

Cadalso testifies (*Cartas* lxvi and lxvii) to the difficulties of writing in a country where censorship was thought to be necessary to protect the *vulgo* from dangerous ideas. By the eighteenth century Spain was so dependent on French taste that its cultural production and its colonies' were similar in their controlled nature.[11]

E. Allison Peers, suspicious of Cadalso's claim that he imitated Young's style, concluded that Cadalso sought to enhance the value of his own work by linking it to Young's; Peers then says: "It would be difficult to find any other reason for a proceeding rather uncommon in literature—the exaggeration of one's debt to another" (414–15).[12] Similarly, in their absorption with Lizardi's sources for *Noches tristes*, critics have debated whether the Mexican imitated Cadalso or Young (Cabañas; Yancey); most have read literally Lizardi's claim that he was inspired by Cadalso's style to imitate it. Thus, they have concluded that *Noches tristes* marks one of the first attempts to import sentimental Romantic ideas into Spanish America and have dismissed Lizardi's work as a poor copy of something of true literary value, European Romanticism.[13] However, I believe that *Noches tristes*, normally considered a minor work in Lizardi's *obra* and the corpus of Spanish American literature, is rather an instructive example of a work whose apparent imitation disguised tough thinking.

Doubt and Belief

In many ways *Noches tristes* is like the Catholic catechism in posing questions about the source of creation and order in the universe, good and evil, man's origins, and so on. After the initial passage in which Lizardi addresses his readers, no narrative voice intervenes in the dramatic dialogues. Yet the book is also a kind of colonial *Candide* in that negative experience constantly contradicts the received lessons of optimism.

Teófilo, the protagonist, undergoes a series of misadventures over four successive nights as a result of which he discusses his faith (and faith in general) with a series of interlocutors. Innocent of any crime, he is jailed in a case of mistaken identity. When he is finally freed, he learns his wife and children have fled in search of him, and he sets off in pursuit. The next night, while traveling through the forest in a storm, he argues with his friend Rodrigo as to which has suffered the greater misfortune. He tries to counter Rodrigo's accusation that some cruel power in the universe delights in seeing him suffer; instead, using a common metaphor of the day, Teófilo insists that God is not Saturn, who devours his own children. Teófilo utters the belief that He is a God who should be understood as the Creator of the universe and who is not disposed to interrupt its order by the working of miracles. Men frequently cause their own misfortunes; and besides, what they often perceive as reverses are really blessings that a benevolent Providence has wisely ordained. Teófilo recoils when Rodrigo reveals he has murdered his father and gives thanks when a providential bolt of lightning illuminates the path and saves him from the abyss into which Rodrigo, unrepentant, has just fallen.

Teófilo continues to encounter tragedy. As it is getting light, he stumbles on Martín and his wife, poor farmers, whom thieves have robbed and beaten. They bring the wife, who is almost dead, home; and on the third night Teófilo goes to request help from a doctor and a priest. Because Martín is too poor to pay them, they refuse to come. The wife dies; her new baby dies; and Teófilo continues to preach God's goodness to the heartbroken husband and father.

On the fourth night Teófilo has sought refuge from a storm in a cemetery. As he is wondering what sin he has committed to bring down heaven's curse, a grave digger comes by to disinter a body he has just buried. He is acting, not out of any perverse passion for the dead woman, which motivated Cadalso's hero in a similar scene, but because the woman is dressed in rich clothing that he can sell to get food for his poor family. When Teófilo sees the dead woman's face, he thinks—mistakenly, it turns out—it is his wife. He faints and is brought back to consciousness in the grave digger's miserable hut. There, he is reunited with his wife, who happens to be passing by with her uncle, a kind clergymen. The story (the only emotionally graphic one of all Lizardi's novels) ends with a sermon by the clergyman that God's justice will ultimately prevail; those who deny charity will be punished and those who share their wealth will be rewarded. Teófilo is happily reunited with his family; and gifts to the needy are dispensed so that those who merely subsist are provided with the means to assure them an ongoing, decent living—for example, a seamstress is given an inn to run.

The dilemma felt by Teófilo, Lizardi might have thought, is one many colonials would have understood. Taught by their religion that God is the ultimate power and the supreme legislator, that everything happens either by his decree or permission in a benevolently structured, just world, colonials would have had grave difficulties adjusting their awareness of contemporary problems to this faithful tenet. Many in 1814 had applauded Fernando's return to the throne as a kind father; yet by 1818, they were alienated by his absolutism.

Lizardi's fiction shows a Mexico where the insecurities of life are such that Teófilo, in jail, scorns life and liberty: "I will live . . . but to what purpose? To be tomorrow again the plaything of fortune or the butt of men's jokes" (128). One understands a country torn by fighting, where one's home could be broken into at any moment by men claiming to represent authority, where one's supposed crimes were, in this case, the result of mistaken identity. Indeed, Lizardi stated in 1822 (*Obras* 11: 565) that Teófilo's experience in jail was not a literary fantasy, but instead a description of his own imprisonment. Lizardi portrays a country of the very wealthy and the very poor, where the latter were so aggrieved that food and sufficient clothing were a constant problem. By depicting a priest's and a doctor's refusal to come to the aid of a poor man, Lizardi metonymically represents the general failure of these professions supposedly offering succor. Colonial readers might have understood that Rodrigo's killing of his father, the ultimate crime, symbolically suggested the colony's rebellion. Yet, even though Lizardi has

Rodrigo argue provocation by making the father vengeful and cruel, he textually condemns the son's deed.

Noches tristes is constructed like the script of a play, in which doubt and/ or denial, and faith, are set out as questions and answers. Readers see each speaker, and his point of view, clearly. Although Teófilo's is the voice of despair in the first part of the book, he later represents the position of Catholic doctrine when others encounter misfortune and doubt, question or curse. Lizardi brackets the blasphemers' viewpoints with their interlocutors' standard formulaic answers; yet the expression of such independent thinking, along with a persuasive dramatization of why the characters' situations have forced them to speak as they do, suggests that the work is not an *apología* for Catholic teaching but instead the thoughtful record of a representative colonial mind not altogether convinced of authoritative explanations of life.

Lizardi's use of the catechism (its question-and-answer format and its subject matter) rewrites the form. A book whose simple language was designed initially to essentialize faith and make learning easy for unbelievers and persons new to Christianity and European ways, the catechism could be seen to be a book that retarded complex thought. Its double voicing, while appearing to resolve conflict and tension, was increasingly recognized to be a false dialogue, guided by the priest. In this time of confusion and contradiction, the catechism, one reads in Lizardi's version of it in *Noches tristes*, was seen to be a tool for controlling revolt by answering all doubt, discouragement, and disbelief by means of magical, linguistic formulae. If earlier the catechism had appeared to authorize questioning by simulating dialogue, now colonials were recognizing how it managed thought by providing its language. The catechism, in a foreign language and coded to different epistemological assumptions, made it difficult, if not impossible, to argue with the terms it imposed. Lizardi, in writing a secular book that imitated the catechism's format, questioned this circular thought and subjected the book's role in the Conquest and the colonization enterprise to scrutiny.

Carlos Monsivais dramatizes the catechism's control through the prior formulation of questions in his contemporary fable "Nuevo catecismo para indios remisos" [New Catechism for Indians Who Are Remiss in Their Obligations]. In it, a priest and an Indian discuss the catechism:

The native responded harshly:

"No, reverend father, no way. I don't like your catechism."

The priest thought at first of calling the Tribunal of the Holy Office (the Inquisition) immediately, but that day he was in a good humor and he waited.

"The Catechism doesn't exist for the pleasure or displeasure of barbarous, foolish Indians, but instead to teach the commandments and holy precepts."

"But not in this way, reverend father, not with this routine of questions and answers that [makes] everyone believe that in heaven they see us Indians as more foolish than we are. It seems like a child's roundelay: 'Who made the heavens and the earth?' And we respond in chorus: 'God made them.' Wouldn't the reverse be much better? You say: 'It was God,' and we answer: 'Who made the Indians, the fish, the rabbits'? (11)

The exchange, in fancifully reversing traditional roles, sets out historic dissatisfaction with answering another's questions.

The catechism has often been overlooked as an early form of colonial consciousness and source for modern literature.[14] Yet I want to argue that decolonization required a rethinking of its immense power. In the first decades of the nineteenth century, the standard catechism used in Spanish America was the one written by the Jesuit Jerónimo Ripalda (1534–1618). Ripalda's catechism figures prominently in the discussion of the way the two cousins were taught in *La Quijotita* (vol. 1, chap. 3); and it is the subject of a long, anti-papal, and anti-Jesuit tract that Lizardi published in 1826 and reprinted in his *Correo semanario de México* in late 1826 and early 1827. There, in "Dudas de El Pensador consultadas con doña Tecla, sobre el *Catecismo* de Ripalda" [The Mexican Thinker Consults with Doña Tecla Regarding His Doubts as to Ripalda's *Catechism*], Lizardi makes clear the religious book's role in the Conquest. "Father Ripalda was Jesuit and Spanish. He wrote his *Catechism* at the same time as the Conquest and thus he had no compunction in persuading of those false and excessively servile ideas those recently enslaved peoples so that they, frightened by the enormous pontifical power, might always be subject to their lords and masters, the kings of Spain" (*Obras* 6: 255).

Antonio de Nebrija's *Gramática* [Grammar] (1492) has often been cited as a colonizing tool because it fixed Castilian as the official language of Spain's Conquest and standardized it for bureaucratic purposes. But I believe Lizardi's identification of the importance of Ripalda's work shows that still another kind of book facilitated Spain's seizure and control of American lands and peoples. Although the catechism had its origins in Augustine's *De Catechizandis Rudibus*, the sixteenth century saw its moment of greatest use in Reformation and Counter-Reformation preaching. Jesuits, in particular, realized its usefulness in evangelizing (in Ireland, America, and Asia). So Lizardi's perception of the catechism's colonizing role is an important clue in explaining why he thought the novel, a secular mode and potentially popular form, could alter colonial habits of reading.

In criticizing Ripalda's catechism, Lizardi notes that its answers frequently do not follow from the questions and that the answers often assert Church practices as articles of faith. The answers are often part of a "vicious circle"; they either avoid answering the question or else use the same mysterious terms as the question and leave the reader as unenlightened as before. Lizardi also sees differences between the Latin Credo (the Apostles' Creed, which is recited as part of the Mass) and the Nicene Creed that the faithful commonly say. He contrasts the two, translating the first from Latin into Spanish for his readers (271); and then he concludes that, because of the differences and because of historical considerations, despite what the Church taught and the devout believed, the apostles (or Jesus, or Moses) could not possibly have been the authors. Lizardi also questions Ripalda's text, which at one point says that passions are bad but at another point holds that four emotions (enjoyment, fear, expectation, and suffering) are virtues. Thus, Lizardi says, the book teaches lies and confuses; and old ladies (who are among those who take its truths most literally or whom he can most easily ridicule) sow hatred when they argue with those who dissent and question Ripalda's authoritative words.

Lizardi wrote this criticism of Ripalda's catechism eight years after *Noches tristes*; Mexico's mood then was pro-British and decidedly anti-Spanish. Catholicism was linked, not only to the colonial past, but also to Spain's ongoing effort, with the help of the Holy Alliance, to reconquer its former colony. Appeals for American obedience by the pope angered many Mexicans; and Lizardi would have remembered his own excommunication as well as the tyranny of the Holy Office in thwarting his publishing efforts. Yet Lizardi, in criticizing Ripalda's catechism, the pope, the clergy, and the Inquisition here and in other places in his writing, does not sound like an agnostic, a Mason, or a Protestant. He sounds like a colonial who resents the historical record of institutional abuse through authoritative language, yet one who also understands the difficulties of getting at truth through language. Lizardi, unlike a Protestant, does not appear to have believed that the Bible was the Word of God; and his textual reproduction of Ripalda's words (along with some of the language of the Mass) may have meant for some the reinvigoration of those forms.

A recent catechism (Bambamarca), written by liberation theologians for use in Peru, shows that the form is still vital in Catholic pedagogy. In this Peruvian catechism, the traditional format has been replaced by a description of a typical situation drawn from Indian life, followed by several open-ended study questions such as "What do you think?." As a consequence, persons seeking a response to injustice, who want some explanation for life's meaning beyond material realities, are forced to try to verbalize for themselves their needs and desires.

However, in the decolonizing climate of early nineteenth-century Mexico, examination of the language of faith had several consequences for Christians. It showed that the "piety" many professed was superstition. "Charity," at the personal level, was often a begrudging, selfish act and, at the corporate level, a palliative for continuing exploitation. "Morality" was a hollow term; only if it were redefined could moral acts take place. "True" religion, therefore, had to distance itself from the royalist rhetoric that had manipulated faith, making it seem synonymous with loyalty to all secular paternalistic structures.

Dialogue as Dialectic

Staging a debate with invented characters was a common technique of Mexican political pamphleteers who wrote when circumstances permitted in the first decades of the nineteenth century. The Socratic dialogue, which was how the device was understood, was brought from the philosophy classroom out into the world of journalism and pamphletry; and aside from the obvious rhetorical benefits of clarifying different points of view and making the exchange sound like lively speech, the patent fiction of the personification was meant to disorient the censors in their assessment of a writer's intent and a reader's belief. Lizardi provides an interesting perspective on the game of fiction he played with his censors in the 1815 prologue to a new journal he was launching; the venture, *Las sombras de Heráclito y Demócrito* [Ghosts of Heraclitus and Democritus], only lasted through two numbers. Lizardi begins by emphasizing to the readers who will buy his newspaper the bearing his fictitious adventures have on present realities: "The strangest thing is that almost all the dreams or fictions that are represented in the imaginations of the dreamers who are both aware and asleep are chimeras and absurdities without any substance. Mine, while being dreams, are evidence of real things" (*Obras* 4: 237).

He goes on to give independent existence to the two philosophers who will speak and calls himself just a copyist:

> Now the reader will see if he should believe steadfastly in my nocturnal conversations, and even more firmly, given the publication in bold type with the necessary approbation and licenses. But if, by some misfortune, he notes some crass error, let him take issue with Heraclitus or Democritus, for they are the legitimate authors of their successful discoveries of truth or deliria. I have no other role in this farce than that of a mere copyist or editor of their conversations, thanks to my excellent memory. And even in this little bit, I do enough for I constantly have to be alert to write and purge my conversation of some expressions that they spill out and I omit in order not to offend chaste ears. . . .
>
> It is my intention that this newspaper appear every Thursday, except when it is detained by the censors, in which case the ghosts and I hope that our prudent readers will excuse us, assured that punctuality does not depend on our will. (*Obras* 4: 237–38)

By acknowledging that censors are reading his material, Lizardi is asking his readers to study the fiction closely. Whether his point was understood might have depended on such factors as the individual reader's experience with fiction, his awareness of the social world referred to, or even his willingness to enter into the terms of the discussion, such as in Lizardi's first dialogue in this newspaper regarding egotism. What is difficult to

know is the extent to which censors were deceived by the pretended debate and the authorial disclaimers. It is clear, though, that Lizardi sought
to neutralize the power of one set of readers to thwart his publication
program—his censors—by alerting his other set of readers to what possible silence meant. In any case, in this 1815 document Lizardi connects
storytelling with the colonial writer's need for ambiguity.

In his career as a journalist and pamphleteer Lizardi frequently used
the dialogue form;[15] sometimes it was an exchange between unequals—an
excuse, for example, for a more worldly person to familiarize a naïve *paya*
with the ways of the city. However, in *Noches tristes* the dialogue form sets
out two separate, and equally valid, interpretations of reality—that of the
believer and the nonbeliever. The nonbeliever (in the persons of Rodrigo
or Martín, or even the jailed Teófilo), rather than arguing as an Enlightenment philosopher in theoretical ratiocinative terms, presents his
doubts and disbelief as a result of Mexican experience. This crisis of belief
might have particularly characterized the criollo, who had been taught to
identify with European culture yet whose inferior status with respect to
the dominant Peninsular class increasingly pushed toward an alliance
with indigenous interests. The bipartite form of *Noches tristes* not only
permits him an expression of conflict but also to some extent resolves the
tension between the two parts of his nature through respectful dialogue.
Although in the *Día alegre* ending Catholic faith is shown to be rewarded,
making it seem that this worldview absorbs the other and triumphs, the
book's dialogue, without authorial commentary on the sincere exchange
between the believer and the nonbeliever, leaves the dispute unresolved.

Style

Agustín Yáñez, as well as other literary critics, have remarked on Lizardi's
unusual use in *Noches tristes* of stilted, artificial-sounding, pretentious language. The style is in marked contrast to that of Lizardi's other works,
which critics perceive as truer to Mexican realities as a result of the use
of frequent slang and rough humor. In his introduction to *Noches tristes*
Yáñez writes:

> The characters and the background of *Noches tristes* are Mexican,
> in spite of a certain ingenuous linguistic artificiality, a little strange in
> Fernández de Lizardi. . . . Between the speech of the characters in
> *Noches tristes* and that of the characters in *El Periquillo Sarniento* is the

difference between the spontaneous and the over-worked, the natural and the learned. And this is one of the most regrettable effects of Romanticism—like that of all literary modes—brought as an import article, [it is] accompanied by set phrases and exalted tones. The false, strange language that even a farmer and a grave-digger speak is on the same level as that of a priest or a maiden. The same language serves for a sermon as for a curse; it does not succeed, however, in disfiguring the indigenous character by robbing it of its distinctive types and regional flavor, or muddying the vein of popular philosophical sentiment which informs the *Noches* and the *Día*. (*Noches* 10–11)

Here Yáñez attributed Lizardi's experiment with literary language to the spread of European Romanticism. Spell in discussing *Noches tristes* is sensitive to the same feature and prefers Lizardi's other works in which a more "realistic" style predominates. Following is Spell's attempt to explain stylistic differences among Lizardi's four novels:

In spite of this lack of finish which prevented Lizardi from attaining a polished style, he recognized and responded to what he considered good stylistic qualities in the works of others. His admiration for the style of Cadalso in *Noches Lúgubres* led him to attempt an imitation in *Las noches tristes*, which was not a success. For the qualities of style which distinguish him as a novelist are to be found in the other novels rather than in this deliberate attempt to attain style. It is in his ability to adapt his form of expression to the demands of the narrative that Lizardi excels. He can write, as he seldom does, in a florid, grandiloquent style, as in the funeral oration in *La Quijotita;* or he can write, as he generally does, in an intimate, chatty, gossipy vein, as when he records the conversation of the "chata" in the same work. Along with its many defects, there are certain admirable qualities in his style. It is realistic in its simplicity; it is fresh; it is spontaneous; and it is not lacking in harmony and rhythm. It was just these qualities that served to endear Lizardi to the common people; and to win for him, at the same time, the hatred of the pedants of his day who were attempting to produce literature. There is, too, in his style, an element which reveals something of his own personality. He is ironic and satiric, but too over-serious to be witty:

he can move us to laughter, for he has a keen sense of the ludicrous, but he lacks the ability to move us to tears; he is sometimes coarse and vulgar, but he is never indecent; and while he is a moralist, he is generous to a fault, and not without sympathy for his weak and shallow compatriots. ("Life" 88)

Both Yáñez and Spell take literally Lizardi's claim that *Noches tristes* is an imitation of Cadalso's book; however, one pauses when one remembers Lizardi's introduction to *Noches:* "the critics should be quiet when they notice the enormous difference there is between my *Noches* and Cadalso's because I do not say that I imitated his style but that I tried to imitate it" (113). Here one understands Lizardi's remark on his style to be a signal to his readers to question why a colonial author would choose this strained, exalted level of discourse. If most of Lizardi's other works, as Spell points out, display both high and low styles, as well as something of Lizardi's own personality, why in *Noches tristes* is there only one style in which all of the characters speak? If class association is a key to one's acceptance of the text, as Spell suggests, does Lizardi's selection of a high style in *Noches tristes* mean he was addressing the "pedants" Spell refers to, and not the people, in this work?

Lizardi's use of varying styles in the *Periquillo* clearly shows a strategy to teach the colonial reader how to read, how to shift one's acceptance of the text according to one's understanding of its changes in language. If this could be accomplished, the colonial would learn to see through the pretense that often characterized the pompous language of the ruling classes; he would also begin to hear the communicative worth of the languages of the lower classes, and thus concede some importance to those speakers in building the nation's future. But, despite Spell's statement to the contrary, the novels Lizardi wrote after the *Periquillo* generally do not demonstrate the great changes of style characteristic of this first novel. For example, in the prologue to *La Quijotita*, a fictitious woman insists that Lizardi understand that the style of a book for women must be different. This style, "which piques us, teaches, corrects and entertains us," must reject the display of erudition, the sententiousness, of earlier moralistic books written to appeal to women's fathers for use in their education; it must also avoid laughter at women's expense. Teaching women how to read, then, perhaps built on Lizardi's observations of colonial readers' experience with the several linguistic styles in the *Periquillo*, a cautionary tale for men. Thus, in *La Quijotita* he followed a middle ground between didacticism and satire.

In *Don Catrín* the tone is consistently ironic. From the very beginning, when the picaresque hero first describes the narrative style with exaggerated braggadocio, Lizardi forces his readers away from the text:

> I would be the most indolent man and the recipient of the execrations of the universe, if I deprived my companions and friends of this precious little book. I have beaten my brains out in writing it, pouring into it my uncommon talents, my vast erudition, and a sublime, sententious style.
>
> No, from now on my friend and companion *El Periquillo Sarniento* cannot glory in the fact that his work found a warm reception in this kingdom for my work, stripped of inopportune episodes, annoying digressions, tired moralities, and cut to a single little volume in *octavo*, will become more valued and better read. . . .
>
> And how could this not happen, when the object that I propose is the most interesting and its methods, the most solid and efficient? The purpose is to increase the number of dandies and method, to propose my life to them as a model. (3–4)

Here Lizardi expects his readers not to take Don Catrín's words literally, perhaps counting on his readers' training with the *Periquillo*. If, in the later book, when a character labels the book's style "sublime and sententious," the character's otherwise slangy language and disreputable identity would have signalled to readers that they should conclude the opposite of what the words actually said.

In light of this review of the styles of Lizardi's other novels, Lizardi's effort in *Noches tristes* to imitate the "eloquence"—as Lizardi phrases it— of Cadalso's work poses a number of interpretive problems. An example of its unmistakably bookish style follows:

> Teofilo:—¡Qué espanto! A la luz de este relámpago he visto despeñarse desde esta cima al infeliz Rodrigo. Rodrigo . . . Rodrigo . . . No responde. El infeliz cayó en un impetuoso arroyo y ha muerto impenitente. ¡Desdichado! Su crimen lo condujo a la desesperación y ésta a la impenitencia final. ¡Terrible estado!

Pero ¡válgame Dios! ¡Qué cerca estuve yo de acompañarlo en tan aciaga muerte, si la atmósfera encendida tan a tiempo no me avisara de mi próximo peligro. ¡Oh Providencia benéfica! Yo adoro tus decretos y, cosida la cara con la tierra, alabaré y bendeciré tus admirables giros.

Mas ¿qué hago aquí? Ya parece que los aguaceros son menos fuertes; dentro de un rato es de creer que cesarán del todo y que, disipándose las ya delgadas nubes, abrirán el paso a alguna claridad. Me volveré por donde vine. Alta Providencia, en quien confío, sostenme en esta espantosa y tristísima noche, y dirige mis inciertos pasos para que no me conduzcan al precipicio. (145)

[Teófilo: "What a fright! In the light of this flash of lightning I saw the unfortunate Rodrigo fall into an abyss. Rodrigo . . . Rodrigo . . . he does not respond. The unfortunate man fell into an arroyo and he has died impenitent. Unhappy man! His crime led him to despair and the latter to final impenitence. What a terrible state!

But, my God! How near I was to accompanying him to such a sad death if the illuminated atmosphere had not advised me of my imminent danger in time! Oh, beneficent Providence! I love your decrees and, as long as I live, I will praise and bless your admirable ways.

But, what am I doing here? It already seems that the showers are less heavy; within a little while one can believe that they will stop and that, when these already thin clouds dissipate, they will open the way to a new clarity. Providence at the Heights, in which I trust, sustain me in this frightful, saddest of nights, and direct my uncertain steps so that they do not lead me to the precipice.]

Obviously, Lizardi here is trying to dramatize the soul's gratitude at deliverance from tragedy, and the attempt at emotional language seems to be part of his desire to make religious and philosophical material meaningful. In many ways, therefore, *Noches tristes* works to draw colonial readers back to a faithful language to which they had become hardened. In *La Quijotita*, written at approximately the same time as *Noches tristes*, Lizardi's fictional counterpart describes how important knowledge of the meaning behind the catechism's words was thought to be for Mexico's development:

> I am tired of hearing some persons respond by heart to some questions from the catechism lightly, like a parrot. For example, if one asks them: "Who is in the Holy Sacrament on the altar"?, they respond with great satisfaction: "Jesus Christ Our Lord in body and glorious spirit, just as in the heavens, in the host as well as in the chalice and in every particle." Very nicely answered; but is the answer equally well understood? Not in the least. Ask them: "Who is this Jesus Christ? What is his body? What is his spirit? What do you understand by glory, particle, etc.?" And you will see them turn silent.
>
> This is a shame. The consequences that follow from this kind of teaching are dreadful. Within Mexico and everywhere people are seen who are very ignorant of their religion, who harbor the most erroneous ideas about it.
>
> And shall we say that this ignorance is to be found in the lowliest of the plebeian class, among ordinary people with no foundational education? No, daughter. I speak to you from experience and I assure you that the decent people who are infatuated with the errors of religion are not few.
>
> If this were not the case, there would not be such corruption of custom as there is today. . . . In short, he who knows his religion fundamentally possesses a great tool for controlling his disordered movements, sufficient motive for recognizing his Creator and a powerful aid for helping him return to the path of righteousness even when he has strayed from it.
>
> But the foolish man, the ignorant man, he who knows nothing of his religion but what the catechism says, without understanding it, has exactly what the Devil needs to distract him. . . . Perhaps there would not have been so much heresy if there had not been so many people ignorant of their Catholic religion. (*La Quijotita* 20–21)

Here Lizardi's concern with the language of religion and catechetical learning conceals several worries. His description of persons who rely on recitation of formulae to show obedience indicts typical colonial thoughtlessness in the use of language. As one disgruntled colonial wrote to *Sud*, an insurgent newspaper, in 1813, "for 293 years we have been deprived of the use of our faculties, and even of our bodily sensations. . . . that's why we are half-witted [*semisopitos*]."[16] Lizardi's awareness of class differences between "ordinary" and "decent" Mexicans suggests still another concern. Many Mexicans were too poor to buy the books that would enable them to learn more about their religion than what the catechism taught them. Consequently, their unreflective language did not stem from their idiocy or hypocrisy but from ignorance, which had an economic explanation. And still another concern, which Lizardi evinces in the above passage and calls "heresy," points not only to the dangers to Mexico of Freemasonry and other liberal philosophies but also to the broad questioning of authority even good Catholics were conducting there.[17]

What seems to be religious discussion, then, is present in *La Quijotita* and *Noches tristes* not only because the censors would have been familiar with this language of authority and belief, set in the context of faith, but also because intellectual questioning for the average criollo, given the educational practices of the day and the books he might have had access to, took a religious form. Social questions pressing on colonial leaders, such as widespread immorality across the classes, civil disobedience, and a society's failure to progress, can be traced, the quote from *La Quijotita* shows, to the population's misuse of a learned language. Colonials commonly spoke of a "soul," for example, without shaping their lives according to a thoughtful regard for this and other words, which taught that one's human conduct would be judged at some point; their unthinking use of this language, therefore, was foolish and dangerous in hindering progress toward true morality.

Colonial bewilderment in the face of restricted language usage, therefore, is at the heart of an explanation of Lizardi's odd language in *Noches tristes*. The elevated level of the discourse suggests he may have been wanting to draw near the colony's elite, many of whom admired Peninsular modes. Evidence that that may have indeed been the case is the fact that the *Ratos entretenidos* volume also included poetry by Mexico's Arcadian group. The name reveals its members' aspirations to high artistry and social status in the reflected light of European fashion. Therefore, it may be argued, Lizardi was attempting to appeal to the colony's elite in gathering the collection; the bookish style of *Noches tristes* fit with their taste. However, it was also the only one he had at hand to convey abstract thought. His discursive world offered no other suitable or respectable means of approaching these colonial leaders and persuading them of his concerns. Cadalso's Romantic sentimental language was new, and Lizardi's use of this unnatural language betrays the colonial writer's dilemma in formulating a convincing literary medium for his readers.

Yet Lizardi's reading public must also have included less powerful persons such as minor clergymen, tradesmen, lesser-ranking military men, farmers, ranchers, and miners. Given the relative scarcity of books and other printed materials in the colony, these readers would have had little or no contact with European literary modes. Indeed, evidence shows that many persons from this social level viewed books with suspicion. By choosing an artificial style as an appropriate expression for the religious subject matter of *Noches tristes*, perhaps Lizardi wished to signal to these less-sophisticated readers that this book was different from his earlier racy stories and the newspapers they were accustomed to, and that its theological and philosophical speculation was more significant.

After calling attention to his stylistic experiment at the outset of *Noches tristes*, Lizardi does not again remark on the level of his language. I therefore conclude from Lizardi's choice of a privileged style and his unexamined use of it for faithful debate that he chose it because he was anxious to please the censors and he was conscious of the dangers of falling below a suitably decorous level of expression. Teófilo's emotional outbursts according to Romantic fashion were meant to divert the attention of upper-class readers from damning pronouncements such as Teófilo's observation to Martín: "You say truly that men are cruel with the poor" (152).

Yet I also think it is correct to see the marked language of Lizardi's book as a typical response whereby a colonial inherits a set of authoritative beliefs and then attempts to apply them with their corresponding linguistic formulae to his specific condition. He can challenge them if he has a basis for creating his own terms and contradicting the discourse; if not, he remains bound to the dominant language and retains some respect for its sacredness even as he is dissatisfied with it. For example, the Mexican had experienced the immorality of a class of *pícaros* such as the *catrín* [dandy] and was therefore prepared with a vocabulary, albeit vulgar and profane, to counter the "sublime and sententious style" with which Lizardi's character represented his life.

Philosophical and theological questions, however, are perhaps more resistant to attempts by men to know and fashion answers; thus uniquely Mexican terminology for such questioning had not yet evolved. Consequently, Lizardi's use of language in *Noches tristes*, which is separate from that of most daily discourse—honest in considering questions as to life's meaning and laden with emotion, yet free of Mexican speech patterns and deliberately strange—suggests an effort to rethink abstract questions while using appropriated terms. If this language strikes Yáñez and Spell as strained, if all the characters seem to speak in the same way, one can conclude that Lizardi had no other language field from which to draw to express this aspect of Mexican life. His secular work reflects the effort by a new national writer to borrow, perhaps awkwardly, the religious language traditionally used to justify authoritative structures and explain absurd happenings and men's failings.

Reception

The only indication as to how Mexican readers responded to *Noches tristes* is Lizardi's comment in the second edition that he was reprinting the book because of its favorable reception the year before. A third edition was printed in 1831 and a fourth in 1843. Subscription records for the first edition indicate that forty-three persons, six of whom were clergymen, signed up in advance for copies in Mexico City; and forty-eight persons, one of whom was a clergyman, in Oaxaca. Added to these numbers those who would have bought the book in installments in the various bookstores, the printing record for *Noches tristes* is respectable. However, a eulogistic commentary on Lizardi's life written by a contemporary at his death in 1827, although it mentions the *Periquillo, La Quijotita*, and various of Lizardi's pamphlets, omits any reference to the work (A. F. A.). The omission is suggestive. By 1827, in a period of independence, the earlier work may have been remembered as too doctrinaire to be considered among Lizardi's more distinguished works; prevailing public opinion may have taken literally Lizardi's statement of the book's purpose: "its moral purpose is none other than to teach the reader to humble himself and to adore in silence the inscrutable decrees of exalted Divine Providence, giving him the assurance that the latter neither prearranges or determines but for our own good, to which it always shows a decided propensity. The Catholic who is imbued with these religious sentiments has a great advantage in overcoming the toils and miseries of this life over the impious and the incredulous atheist" (*Noches tristes* 114). By situating his work in the discourse of pious literature, Lizardi invited a superficial reading. By declaring his intention to imitate Cadalso's mood-inspiring *Noches*, Lizardi might have drawn the attention of some readers to the eloquence of his attempt at voicing personal suffering (Spell, *Noches* xiii). But in the postcolonial period some might have been offended by this connection with an imperial author.

What message contemporary readers may have read in *Noches tristes* is purely speculative; but the oblivion into which the work fell suggests that they and later taste-makers did not understand Lizardi's profound attempt to rethink colonial identity at a critical moment in Mexico's history. Why they failed in this may be explained by Lizardi's misleading instructions as to how the work was to be read. Their inattentiveness to the book's structural meaning may also have been part of a general unwillingness to question the premises on which political, and then later, cultural colonialism rested.

9

Don Catrín de la Fachenda

A Modern Discourse: Machiavellianism

Lizardi must have written *Don Catrín de la Fachenda* [Sir Dandy from the Land of Vanity] sometime in 1819 because the censors' approval is dated February 22, 1820. Their comment reveals their reading of the novel's apparent orthodoxy: "The life and deeds of D. Catrín de la Fachenda with the notes of the American Thinker is a tragicomedy with which the vicious persons who deserve this epithet on account of their libertine life are ridiculed. One also deduces a healthy moral with which the sentiments and obligations are brought into conformity with those of religion." However, when freedom of the press was declared in Mexico on May 31, 1820, Lizardi dropped the project of publishing *Don Catrín*. He did so, Spell speculates, because he was then free to express his opinions and no longer needed fiction's disguise for his politics ("Life" 33). In fact, Lizardi wrote no other novels after *Don Catrín*.

Nevertheless, in 1822, at the end of one of his pamphlets, Lizardi did announce his intention to publish *Don Catrín*, saying that he already had enough subscriptions for an *imprentita*.[1] But, perhaps because of his excommunication in February 1822, he did not carry his plan through and *Don Catrín* was only published after his death. Yet, as the 1820 political pamphlet I quote from in chapter 1 reveals, the character of Don Catrín seems to have been familiar to Mexicans, thus leading one to question whether there was a network of readers at this late colonial moment through whose hands often censored, unpublished material commonly passed (Vogeley *La literatura manuscrita*).

At the outset of *Don Catrín*, Lizardi states how he wants to strip from the text the "annoying digressions" and "tired moralities" of the earlier *Periquillo*.[2] Free of these, the *Catrín* narrator predicts, his story "will fly on the wings of fame through all parts of the inhabited world—and even the uninhabited world. It will be printed in Spanish, English, French, German, Italian, Arabic, Tartar, etc" (3).[3] This broad distribution, although its overstatement helps set the book's ironic tone, significantly connects Don Catrín's story to Europe and beyond, in contrast to Periquillo's tale, which is only known in Mexico. The list of tongues directs readers toward Lizardi's imaginative leap—a relationship between the Mexican *catrín* [dandy] and foreignness. This internationalism pointed to foreign Enlightenment thought, which was sweeping Europe and entering the Spanish colony as progressive; the *catrín*, a segment of the colonial population whose stylish dress and rash speech were condemned by some yet also admired by many others, symbolized this new cosmopolitanism and liberalism.

Between 1814 and 1820, when Fernando VII tried to close Mexico off from foreign influence, Enlightenment thought, which had become familiar to Mexicans in the first years of the nineteenth century, officially disappeared. French and British ideas, which had previously entered Mexico and were regarded as "civilizing," "modernizing" and "useful," were banned. Liberal thought, therefore, became a bone of contention in Mexico. Many traditionalists had always considered it subversive since it often entered the colony clandestinely via travelers' reports and illegal traffic; the Inquisition routinely questioned persons who gave evidence of familiarity with French writers such as Voltaire. But new ideas had also come in openly through Christian writers who restated the views of so-called Godless authors. Scientific thought, such as mining technology, had been imported under official auspices; and new political and economic ideas were introduced during the rule of Carlos III, whose efforts to modernize conditions and loosen the monopoly on colonial trade reflected advanced theories. Innovative thinking had also filtered in with news of Napoleon. The legislative reforms he implemented—but most especially, his energetic, overreaching person—brought the message that the French revolutionary model and republican values, like it or not, would increasingly prevail. However, Fernando VII, together with the other monarchies of Europe, condemned Napoleon and all he stood for at the Congress of Vienna. Yet when Fernando returned to Spain and imposed absolutism throughout the empire, his repression soon angered many of his Mexican supporters and they expressed exasperation by joining with insurgents and again seeking out modern ideas.

Mexicans were thus battered by these political reversals and philosophical swings. Had not Napoleon fought against Protestant England, Spain's traditional enemy? And had not the Spanish Cortes and regional juntas, which were variously attempting to democratize Spain yet also preserve the monarchy's authority while Fernando was in a French prison, sought an alliance with England during the country's "War of Independence" (terminology that seemed to rob America of its right to use that phrase)? Spain's return to religious and political orthodoxy and repudiation of modern thought left many Mexicans in a mental quandary. And the 1814 exodus of the Spanish *afrancesados*, many of whom were among that country's intellectual elite, added to Mexicans' confusion over Spain's moral and intellectual leadership.

Lizardi's story of the *catrín* dramatized this colonial philosophical conflict. Its fictional rebellion against traditional morality posed the problem of what the Mexican insurgency (that is, thinking for oneself) meant and what it might lead to. The book's ending seemed to promise tragedy. Yet the textual sense of an alternative set of values suggested some imaginative agility and defense of Mexican actions; many Mexicans believed that their recourse to violence, rather than a crime, was a justifiable response, a moral assertion of the colony's basic rights in the face of Spain's historic immorality. So the book's portrayal of doubt and rebellion, in voicing rejection of authority, might be supposed to have performed some satisfying role in acknowledging fears and confusion.

Don Catrín is the culmination of Lizardi's fictive experimentation in four novels, written over six years. In each, a mode, now regarded as "picaresque," variously expressed transgression. In the *Periquillo* and *La Quijotita* the delinquency of the young people was the result of an improper education, ruinous friends, and unwise judgment. In *Noches tristes* cynicism questioned faith. In *Don Catrín* Lizardi also explored disobedience; but in this story of a character's departure from Catholic faith his delinquent died unrepentant. Thus, in this last work, which seems superficial and slight, a potentially more threatening, and unresolved, historical dialectic was enacted.

The complexity of Don Catrín's *picardía* is structurally set out in contradictions between the text's irony and obvious truths, and by a lack of authorial signals, which Lizardi had provided in the *Periquillo* to guide his readers. These signals—correcting sermons and restatements of the moral, serious, and uplifting discussions of culturally broad topics—were intended to offset the textual space of Periquillo's descent into an underworld of commoners and criminals. In answering the charges of contemporary critics (readers who thought themselves sophisticated) that these digressions in his first novel were tedious and distracting, Lizardi admitted that he knew the moral should be contained in the action of the story. But he argued that he had broken narrative rules because his colonial readers required the guidance of authorial commentary. The explicitness of the *Periquillo* suggests that the author was reaching for a broader, more plebeian readership, unfamiliar with literary indirection. However, one can also suppose that Lizardi meant that all of his readers, regardless of class, required direction in learning to reconsider a book's authority; they had to be instructed in how to accept a literary portrayal of the world around them.

Don Catrín's announcement, then, at the beginning of the novel, that his story will omit these digressions, although it seemingly acquiesces to the Mexican critics' demands for subtlety, challenges them to interpret the ne'er-do-well's story. On one hand, Don Catrín's exaggerated self-grandeur signals humor and suggests Lizardi is asking his readers to distance themselves from the ideas flowing from that point of view. On the other hand, some of his speeches reproduce aspects of modern thought which colonials, in their increasing rejection of Spanish tyranny and awareness of domestic needs, were beginning to take seriously.

I believe, therefore, that there is considerable ambiguity in the author's use of irony and that textual devices such as allegorical names and the story's pious ending are not to be trusted. The novel's ending especially must have taxed the interpretive capabilities of Lizardi's readers. Before he died, Don Catrín went through the motions of confession and the last rites of the Church. But he mocked them, refusing to believe in the rewards of heaven or the eternal sufferings of hell; and he seemingly died calmly, saying that a "fanatic" friend would finish writing his story. The adjective "fanatic," in the discourse of the day, suggested an old-fashioned Catholic whose faith was unthinking. So, when readers confronted the last pages of the book, written by this friend whose credibility has been undercut by Don Catrín's words and whose account of Don Catrín's death tells that he suffered "the most atrocious remorse," they would have had to resolve for themselves the textual contradiction.

The irony of *Don Catrín* is more than the ambiguity or "sly civility" that Homi Bhabha has claimed often characterize colonial discourse. It is true that the irony's double meaning suggests the cautious public expression of dangerous ideas. But the resulting impreciseness also conveys the colonial dilemma of moving gingerly between foreign words and American material realities. The uncertainty as a result of two conflicting testimonies reproduces the crisis of faith that Mexicans, taught a credal religion and a totalizing political ideology, would have faced. The mixed way in which the reading may allow positive and negative attitudes toward Don Catrín's thoughtful rejection of traditional belief and acceptance of worldly notions discharges some of the intellectual tension of Lizardi's colonial world.

The Dilemma

I have already referred to A. A. Parker's valuable work on the picaresque, calling particular attention to his discussion of changes in the mode during the eighteenth century. Although I do not agree with Parker's judgment that with works by Defoe and LeSage, "The picaresque tradition has moved away from a religious-moral preoccupation to humanitarianism and thus . . . it constitutes a literary world of lower intellectual and emotional significance" (110), I believe Parker rightly pins changes in this narrative form to secularizing forces in Europe.

The Christian language of vice and virtue was especially affected by secularization. The virtues David Hume identified as "monkish" (celibacy, fasting, penance, mortification, self-denial, humility, silence, solitude, etc.) were instead vices, Hume thought, if one applied capitalist standards of social usefulness (quoted in Parker, 133–34). The *philosophes* in France, as Carol Blum has shown, were instrumental in transferring the concept of virtue from the person of the monarch to the body politic by means of their advancement of republican values; and Rousseau's notion of virtue was uniquely transformed when Robespierre appropriated it to call violence public justice in the reign of terror. Americans in the Spanish colonies, taking up arms against Spain, made use of these redefined, politicized concepts of vice and virtue in vindicating their crime against God and king.

New art forms in Europe had helped extend these revisions. In the works of genre painters and printmakers like Hogarth, Greuze, and Goya, individual sins like alcoholism and profligacy were portrayed because they had large consequences for the family and society. Bourgeois art took over the function of the Church in spreading lessons of the new domestic morality such as thrift. And the novel's images, also, via the story and the book's illustrations, taught a new, personally decided morality—one, however, dictated by social requirements—as the private act of reading eliminated institutional middlemen.

However, if Lizardi's novel owes a debt, as I believe it does, to the sixteenth- and seventeenth-century Spanish novel,[4] that early use of realism to correct idealistic myths was a powerful example of the novel's capacity for bringing about social change. Yet one can argue[5] that the early Spanish form, which questioned gentlemanly honor and service to king, also validated those elitist codes by catering to a taste for elegant language. It reinforced wealth's hold on the society by erasing poverty's ugliness. The pretense of a homeless waif robbed the real-life poor of their true voice. Their sorry story was distorted by the novel's humor and word play; their social problem was circumscribed and trivialized by the book's package. Similarly, Lizardi's adaptation of this Spanish literary structure, while it permitted a critique of the terms of Spanish control and depiction of American realities, was responsible for shaping colonial thought at this strategic moment. In the Mexican development of a new social and political consciousness, the fictional discussion of "vice" and "virtue" (or socially unacceptable/acceptable behavior), while permitting public discussion, dictated the terms for the discussion.[6] Consequently, *Don Catrín*'s dilemma was bounded by the language terms Lizardi knew and the publishing conventions he could use, but these, in turn, might be considered to have determined Mexican categories of morality in the post-colonial period.

Don Catrín's satiric tone, while seeming to discredit the hero's cavils and vacillations, paradoxically validated the discourse of doubt, and thereby the novel, as the battle site for the profound struggle between Christian faith, ethics, and traditional idealism, on the one hand, and materialist, utilitarian philosophies with secular underpinnings, on the other. The satiric novel was an important discourse space in which the colony's inherited religious belief could collide with new thought. Yet many colonials were troubled by ideological, discursive combat, seeing in it scholasticism's pretense that truth, according to propositional logic, flowed from the working of man's mind; what was often called "truth" was only the product of the manipulation of rhetorical strategies and words.[7] Dialectics suggested debate; but this debate, as critics increasingly charged, usually took place in a performance setting where jealousies and animosities between personalities and schools, rather than any desire to know the truth, controlled the outcome.[8]

Throughout the colonial period, theology ruled the university as queen of the sciences; its values forced all intellectual and moral conclusions. Despite the occasional enlightened investigator,[9] educational practice was generally based on the deductive method of inquiry and featured the teaching of classical philosophy and Catholic orthodoxy. Colonial schools emphasized memorization and mechanical recitation of standard arguments.[10] As Lizardi testifies to in the *Periquillo*, the Latin-based curriculum and rote learning contributed to general weariness with scholasticism and institutional thought (part I, chaps. 4–6). His portrayal of professional educators, whose own inadequate formation and mediocrity made them poor teachers of the young, contrasts with the picture of enlightened scholars and investigators that historians of the period provide[11] and causes one to conclude that Lizardi was providing a picture of common practice not yet affected by modern thought. If a few men gathered together in literary and economic societies to discuss Mexico's problems in light of new ideas, thus providing the nuclei from which intellectual leadership of the revolution emerged (Shafer), it must be said that many others at the intermediate level of education were stunted in their growth by servile schoolmasters and stagnant tradition.

Yet elimination of the traditional books, their theologically grounded epistemology and methodology, threatened colonial thinkers uniquely. If colonials disallowed metaphysical presuppositions, they were left with the degraded, material realities of their colonial existence. If they called religious faith pious superstition and criticized the Catholic Church for backwardness in its teachings on revelation and the sanctity of tradition, they opened up a void that modern humanist, materialist philosophies had difficulty in filling. If, as one character argues to Don Catrín, "honor" is only a word (23), on what ideals does a colony aspiring to independence base its civic life?

Most troubling of all would have been the question of justice for, if God's justice was not be relied upon, if *eternity*, too, was only a word, the evidence of colonial juridical practice demonstrated that manmade legal systems were not to be trusted. Colonials could only despair when they believed that the cruelty they witnessed around them would never be punished; they could only cope with that dog-eat-dog world by selfishly living for their own pleasure and emotionally cutting themselves off from their fellows. The same intellectual dilemma underlay *Noches tristes;* and in that book Lizardi resolved it happily through the *Día alegre* ending in which the *cura* affirmed faith in God's existence and power to settle all conflict and right all wrong. But in *Don Catrín* the dramatization of a character who holds himself above men's laws and denies God's laws, whose end is tragic, bespeaks another, darker conclusion.

There is nothing in Don Catrin's character to suggest that he is inherently bad; instead, he appears as the product of society's making. His selfishness begins as the result of indulgent parents. His idleness originates in the scornful attitudes toward work characteristic of his well-born economic station; his blind pride also has its source in the criollo's belief that family name guarantees one's worth. If, like Don Quijote, whose title the Mexican's ironically imitates, Don Catrín lacks judgment [*juicio*], this incapacity seems more a function of his colonial bewilderment as to what to believe than any inability to distinguish between reality and illusion.

Lizardi uses the language of Fortune characteristic of the Golden Age picaresque to develop the story of Don Catrín.[12] In a chapter heading "In which it will be seen how Fortune began to pursue him and the methods he used to outwit her," he invokes that expectation for a character's story. Yet his message is clear that "Fortune" for the nineteenth-century Mexican is not fate or providence; instead, it is a historical process that individuals set in motion. Don Catrín is shown to bring about his own tragic end when he chooses to reject his elders' advice. However, his "choices" are limited by his colonial birth and opportunities for honorable work and success in the American field. If Don Catrín tries to live like the Mexican nobility and assumes the external signs of that class, as a criollo he does so without the economic base to sustain such luxury. If he seeks nobility in virtuous living, as traditional Christianity teaches, he must have recourse to that mental system that colonial practice demonstrates yields no rewards and that new materialist philosophies tell him is only the spurious use of manmade, evanescent language.

At one point in the novel Lizardi arranges a discussion between an old man and a clergyman (creditable voices) and Don Catrín, so as to define the term *catrín* (chap. 8).[13] The older men blame *catrines* for the decadence and corruption of the period. Yet Don Catrín asks what harm there is in dressing according to the latest fashion, dancing, behaving as a gentleman, and so on.

The exchange evinces colonial confusion regarding attempts at style and innovation.[14] Dress signalled one's ideological loyalties. Old fashion at this moment revealed allegiance to Spain and traditional values; the new mode meant one espoused the modern ideas of France, England, the new American nation to the north, and related independence movements throughout Spanish America. Each group, which would develop into a political faction in the national period, criticized the other and made common cause seem impossible. Faith meant fanaticism and the superstitious beliefs of women and the lower classes; modern thought connoted materialism, the egoism associated with absolute liberty, and the unconsidered approval of callow youths such as Don Catrín.

The *catrín*'s identification with European Enlightenment thought is apparent when Don Catrín describes his picaresque education: "I became so enlightened" (73). Amid traditional-thinking Catholics who are discussing the truth of the Catholic faith, Don Catrín celebrates his rebellious identity as an *espíritu fuerte* [free spirit], emboldened by "the Enlightenment of this century."[15] In the following ironic defense of *catrines*, Lizardi has his character reassure a priest that such attitudes and behavior are inoffensive because they are to be found among the most noble, Christian, and enlightened members of society:

> Dear father, calm down. Dandies are noble, Christian, gentlemanly, and educated; they know very well what they are talking about. Many fanatics blame them with no reason. What evil does a dandy do in dressing decently, however that may be, in not working like the plebeians, in gambling with his own money or someone else's, in seducing as many women as he can, in subsisting at the expense of others, in being lazy, in enjoying himself and living in cafes, salons and billiard parlors? Perhaps this, or much of this, is what a thou-

sand others do, although they don't have the honor of being dandies?

Now, why must they be called impious or irreligious only because they never go to confession, they don't respect priests or churches, they don't kneel in front of the Viaticum, or at the time of the Mass they don't touch their hat when the Ave María sounds, or other similar foolishness? (74)

Here Lizardi locates the *picardía* that most concerns him at the level of the upper and middle classes. The *catrín*'s question—whether noncompliance with external signs of faith is serious—suggests modern man's religious confusion, but also, specifically, colonial difficulty in breaking with habits of mechanical ritual. After all, colonial authorities had really only cared whether the population conformed to external appearance, not whether their subjects understood and subscribed to the spirit behind the rules.[16]

The narrative line in *Don Catrín*, therefore, develops the colonial ideological dilemma. The book proceeds according to a series of dialogues in which Don Catrín, at first, echoes the teachings of the Church on faith and morality because an inner voice constantly reminds him of what he learned from his uncle, an honest, scrupled priest. However, his interlocutors, established *catrines*, argue the foolishness of such views. They hold up as civilized their amorous behavior with the ladies in polite society; they exult in their personal happiness as they realize their own ambitions at the expense of others; and they boast of the impunity they seemingly enjoy as a result of the lack of any court to judge them. Finally, Don Catrín silences his conscience and yields to their arguments. As a libertine he indulges in the behavior typically censured by a bourgeois society—drunkenness, idleness, gambling, and a common-law marriage. Unlike the Golden Age *pícaro* whose decision to steal food seems a spontaneous reaction to material deprivation, Lizardi's Mexican counterpart engages in semitheological and philosophical debate before becoming a *catrín*.

One character indignantly describes this variety of *pícaro* as *sin ley y sin rey* [lacking a code of law or allegiance to king] (45). Once free of the restrictions Spanish colonial institutions imposed, Mexico was going to have to look elsewhere for standards of behavior; and an obvious source was the theories and philosophies being put forth in other, advanced European countries. The number of these theories, their often conflicting conclusions, their statements of relativism, and their rejection of old authorities—all made Mexicans believe that there were no longer any rules. Remaining within the world of Spanish traditionalism, however, seemed like adherence to an outmoded feudalism. Trying to convert Don Catrín to new ideas and playing on his colonial sense of estrangement and inferiority,[17] a *catrín* argues: "your world is very small and you are unacquainted with the enlightened century you are living in" (38).

By 1819 the institutional Church, even in the eyes of many faithful, was so discredited that anticlericalism and secularism were rampant. Many disaffected Mexicans embraced Freemasonry to experiment with foreign modernizing ideas and satisfy religious needs. Yet ideas were not free of the European nation whose thinkers proclaimed them, and Mexicans alternately admired foreign ideas and found fault with them. France, as I have indicated, was usually characterized as torn by irreligion; England was tainted by its slave trade, as well as its reputation for having a large middle class that attempted to deceive through appearances.[18]

Centrally placed in Lizardi's novel is a list of ten rules for the *catrín*'s behavior, supposedly the *Decalogue* of Machiavelli (70–72). A fellow *catrín* is Don Catrín's instructor, and the numbered format of the ten commandments on the page invites attention. After reading them, the reader is guided to censuring the code by Don Catrín's comment, showing that he is still bothered by Christian scruples, that what many do can be seen to be outrageous and offensive when their behavior is spelled out.

The rules, badly stated, rewrite Machiavelli's philosophy of evil; they adapt Machiavelli's advice to princes for use by the average modern man. Lizardi says in a footnote that Machiavelli and then later "a false politician from France" passed them on to the members of their sects; the rules were also reproduced in the preface to a work by Albertus Magnus. Lizardi's sense of chronology here seems mixed up, yet the attributions apparently rang true for contemporary readers. For them Machiavellianism was a much-cited discourse term, synonymous with political expedience and religious heterodoxy, if not atheism.

Don Catrín's friend calls particular attention to the precept that advises taking on the character of associates when it is useful: "in a short space of time I was a Christian among Christians; Calvinist, Lutheran, Arian, etc., with those of those sects; a thief among thieves; a drunkard among drunks; a gambler with card sharks; a liar with the trickster; impious with the immoral man; and an ape of all" (72–73). The most important lesson of Machiavellianism, ironically formulated in Lizardi's book as a creed, was that an individual should abandon all creeds, all a priori statements of truth and rules of conduct. A *catrín*, as Lizardi has his character argue, will support heresy, "alleging the difference of opinions that each day are applauded and scorned" (64). A *catrín* will excuse any manner of crime in the name of tolerance and sentimental love for one's fellow man. Thus, it is clear that behind Lizardi's parody are the very ideas of modernity, of experimentation and pragmatism, of new attitudes of community and mutual regard, that Mexico was entertaining for its independent future.

However, the term *Machiavellianism*—although Lizardi does not explicitly say so in the novel—also would have suggested to colonial readers the politics of the American Conquest and Spanish government of the colonies. This meaning for Machiavellianism was made clear in *La Quijotita*, as I discuss earlier; and the same associations are repeated in an 1820 political pamphlet,[19] in which Lizardi defines Machiavellianism. There he cites a popular maxim which said that, despite what was generally believed about a kind king and his wish that his subjects be educated, his ministers and probably even the king's policies deliberately kept colonials ignorant so as to prolong their dependency. However, Lizardi exculpates Machiavelli by saying that his advice to rulers to take advantage of their colonies by preaching one thing and doing another did not originate with him. Machiavelli merely put into words what he saw tyrants doing (406).

Machiavelli's influence on the fifteenth-, sixteenth-, and seventeenth-century Spanish jurists (such as Francisco de Vitoria and Francisco Suárez), who were instrumental in writing the treatises of imperial rule, has been documented.[20] Even though their efforts took the form of thoughtful anti-Machiavellianism, that realistic philosophy is apparent in their insistence that men's laws be made to conform to natural law (which was supposed to flow from God's eternal law) and therefore that, in the transfer of political institutions to the new lands, laws could be an important restraint on the monarch's power. Vitoria's ideas, in particular, extended the secularity of law in his focus on international order and the creation of the state (which is not necessarily coincidental with the monarch's power); he also invested law with the notions of rights and justice.

When later, in the eighteenth century, the Bourbon government attempted to modify the old authoritarianism, it called into question the seemingly inalterable relationship between the king and his vassals, according to which the Reyes Católicos and the Hapsburgs had founded the empire (MacLachlan, *Spain's Empire* 123–35). The Crown itself, by instituting reforms, officially introduced the possibility that its imperialism was imperfect and might be criticized. Its expulsion of the Jesuits from Spain and the American colonies in 1767 made clear animosities between altar and throne and communicated a sense that the traditional notion of one ruler who combined divine and temporal powers could be rethought. Mexico's upper classes lamented the loss of academic and intellectual leadership when the Jesuits left the colony.[21] And the Indian classes were confused when they suddenly lost their missionaries.

The eighteenth-century Spanish essayist, Padre Benito Feijóo, contributed to this discussion of the monarchy, significantly also couching his criticism in a discussion of Machiavelli and his philosophy. In two *discursos*, "La política más fina" [The most refined politics] and "Maquiabelismo de los antiguos" [The machiavellianism of the ancients], he apparently chose the philosophy for its amplitude in connoting unspoken Spanish governmental policies, yet also new political and economic views, free of traditional morality. Feijóo asked what, at first glance, seem to be literary questions: What was Machiavelli's real intent in writing his book? Did he want to advance the power of princes if his other writing showed that he condemned tyranny? Might he not have been helping the people by exposing how their rulers manipulated them? So as to have his book published, might Machiavelli not have disguised his purpose to educate the people behind his stated goal of offering advice to princes? Machiavelli's book, then, thought to be evil, might be considered moral if the populace benefitted from reading it. Perhaps the author was not evil if he did not invent the rules he listed; he was merely copying down the tactics of the rulers he observed. Among other lessons, Feijóo's essays, at one level teaching that vice and virtue were often not what they appeared to be and that a book's morality might be subjected to several readings, at another level verbalized the possibility of an immoral monarch.[22] The essays were well known in Mexico, influencing Lizardi (Spell, "Lizardi, The Mexican Feijoo").

Machiavellianism, for *Don Catrín* readers, then, would have evoked this discussion of political authority in defense of a Christian empire, a concern that was at the root of their historical identity. The philosophy would have aroused issues of a good king versus a tyrant, the primacy of king or people in the social contract, and the trustworthiness of metropolitan language in promising proper colonial management and education. Machiavellianism, although its statement in *Don Catrín* seems to suggest individual ethics and the dangers of the new humanistic, pragmatic philosophies entering the Spanish American colonies from liberal and Protestant Europe, would first of all have connoted the record of Spanish colonialism in Mexico—not only situational compromise and manipulation, but also downright malevolence in the treatment of innocent peoples.

J. G. A. Pocock in his work *The Machiavellian Moment* has studied the way in which Machiavellian vocabulary affected political thought in the Atlantic English-speaking world in the eighteenth century. Particularly suggestive for my reading of *Don Catrín* is Pocock's discussion of the ways the terms *virtue* and *corruption* were revised then, permitting the development of republican concepts of individualism and capitalistic notions of self-interest. Machiavelli's political philosophy, instrumental in the development of the Florentine and Venetian republics, can be seen to have contributed to their successes; their societies, based on commercial values rather than on religious and monarchical definitions of civic life, Pocock argues, were increasingly attractive as historical models to the newly forming American nations as they considered their identity and plans for modernization.

However, Lizardi's use of the term *Machiavellianism*, although in various places in his writings it suggests the self-interest of commerce and motivations that might inspire Mexicans in a postcolonial development, differs from the term's use in Protestant America. Mexican discussions of self-interest rather displace the debate onto Spanish colonialism, English capitalism, and Mexico's undisciplined masses. Elite self-interest, which became manifest later as Mexican independence and economic maneuvering for domestic, individual gain, was allowed to remain unspoken.

Some of the eighteenth century's revision of Machiavellianism, its rethinking of immorality according to a new worldly, or realistic, ethic, appear to have been acceptable to many Mexicans in the early nineteenth century. Newspapers, for example, show that a spendthrift son who dispersed his father's fortune was commonly understood to be useful to so-ciety;[23] actions that at one time had seemed sinful were now in the process of being reevaluated in terms of the greater good, colonial advantage, or a useful end. The title of an 1810 anonymous pamphlet shows this will-ingness to rethink the old according to the new in its pragmatic justifica-tion of imperialism (the union referred to is the empire): "Evils of Dis-union and the Useful Benefits Which Confraternity Can Produce."

Yet many Mexicans appear to have had difficulty in seeing self-interest favorably. In two newspaper articles published in 1815, Lizardi identified *egoísmo* [self-interest or selfishness] as a philosophy whose many adher-ents believed they could satisfy their individual passions at the expense of others.[24] In the first article, Lizardi's fictitious voices associated *egoísmo* with an uncaring monarch, a tyrant, or indeed any abusive authority: "Every tyrant is an egotist; and every egotist, if he had authority and force, would be a tyrant" (244). However, in the second, the voices dis-played a criollo awareness that egoism was widespread and that money, in various ways, was at the root of everyone's selfishness: "Almost always money is the motivation or the reward for most of our actions—good or bad." Thus, self-interest, which Machiavellianism taught, threatened the Mexican social fabric. Throughout the colonial period, despite an official Christianity, Mexico had suffered greatly as the result of social inequities. However, if the common ideal to which men might aspire, the law the Catholic faith taught, that one love one's neighbor as oneself,[25] was re-placed by a new lawlessness and matter-of-fact acceptance of greed that the new utilitarian and commercial philosophies seemed to promote, then many Mexicans feared an even worse situation.

The American intellectual predicament may be similar to the Euro-pean at that moment. As previously religious societies became secular, such a shift sowed seeds of doubt and confusion among ordinary persons on that continent, too. As feudal economic practices gave way to capital-ism, the European peasantry began to feel the effects of impersonal mar-ket forces and theoretical discussions ranging at higher levels. However, the American predicament, especially in the Spanish colonies, as I have been arguing, was different. There the essence of colonialism was con-nected with the language colonials inherited, with intangibles that func-tioned as realities; the very roots of colonial existence were deep in the individual's sense of his spiritual well-being. The religious character of the Spanish colonial enterprise had created an official loyalty based on the double notion of God and king. Consequently, any crime committed against the one automatically suggested an attack on the other.

The *catrín*'s problem, Lizardi tells his readers, is generational and widespread (50). This diagnosis means that the *catrín* must be listened to; Lizardi's full rendering of the logic behind all of the characters' voices, even though some might seem to have been discredited, suggests their power. But Lizardi's choice of Machiavellianism to symbolize the *catrín*'s new belief system is particularly interesting because Lizardi, in taking that philosophy which Spanish Catholicism had taught symbolized earthly greed and power to talk about the colonial past, turned the language around to accuse Spain. Antonio Gramsci, studying the vitality of Machiavelli's work in the modern period, has focussed on *The Prince* as "a creation of concrete fantasy which works on a dispersed and pulverised people in order to arouse and organise their collective will" (135). Gramsci's work helps one to understand how the Mexican reception of Machiavelli's political ideology was something more than a look backward at a detested philosophy.

Intellectual Crime

Don Catrín's religious and ethical dialogues reveal the dilemma of the individual Mexican, who agonized because he thought his soul in jeopardy if he participated in the collective crime of opposition to the Crown. Ecclesiastical authorities had made this religious dimension of the political crime clear in 1810 when they excommunicated Hidalgo and other insurgents for their treason. Thinking colonials, however, could see the inappropriateness of religious punishment for the political act; and they also were beginning to understand that religious teaching often deteriorated into tyranny, intended to keep the colonial childlike in his fear of powerful words and paper. As a friend of Don Catrín argues: "Your uncle, that stale old guy, pestered you with sermons, and that's why you still believe that they are coming at you after he's dead. You are a big fool; you get scared, like children with the bogey man. But courage, friend, assume an air of confidence and importance and scorn those illusions which fear causes. Don't you know that the dead don't talk? In your sad fancy, agitated by your misery, these paper specters are formed. . . . Let's enjoy all the pleasures that are in our grasp" (69–70).

Taught to be a *mono* [ape, monkey], Don Catrín did not think for himself. He had no essence beyond that of an imitator. Deprived of any power to affect religious discourse, or indeed any other hegemonic discourse, the colonial historically had learned to gesture, to pay attention to symbols of obedience such as the correct use of language, and to invoke them in moments of crisis. Throughout his life, the individual colonial, who had internalized the voices of authority, heard their echo and suffered guilt when he transgressed; faced with death, he listened again to the words of Catholic faith and according to how he had lived his life was either comforted or horrified.

Documents of the period show that Mexicans, in attempting to end their dependency on Spanish Catholicism and reach a collective maturity, grasped at the philosophical language of *librepensamiento* [free thought].[26] In *Don Catrín*, however, Lizardi shows how accepting linguistic abstractions out of this other European experience was only another kind of American *servilismo* [subservience]. Lizardi dramatizes how Don Catrín, in listening to his friends and following their example of self-gratification and disobedience (44), confusedly understood the lessons of the European Enlightenment, perhaps because as a colonial he still only mimicked its external signs. In seeking to acquire the veneer of civilization, he equated waste and debauchery with civility and gallantry.

The plot of the novel, however, shows Lizardi's understanding of the Enlightenment's profound challenge to all modern men. Once free of a belief in God's justice, men must rely on their own manmade systems to introduce order into their lives. Once released from social obligation to a monarch, men have difficulty rethinking their duties to family or to the poor—and still greater difficulties understanding their relation to impersonal laws. Once enlightened by the idea that words and pieces of paper are men's inventions, men face an overwhelmingly material, and ugly, world; and the *catrín*'s solution, to maximize his own earthly happiness, is that of many others.

Don Catrín can be understood as a fool. His susceptibility to the words of others, his gullibility, and his literal understanding are often the substance of comedy. In sophisticated metropolitan circles, the provincial who does not understand the concealed play of meaning among the instructed is often made the target of jokes. In creating a colonial *pícaro*,

Lizardi showed that the colonial was vulnerable to such charges because of his intellectual indebtedness. The colonial's *picardía* was the result, not of naïveté or rebelliousness or willful disregard of authority, but of the conflict, felt personally and collectively, between opposing language constructs and inner needs, between sound and silence.

Roberto Fernández Retamar has described the American as Caliban, the slave who, robbed of his own language by the Conquest, used the language of his master to curse him. *Don Catrín*, in many ways, is this linguistic creature whom Fernández Retamar identifies; the Cuban author's linkage of colonial history and the psychosocial formation of the individual colonial helps us to understand Lizardi's fictional construct. However, *Don Catrín* goes beyond Fernández Retamar's analysis by extending the notion of "slave" and opening up the questions of the degree to which the various classes in the American colonies were linguistically penetrated, or ideologically trained, and of the kinds of language activity characteristic of each class. Habituated by the colonial education system to the Spanish mindset and professionalized to the legal, administrative, theological, and educative work that made a business of words, the criollo class to which Don Catrín belongs would have been closer to the Spanish discourse system than those Mexicans of the lower classes who worked with their hands and who may have maintained their own Indian or African languages. The criollo intellectual, in particular, would have had difficulty "cursing" Spanish usage—to use Fernández Retamar's term—because the character of his work prevented him from creating an original discourse with which to counter the dominant form.[27] Thus, although Lizardi's use of the picaresque must be seen to have provided an imaginative channel for dialogically exploring the Enlightenment set of terms (an alternative language of vice and virtue) at this key moment, it is clear that borrowing was predictable. For various reasons the criollo still preferred a European philosophical system to one of his own making.

However, surrounded by a natural world that challenged the European naming system and by social ills that demanded solutions (as well as by an oral world with which he was sometimes more familiar), the American in the first decades of the nineteenth century was beginning to learn to distrust European knowledge and its forms. One colonial who wrote to the *Diario de México* suspected, for example, that European humanism was merely another word system incapable of understanding American realities: "It does not matter to [those abroad who concern themselves with worldly, human knowledge] that we have little commerce, that agriculture is backward here, that because the area is unpopulated, science and the arts do not flourish. But it does matter to them to declaim that we are ignorant because there is no liberty to write, to think like libertines do, that we lack population because celibacy is permitted and protected, and that commerce, industry and agriculture are missing because we are fanatics and we house *the horrible monster of intolerance disguised under the respectable cape of Religion.*"[28] This cynic believed that foreign humanist philosophers were just another variety of Europeans who were using secular philosophy to discredit America. Thus, the revolution in thought, which the Enlightenment particularly in France and England represented, attractive though it was to Mexicans exasperated with Spanish Catholicism, caused great defensiveness and, therefore, intellectual uncertainty in Mexico.

In illustrating the complexities of accepting Enlightenment thought, Lizardi examines in his novel "knowledge" [*las ciencias*], the Spanish word suggesting an Enlightenment understanding of new scientific fields of inquiry. The priest/uncle is lecturing Don Catrín on the need to study and acquire knowledge, yet also the vanity of aspiring to be completely wise in "theology, jurisprudence, medicine, chemistry, astronomy, or in any other field of study that we know and understand" (14–15). In his traditional-sounding lecture, the priest cites Rousseau's *Discourse on the Arts and Sciences* in which the philosopher demonstrates through logical proofs that knowledge is antithetical to the practice of virtue. The priest rejects such a finding, and then says that Rousseau, the product of a superior education, was motivated by vanity to argue falsely. He perverted reason and abused his skill with words. The priest asserts that great social harm was done by the Dijon Academy's award; indeed, knowledge and virtue are compatible.

The discussion opens up the question of whether knowledge (as the priest's criticism of Rousseau suggests) was perceived in the colony as just the dazzling display of language, regardless of false conclusions.[29] Did the debate of the Mexican intelligentsia, its special access to speculative activity, injure lesser minds? Should a concern for virtue be separated from the increasing business of pursuing knowledge? If such was the case, then, did a concern for virtue, that is, a respect for certain fixed beliefs according to which the general population lived, override the publishing of contradictory findings?

If an important aspect of the Conquest had been the despoliation of language, the struggle for independence meant fighting, not just militarily, but also linguistically, against colonial status. Lizardi gives evidence of this consciousness throughout *Don Catrín* as his character questions priests' sermons, the Gospel, legal strictures, and moral codes—words that signified the imposition of law and a consequent loss of local and individual control. The injustices of colonial life had seemed to call for law, yet the special privileges enjoyed by many were causing Mexicans to examine the bases of present laws and ask why there were so many exceptions.

Military men, in particular, associated with Spanish rank and privilege, lived self-indulgent, free lives. Significantly, Don Catrín pauses as he is considering a military career and *catrines* tell him that a military officer who serves the king is not subject to the same laws as the civilian population (38–39). Taravilla (his name suggests vices of the town) then describes the freedom he has to use language: "enjoy yourself in the style of those they call libertines . . . [so that] there is no virtue exempt from your force, or religion or law that your tongue tramples on." Loose language was a particularly abhorrent sin for Lizardi; he has Don Catrín say: "Within a few days I devoted myself to being frank, to enjoying myself with women and at cards, to not letting anyone push me around, whoever it may be, to speaking with abandon about affairs of state and religion, and to making money at any cost" (37).

The ongoing insurgency war would have suggested to readers both the deterioration of idealistic military language (the source of much talk about patriotism, heroism, etc.) and the ideological phraseology of rebel troops. The latter could not continue to be "servile sycophants to the taste of the sanctimonious and rigid moralists" (39), but instead they had to attack the language that perpetuated a corrupt system and invent their own set of inspirational terms.[30] However, in the name of larger issues, intangibles that were being made known by their linguistic tags, both sides were terrorizing the Mexican population and destroying the country. Public opinion, the regard in which one was held, depended on the language used by the particular set of friends one chose (Lizardi shows the polarization in Don Catrín's world by contrasting Precioso, Taravilla, and Tronera with Modesto, Prudencio, Constante, and Moderato).

The role of language in the colony's public discourse space, therefore, is of concern to Lizardi in *Don Catrín*. As he makes clear, Don Catrín's greatest offense is not his conduct but his blasphemous, impious use of language, his attack on sacred beliefs of the Catholic faith. Modesto lectures Tremendo:

> The king permits you no license to offend the peaceful civilian, to ride roughshod over his honor or that of his family members. . . . Be advised, friend, that when you commit these crimes, your aiguillettes, your epaulets, your military stripes and your braid won't serve you for anything else but to make you more abominable in the eyes of the wise, the virtuous, your superiors and everyone; because everyone resents the conduct of a *pícaro*, however fortunate he may be to pass for a gentleman. In such a case, those above him will shun him, those who are equal to him will loathe him and those beneath him will curse him.
>
> If anyone becomes detestable because of these crimes, what will happen if to them are added being a blasphemer and an infidel, who speaks out publicly and scandalously against our Catholic religion, the holiest of religions, the only one [that is] true and justified? Isn't it enough to be violators of the law? Is it necessary to destroy dogma, to laugh at the mysteries and to make a shameless mockery of what is most sacred, under the guise of [being] buffoons, fools and libertines? (24–25)

Each age defines *picardía* according to what is most feared. In fictionalizing a world of competing language systems, where one discourse is seen as corrupt and outmoded and the other threatens anarchy and offers the individual no consolation in the face of adversity or death, Lizardi expresses confusion, despair, and existential terror. In the above quote, the *pícaro*, whose rich and official clothes invite respect, is the Mexican who, in embracing the new thought, not only himself transgresses but also corrupts others. By verbalizing his personal belief in the public arena, the individual destroys the bases of society and sows unhappiness. His ridiculous talk is not harmless, but dangerous. And although, as Lizardi says, such a person may appear to be a buffoon, a fool, or a libertine, this *pícaro* may also be the person of high rank and/or profound thought whose deviance is serious.

Lizardi's novel textualizes the author's understanding of the importance of public opinion in an evolving nation, his awareness of the public places and spaces where discourse is susceptible of change. Newspapers and cafes, as I have shown before, were only some of the new situational modes bringing Mexicans together across class lines and under circumstances that challenged the old order. Lizardi as the first Spanish American novelist, in intervening in this new public discourse space, therefore, was himself a kind of *pícaro* in giving voice to such a deviant *persona* and concretizing through his writing the possibility—and the dangers—of oppositional thought.[31] If philosophical questions had been the prerogative of only a few philosophers and theologians in the past, the novel writer now introduced some of the same questions, albeit vulgarized, to a broader and more diverse section of the population. Earlier theoretical formulations were now subjected to the probings of colonial minds, increasingly aware not only of pragmatic concerns and material realities[32] but also of the language in which theoretical formulations were couched. Lizardi's use of the pen name "El Pensador Mexicano" [The Mexican Thinker], therefore, stands as the declaration of his own thoughtful role in the new society.

10

Conclusion

The birth of the novel in Spanish America implies, I believe, the death of the catechism. Associated with the imperial past, with dictated language and fanatical belief, the catechism symbolized the invasion of Mexico by a European power and continuing mental oppression. Decolonization could only be accomplished if Mexicans could learn to question its tyranny, if its terms of domination and subordination could be rethought.

Independence, although Mexicans were divided about ties to the institutional Church, generally promised the end of the Inquisition and a lessening of papal control. Orthodox language, which throughout the colonial period condemned as "heretical" and "blasphemous" thought that threatened doctrinal supremacy and monarchical rule, now seemed to be waning in influence. A new secular state appeared to be the guarantor that religion could be something other than the old fanaticism. At the personal, but also at the corporate level, decolonization required that a new openness be learned; old obedience (which had depended on cowardice, apathy, and ignorance) had to be transformed into a new loyalty based on civic awareness and responsibility. Ordinary persons who previously had shouted "Viva" with each change of *virrey* or government, confident that politics did not much matter to them, now had to be taught that new relationships did require their participation and republican ideals of education did mean changes in thoughtless language.[1]

Lizardi's interest in the catechism is more than just the professional concern of a writer for language; he understood the book to be the supreme example of cultural imperialism. Even if some of its lessons were intrinsically good and perhaps useful in the new society, its dogmatic assumptions about language acquisition represented much that the new decolonizing mentality was trying to combat. Yet he recognized that some colonials, who were among the most fervent of the advocates of Mexican independence, could not separate themselves from its statement of religious truth. Perhaps realizing that it was difficult to formulate alternative language, they left intact the set expressions of the Our Father, the Ave María, and the Gloria Patri. After all, how could one challenge the Church's legal language, which declared differences between "commandments," "precepts," and "laws"? How could one argue with its righteous appropriation of goodness? How could one have any other access to the mysteries of faith than what the Church held out?

One response to the interconnectedness of political and religious language, then, was silent obedience, retreat behind the protective shield that Octavio Paz has described as concealment behind a mask (*El laberinto*). Still another was loud proclamation of loyalty and belief. The price of that was careful separation of one's private feelings of pain and fear from one's public, dutiful behavior, detachment of the more meaningful personal and familial language from scripted forms that society required. If expression in the home, as the quote with which I began this book suggests, meant giving release in that setting to frustration and instructing the young, then language only worked confidently, and maybe honestly, in that sphere.

Lizardi's novels showed how official, public language usage might connect with individual lives. The novels, if they did not offer an alternative explanation of life to the Church's catechism, at least attempted to begin decolonization by opening up questioning of that form and authoritative language. However, in phrasing the debate in language of the Church's teaching, they helped to perpetuate that institution's control. In his novels Lizardi dramatized transgression; but he did so by drawing on his bookish knowledge of personal sin from the catechism's categories. Although experience may have given him a personal knowledge of sin, it seems clear that he defined individual and corporate sin according to Church morality. The catechism helped Lizardi to think of specific instances of vice and virtue; its language, for example, of spiritual and corporal acts of mercy— correcting the one who errs and consoling the sad or giving food to the hungry—could identify problems within the colony and indict those colonialists and imperialists who regularly flaunted the catechism's moral teachings. And Lizardi relied on his readers' familiarity with Ripalda's special charge to the privileged—that the wise, for example, instruct the foolish—for convincing them of his satire. By positing the Christian instruction of most of his readers, Lizardi could show the discrepancy, not just between these privileged persons' faith and their works (which would only have proven their hypocrisy), but between their public words and their private selves.

Ripalda's catechism was illustrated with *láminas* of scenes from both the Old and New Testaments, and its question-and-answer format was extended by narrative examples of the virtues and vices.[2] "Avarice," for instance, was depicted, connected to Christ's parable of the rich man; and then that parable was retold. "Largesse" or "liberality" (not to be confused with its excess, "prodigality") was shown by the patriarchal figure of Abraham. Thus, I believe that, in addition to the literary and other discursive antecedents for his novels that I have mentioned, Lizardi was inspired by these pictures-through-words in the catechism. His *narratio* of colonial vice and virtue is designed, like the catechism's, to interpret the abstract language of morality. His novels' alternating of stories and summaries reproduces the catechism's structure.

From one point of view, then, Lizardi's recontextualization of the catechism reinforced religious language's power. The Credo, reprinted in Lizardi's political pamphlet of 1826–27 with its glossed discussion of authorship, resituates the sacred text in the Mexican world at the same time it treats it as secular literature and questions its making. The words of traditional morality of Lizardi's novels, while they gain new meaning as the catechism's solemn style is altered to fit the humor and familiarity of the novel, continue to hold men to the Church's ethical standards.

However, from another point of view, Lizardi's new novelistic depiction of contemporary, domestic realities had the distinct advantage of intervening in the process of interpellation to which colonials had been subjected. Through fiction Mexicans could see themselves as other than loyal Spaniards and faithful Christians. Through novel reading, they could imagine that they could appear outside the bounds of official discourse and that therefore there might be other ways in which their existence might be constructed. This self-representation, in which their deviation from standards of good taste and good behavior was developed in the picaresque stories, brought home to them the complexity of making a life without the help of prescriptive books. The exercise of reading a novel—in which one alternately saw oneself and saw others, approved and disapproved of the fictional characters, drew near to and distanced oneself from the text—encouraged independent thinking.

Showing rather than telling was common to religious discourse. Yet many secular thinkers were also exploring this route to knowledge at that moment. The value of the senses in acquiring knowledge—the importance of the ear and the eye in finding specific instances of a rule's abstractions—are apparent in Condillac's *Lógica* (Madrid, 2nd ed. 1800). In this Spanish translation by Valentín de Foronda of what appears to be the *Cours d'études pour l'instruction du Prince de Parme* one reads some of the same concerns that occupied Lizardi: the process of observation as it satisfies curiosity and gives visual pleasure, the procedure whereby images pass through language to the stage of ratiocination, the detection of error in such ratiocination, and the authorities who claim to perform it for us. Language, Condillac says, is not innate (86); we are taught it by Nature. And then he describes his analytic method with the aid of the following definition of thought [*pensamiento*]: "The word *thought*, being yet more general, includes in its meaning all the faculties of understanding [*entendimiento*], because to think is to feel, to pay attention, to compare, to judge, to reflect, to imagine, to ratiocinate, to desire, to have passions, to hope, to fear, etc." (46–47). Thus, we must constantly decompose (Condillac's translator uses the Spanish word *descomponer*) our language so as to make it fit with our experience; signs are provisional and language is artificial.

If one understands Lizardi's pseudonym "El Pensador Mexicano" [The Mexican Thinker] with this meaning for "thought," one then better appreciates the purpose of his writing. As the European author counselled detachment from self-interest in pursuing the truth, in recognizing the ethnocentric dangers of arguing from ignorance and assuming all men are like one's fellows (196–97), so, too, Lizardi wanted a new kind of "thought" to interrupt old, religiously defined procedures of thought and habits of language.[3] Lizardi's thought, like Condillac's, new in its scope and methodological challenge to traditional authority, made it seem as though, with the exercise of their minds, men could clear up old mysteries and that a perfect world was very near.

Lizardi's modernizing task, then, depended on bringing "language" toward this new meaning for it as a sometimes-imperfect tool of thought, a medium in which one might discover personal or cultural biases. The Church's explanation of language—that it was thought's external reflection, the God-given faculty by which men formed into communities and extended through writing their rational thought—produced the faithful belief that men acquired their reason as an "emanation of the sovereign reason of God." One then deduced that "reason" and "language" were somehow fixed, a priori attributes.[4] This syllogistic explanation of language presupposed the existence of God and placed language as a function of reason.

However, Lizardi, although modern, was also a colonial; and he and his readership, in their attitudes toward language, appear to have fallen somewhere between Condillac's theories and the Church's teachings. Criollos and others who used Spanish had been given Spanish; they knew it was not their language and that any invention they might introduce carried with it the probability that some would accuse them of incorrectness. In the midst of a multilingual society where illiteracy and semi-literacy were the norm, they understood their language to be one more sign system. Often several steps down the social ladder, they distrusted powerful "language," yet they envied those who owned it and knew how to use it. As I have shown, colonial reception of hegemonic language was a mixture of sensitivity and numbness. Mexicans, accustomed to official discourse, were intimidated into receiving it and reproducing it obediently, yet they were also critical of the discrepancy between words and deeds.

Noting this mixed consciousness toward language of his fellow Mexicans, Lizardi used the multivoiced novel to heighten this consciousness and direct it. By varying the style levels of his book, particularly in the *Periquillo*, he could make colonials aware of the range of expressive voices around them. By using print to bring the Mexican world into view, by giving readers the opportunity to consume privately a book designed for them, he could subject "voice" to scrutiny. By using the book as a seemingly entertaining mode and form of secular education, he appropriated a tool of the powerful classes and used its authoritative "voice" to contrast with de facto exchanges.

Yet Lizardi's "voicing" was not easy.[5] He might have been silenced by habits of obedience and fear. His domestic voice could only resonate intertextually against satire and imported novel forms, periodical literature, and the catechism. His "voice," recalling literally the varieties of Mexican speech,[6] worked dangerously close to being an ungrateful attack on colonial institutions, a personal diatribe, and a disclosure of colonial realities that everybody knew but preferred to hide. His technique of "reported speech," while it imitated Spanish and non-Spanish novelistic antecedents, was audacious in inserting a lively Mexican language into what had been a static, monologic, monumental form.[7]

That Lizardi overcame colonial obstacles to writing and publication is a measure of his, and the age's, progress toward decolonization. Lizardi's decolonizing "voice" was part of the campaign for honesty, for reexamination of accepted tradition, that some had launched in Mexico in the first decades of the nineteenth century. Replacing the authority of the Church and the monarchy, the new Enlightenment creed of reason gave men to believe that they could escape from the tyranny of those institutions and the hold their own passions had on them.[8] Armed with a new knowledge of the imperial language that had enslaved them, colonials seem to have been empowered to bring about changes.

How, then, were these first, fresh "voices" silenced and apparent consciousness lost? Do we post-Enlightenment societies, as Horkheimer and Adorno have argued, trust too much that the development of consciousness will bring about progress? Although the answers to these questions presuppose a postcolonial perspective, a study of Lizardi's decolonizing discourse is not complete without trying to find to what extent Lizardi's writing contained the seed of its eventual demise, to explore the way residual habits of language in the Mexican experience interfered with finding a critical point from which to view old institutions and judge new foreign intellectual systems.

What emerges in the discussion of the newspapers of the period and in Lizardi's novels is an impression of a society that, in stripping men of the individual comforts of religious faith[9] and trust in a father figure, substituted new social myths. While old myths had been perpetuated unknowingly, new ones were embraced consciously, at least by some. Supposedly society needed these new national myths to inspire individuals to put aside selfish goals. In a contemporary description of "civility" in the *Diario de México* the author identifies this "ingenious lie" which throws a necessary cloak over ugly human emotions; his discussion suggests other ways in which deception might have been tolerated, and even encouraged, if a few retained some awareness of the moral compromise:

> Civility reigns supreme; and it has become extensive throughout almost all the classes. That is because it has been observed that it produces an infinite number of good effects in society. People who may not see one another any longer than for a moment have the right to require that this fleeting exchange be agreeable. Without this ingenious lie meeting would be a wrestling match in which the low, petty passions would be present with all their deformities. This type of politics, which has been generally adopted, masks the ferocity of pride and the urgings of self love. . . . A light cloak, thrown over morality, is as necessary perhaps as a garment over the body. (Unsigned, March 27, 1809)

This superior awareness is a reminder of the way a domestic elite would later legitimize governance because it thought it knew more than the populace. The discussion also suggests the way the new activity of politics might require conscious hypocrisy.

The most important metaphorical construct to be demythologized and then reconstituted as the power of the state was the notion of the monarchy. As the king became less of a god and more of a human father, his subjects were transformed from a community of believers into a family, the empire into a union of brothers. Then, when his person was eliminated as a unifying principle, the *patria* with its range of symbols had to supply the necessary social structure. Yet the *Diario de México* and Lizardi's novels show that not everyone understood the same thing when this word was used; and the complexity foreshadows the tensions between liberals and conservatives in the postcolonial period.

Peninsular usage defined patriotism as the conserving force that defended Spain from Napoleon,[10] pitying France where irreligion had so destroyed social ties that force was necessary to hold the nation together.[11] "Patriots," in Mexico in the early years of the Mexican Independence War, were those Spanish and Mexican soldiers fighting in the royalist armies.[12] But decolonizing efforts had to rewrite these meanings for the term so as to signify Mexican affiliation. Perhaps because Spanish usage had emphasized social distinctions according to one's birthplace, independence-minded Mexicans fell back on understanding *patria* as one's place of birth; and they increasingly expressed love for that physical site. Yet others argued that this definition of *patria*, common among ordinary persons, was false: "it is necessary to distinguish the true *patria* from the vulgar *patria*, which everyone mouths. . . . The place, the city, the province, the kingdom, the state where we are born we call rightly and properly our *patria;* and we owe them respectively love and reverence. Having said this, we make it clear that it is not the walls and the streets, or the cliffs and mountains, or the valleys and the forests, that which we must love as *patria*. Because material and inanimate things are not the object of rational love."[13] This pro-Fernando writer, reminding Mexicans of Spain's gifts to its colonies over three hundred years, attempts to garner support for the junta, which in 1809 was governing in the name of the monarch. However, this distinction between tangible and intangible patriotism is one that leaders in the postcolonial state would repeat in their substitution of a legal code for a king.

Patria was defined as civil structures.[14] In one letter to the *Diario* a concern for law equated *patria* with civil liberties, that is, the abolition of slavery.[15] In many others, as I have shown, *patria* was defined as a linguistic unity, although Mexicans differed as to what that meant. Love was a strong force in patriotism, and the sense of several letters is that this passion was connected to a desire for the well-being of all members of the family and self-sacrifice for that body.[16] Yet Lizardi took this language and in an 1814 essay insinuatingly asked how large an emotional circle this family might be; he also questioned who, over three hundred years, had been responsible for the ills of "América septentrional" (North America, a common referent to Mexico that avoided the Indian connotations of that latter term, *Obras* 3: 379–84). Later, in 1820, when the restored Spanish Constitution offered some hope that the empire might be preserved and Mexico's problems might be solved by that legal change, he used the idea of "love of *patria*" facetiously to reproach the Spanish monarchy for inadequate Mexican representation in the Cortes (*Obras* 4: 399–402). As the *Periquillo* shows, Lizardi thought of *patria* as a place where a man developed into manhood and worked.

After Independence a domestic elite found national symbolism in Hidalgo and his revolt (Turner, chap. 3), the Virgen de Guadalupe (Lafaye), and the Indian past. The criollo connoted Mexicanness; and

Lizardi's person, too, became identified with the Mexican people. However, as I have shown, once he was lowered to that level, critics from Mexico's upper classes could reject Lizardi's novels as bad art. They could silence his voice by invoking his book but forgetting its message, thereby ignoring the social criticism in the *Periquillo* and in Lizardi's newspapers and pamphlets.

A novel, unlike the ephemera of political pamphlets, has the advantage of pedigree and certification that allow the statement of the work to last. Thus, the circumstantial anger and direct confrontation of political and religious issues in Lizardi's journalism were largely lost. In 1822, in a newspaper article, he attacked the record of Spanish plunder in the Americas.[17] In 1823, while excommunicated, he published the text of the Papal Bull, in which Mexican readers could read for themselves how Alexander VI had carved up America for Spanish and Portuguese colonization; in an editorial postscript he then questioned the pope's authority and asked whether faithful Christians had to believe that the Mexican Conquest was just.[18] In 1824 he sarcastically asked whether, after three hundred years of seeming protection as "new Christians" (they were conceded the "privileges" of working on Sundays and feast days, and not attending Mass), Indians could not be considered "old Christians" and their "privileges" acknowledged as a fraud.[19] These outright statements about politics and history were omitted from literature in its ensuing development; thus, the mechanism of "artistic" selection can be seen to have worked to stifle the message of Lizardi's pamphletry and journalism.

In his novelistic story of a son's rebellion to express the Mexican war, Lizardi, while advancing decolonization, can also be seen to have retarded it. Reading the *Periquillo*, the novel for which Lizardi is best remembered, one gathers that the relationship between father and son is intact at the end. The book teaches that Pedro, now a good father, transmits a new kind of experiential knowledge to his sons. Thus the trust encouraged in the voice of experience and concern suggests a basic acceptance of the father/son continuum. The family metaphor so absorbs the idea of historical growth that any change in the personal relationship takes on the connotation of disobedience and betrayal of one's kin. The metaphor, therefore, while permitting some flexibility of thought, forecloses any radical alteration of social bonding.

Paternalism is a difficult metaphor for the nation—and the individual—to break away from in constructing a separate identity. Some new attempts to accomplish the task have tried to show how "acquiring the idiosyncratic" (Sefchovich 22), that is, emphasizing the uniqueness of Mexico's Indian culture, or the mestizo mix, of the new nation can permit affirmation of a new identity. Although my discussion of decolonizing discourse in the context of Lizardi's novels implies the formation of a new nationalism,[20] I prefer to return to Zea's idea of discovering humanity in the process of decolonization, which is importantly embedded in Lizardi's use of the novel form and his choice of fictional language.

Decolonization tends to suggest a macrocosmic process when post-colonial critics describe it with phrases such as "the empire writes back" (Ashcroft et al). Yet *liberation* and *emancipation* have their personal counterparts; and, if the term *colonial discourse* is to describe the language of an individual to escape his or her subordination, then *decolonization* must also face such microcosmic considerations as verbalization and the psychosocial consequences of appropriating or rejecting a community's majority discourse.

As Louis-Jean Calvet asserts, the right to name belongs to the colonizer (56–79). The colonized, then, who has remained silent when others have spoken, is not only claiming a human right in speaking out; he is also attempting to put into words—and words of his own—what he especially wants to say. Freudian theory, as I have mentioned, understands word emergence in terms of auditory memories, and the formation of the superego as the result of parental and other authoritative admonitions. Similarly, Marxist theory, in the person of V. N. Volosinov, suggests that "inner speech" is related to factors outside the individual such as experience, and dialogic validation of one's language through utterances and exchanges with others; Volosinov describes how the individual psyche appropriates signs (words) whose meaning is very much a function of the materiality of the sign (28). He continues: "Any psyche that has reached any degree of development and differentiation must have subtle and pliable semiotic material at its disposal, and semiotic material of a kind that can be shaped, refined, and differentiated in the extra-corporeal social milieu in the process of outward expression" (29). But, as I have shown, the colonial is characterized by his limited access to "subtle and pliable semiotic material." Thus, the colonial subject's ability to self-reflect and alter his nomenclature, or penetrate the world of writing, must be seen to be difficult. One's ability to imagine one's human nature and stretch the use of one's language, therefore, appears to be key to individual decolonization.

The power of language over the individual and the residual linkage between one's language and one's political loyalties (or one's sense of belonging to a community) are apparent in the following letter to the *Diario de México*, in which the writer responds to a suggestion that Indian languages could be used in Mexico:

> "Campamocha" old uncle? . . . But I don't know by your language if you are Mexican or Otomi. . . . [Y]ou must be Tarascan, right? At least if you aren't *"dragón"* [oafish, plebeian] in your use of language, in your way of expressing yourself, you strike me as such. . . . So we children of Spaniards cannot say that Castilian is our language, eh? . . . then, little uncle, what is it? Because I and all American Spaniards, if there is not a special contingency or special dedication, speak no other.
>
> And if the only language we speak, as soon as we leave the cradle, we cannot call our own, my God! We are men without a language. . . . Look, my dear man, you are very far from knowing what *patria* means. ("Anti Hermogene mexicano" "Jorobita," August 31, 1809)

Criollo Mexicans, indeed most Spanish speakers in the colony, seemed to be locked into a belief that their identity was tied to their Spanish language usage, their membership in that *patria*.

Lizardi's novels show, I believe, that the individual works with great difficulty in the upper registers of language—the abstractions of intellectuals, the refinements of upper-class speech, the seemingly obvious and good notions connected with *patria*, even the vocabulary of "art." Lizardi's fictional references to the catechism in *La Quijotita* and *Noches tristes*, and his exploration of Enlightenment thought in *Don Catrín*, suggest the dependency of believers, intellectuals, or even doubters, on religious and secular thought systems. Octavio Paz's phrase *las trampas de la fe* [the traps of faith], although he uses it to allude to Sor Juana's difficulties with Church government, points to a dimension of language I believe Lizardi's novels—in their content and in the fact of their publication—make clear: Language that touches particularly on intangibles in human life often binds its users tightly to it. This kind of language, frequently transmitted through print, is highly vulnerable to social manipulation because it affords little or no opportunity for questioning.

While Lizardi's use of the catechism form as a basis for his novels is unstated and critical, other writers of the time and in the postcolonial period borrowed prestige for new ideological ventures by openly calling their works "catechisms." Although Mexico during the period of Independence struggle saw parodic versions of set religious expressions such as the catechism and the Our Father, one writer, attempting to instruct the Mexican citizenry in the doctrine of the Spanish Constitution of 1820, seriously titled his unsigned political pamphlet "Cartilla o catecismo del ciudadano constitucional" [Catechism for the constitutional citizen]. His "confession of sins" follows: "I, a Spanish citizen, confess before the Nation and you, holy Code of the Constitution and the most blessed heroes of the *Patria:* García Herreros, Martínez de la Rosa and Cepero, that I have sinned by thought, word, and deed against the Constitution, through my fault, through my fault, through my most grievous fault. Therefore, I beg the Mother Country, the supremely wise Constitution, the blessed defenders of our legitimate rights and all good citizens to pardon me." This political catechism, although the author insists he is using the form only because it is simple and he intends no profanation of religious confession, rewrites the discourse of patriarchy to teach loyalty to the Spanish Constitution; as in a religious catechism, the ritual language admits no deviation.[21]

Secularization is a term often used to describe a society's loss of a sense of transcendence, the conversion of its religious vocabulary into political terms (Chadwick). Yet the process may not be as neat as theologians, historians, and sociologists have made it seem, for, at least in the decades of Mexico's movement to independence, some of the changes in language attempted to preserve an aura of divine legitimacy by deliberately confusing the religious and the profane. Secularization, too, is often linked to the process whereby a military, aristocratic society becomes civilian, an economy based on trade monopolies is forced to integrate into a mercantile system, and new legal structures forsake the use of Latin for vernacular forms. The ideological state apparatus (to use Althusser's term) may change at the moment of decolonization.[22] Yet the several ideological codes these apparatus have taught to ensure their reproduction continue to work through language beyond the historic moment of rupture. As I have attempted to show, habits of language—and thereby, habits of thought—imposed themselves on the new Mexican nation; and even though Lizardi's efforts to rethink the forms by which Mexicans understood their world and themselves (novels, sermons, catechisms, paternalistic structures, Enlightenment thought, etc.) were valiant, powerful competing and enemy voices then and later acted to silence his voice and erase the generation's problematic consciousness.

Notes

Introduction: Decolonizing Discourse

1. In 1820, after a period of repressive rule, Fernando VII was forced to placate liberals by swearing allegiance to this constitution written in Cádiz. Its implementation in Mexico encouraged reactionaries there to proclaim Mexican independence so as to isolate that country from the infection of liberal European ideas (Parkes, chapter 4). For the debate in the Cortes de Cádiz and related discussion of the abolishment of the Inquisition, see *Actas de las Cortes de Cádiz*, 1: 19–31, 2: 1027–1229.

2. The pattern is similar to the code switching of bilingual speakers and the double voicing associated with African Americans. Yet, unlike those alternating behaviors, colonial public and private language usage suggests one language and its function or not.

3. "Segunda parte del Indio Constitucional, o Idioma de la sensibilidad" (Mexico City: Oficina de D. Alejandro Valdés, 1820).

4. The phrase is drawn from the prospectus of the *Correo americano del sur*, the insurgent newspaper that reflected the views of José María Morelos.

5. For a study of this 1820–21 period, see Rodríguez O. ("La transición de Colonia").

6. I am assuming the writer was a man for two reasons: (1) Although women wrote letters to the *Diario de México* in the early decades of the nineteenth century, most pamphletry was written by men even though these male writers sometimes adopted a fictitious female identity; and (2) the economic concerns expressed suggest a male breadwinner.

7. My phrase borrows from Anderson, who discusses the role of Lizardi's novel in creating a new Mexican identity.

8. Here I am mindful of Condillac and Volosinov (see later references in my text), but also Paulo Freire's discussion of schooling and deschooling in, on the one hand, using literacy to fill with words an individual's vacuum and, on the other, ridding him of conformity to authoritative language so that he can read the world himself.

9. Typical is Alegría's pronouncement that Lizardi was "chronologically the first Spanish American novelist" (16). However, some scholars have variously argued for the following as Spanish America's first novel: *El carnero* (Juan Rodríguez Freile, ca. 1638); *El desierto prodigioso y prodigio del desierto* (Pedro de Solís y Valenzuela, ca. 1650); *Infortunios de Alonso Ramírez* (Carlos de Sigüenza y Góngora, 1690); and *Lazarillo de ciegos caminantes* (Alonso Carrió de la Vandera, 1773). See Orjuela, 19–83; Pérez Blanco, 20–23.

10. Alegría's discussion of why there was no domestic novel in Spanish America during the colonial period (9–15) remains an excellent survey of attitudes toward fiction writing and reading in Spain's American colonies. Recent efforts by González Echevarría and Pupo-Walker to convert the *cartas de relación* into early forms of the Spanish American novel, which draw to a large extent on Sánchez's thesis (78–104), have also contributed to an understanding of its emergence there.

11. The scholarship on decolonization is vast; Betts provides a summary. For representative African titles, see Gifford and Louis, Birmingham, Oliveira e Castro; for Britain, Darwin; for France, Labouret, Sartre. Also see Fanon's *A Dying Colonialism*. In the case of Spanish America, and particularly Mexico, Sims is the only one I am familiar with who describes post-Independence in terms of decolonization. Zea, as I discuss, uses *decolonization* to refer to a mental process.

12. In his 1838 work, Howitt provides an early comparative view of how, in the name of Christianity, Catholics and Protestants in Asia, Africa, and the Americas perpetrated "the most extensive and extraordinary system of crime which the world ever witnessed."

13. For a discussion of the two terms, see the introduction to Williams and Chrisman, 1–20. Also see Chrisman's essay in the same volume, "The Imperial Unconscious? Representations of Imperial Discourse," 498–516. Said (*Culture and Imperialism*) acknowledges the importance of the latter term.

14. In using this vocabulary of "First" and "Third" Worlds, I am mindful of Fernández Retamar's attack on such categories in his essay on Martí in *Algunos usos de civilización y barbarie* (30–66). However, I use this shorthand to evoke the differences between worlds he sees in the Leninist terms of *imperial* and degrees of *colonial*. Ahmad's discussion of First and Third Worlds is also valuable. He makes it clear that the distinctions are not absolute since colonialism exists within so-called First World countries in racial and gendered differences.

15. These categories were specifically discussed in sessions labeled "Representations of Colonization: Class, Race, Gender, and the Fate of the Humanities" at the 1984 meeting of the Modern Language Association.

16. See Fernández Retamar, *Caliban*. For Caliban as symbol, see Vaughan.

17. Niranjana uses the term *siting* in his discussion of "translation," a concept he means broadly to cover imperializing strategies for absorbing the histories of colonized peoples. The collection by Godlewska and Smith is pertinent; in particular, see Crush's essay, "Post-colonialism, De-Colonization, and Geography," in which he asks the question: "What would a de-colonized, de-whitened, post-colonial geography actually look like?" (333–50).

18. Faced with many native tongues, particularly East Indian and African Luso-phone writers have seen the colonized language to be a unifying form of communication.

19. Adorno, Mignolo, and Zamora are among the most prominent Latin Americanists who have argued for the importance of "discourse," rather than "literature," in considering Latin American texts. For a helpful discussion of discourse, see Zamora, 7.

20. For the significance of Las Casas among this generation of Mexicans, see the unsigned writer in *Sud*, Oaxaca, January 25, 1813; see the *Diario de México*, November 15, 1812, for the life of Las Casas. Fray Servando Teresa de Mier was instrumental in this reconsideration of the foundational ideas of Las Casas in a definition of American nature. See my chapter 3, note 22.

21. Here I recall Spivak's question, "Can the subaltern speak?"

22. See Fernández Retamar *Caliban*. Also, Greenblatt's emphasis on "learning to curse" is suggestive of this view of the colonial's language. Greenblatt's title points to two aspects of the colonial self I develop later—anger directed not only at the colonizer but also at the self, and a language deprivation such that formulation of thought beyond the "cursing" level is difficult.

23. What the European Romantics were defining at this moment as the emotional release of individual sensibility or subjectivity, often in poetry, this American pamphleteer understood to be the historically determined, everyday response of the average colonial.

24. See José María Morelos's insurgent newspaper, *Correo americano del sur* (August 26, September 6, 9, 1813).

25. Vogeley, "The Discourse of Colonial Loyalty: Mexico, 1808" and "Colonial Discourse in a Postcolonial Context: Nineteenth-Century Mexico."

26. See Brading (*Mineros y comerciantes*, part 2, chapter 5); Hamill (*Hidalgo*, chapter 2); Ladd, Villoro (25–29); Flores Caballero (chapter 1). Hamill describes two types of criollos: the European and the American. Among the latter he finds "criollos de la plebe." Hamill also usefully documents stereotypes of the day, which disparaged the criollos as indolent and degenerate because of the American climate.

27. Brading (*Orígenes*) also emphasizes the role of Jesuit historians (Carlos Sigüenza y Góngora and Francisco Javier Clavigero) and writers (Rafael Landívar) in the formation of a Mexican consciousness; see also Navarro B. (chapter 6).

However, Mexicans also learned of their special nature through the writings of Alexander von Humboldt, discussed in the pages of the *Diario de México* as early as January 10, 1806.

28. The phrase is borrowed from the title of Domínguez's book.

29. His use of the term refers indistinguishably to both the languages of the governor and the governed.

30. On "colonial resistance," see the special number of *Modern Fiction Studies*, edited by Brennan. Lazarus, in his study of postcolonial African literature, also emphasizes resistance in his chapter on decolonization (1–26).

31. See Harlow for a seminal study of resistance literature.

32. For an understanding of Althusser and a valuable commentator on Althusser, Michel Pêcheux, I have relied on Macdonell. Macdonell valuably links Pêcheux's material view of the way words change meanings with Althusser's emphasis on class conflict in language and his focus on "interpellation." For a fuller discussion see Pêcheux (parts 2 and 3) and Althusser, 127ff.

33. Carrió de la Vandera's *Lazarillo de ciegos caminantes* (1775) is an important example of the debt colonial literature owes to the experiences of mail routes.

34. My definition depends to a great extent on Turner's anthropological approach to communication in the development of social structures. His emphasis on tangible objects, on the happening, on ritual, have made me think about the surrounding facts of colonial discourse. In the chapter "Hidalgo: History as Social Drama" in *Dramas*, Turner, among his many telling points with respect to the revolutionary moment and its message, calls attention to the Spanish road system (128) in tracing a flow of information in that social world.

35. Here I rely on Pratt's description of speech act theory: "speech act theory provides a way of talking about utterances not only in terms of their surface grammatical properties but also in terms of the context in which they are made, the intentions, attitudes, and expectations of the participants, the relationships existing between participants, and generally, the unspoken rules and conventions that are understood to be in play when an utterance is made and received" (86).

36. Studies of colonial representation (Merrim; Iris Zavala; Said, "Representing the Colonized"; Bhabha, "Stereotype") have variously considered the task of naming the Other, of imaginatively capturing the new. My focus, while remembering the first colonizers of the New World—the major theologians, priests, explorers, naturalists, military men, historians, and so on—whose words attempted to bridge the gap to the Old World, also attempts to consider as colonial discourse the production of later, lesser officials. These, perhaps no less noble, were often more caught up in the bureaucracy of the colonial enterprise; and their de facto power to interpret policy was arguably as important as the intellectual contributions of the first colonizers. Writing at long distance but also, increasingly, writing and speaking to a home readership and audience, they must be studied for the representation they provided of the king and the far-off court (Marin, *King*) and for the self-consciousness they taught colonials.

37. Vidal's discussion of the colonial's fascination with Baroque language perceptively links the taste to political and economic realities: "In social gatherings and palatial soirees one impressed viceregal authority by means of a verbal brilliance that could lead to the granting of favors and gifts within the bureaucratic scale" (108).

38. Patrick Taylor has a pertinent discussion on the importance of fear, in Kierkegaard's sense of jumping off into the abyss (84–87). However, Taylor's description of the slave's leap into history, even Taylor's recognition of the "risk of self" (86) that such a leap means, does not consider religious belief in an afterlife where one's actions may be judged.

39. For a rich collection of studies of this period, see González Stephan and Costigan.

40. Memmi prefers the term *colonialists* to *colonials* because he sees privilege perverting their viewpoint in such a way that they identify with the colonizers rather than with the lower-class colonized. Working from the historical example of Tunisia, Memmi, however, defines "colonials" as European-born; Tunisia's shorter colonial history does not suggest to his thought the emergence of a criollo type, such as evolved in Latin America over a longer period of time, caught more profoundly between two worlds.

41. For this discussion I am indebted to Heath. She emphasizes that the Franciscans, Augustinians, and Dominicans learned Nahuatl to use as a lingua franca among the many Indian tongues in Nueva España (23–27). Early experiments by the Franciscans and the Jesuits to teach a select group of Indians theology and classical culture in Latin were criticized and quickly abandoned.

42. "Alacena," "Allá va ese vocadillo para el guapo del tapado" (Mexico City: Oficina de D. José Maria Ramos Palomera, 1822).

43. "El Patan de Managua, J.J.G.," "Humanidad," reprinted from *Diario de La Habana*, *Diario de México*, November 7, 1810.

44. See Dhareshwar; the exchange between Jameson and Ahmad in *Social Text*; and *Yale French Studies*, the double volume "Post/Colonial Conditions: Exiles, Migrations, and Nomadisms."

45. Hechter in his valuable study of internal colonialism does not speak of decolonization but instead of national development according to which a peripheral group either seeks greater union within the larger core or else decides to separate (3–43). Hechter's sense of collective consciousness is broad in encompassing the cultural components of language and religion that may form it, and his use of the notion of *national* implies a deeper meaning for *nationalism* than nineteenth-century usage often allows. Yet my use of *decolonization* is meant to suggest a larger process than just state formation.

46. These categories are somewhat misleading, as Jennings shows in his description of the work of French Jesuits among the Iroquois.

47. L. M., "Solfeada y palo de ciego á todo autorcillo lego, ó Memorias para servir a la historia de la literatura de Nueva España, ó sea Examen crítico-apologético de los escritores del dia" (Mexico City: Oficina de M. Ontiveros, 1820). Lizardi's use of *mexicanismos* is important for many latter-day critics; see Davis, "Americanismos."

48. Strangely, only one copy of one volume has ever been found; it is part of the Sutro collection.

49. Yáñez also called Lizardi "patriarch and prophet in the country's list of saints" (Lizardi, *El Pensador Mexicano* vi). Yáñez's essay is indispensable for a post-Revolution analysis of favorable and unfavorable attitudes toward Lizardi and his work. Yáñez finds the disdain national critics show for Lizardi at odds with their professed interest in "lo mexicano" and "lo popular" and blames their rejection of his work on a continuing preoccupation with inherited formal standards for literature.

Yáñez also discovers in the mestizo identity of both Lizardi and his fictitious creation reasons for the book's truth as well as for ambivalent attitudes toward the public statement of this truth. Yáñez's highlighting of this symbolic aspect of the book's meaning—its portrayal of *mestizaje*—is borne out by a recently reprinted novel, *Perucho, nieto de Periquillo* (which first appeared in a Mexico City newspaper in installments in 1895–96). In it the anonymous author, signing himself "un Devoto del Pensador Mexicano," refers intertextually to the earlier work, mentioning specifically the importance of the mestizo portrayal of the national self for the late nineteenth century (see my "Intertexuality: *Perucho*").

50. See also Reyes's essay, "Categorías de la lectura," in *La experiencia literaria*, 145–50, where he traces reading to class and access to education.

51. I have discovered in the British Library seven *calendarios* dated 1866, which include excerpts from Lizardi's four novels, fables, newspaper writing, and last will and testament. Lizardi bibliographies have never recorded these *calendarios*, and I believe they are additional evidence of the diffusion of Lizardi's works in a form suited to readers of lesser education and income. The 32–page *calendario* devoted to the *Periquillo*, for example, includes the first two chapters of the novel and promises to be continued; but I find no sequel, which is not surprising, considering the political turmoil the country was thrown into the following year.

52. In his edition of Lizardi's *El Pensador Mexicano*, Yáñez's discussion of realism (xvi–xviii) and "bad taste" (xviii–xix, xxx–xxxiv) covers this point.

53. For an alternative view, see Stolley, who studies *El Periquillo Sarniento* and *Don Catrín* in terms of their "genealogy," their linkage to the Spanish picaresque novel.

54. See, for example, Urquhart on the role of the United Nations in bringing about peace in the postcolonial world.

Chapter 1. Lizardi and Print Culture

1. However, the oficial *gaceta* was sometimes under the direction of enlightened men; Antonio León y Gama, a noted scientist, edited five issues in 1784. Examples of semi-official *gacetas*, which to some extent also served as precedents for the *Diario* in considering all manner of scientific and commercial topics, were those edited by José Antonio Alzate y Ramírez from 1788 to 1795, and by Jacobo de Villaurrutia, while still in Guatemala (Liss, "Late Colonial Intellectuals").

2. For biographical information, I have relied largely on González Obregón's studies and Spell's "Life."

3. Rangel: "he enrolled in the *curso temporal de artes*," 47. Rangel's wording makes it seem to be a temporary course in the arts. Spell, basing his information on Rangel's research, has changed the meaning by expressing it this way: "on that day, he enrolled in the course in 'temporal de artes'" ("Life" 12).

4. "Respuesta del Pensador al defensor del Payo del Rosario. Ciudadano José Maria Aza" (Mexico City: Oficina del finado Ontiveros, 1825), reprinted in *Catalogue of Mexican Pamphlets in the Sutro Collection*, 442–49.

5. Radin, *Bibliography: The First Period*, 4–5. For information on the printing press, Radin cites Lizardi, "Breve sumaria por el Pensador al Señor Don Antonio Leon" (Mexico City, 1824), reprinted in *Obras* 13: 85–97.

6. For this information González Obregón (*Novelistas Mexicanos* 19) and Spell

("Life" 12–13) rely on a memorial published at the time of Lizardi's death (A. F. A., "Muerte del Pensador y noticia histórica de su vida," Mexico City: 1827).

7. Spell, "Lizardi and Taxco," reports the reasons for the conflicting views that (1) Lizardi had supported the insurgents and (2) he had remained faithful to his viceregal appointment as *teniente de justicia* in Taxco. Accused of turning over "without protest, all the available arms, powder and ammunition" to Morelos, who was besieging the town, Lizardi was imprisoned. However, he explained to authorities that a town council had adopted this ruse to protect the citizens and that, as soon as the insurgents left, they planned to proclaim their allegiance to the crown again. Apparently, the authorities believed him and he was set free.

McKegney refers to this dispute over Lizardi's loyalty, as it surfaced later, in "El Payo del Rosario y la riña de Lizardi con José María Aza." In 1823 those who had assisted the revolutionary cause were eligible for a government pension; and when Lizardi applied for his on the basis of the Taxco incident and it was granted, his "patriotism" was contested by many.

8. Jorge Flores, "Mosaico histórico," *Excélsior*, December 17, 1959. Quoted in Lizardi, *Obras* 1: 21.

9. The dialectical form originated with the dialogues of Plato, but the "dialogues of the dead" are a satirical invention of Lucian in the second century. In England and France in the seventeenth and eighteenth centuries there were many imitations of the classical form, in which persons from antiquity or from recent history spoke and often commented on contemporary events.

10. James McKegney, "El Payo del Rosario y la riña de Lizardi con José María Aza."

11. See "El Melancolico," "Literatura," *Diario de México*, October 19, 20, 1805; "El Semi-Sabio," *Diario de México*, January 18, 1806.

12. See "El Ex. D. P.," *Diario de México*, November 3, 1805.

13. Calleja, "Humanidades," *Diario de México*, February 4, 1806.

14. "Pronunciacion," April 19–20, 1806.

15. Lizardi touches on this and other issues in the *Diario*, February 14–16, 1812.

16. "El Criollo Pueblano," "Pronunciacion," *Diario*, February 8, 1806.

17. See "El Escuelero de Tierradentro," "Educacion de Querétaro," *Diario*, December 3–5, 1805; also "L. P.," "Pronunciacion," *Diario*, January 27, 1806.

18. "Idea de un manuscrito," *Diario*, November 8, 1807.

19. *Efemerides de España*, Núm. 315, "Sobre el buen tono," reprinted *Diario*, January 1–2, 1810.

20. J.M.W. Barueq. (Barquera), "Carta segunda," *Diario de México*, November 20, 1805.

21. Unsigned, "¿Las ciencias han corrompido las costumbres?" *Diario*, February 15–17, 1813.

22. Unsigned, "¿Las ciencias han corrompido las costumbres?" *Diario*, February 15–17, 1813.

23. This idea is developed in an article by Andrés Zarquechabala on the "papeles públicos," *Diario*, November 4, 1809.

24. Lizardi had 217 subscribers for this venture, with several receiving more than one copy. A few women's names appear on the list.

25. "De V. el Litigante," *Diario*, November 12–24, 1805.

26. Seijo Leuman Báñez, "Sobre la historia de las plantas americanas," *Diario*, September 23–24, 1806.

27. "Idea de las diversiones públicas en México," *Diario*, March 11, 1806. This follows a series on "Exâmen historico de las diversiones públicas de las naciones." Another significant way in which culture was democratized and spread at this time was the *retablo* industry, which was flourishing in Mexico then. By this means iconic images of Spanish Catholic forms were reproduced and sold cheaply. The image of the Virgen de Guadalupe, in particular, became the symbol of the insurgents (Giffords 19–44; de la Torre Villar and Navarro de Anda; Guedea).

28. "Tablas de Humboldt," *Diario de México*, May 18–20, 1807. This article quotes Humboldt's statistics that in 1803 the population of Nueva Espana was 5,764,731 and was divided approximately as follows:

75,000	Europeans
1,000,000	Spaniards or white Americans
2,300,000	Indians
2,385,000	Persons of other castes ("castas mixtas de indio, americano, europeo, asiático, africano & resultado bien diverso de lo que hasta ahora se ha creido")
5,760,000	

29. "El Melancólico," "Sobre las bellas artes," *Diario*, December 27, 1805.

30. "Proyectista," *Diario*, October 6, 1805.

31. See "El Bascongado," "Lenguage del Silbido," *Diario*, November 9, 1805; "El Ex. D. P.," "Costumbres," *Diario*, December 7, 1805, defends the *silbido*.

32. The technical mastery of the poetry of many "songs" and "marches," which were intended to circulate orally, suggests authors from the learned culture (González Casanova and Miranda).

33. See Bernstein, Castanien, and the two studies by Gómez Alvarez and Téllez Guerrero.

34. "Edicto del Santo Tribunal de la Fe. Prohibidos aún para los que tienen licencia," *Diario*, September 24, 1809.

35. To be found in the AGN Ramo de Inquisición, vol. 1409. The author in question was Pedro Nicole.

36. The collection is also valuable because some of the used copies have the names of their owners.

37. "J. L. M.," "Discurso sobre el uso de la mitologia en las composiciones poeticas," *Diario*, September 20, October 6–9, December 20–21, 23–24, 26, 1808.

38. "Son superiores las bellas letras à las bellas artes. Alegoria por Mr. Klopstock," *Diario*, March 1 and 3–4, 1809; see also "El Quixote del Parnaso," "Poesia," February 19, 1806.

39. Eastern peoples were usually associated with language that hid several meanings. An article in the December 25, 1812, issue of the *Diario*, "De la alegoría," develops this idea: "One of the most decorous stylistic devices, when a man is forced to speak or write about an ugly vice, or a person who displays some weakness, is

allegory. . . . Orientals, whose ostentatious customs have accustomed them to speak with a certain loftiness, and whose use of the Koran has taught them to express themselves with mystery, excel in allegories."

40. An article in the *Diario de México*, November 8, 1806, discusses Blair at length. See also my article, "Mexican Readings of Hugh Blair's *Rhetoric.*"

41. October 15, 16, 1805. See also O'Kane.

42. See my article on Lizardi's "Concept of 'the People.'"

43. For a discussion of La Malinche as a national symbol, see Paz, *El laberinto de la Soledad*; Cypess; Phillips; also Leal, *Aztlán y México*, 168–69.

44. Montesinos's bibliography of translations of foreign works remains one of the best sources for this study.

45. "El Ex-D.P.," "Inscripciones," *Diario de México*, November 3, 1805.

Chapter 2. Lizardi and the Satiric Novel

1. Fuentes elaborates these views in *La nueva novela hispanoamericana*. Fuentes, Cortázar, and Cabrera Infante express similar ideas in interviews in the collections by Guibert and by Harss and Dohmann. See also Dorfman for the importance of teaching new reading habits to the Latin American reader.

2. See "La afeta á ler," *Diario de México*, March 2, 1806, in which the female writer asks for reading material befitting her interests. The letter's orthography suggests substandard language, thus hinting at unfamiliarity with grammar and print.

3. See "B," November 8, 1805, who asks why nudity is peculiar to Mexico, why the Indian, no matter how poor he is, is always dressed but persons of mixed blood are usually naked, and why haulers go about nude when clothing costs so little.

4. "El Tocayo de Clarita," "El Gran Hospital del periodico titulado: La Canoa" (Mexico City: Oficina de Juan Bautista de Arizpe, 1820).

5. See, for example, the August 29, 1815, edition of his *Alacena de Frioleras* (*Obras* 4: 117–22) in which Lizardi sketches himself: "His manner was affable and courtly, but his features [were] somewhat hard since his face showed his hypochondria in its darkness. The shape of his face was elliptical or longish, his black eyes sad and a little unequal in their symmetry; his beard sparse and his teeth even more so; his nose regular."

6. See my "The Discourse of Colonial Loyalty."

7. This one-page announcement is bound in the Bancroft Library's run of the *Diario* after the March 16, 1808, issue. A later reference to the announcement (April 25, 1808) suggests that it came out in the *Gazeta Política de México* on March 12, 1808.

8. Lizardi fictionalizes an exchange between an "Autor" and an "Impresor" in no. 2 of vol. 1 (1812) of *El Pensador Mexicano* (*Obras* 3: 42–45).

9. "F. de la P.," in a letter to the *Diario* (dated July 23, 1809, Tuyahualco, and printed August 4, 1809), records his reading: "el Quixote, ya la Casandra, ya la Pamela, el Telemaco, el Robinson, los Cuentos Tártaros, y otros." A request to buy "*Clara y Grandison* (Richardson)" appeared in the December 1, 1805, issue of the *Diario*.

10. Any work will have to begin from the base of Pérez Marchand's excellent work

on the eighteenth century. There she describes the nature of prohition and censure: how proscribed works entered Mexico and were circulated; in addition to giving titles of banned books, she lists owners and readers of illicit books. Based on extensive research in Inquisition archives, she defines the terminology of edicts (atheism, tolerantism, sedition, etc.). However, she observes that the Inquisition began to lose control in the colony toward the end of the eighteenth century. See also Longhurst; and Vogeley, *La literatura manuscrita*.

11. J. M. L., *Diario de México*, January 22, 24, 1812.

12. Lizardi wrote in 1820 ("Quien llama al toro sufra la cornada," *Obras* 1: 242) that it sold for three times more. A biographer at the time of his death in 1827 said that it sold for two times more (A. F. A., "Muerte del Pensador y noticia historica de su vida" [Mexico City: Imp. de la Ex-Inquisicion á cargo de Manuel Ximeno], reprinted in *Catalogue of Mexican Pamphlets in the Sutro Collection*, 489–94).

13. González Casanova y Miranda; Vogeley, *La literatura manuscrita*.

14. Of those critics who interpret the *Periquillo* according to the picaresque form, many tie Lizardi's book to LeSage's eighteenth-century work *Gil Blas*, which Lizardi probably knew in Padre Isla's translation. See Alegría (19), as well as Casas de Faunce, Lozano, and Lizardi's *Obras* 8: xiii (comments by Reyes Palacios).

15. Blanchard makes this point (3: 190).

16. Johnson in her fine book on satire in colonial Spanish America follows its development over three centuries in the works of identifiable authors. However, to those, it is necessary to emphasize, must be added satire's underground development as anonymous (see González Casanova y Miranda).

17. For a further discussion of "colonial reader," see my article on the subject.

18. This exchange in which Lizardi quotes Terán verbatim and answers his criticism was published in the *Noticioso General*, February 12,15, 1819. This "Apología de el Periquillo Sarniento" is reproduced in *Obras* 8: 17–27. I refer to this exchange again later.

19. See Tanck de Estrada, "La enseñanza de la lectura," and Staples, "La lectura y los lectores."

20. I quote here and elsewhere from the 1974 Editorial Porrúa edition of the *Periquillo*, readily accessible in the Sepan Cuantos series.

21. "Aquel," "Lectura," *Diario de México*, July 16–18, 26, 1809; Unsigned, "Carta á una señorita sobre el modo de aprovechar la lectura de los libros," *Diario de México*, July 16–18, 1809. These newspaper essays, as I have suggested, seem to have been an important means of introducing contemporary philosophy. This series, for example, mentions the "respetable Loke" [respectable John Locke].

Chapter 3. El Periquillo Sarniento: *The Family: Sons and Fathers*

1. Dictionary definitions of *sarna* today suggest "scabies." Yet the *Diario de México* (November 13–16, 1806) in a discussion of smallpox vaccination and the plague killing thousands of Mexico's Indians uses *sarna* to describe that contagion. Consequently, the word may have connoted that contemporary problem, particularly associated with America's Indian population.

2. In an exchange in the *Diario* (July 4, August 19, 1807) that criticizes the editors for their choice of letters to print, *perico* and *papagayo*, varieties of parrots, are invoked humorously as types of human speakers: "These animals [*pericos*] don't know what they are saying" and "I have spoken *a lo perico* [uttering words foolishly], without a knowledge of cause."

3. "El Arlequin. F." in an article in the *Diario de México* (August 7–8, 1806), "Nomenclatura," also protested against this Mexican custom of giving *malos nombres* [vilifying nicknames].

4. In the *Periquillo* Lizardi says: "Los niños son los monos de los viejos" [children ape adults] (27). I quote here from the 1974 Editorial Porrúa edition of the *Periquillo*, readily accessible in the Sepan Cuantos series. The translation from the *Periquillo* is largely my own, although I have borrowed from the translation by Katherine Anne Porter and Eugene Pressly.

5. Signed "D," "Historia natural," *Diario de México*, July 19, 24–25, 1806.

6. Liss discusses divine right of kings in her study of Jesuit contributions to the ideology of Spanish empire in Mexico, particularly questioning Jesuit loyalties in the eighteenth century to pope and king. Did the Spanish king's right to rule a Christian empire come directly from God or did it come via the pope? This discussion, initiated by legal scholars like Francisco de Vitoria and Francisco Suárez, trickled down as a general reverence for the king's authority.

7. *Obras* 3: 219–51. This essay is interesting for various reasons. It shows an increasing sense that Spain, invaded by the liberal French and allied with Protestant England at that moment, was no longer the pure source of Catholicism that it once was. Americans, such as the morally indignant Lizardi who denounces European crimes, are the true Catholics.

In addition, the careful discussion of heretics, apostates, atheists, unbelievers—and the contemporary categories of deists, materialists, liberals, Jansenists, *espíritus fuertes*—Americanizes and updates Las Casas's analysis of the different kinds of barbarians in *In Defense of the Indians* (see Las Casas, *Colección*).

Finally, Lizardi's defense of the rebellious priests Hidalgo and Morelos, on the grounds of their ecclesiastical status and their secondary role in bringing to a head resentments caused by past injustices, dexterously turns the tables on the officials who excommunicated them.

8. Lizardi's awareness of the Inquisition figures importantly in his writings throughout his career. As a writer he particularly understood the control this body had to outlaw imaginative literature. The following appeared in his *El Pensador Mexicano* on September 30, 1813: "I have heard many wise men dispute the prohibition of *Eusebio, Iglesias*, and some verses of the *Arriaza*, etc.; and they wanted to know why they were prohibited. But the Inquisition was not concerned with satisfying [curiosity] but with ordering; and it was not licit for us to inquire but to obey totally and blindly, what was just or unjust, for this is the character of despotism and the distinguishing feature of all ignorant, enslaved peoples" (*Obras* 3: 181).

Similarly, in the introduction to the *Periquillo*'s second edition (1825), he stated: "It is necessary to remember that this work was written and published in 1816, under

Spanish domination. Its author was viewed critically by the government as a patriot; there was no freedom of the press; we were subject to the censorship of *oidores*, canons and friars—and beyond anything else, with the foolish and despotic Inquisition on top of us."

During the period 1810–1820 the civil war must have increased the Inquisition's power to dictate public morals without appeal. Indeed, the *Noticioso General* (February 23, 26, 1816) published a list of 173 books, newspapers, pamphlets, speeches, and plays that were gathered up as dangerous; another seventeen items were prohibited even for those who had a license to read borderline material. Thus, the Inquisition controlled reading and thought.

9. Juan Camargo y Cavallero, p. 29. This statistical report by a Spanish military engineer also provides impressions of the various classes in the Mexican population.

10. J. W. Barquera, "Reflexiones filosofopolíticas," *Diario*, November 1, 1808.

11. See, for example, "El Melancólico," "Resumen histórico político de los sucesos de la Europa desde la declaracion de la guerra con la Alemania hasta la toma de Viena," *Diario*, February 23–25, 1806; then the biography of Napoleon, Unsigned, "El Tirano de la Europa," *Diario*, October 10 and 13–16, 1808; also Unsigned, "Idea histórica de Bonaparte," *Diario*, December 2–3, 1808, which is favorable to him in describing his military exploits.

12. See, for example, "Contra la igualdad de la Francia," *Diario*, May 16, 1810.

13. J. W. Barquera, "Reflexiones filosofopolíticas," *Diario*, October 31, November 1–2, 1808.

14. *Representacion que hizo Nuestro Soberano El Señor D. Fernando VII a su Padre el Señor D. Carlos IV.* En octubre de 1807. Reimpreso en Cadiz, y por su original en la Oficina de Doña Maria Fernandez de Jauregui. Año de 1809. Mexico City.

15. In his "Carta primera de el Pensador al Papista" (Mexico City: Oficina de Betancourt, 1822) (*Obras* 9: 537–51), Lizardi describes how the bishop of Oaxaca said, "Señor Morelos had horns and a tail."

16. Arzobispo D. Francisco Xavier de Lizana y Beaumont, "Edicto," *Diario*, October 22, 1810.

17. Unsigned, "Sobre los medios de promover mayor número de matrimonios," *Diario de México*, March 12–23, 1813.

18. See, for example, *Obras* 3: 67: "The cause, then, of the insurrection is the complaint of Americans. This relative to bad government in the past; the latter was the most impolitic which has ever been seen. And the complaint comes down to the fact *that the hands of Americans have been tied [preventing] industry and the doors to their employment have been closed.* There you have it in a few words, the explanation for the source of the revolution; and with the evil exposed, and reason and justice in favor, the beginnings of the remedy."

19. In the *prólogo* Lizardi's mature protagonist says: "When I write my life it is only with the healthy intention that my children be instructed in the matters of which I speak to them" (5).

20. Taylor (*Drinking*, 206–16) describes these *gavillas*, or gangs of thieves and cattle rustlers. Some, like the group that Lizardi's fiction describes, included women.

21. In the forefront of resurrecting this debate between Las Casas and Sepúlveda was Fray Servando Teresa de Mier. Mier wrote the prologue for the Spanish edition of *Breve relación de la destrucción de las Indias* (London, 1812). Mier also made the historical debate an important defense of American nature in his *Cartas de un americano* (London, 1811–1812), documents that were circulated widely in the Spanish colonies; Calvillo, Mier's editor (1987), calls Mier "el nuevo Las Casas." See particularly *Cartas* 101–3, 103–7, 139–216, 219–22, 232–47.

Las Casas was especially promoted in Europe in the last decades of the eighteenth century and the first of the nineteenth by the Abbé Henri Grégoire, who contributed several letters and essays to a two-volume Spanish edition of the *Obras* of Las Casas, published in Paris in 1822 (ed. Juan Antonio Llorente, Casa de Rosa). Among these documents are letters between Grégoire and Mier on the subject of Las Casas. Grégoire, imbued with the liberal ideas of the French revolution, was particularly interested in Las Casas's rationale for introducing black slavery into the Americas.

22. Reprinted in the introduction to *El Periquillo Sarniento*, José Joaquín Fernández de Lizardi (Barcelona: Editorial Sopena, 1901), 2: 6.

23. See in the *Actas de las Cortes de Cádiz*, "Las provincias de Ultramar. La representación igualitaria. La discriminación social y racial" (1: 93–160) and "Los españoles que por cualquier línea traen origen de Africa" (1: 161–292); also David T. Garza, "Mexican Constitutional Expression in the Cortes of Cadiz," in Benson, 43–58.

Chapter 4. El Periquillo Sarniento: *Law and Utopia*

1. Franco, *Introduction*, is the only one, so far as I know, who identifies the island as Utopian, thereby implying that Lizardi is portraying a nonreal world, a vision of Mexico's future if independence were achieved (37). Sánchez, for example, does not find a voyage to the Pacific unusual for a Mexican and suggests a literary precedent in Sigüenza y Góngora's *Alonso Ramírez* (111, 114).

2. These issues concern Lizardi, as shown by articles throughout *El Pensador Mexicano* (1812–14).

3. Here Lizardi deviates from the standard definition of criollos—European-blooded persons born in the Americas.

4. A series of *bandos* from the viceroy, Félix María Calleja, published in the *Noticioso General*, June 7, 10, 14, 1816, provides a possible explanation of this fictional title. During the period from 1813 to 1814, the trading monopoly that Manila merchants enjoyed had been discontinued and English cotton and other textiles had entered Mexico and the Caribbean at a much lower price. The viceroy was interested in selling off these cheap goods quickly so that the king could resume his protection of the Philippines (and prices could be raised).

5. "Reflexiones al proyecto de reglamento criminal presentado a las Cortes," *Diario de México*, July 3, 1811.

6. Unsigned, "Examen histórico de las diversiones públicas de las naciones," *Diario de México*, March 10–11, 1806.

7. See the *Periquillo*, 354.

8. See the *Periquillo* when a worthy citizen speaks, 196–97: "I, for example, speak

Spanish reasonably well because I was reared alongside a wise friar, who taught me to read, write and speak. If I had been reared in the house of my aunt, the tripe-seller, surely today you would not find anything to admire in me."

9. The *Periquillo*, 369: "I remember having read in Plautus where, speaking of how useless or at least of how little respected laws are in a land where customs are relaxed, he says. . . ."

10. Unsigned, "Dinero llama dinero," *Diario de México*, November 6, 1806.

11. Historians who study Latin American revolts have devoted much attention to rural unrest in Mexico over the centuries in an effort to see why that country seems to show such a pattern; see particularly Katz; Tutino; Van Young "Agustín Marroquín"; W. Taylor (*Drinking*). Speculation as to the rebel troops' motives for fighting generally concludes that no hard historical evidence exists to determine what might have been ideologically based conflict and what might have been purely criminal fighting.

12. For an ironic discussion of criminality among the white upper classes, see the *Periquillo*, 174–75.

13. J. H. Hexter states in "Utopia and Its Historical Milieu" that because an author criticizes one social group it cannot be concluded that he automatically favors another group (Surtz and Hexter 4: lix–lv).

14. Unsigned, "Prólogo," *Diario de México*, August 21–23, 1806.

15. Unsigned, "Cap. 26," *Diario de México*, July 20–25, 1807.

16. P. P., "Señor Diarista. Acabo de presenciar un diálogo . . . ," *Diario de México*, May 4, 1808.

17. *El Periquillo Sarniento*, 2nd ed. (Mexico City: J. Valdés y Cueva, R. Araujo, 1885), 4: 48. This editorial footnote is usually abbreviated in modern editions of the novel.

18. The importance of work in constructing an ideal society would have had resonances for Mexicans. In the sixteenth century the Dominicans, who were some of the most outspoken critics of Spanish abuses in the New World, sent one of their friars, Vasco de Quiroga, to Michoacán to found a community in which Christian ideals would be taught to the Indians (see Tena Ramírez). This order's emphasis on work to bring about the City of God on earth relates to the Augustinian concern for the will; and it suggests that, particularly after the Reformation, Catholic theology was not as uniformly committed to a Stoic acceptance of conditions in this world, the supremacy of faith, and a mystical ideal as may be popularly thought (for a discussion of the ideological differences between the various religious orders see González Casanova, *Misoneísmo*, chapter 1).

19. Indeed, Gonzalbo Aizpuru (*Historia de la Educación* 11) writes: "In the Renaissance Hispanic world, and throughout the Golden Age, the dispute between arms and letters was more than a literary recourse or a theoretical discussion. . . . Arms, in the service of a monarchy with imperial arms, gave glory to soldiers and contributed to enlarging the Crown's territory; letters, destined for public service or to the embellishment of the language, consolidated the conquered lands and facilitated good administration."

20. Knowlton's discovery is an amazing linkage. However, his work is largely textual in its analysis of language, and his speculation is limited. He says it cannot be concluded from his evidence that Lizardi traveled to Manila, and he does not read Lizardi's portrayal of the Chinese literally. Instead he emphasizes the author's desire to criticize conditions in Mexico through the depiction of an island society; because life in the Philippines could not be the epitome of social perfection Lizardi required, he chose the relatively unknown Chinese society.

21. Félix García, editor of the 1947 edition, records the book's popularity throughout Europe in the sixteenth and seventeenth centuries (González de Mendoza, xxxiii–xxxv).

22. See my article on González de Mendoza, "China and the American Indies: A Sixteenth-Century 'History.'"

23. See Lizardi's political pamphlets: "Segundo sueño de El Pensador Mexicano" (1822) (*Obras* 12: 25–43), "Impugnación que los gatos . . ." (1824) (*Obras* 13: 31–59), "Dentro de seis años o antes hemos de ser tolerantes" (1825) (*Obras* 13: 537–46); and No. 6 of *Correo Semanario de México* (1826) (*Obras* 6: 90–104).

24. See Benot for a discussion of the participation of other authors in Raynal's book (Denis Diderot, for example), and how the French *philosophes* compacted into this economic treatise questions of human nature, competition between world empires, laicization of the state, the means toward a Utopian future, and so on.

25. Neither Raynal's name nor Eduardo Malo de Luque, the pseudonym under which the Duque de Almodóvar translated Raynal's work into Spanish (*Historia política de los establecimientos ultramarinos de las naciones europeas*, Madrid, 1784–1790), shows up in the Abadiano collection.

26. Regueiro provides a valuable analysis of how the Duque de Almodóvar, in translating Raynal's work into Spanish, softened or eliminated entirely the criticism of Spanish colonialism found in the French work, with the result that the Inquisition prohibited the French version from circulating in the Americas but permitted the Spanish (186).

27. Baudet (1976, 43ff) emphasizes Chinese atheism as an important factor in the appeal that that civilization had for eighteenth-century French philosophers, such as Voltaire. Baudet sees the Chinese role in a European process of "dechristianization." However, in Spain and its American colonies, because of the fact that ethnographic accounts of American Indian and Moslem peoples were being produced largely by exiled Jesuits, their humanism was still tempered by considerations of these peoples' religious beliefs.

28. For a pertinent discussion of Spaniards' use of the term *Indian*, see Reissner.

29. See, for example, "Rasgo filosófico," *Diario de México*, January 14, 16, 1810.

30. "Apuntaciones político-morales. Sobre la obediencia popular," *El Mentor Mexicano*, October 11, 1811.

31. A. A. G., "Política: Articulo comunicado a los editores de la Tertulia patriotica de Cádiz, sobre que la soberania de la nacion no es contradictoria a la monarquia," *El Mentor Mexicano*, February 11, 1811; reprinted in the *Diario de México*, July 10, 1812.

32. Here I diverge from writers like Cordero who describe Lizardi in the *Periquillo* as "a tranquil and serene propagandist for ideas in favor of the independence of his *patria*" (26). Hale in his discussion of the growth of Mexican liberalism valuably warns that the equation of *liberalismo* with *patria* is misleading, that the desire of Mexican criollos for social reforms did not necessarily translate into a wish for independence from Spain.

Chapter 5. El Periquillo Sarniento: *Education*

1. For background on Mexico's educational practices throughout the colonial period, see among others: Gonzalbo Aizpuru (*Historia de la educación*) and Tanck de Estrada (*Educación ilustrada*, "Tensión," "Enseñanza de la Lectura").

2. For an attempt to merge Christian and humanistic meanings, see Almeida, *Armonía de la razon y la religión, ó respuestas filosóficas a los argumentos de los incrédulos*. This book is to be found in the Sutro collection.

3. See, for example, J.M.W. Barueq. (Barquera), *Diario de México*, December 13, 1805: "Fathers are the providers of a proper education for their children and their domestic help, as we recommend according to the rules of Providence for this end. Fathers sow the good seed, and mothers with their nurture cultivate it."

4. However, Lizardi gives evidence of having read some of Rousseau's ideas on education, as transmitted through Padre Blanchard, in writings like "Continúa el proyecto sobre las escuelas" (*Obras* 3: 424–29). There he urges that children not be confined to schools in their early years but instead be allowed to develop physically by playing in the country.

5. See, for example, the letter by "El Criollo Mexicano" in the November 9, 1805, issue of the *Diario de México:* "I want to know from you, or from someone else who may know, what is the reason that we *criollos* generally do not pronounce correctly our Spanish language. Is it because our parents did not teach it to us from the time we were very young? . . . What advantages society would have received if our forebears had spoken the language of their origins! Perhaps this circumstance in a *criollo* of good education would be a quality that, among people of politics and character, would bring him some consideration in benefits and esteem."

6. Lizardi develops the idea of imitation in the educational process in his essay "Educación," *El Pensador Mexicano* (*Obras* 3: 106–10).

7. Lizardi describes, for example, in *El Pensador Mexicano* (*Obras* 3: 225): "the constant tradition which has come down to us from father to son has removed all doubt in the particular, and to deny assent to these truths would be to incur the greatest stupidity and barbarism."

However, the passage of women's knowledge from mother to daughter, which Lizardi explores in *La Quijotita*, seems not to qualify as "tradition."

8. Lizardi explores this issue in several essays in *El Pensador Mexicano*, in particular the essays written between November 11 and December 9, 1813 (*Obras* 3: 218–51).

How one viewed "tradition" depended to a great extent on whether or not one approved of the revolutionary priests, Hidalgo and Morelos.

For a helpful, related discussion, see Hobsbawm and Ranger.

9. "El nuevo arbitrista," *Diario de México*, November 20, 1805.

10. *Periquillo*, 113.

11. A contemporary of Lizardi's, whom Moore ("Bibliografía" 391) hypothesizes may have been Mariano Galván Rivera, wrote the following about Lizardi, thereby suggesting the element of paternal supervision in a son's education was autobiographical:

> Don José Joaquín Fernández de Lizardi is one of the men whose knowledge and writings would have been the pride of his *patria*, if his literary education had kept pace with the clarity and quickness of his talent and his extraordinary facility with writing. But unfortunately for his country, the first years of his youth were wasted, not so much because of indolence but because of the slender resources of his father, who did not give him the best teachers or exercise over his activities and studies that untiring vigilance that is necessary for children and young people until the hardness, aridity, and boring monotony of primary instruction are overcome. Thus it is that, despite the fact that when he was older he applied himself with the greatest dedication to the reading of good and bad books indiscriminately, he could not acquire that solid instruction that foundational studies, followed in an orderly way according to a proper distribution, give. This [proper education] forms the correct and sure judgment which characterizes the production of wise men, and everyone bemoaned the lack [of this judgment] in his innumerable writings. Another failing, no less important, was the lack of correction and polish in what he wrote, something he never could achieve, which he himself confessed at the end of the last chapter of the *Periquillo*. (Quoted in "Ligeros apuntes para la biografía del Pensador Mexicano," preface to *El Periquillo, por el Pensador Mexicano*, 4th ed. [Mexico City: Librería de Galván, 1842.] iii–iv)

12. Lizardi writes in an essay in vol. 2 of *Ratos entretenidos* that "All men are possessed of ignorance; but ignorance is not one and the same thing in all men" (13–26).

13. For Rousseau's influence in Spanish America, see Spell's valuable *Rousseau in the Spanish World Before 1833*; also Miranda, 213–33. For Enlightenment influences on Spain's American colonies, see Whitaker; and Aldridge.

However, see Lanning (*Academic Culture*) for a valuable qualification:

> It has long been the custom of specialists to assume that the theoretical foundation of the revolt against Spain rested solely upon the ideas of the French political doctrinaires of 1789. A man dropping from Mars to investigate that subject, with all second-hand treatises destroyed and forced to use original papers exclusively, would perhaps not regard the names of Rousseau, Voltaire, Montesquieu, or even Raynal as significant enough to emphasize. . . . No doubt these last gave

the late colonial period a definite slant, but the names which would seem of transcendant importance in this hypothetical book would be, instead, St. Thomas Aquinas, Descartes, Newton, Condillac, Pierre Gassendi, and Malebranche. Without them Raynal, Condorcet, Diderot, Benjamin Franklin, and Thomas Paine would scarcely have been heard and certainly not understood" (87).

All of this is to say that these revolutionary writers, because of the prestige of the Church in the Spanish colonies, passed through the filter of more innocuous thinkers and Christian intermediaries such as Padre Blanchard.

14. See, however, Jacobo Chencinsky, "Estudio Preliminar," in Lizardi's *Obras* 1: 68–69; also Guiton.

15. See, for example, Lozano, whose analysis depends on finding a link to a similar character in *Gil Blas* and to establishing the satire of colonial medicine: "Doctor Physic in *Periquillo Sarniento* is a caricature of the quack doctors of Lizardi's time but doubtless he is also patterned after Doctor Blood-letting [Doctor Sangrado] in *Gil Blas*" (265).

16. See, particularly, chapter 2, in which Parker attributes the insight that the picaresque novel had its origins in the Counter-Reformation to Enrique Moreno Báez, "Lección y sentido del *Guzmán de Alfarache*," *Revista de Filología Española*, Anejo 40 (Madrid, 1948).

17. For a detailed analysis of Lizardi's religious beliefs see Piana, chapter 4.

18. Lizardi discusses Deist thought at length in *El Pensador Mexicano* (3: 219–51).

19. See my article on Lizardi and the Inquisition.

20. On ocular learning, discussed as part of the vulgarization of science in eighteenth-century France, see Stafford, chapter 2, 4.

21. However, one notes a certain defensiveness with respect to a writer's access to books in a political pamphlet, "Defensa del Pensador Mexicano por su aprendiz" (Mexico City: Imprenta Imperial, n.d.). In it the author tries to list how many books Lizardi himself owned, and he describes Lizardi's habit of reading in public libraries.

22. The same essay appeared, credited to this French philosopher, several times: in Almeida's *Armonía de la razon y la religión* (1: 78–80); and in the May 14–15, 1832, issues of *La Antorcha*.

23. See, for example, Spell, "Life": "Lizardi treated his material with such attention to detail and local color as to foreshadow definitely the *costumbrista* movement which gained ascendancy in Spain only a short time later" (112). Sánchez in his discussion of Lizardi and the *Periquillo* (105–23) also links them to *costumbrista* developments in Realism.

24. See, particularly, Bhabha, "Representation and the Colonial Text."

25. This indictment of three hundred years of Spanish colonial government—rather than the crime of individual Mexicans—is openly stated in the first numbers of *El Pensador Mexicano*. Also see my "The Concept of 'the People' in *El Periquillo Sarniento*."

26. "Salvo sea el lugar," "El de las Batuecas," *Diario de México*, November 13–14, 1811.

Chapter 6. El Periquillo Sarniento: *Adolescence, Gratitude, and Whimsy*

1. For a discussion of differing views, see Hiner; Spacks. Kiell goes back to Aristotle and Augustine for evidence that adolescence, because it is tied to biology, is a universal experience.

2. One of the debates at the Cortes de Cádiz was "Sobre la libertad para contraer matrimonio y la mayoría de edad" (*Actas* 1: 293–334).

3. I have consulted the original printing of this pamphlet, and "consistente" is used there. It is not clear if this is a misprint for "consintiente" [consenting], or if Lizardi intended "consistente" to mean "solid, stable and lasting," as in dependable manhood. I have tried to incorporate both senses in my translation.

4. See also the unsigned "Rasgo sobre la amistad," *Diario de México*, February 2–3, 1811.

5. "Orah," "De la amistad," *Diario de México*, August 5, 1806.

6. This counsel is to be found in a contemporary edition, *Los oficios de Ciceron.* This book is part of the Abadiano collection. Almeida, too, speaks of an inner voice, calling it the voice of reason and God (1: 88ff.)

7. This chapter, only published after Lizardi's death, is chapter 2 in vol. 4 of the 1830–31 edition.

8. For a discussion of intermarriage in binding together Mexican wealth, see particularly Ladd (25–27) and Kicza (chapter 7). The latter is useful for a study of marriage into Mexican families by enterprising foreigners.

9. See my article, "La figuración de la mujer."

10. For a discussion of homosexuality in the *Periquillo*, see Irwin.

11. The *Diario de México* is full of essays and poems devoted to "gratitude" and "ingratitude." See particularly [Juan María Wenceslao] Sánchez de la Barquera, "La piedad filial. Anecdota curiosa," July 29, 1806; "Tirsis," "El amor y la ingratitud," August 15, 1811; "Tirsis," "La ingratitud. Romance endecasílabo," September 21, 1811.

12. For a typical colonial statement, see Lic. J. T. Villalpando, "Reflexiones filósofo-cristianas echas â los Americanos," *Diario de México*, October 11, 1810.

13. See the versions by Louis Hersent (1808) and Jean-Jacques-François Le Barbier (1810). Hugh Honour in *The European Vision of America* reproduces Hersent's painting (exhibited in Salons in 1808, 1814 and 1824) and provides the source for the several versions of the scene (269). It is Jean François Marmontel who, in his *Les Incas ou la destruction de l'empire du Pérou*, tells the story of how an Indian *cacique* urged his wife, whose baby had just died, to generously nurse with her milk the dying Las Casas so as to show their gratitude. The illustrator for that first edition, Jean-Michel Moreau the Younger, depicted the scene; and engravings in 1808 and 1823 spread the image. Honour reproduces Le Barbier's painting in his *The New Golden Land* (161).[Juan María Wenceslao] Sánchez de la Barquera invokes the classical source for this model of virtue, Valerio Maximo, in his essay cited above, "La piedad filial," in the *Diario de México*, July 29, 1806.

14. On February 21, 1809, in an article on Pestalozzi by Juan Bernardo O'Gavan, reprinted from a Havana newspaper, the names of Locke and Condillac appear but

are inked out in the Sutro copy. On October 3, 1809, Locke is praised, along with Leibnitz and Newton, in a list of modern philosophers.

15. Porter's role in the translation is interesting. Pressly was Porter's third husband and they collaborated on the project. Her participation is documented in an exchange of letters between the two, and the translation is shown to be essentially Pressly's. Her role seems to have been that of editor and publishing agent. She tried to have the whole of the book published, but Doubleday wanted the digressions cut.

16. I have used Pierre Larousse's discussion of sensualist philosophy's contribution to the meaning of "voluptuousness" in *Grand Dictionnaire Universel du XIXe Siècle*, vol. 15 (Paris: Administration du Grand Dictionnaire Universel, 1876), 1186–87.

17. See Navarro B., particularly chapters 6–9.

Chapter 7. La Quijotita y Su Prima: *Colonial Nature*

1. My study of *La Quijotita* uses the Ruíz Castañeda edition (1967); all quotes are my translations from that edition.

2. Watt makes the point that, because the middle class enjoyed new leisure in the eighteenth century in England, the women of that class particularly became novel readers and their tastes began to shape the genre (43–45, 151–52, 298–99). However, McKeon questions the assumption that "'the rise of the reading public' in early modern England . . . influenced the rise of the novel" (51). He wonders how much of this new leisure was actually spent reading; and he suggests that the novel's association with women at this time owes more to "a fear that women's morals will be corrupted by reading romances" and a "persistence of anxiety about women" (52).

E. Jennifer Monaghan in her essay "Literacy Instruction and Gender in Colonial New England," in Davidson, *Reading* (53–80), helpfully focusses on the schooling of women in trying to determine gender in the early novel in British America. Several of her conclusions point to differences in Spanish America; in British America, for example, "[b]ecause writing was considered a job-related skill, society only required that it be taught to boys" (70). As I have shown, traditional education in Spanish America did not usually aim to prepare the upper-class boy for work. And girls in British America did not, as a rule, have the additional impediment of racial difference that many of that sex had in Spanish America.

In *Historia de la educación en la época colonial*, Gonzalbo Aizpuru, particularly in chapter 2, emphasizes that boys and girls were schooled separately (the girls in *migas*). However, her point that girls were prepared for marriage, that they often were trained for a skill (41), suggests a practical attitude toward their education that often did not extend to boys.'

3. Reprinted in the February 16, 1816, issue of the *Noticioso General*.

4. See Bárbara Laso Manay, "Desagravio de la poesía," *Diario de México*, April 16, 1806; "Carta escrita por Doña María Josefa de Padilla en Guadalajara a 14 del corriente a una Señora de esta Capital," *Diario de México*, April 26, 1806.

5. Ruíz Castañeda traces Lizardi's inspiration for *La Quijotita* to an anonymous

work (which she attributes to Sánchez de la Barquera) appearing in the *Semanario Económico de México*, "Diálogo entre Cecilia y Feliciano sobre educación de las niñas" (January 4, 1810), xvi. Her discussion of Lizardi's various sources for *La Quijotita*, contained in the prologue to her edition (1967), is generally excellent.

6. Unsigned, *Diario de México*, May 18, 1806.

7. "El Casado," "Parteras," *Diario de México*, March 1, 1806.

8. L. L. J., "Sobre que las mugeres no coman tierra," *Diario de México*, January 20, 1806.

9. Franco in "Women, Fashion and the Moralists in Early Nineteenth-Century Mexico" calls attention to dress in *La Quijotita* as a way of talking about modernity. She sees Lizardi's book as instrumental in teaching a new paternalism in which the family replaces the monarchy in dictating new structures of dependency. However, Franco reads the bourgeois family as portrayed in *La Quijotita* (she focusses on the model family) as a blueprint for change; she quotes Arrom's statistics that in 1811 "[m]arried women living with their husbands and children were ... not in the majority" (423).

However, I read Lizardi's treatment of women's role in this new bourgeois unit as problematical at the same time it may be prescriptive. Also, Lizardi's fictional focus is not the total population but the more limited social world of the two girls.

10. This article appears in the anonymous collection, *Miscelanea instructiva, curiosa y agradable*, vol. 3 (Alcala: Oficina de la Real Universidad, 1797). The article itself (191–214) is credited to Abate Nadal.

11. Franco makes this point in *Plotting Women*, 84.

12. Although Franco in *Plotting Women* (87–88) remarks on the power of Eufrosina's role in the narrative—Franco describes her as a "debating opponent" rather than a "character," she appears to read Lizardi's view of women and the bourgeois family as decidedly in favor of traditional values. However, I understand Eufrosina's voice as one aspect of Lizardi's unsettled mind, not only with respect to women's role in the new Mexico but also the modernizing influences Eufrosina represents.

13. Lizardi may have been inspired to write of the "heroínas mexicanas" by a series on "Las Ilustres Americanas" that was reprinted in the *Indicador Federal, Diario político, económico y literario* (June 17–27, 1825). The long article, signed by "P.C.," claims to be drawn from *La Biblioteca americana, ó Miscelanea de literatura* (London, 1823; reprinted Philadelphia). In the series, the role of women in a nascent society, as well as the contribution to Independence of extraordinary women, are examined. A copy of this issue of *La Biblioteca americana* (September 1823) is to be found in the Sutro Library.

14. See Lanning in his chapter on "The Last Stand of the Schoolmen" in *Academic Culture* for a pertinent discussion of university theses, done in Mexico, Guatemala, Caracas, Chile, and Cordoba between 1750 and 1810, in which he finds this topic of the relationship between mind and body a vital concern.

15. For a thoughtful discussion of unequal status in marriage in Mexico, see Seed, *To Love, Honor, and Obey*, particularly 237–41.

16. As I have said, Ruíz Castañeda in her introduction to the Porrúa edition of *La*

Quijotita reviews the possible sources for Lizardi's adapation of the *Quijote*. However, she does not mention the Spanish translation of Charlotte Lennox's *The Female Quixote or The Adventures of Arabella* [*Don Quijote con faldas; ó Perjuicios morales de las disparatadas novelas, escrito en inglés, sin nombre de autor*] (Madrid: Fuentenebro, 1808), trans. Bernardo María de Calzada. This book does not appear in the Sutro's Abadiano collection, and it is only conjecture that Lizardi knew of Lennox's female Quijote and was inspired by it to create his own character so as to ridicule colonial reading practices.

17. See de Alba-Koch for a discussion of the illustrations for Lizardi's novels. Her work is also valuable for information on this aspect of Mexico's developing print industry.

18. Facundo Casares y Farria (Mexico City: Oficina de D. José María Ramos Palomera).

19. Peña's important study passes over this political dimension of the text.

20. The relevant documents by Mier, Muñoz, and Guridi y Alcocer are reproduced in de la Torre Villar and Navarro de Anda; see also Lafaye, chapter 10. I have consulted the Bancroft Library's copy of Guridi y Alcocer's "Apología" for the subscription list. For another view of Muñoz, see de Onís, ed., Muñoz's *Las polémicas*.

Chapter 8. Noches tristes y día alegre: *The Catechism and the Language of Faith*

1. Cadalso's *Noches* ends on p. 104 and Lizardi's begins on p. 105. But between the two, in unpaginated sheets, is the new conclusion to Cadalso's "Noche tercera," which Lizardi claimed he had just seen in the 1818 Valencia edition and wanted to include for his Mexican readers. At the end of these sheets Lizardi also printed six poems, presumably by Cadalso, on the tragic love of his prose story; a seventh poem, which Lizardi says he wrote, also deals with the unhappy love of Cadalso's hero.

Helman (51), the editor of *Noches lúgubres*, says that the 1815 Repullés edition (Madrid) of Cadalso's *Noches* introduced the new conclusion, which all later editions reprinted.

2. Abad y Queipo set the tone for the debate with his December 11, 1799, "Representación sobre la inmunidad personal del clero, reducida por las leyes del Nuevo Código, en la cual se propuso al rey el asunto de diferentes leyes, que establecidas, harían la base principal de un gobierno liberal y benéfico para las Américas y para su metrópoli" (33–86). See also Mier, *Cartas*, "Sobre las excomuniones y la Inquisición" (132–38) and "Sobre el fuero eclesiástico" (217).

Lizardi wrote about the topic in his "Apología compendiosa de nuestra sagrada religión y de la dignidad del estado eclesiástico" in *El Pensador Mexicano* (*Obras* 3: 219–51). See also "Discurso dogmático sobre la jurisdicción eclesiástica" by the unsigned author (Mexico City: Imp. de D. Mariano Ontiveros, 1812, 23 pp.).

3. For a history of the Inquisition in Mexico, particularly in the last years before it was abolished, see Medina.

4. I cite the 1970 Porrúa edition, *Don Catrín de la Fachenda y Noches tristes y día*

alegre, ed. Jefferson Rea Spell, throughout this study; page references to it are given in my text.

5. However, included in the *Ratos entretenidos* collection is also a poem, "Noche triste," by the much-admired Mexican priest, Fr. Manuel Navarrete, which Lizardi does not link to his prose work.

6. Torres-Ríoseco, in his influential survey of Spanish American literature, set the tone for later scholars in his chapter on "The Colonial Centuries." He rightly pinned the obsession for imitation to an oppressive political system that prevented any other form of expression, an exploitive economic structure that provided luxurious living for the colonial elite, and a cultural life in the viceregal capitals dominated by universities founded and run according to European models.

7. González Peña typically represents Mexico's literary production in the eighteenth and early nineteenth centuries. At this critical moment when political events will end Mexico's colonial status, Mexico's writers, according to González Peña, not only imitate and exhaust outmoded Peninsular forms but for some reason they do so ignoring more recent developments.

What is certain is that, when the nineteenth century began, the classical renovation had not yet been completed. *Culteranismo* and *conceptismo* [Baroque aesthetic modes], as a secular inheritance, continued to persist in an anemic, circumstantial literature, in spite of the influence of the rhetoricians of the school of Luzán, the favor that Meléndez Valdés and Moratín the elder enjoyed in verse and Feijoo and Cadalso in prose. In the pulpit the flowery orators predominated. And jointly with the convoluted, empty rhetoric of a Góngora stripe that refused to die, dullness had begun to thrive and prosper.

Book production had fallen to a new low; few books were being printed and almost none of a literary character. (*Historia de la literatura mexicana*, my translation 112)

8. In my discussion of imitation and originality I wish to sidestep much of the debate regarding the emergence of the novel in Spanish America. Both Alegría and Sánchez credit Lizardi with writing the first Spanish American novel, yet both discuss nineteenth-century novelistic production in Spanish America using European critical terms such as Romanticism and Realism. Sánchez, in particular, as late as 1953 refuses to see an American "*novelística*" [novelistics] even though he acknowledges there may be individual American novelists; describing the situation in Spanish America, he blames imitation of the French form for the lack of development (48).

9. Spell's theory seems wrong. Lizardi's *Día alegre* resolution is generally read as an optimistic view of faith and the Church. Yet Cadalso's ending to the "Noche tercera" describes an unrepentant hero, who never stops scorning life and is sentenced for his crime of passion into exile by a judge who calls himself loving.

10. Although Helman also cites this passage in her thoughtful discussion of Young's influence on Cadalso in his *Noches lúgubres* (29), she fails to develop her observation on the pertinence of political realities and takes Cadalso at his word that he was imitating Young.

11. Arce reflects this attitude in his judgment: "Precisely the radical innovation of the work consists of having tried to acclimatize in Spanish literature the sepulchral genre. Cadalso is, in a word, he who introduced into Spanish literature what has been called Preromanticism" (in Cadalso, *Cartas marruecas* 47).

12. Sebold discounts completely the importance of Cadalso's invocation of Young's work: "The slight resemblance between the *Night Thoughts* and the *Lugubrious Nights* did not justify the observations of Cadalso with respect to imitation in any strict sense. The recognized name of Young was simply an easy way of alluding to the sepulchral tone that was becoming increasingly more frequent in English literature" (160).

13. For example, Alegría pronounces sentence on *Noches tristes:* "It can be said unequivocally that, in spite of its aim, it is a mediocre novel and, at times, very bad. Nevertheless, its historic importance is undeniable. It not only forecasts the romantic novel of the second half of the nineteenth century, but in its allegorical character, the *First Night* especially, it antecedes certain modern creations" (22).

14. Adorno (*Guaman Poma*) perceives the importance of the catechism in her discussion of the literature of conversion (65–68); and Harrison uses the catechism in her crosscultural work.

15. "El Indigente J. M. B.," in his political pamphlet, "Dudas del indigente para alivio de sus penas" (Mexico City: Imprenta de D. Juan Bautista de Arispe, 1820), provides the following testimony: "Mr. Thinker, my friend: You have already provided us with a vocabulary of questions and answers, with which more than once you have clarified our doubts and developed various useful thoughts."

16. Reproduced in *Correo americano del sur*, 2.

17. Mateos describes the introduction of Masonry into Mexico (particularly in terms of the traditional Scottish rite, which came in 1813 and to which many Mexicans loyal to Spain belonged) and then the arrival of the more revolutionary York Lodge in 1826; see also Sims; Green (chaps. 4, 6).

Chapter 9. Don Catrín de la Fachenda: *A Modern Discourse: Machiavellianism*

1. See Lizardi, "Hemos dado en ser borricos y nos saldremos con ello" (Méjico: Imprenta del Autor, 1822) (*Obras* 11: 495–99).

2. Although *Don Catrín* has lived in the shadow of the *Periquillo*, some critics have recently argued that *Don Catrín* is the better novel. Because *Don Catrín* omits the long didactic digressions of the *Periquillo*, they reason that the picaresque story emerges more artistically. They also admire the ironic mode that Lizardi uses consistently throughout the work, in contrast to the textual shifts of the *Periquillo;* they say that the play of meaning thus achieved is more interesting and shows a more sophisticated narrator and readership. See R. Bancroft; Pawlowski, "Comparison and Contrast"; Borgeson; Anderson Imbert, 187–88.

3. Here and elsewhere I base my quotes on the 1970 Porrúa edition.

4. I understand the eighteenth-century Spanish novels, such as those by Torres

Villarroel and Isla, to also have their origins in the sixteenth- and seventeenth-century forms.

5. The contemporary work *Lumpen, marginación, y jerigonça* by Alfonso Sastre rewrites the Golden Age picaresque novel and makes this point. See my article "Updating the Picaresque Tradition."

6. Taléns takes issue with Parker's translation of *pícaro* as "delinquent" if it leads Parker to conclude that the *pícaro*'s behavior is "dishonourable and anti-social" (quoted in Taléns, 21). Taléns concedes that this may be so, but that the *pícaro* is forced to be this way. However, Taléns's use of the term *transgresion* throughout his discussion of the picaresque appears to indicate that he shares Parker's view of the individual and his troubled relation to society.

7. See González Casanova, *Misoneísmo;* Lanning, *Academic Culture,* particularly chapter 3; Stoetzer, *Scholastic Roots.*

8. Feijóo has several essays, among which are "Abusos de las disputas verbales," "Desenredo de sofismas," "Dictado de las aulas," and "Argumentos de autoridad" (Biblioteca de Autores Españoles), which criticize these philosophical and educational methods. See also E. E., "Actos literarios," *Diario de México,* April 22–23, 1806.

9. See Moreno, who typically focusses on stellar figures like Sor Juana Inés de la Cruz, Carlos Sigüenza y Góngora, and the circle of Jesuit scholars.

10. Perhaps the best record of the effect of this colonial education on the average university student is that to be found in the pages of the *Periquillo.*

11. For a succinct summary of Mexico's intellectual life on the eve of Independence, see Liss, "Late Colonial Intellectuals."

12. In an article, "Discútese sobre lo que se llama fortuna de pícaros y en qué consiste ésta, entre Claudio y Benito" (published in his newspaper *Cajoncitos de la Alacena,* September 16, 1815), Lizardi raises the same question. "Fortune," or the apparently favorable visitation of luck, is shown to be rather the result of the lucky person's craftiness [*maña*]. Claudio, who is honest and poor, bemoans the fact that many in Mexico unjustly enjoy wealth and noble privilege; Benito offers the alternative Christian term "providence" to explain the distribution of differences and finds his solution in the traditional argument that virtue is rewarded and one should not envy a *pícaro*'s ill-gotten "fortune."

13. Sefchovich uses the term *catrín* to refer to those post-Revolutionary Mexican leaders, working principally in the 1940s, whose version of a modernization project was the development of capitalism. She also sees their equivalents in a generation of novelists. She is consciously invoking Lizardi's use of *catrín* (see her chapter 4, "El triunfo de los catrines").

14. *Catrín,* favored over the Frenchified *petimetre,* seems to have come into Mexico and Central America at this time. Its spread appears to be limited to those areas.

15. Caillet-Bois discusses Lizardi's use of this French term in the introduction to his edition of *Don Catrín.*

16. Taylor, *Magistrates* (48ff), helpfully touches on this point. However, his study of rural priests and parishes, focussing as it does on Indian religious understanding

and performance, takes on issues irrelevant to the criollo, such as syncretism. What Taylor sees as the state's willingness in the eighteenth century to allow private forms of worship so long as fees were paid and externals were observed (51), Lizardi, however, understands to be the failure of religious language to be taken seriously, to be used as a moral force in solving Mexico's problems. Taylor's interest in contact between Spanish Christianity and native beliefs leads him, as it does Gruzinski in his study of "colonizing the imaginary," to suppose that the Indian mind throughout the colonial period remained full of its own religious structure. But the criollo's religious consciousness, Lizardi is saying, was furnished only by Spanish words that spoke of obedience and was therefore ill-equipped either for political independence or the satisfactory practice of individual religious faith.

17. The question of the psychological makeup of the colonial is complex. Memmi studies the phenomenon in *Colonizer* and *Dominated Man*. See also Mannoni. To appreciate the specific question of the identity of the criollo in Mexico, see Frost. Particularly in chapter 2 she discusses the question of the imitativeness of Mexican culture in terms of "dependency" and "reflection."

18. See Unsigned, "Exterioridad," *Diario de México*, September 7, 1810.

19. "Carta de los indios de Tontonapeque a el Pensador Mexicano" [Letter from the Indians of Tontonapeque to the Mexican Thinker] (*Obras* 10: 401–8).

20. Stoetzer *Scholastic Roots*; Liss, "Jesuit Contributions"; Fernández-Santamaría.

21. H. H. Bancroft estimates that there were well over five hundred Jesuits who left Mexico in the four evacuations (chap. 23). The literature describing the event is vast: see Liss, "Jesuit Contributions"; Batllori; Navarro B.; Moreno; Méndez Plancarte.

22. See Kahn for various readings of Machiavelli's philosophy.

23. Unsigned, *Diario de México*, November 6, 1806.

24. "Las sombras de Heráclito y Demócrito," "Refútase el egoísmo, y trátase sobre las obligaciones del hombre," in *Obras, Periódicos* vol. 4: 229–47. McKegney found a copy of the second number of "Las sombras de Heráclito y Demócrito" in the British Library, and it is published in his "Dos obras," 193–220.

25. Don Catrín's uncle, the priest, repeats this teaching (21).

26. Typical is the language of the "Acta solemne de la Independencia de la America Septentrional," in which the Congreso de Anáhuac (November 6, 1813, Chilpancingo) declares Mexican independence: "The Congress of Anáhuac . . . declares solemnly . . . that under the present circumstances in Europe it has reclaimed the exercise of its sovereignty which has been usurped, and that, according to such a concept, dependency on the Spanish throne has been forever broken and dissolved," quoted in Herrejón, *Morelos*, 140.

27. I owe much of my thinking here to Macdonell's discussion of Pêcheux's discourse notions (39–40). See my chapter 1. Many Mexican criollos in the early nineteenth century appear to have been struggling with "disidentification."

28. Unsigned, "La intolerancia civil. Reflexiones sobre sus perjuicios y utilidades," March 25–28, 1813.

29. Liss ("Jesuit Contributions" 453) emphasizes how Jesuit education in Mexico emphasized drama, literary acts, and disputation.

30. However, Villoro, in discussing the direction provided the insurgency by the local clergy, shows their motivation to defend their downtrodden Indian parishioners to be anything but Enlightenment thought (85). Villoro thus demonstrates the ideological complexity of the insurgency movement.

31. Here I am mindful of Sieber's important study of the *Lazarillo*, in which he argues that the story plays out the *pícaro*'s discoveries about language and the book's writing confers status on the basically oral narrator. I find some of the same structure in *Don Catrín* that Sieber discovers in the *Lazarillo;* but whereas Sieber considers the sixteenth-century work as a "semiotic project" and understands historical and sociological concerns to be secondary, I judge the latter paramount in explaining the importance of language in both the making of the text and the book.

32. Today's liberation theology in Latin America shows this same need to incorporate material considerations and a desire for praxis into a religious belief structure. See Silva Gotay.

Chapter 10. Conclusion

1. Lizardi develops this idea in "Chamorro y Dominiquín. Diálogo jocoserio sobre la Independencia de la América," *Obras* 11: 108.

2. I have consulted Ripalda's *Catechism* in the edition *Catecismo de los Padres Ripalda y Astete,* 4 vols. (Madrid: Imprenta de la Administracion del Real Arbitrio de Beneficencia, 1800). This edition is to be found in the Abadiano (Sutro) collection. Although it combines Ripalda's and Astete's catechisms, the book, in its printing format which distinguishes between the two, allows one to know what Ripalda's portion was.

3. Foronda rewrote much of Condillac's text; the full title is: *The Logic of Condillac, put into dialogue by D. Valentín de Foronda, corrected with the greatest care and added to by a short treatise on all kinds of arguments, sophisms, with the various observations of Locke and Malebranche so as to find the truth. And with some reflections on the moral arithmetic of Buffon on how to measure uncertain things, on the way to appreciate the relations between verisimilitude, degrees of probability, the value of witnesses, the influence of causalities, the inconvenience of risks, and on forming a judgment so as to [ascertain] the real value of our fears and hopes.* The influence of Condillac on Mexican society at this time is hard to measure. The first issue of the *Diario de México* (October 1, 1805) names him and mentions favorably another of his books, *El comercio y el gobierno mirados con relacion reciproca,* saying that the translator wanted to Spanishize [*castellanizar*] it too much. Condillac and Locke are mentioned in the February 21, 1809, issue of the *Diario;* in the Sutro copy of the *Diario* these names are inked out.

4. For this summary of the Church's orthodoxy, I am drawing on the translator's preface by D. Gabriel Quijano to *Verdadero antidoto contra los malos libros de estos tiempos ó Tratado de la Lectura Christiana* by Nicolás Jamin.

5. "Voicing" conveniently describes the intervention of previously silenced per-

sons or groups into the public discourse space; see Kristin Herzog, *Finding Their Voice: Peruvian Women's Testimonies of War.*

6. Certeau, Julia, and Revel record a similar phenomenon to the colony's consciousness of "voice" in their description of the inquiry the Abbé Grégoire conducted in postrevolutionary France (1790–1792). This survey of the various provincial patois so as to standardize the educational system in the service of the state noted the preeminence of the sounds of language, apart from their graphic signs, and attached importance to voice as the originator of language (95–98).

This consciousness of "voice" would have been particularly acute in the multilingual context of Spain's American colonies, where the energies of the Spanish missionaries had historically been devoted to capturing Indian orality in dictionaries and literature for religious instruction.

7. Here I am indebted to Volosinov's discussion of these terms in his chapter 2.

8. Benot studies these optimistic sophistries of the eighteenth century in his study of Diderot (176–78).

9. See, for example, "El A. de la V.," "Abusos en la devocion de los santos," *Diario de México*, November 8, 1811. Lizardi discusses at length the recommendations of the Council of Trent in the *Periquillo* 70–71, 270, and in *Obras* 3: 310.

10. "Veranio," "Carta dirigida a los señores editores de este periodico, Vitoria, 20 de septiembre de 1808," *Semanario patriótico* no. 11, reprinted in *Diario*, August 28, 1809.

11. *Diario*, October 10, 13–16, 31, 1808.

12. See the illustration of the broadside "La visita de Chana a Pepa. Elogio a los patriotas" (Mexico City: Oficina de Doña María Fernández de Jauregui, 1810).

13. "Filopatro," "Discurso dirigo *[sic]* a los señores regidores de . . . Sobre la eleccion de diputados de la Nueva España, en cumplimiento de la real orden de la Suprema Junta Central de 29 de enero de 1809," *Diario*, July 19, 1809.

14. J. M. de V., "Amor á la patria" (reprinted from the *Diario de la Habana*), *Diario*, February 6, 1812.

15. Unsigned, "Patria," *Diario*, March 1, 1812.

16. "Reflexiones sobre el patriotismo" (reprinted from *Semanario patriótico número 3*), *Diario*, July 31, August 1, 1809.

17. "Vida y entierro de D. Pendón. Por su amigo el Pensador" (Mexico City: Oficina de D. José María Ramos Palomera) (*Obras* 12: 107–13).

18. "Bula del Sto. Padre contra la independencia de la América, o sea la Bula del Sr. Alejandro VI de feliz memoria, en la que donó toda la América á la corona de Castilla, excomulgando á quien siquiera interesase acercarse a ella sin especial licencia de los reyes catolicos" (Mexico City: Imprenta del Autor).

19. *Calendario histórico y pronóstico político. Para el año bisiesto de 1824* (Mexico City: Oficina del Autor).

20. Studies of postcolonial discourse have mainly focussed on this new nationalism; see, for example, Arnold; Chatterjee; Franco, "The Nation as Imagined Community"; Sommer.

However, works that have usefully emphasized other facets of the decolonizing process, in Mexico and elsewhere, are Franco, "En espera de una burguesía"; Harlow; Rodríguez O., "Down from Colonialism"; Sims.

21. Staples, "El catecismo como texto," studies the use of the religious catechism for civil purposes in Mexico in the nineteenth century.

22. See Seed, "The Colonial Church as an Ideological State Apparatus," for a pertinent discussion.

Select Bibliography

A., A. F. "Muerte del Pensador y noticia histórica de su vida." Mexico City: Imprenta de la Ex-Inquisición á cargo de Manuel Ximeno, 1827.

A. A. A. "Viaje de Fr. Gerundio a la Nueva España." Mexico City: La Imprenta de D. Alejandro Valdés, 1820.

Abad y Queipo, Manuel. *Colección de escritos.* 1813. Ed. Guadalupe Jiménez Codinach. Mexico City: Consejo Nacional para la Cultura y las Artes, 1994.

Actas de las Cortes de Cádiz. Antología. Ed. Enrique Tierno Galván. 2 vols. Madrid: Taurus, 1964.

Adorno, Rolena. *Guaman Poma: Writing and Resistance in Colonial Peru.* Austin: University of Texas Press, 1986.

———. "El sujeto colonial y la construcción cultural de la alteridad." *Revista de crítica literaria latinoamericana* 28 (1988): 55–68.

Aguirre Beltrán, Gonzalo. *Lenguas vernáculas. Su uso y desuso en la enseñanza: la experiencia de México.* Mexico City: Ediciones de la Casa Chata, 1983.

Ahmad, Aijaz. "Jameson's Rhetoric of Otherness and the 'National Allegory.'" *Social Text* 17 (1987): 3–25. Followed by F. R. Jameson's response, 26–27.

"Alacena." "Allá va ese vocadillo para el guapo del tapado." Mexico City: Oficina de D. José Maria Ramos Palomera, 1822.

Aldridge, A. Owen, ed. *The Ibero-American Enlightenment.* Urbana: University of Illinois Press, 1971.

Alegría, Fernando. *Historia de la novela hispanoamericana.* 1959. 4th ed. Mexico City: Andrea, 1974.

Almeida, P. D. Teodoro de. *Armonía de la razon y la religión, ó respuestas filosóficas a los argumentos de los incrédulos.* Trans. P. Don Francisco Vazquez. 2 vols. Madrid: Imprenta de Villalpando, 1802.

Altamirano, Ignacio M. *La literatura nacional: Revistas, Ensayos, Biografías y Prólogos.* Ed. and prol. José Luis Martínez. 3 vols. Mexico City: Ed. Porrúa, 1949.

Altbach, Philip, and Gail P. Kelly, eds. *Education and the Colonial Experience*. New Brunswick, N.J., and London: Transaction, 1984.

Althusser, Louis. *Lenin and Philosophy and Other Essays*. 1966–71. Trans. Ben Brewster. New York: Monthly Review Press, 1971.

Alvarez de Testa, Lilian. *Ilustración, educación e independencia. Las ideas de José Joaquín Fernández de Lizardi*. Mexico City: UNAM, 1994.

Anderson, Benedict. *Imagined Communities: Reflections on the Origin and Spread of Nationalism*. London: Verso, 1983.

Anderson Imbert, Enrique. *Historia de la literatura hispanoamericana*. Vol. 1. 1954. Reprint, Mexico City: Fondo de Cultura Económica, 1961. 2 vols.

Andrés, Juan. *Origen, progresos y estado actual de toda la literatura*. 4 vols. Madrid: Antonio De Sancha, 1784–87.

Ansprenger, Franz. *The Dissolution of the Colonial Empires*. 1981. New York: Routledge, 1989.

Archer, Criston I. "Where Did All the Royalists Go? New Light on the Military Collapse of New Spain, 1810–1822." *The Mexican and Mexican American Experience in the 19th Century*. Ed. Jaime E. Rodríguez O. Tempe, Ariz.: Bilingual Press/Editorial Bilingüe, 1989.

Arnold, Linda. *Bureaucracy and Bureaucrats in Mexico City, 1742–1835*. Tucson: University of Arizona Press, 1988.

Arrom, Silvia Marina. *The Women of Mexico City, 1790–1857*. Stanford: Stanford University Press, 1985.

Ashcroft, Bill, Gareth Griffiths, and Helen Tiffin, eds. *The Empire Writes Back: Theory and Practice in Post-colonial Literatures*. London and New York: Routledge, 1989.

Azim, Firdous. *The Colonial Rise of the Novel*. London and New York: Routledge, 1993.

Azuela, Mariano. *Obras completas*. Vol. 3. Mexico City: Fondo de Cultura Económica, 1960. 3 vols.

B., D. A. [Antonio Ballano]. *Diccionario de medicina y cirugía, o Biblioteca manual médico-quirúrgica*. Vol. 7. Madrid: Imprenta Real, 1805–1807. 7 vols.

Bakhtin, M. M. *The Dialogic Imagination: Four Essays*. Ed. Michael Holquist. Trans. Caryl Emerson and Michael Holquist. Austin: University of Texas Press, 1981.

Bancroft, Hubert Howe. *The Works of Hubert Howe Bancroft*. Vol. 2, *History of Mexico, 1600–1803*. San Francisco: A. L. Bancroft, 1883. 39 vols.

Bancroft, Robert L. "El 'Periquillo Sarniento' and 'Don Catrín de la Fachenda': Which Is the Masterpiece?" *Revista Hispánica Moderna* 34 (1968): 533–38.

Batllori, Miguel, S. J. *La cultura hispano-italiana de los jesuitas expulsos. Españoles, hispanoamericanos, filipinos, 1767–1814*. Madrid: Ed. Gredos, 1966.

Baudet, Henri. *Paradise on Earth: Some Thoughts on European Images of Non-European Man*. 1965. Trans. Elizabeth Wentholt. Westport: Greenwood Press, 1976.

Baudot, Georges. *Utopía e historia en México. Los primeros cronistas de la civilización mexicana (1520–1569)*. Madrid: Espasa-Calpe, 1983.

Benítez, Fernando. *El libro de los desastres*. Mexico City: Ediciones Era, 1988.

Benot, Yves. *Diderot: Del ateísmo al anticolonialismo.* 1970. Trans. Sergio Fernández Bravo. Mexico City: Siglo XXI, 1973.

Benson, Nettie Lee, ed. *Mexico and the Spanish Cortes: 1810–1822.* Austin: University of Texas Press, 1966.

Beristáin de Souza, José Mariano. *Biblioteca hispanoamericana septentrional 1816.* Ed. Emilio Azcárraga Milmo y Valentín Molina Piñeiro. Facsimile ed. Vol. 2. Mexico City: UNAM, 1981. 1980–81. 3 vols.

Bernstein, Harry. "A Provincial Library in Colonial Mexico, 1802." *Hispanic American Historical Review* 26 (1946): 162–83.

Betts, Raymond F. *Decolonization.* London and New York: Routledge, 1998.

Bhabha, Homi. "Of Mimicry and Man: The Ambivalence of Colonial Discourse." *October* 28 (1984): 125–33.

———. "The Other Question . . . Homi K. Bhabha Reconsiders the Stereotype and Colonial Discourse." *Screen* 2 (1983): 18–36.

———. "Representation and the Colonial Text: A Critical Exploration of Some Forms of Mimeticism." *The Theory of Reading.* Ed. Frank Gloversmith. Sussex: Harvester Press, 1984, 93–122.

———. "Signs Taken for Wonders: Questions of Ambivalence and Authority Under a Tree Outside Delhi, May 1817." *Critical Inquiry* 12 (1985): 144–65.

———, ed. *Nation and Narration.* Routledge: New York and London, 1990.

Birmingham, David. *The Decolonization of Africa.* Athens: Ohio University Press, 1995.

Blair, Hugo (Hugh). *Lecciones sobre la retórica y las bellas letras.* 1783. Trans. Don Josef [José] Luis Munarriz. 4 vols. Madrid: Imprenta Real, 1804.

Blanchard, Jean Baptiste. *Escuela de costumbres, o, Reflexiones morales é historicas sobre las maximas de la sabiduria. . . .* 1772. Trans. by Ignacio Garcia Malo of *Ecole des Moeurs.* 4 vols. Madrid: Imprenta de Villalpando, 1797.

Blum, Carol. *Rousseau and the Republic of Virtue: The Language of Politics in the French Revolution.* Ithaca and London: Cornell University Press, 1986.

Borgeson, Paul W., Jr. "Problemas de técnica narrativa en dos *novellas* de Lizardi." *Hispania* 69 (1986): 504–11.

Brading, David. *The First America: The Spanish Monarchy, Creole Patriots, and the Liberal State, 1492–1867.* New York: Cambridge, 1991.

———. *Mineros y comerciantes en el México borbónico (1763–1810).* 1971. Trans. Roberto Gómez Ciriza. Mexico City: Fondo de Cultura Económica, 1985.

———. *Los orígenes del nacionalismo mexicano.* 1973. Trans. Soledad Loaeza Grave. Mexico City: Ediciones Era, 1988.

———. "Tridentine Catholicism and Enlightened Despotism in Bourbon Mexico." *Journal of Latin American Studies* 15 (1983): 1–22.

Brennan, Timothy, ed. "Narratives of Colonial Resistance." Special number of *Modern Fiction Studies* 35 (1989).

Briseño Senosiain, Lillian, Ma. Laura Solares Robledo, and Laura Suárez de la Torre, investig. and comp. *La independencia de México, Textos de su historia.* 3 vols. Mexico City: Instituto Mora, SEP, 1985.

Brookner, Anita. *Greuze: The Rise and Fall of an Eighteenth-Century Phenomenon.* Greenwich, Conn.: New York Graphic Society, 1972.

Brushwood, John S. "The Mexican Understanding of Realism and Naturalism." *Hispania* 43 (1960): 521–28.

———. *Mexico in Its Novel: A Nation's Search for Identity.* Austin: University of Texas Press, 1966.

Bueno, Salvador. "El negro en *El periquillo sarniento:* Antirracismo de Lizardi." *Cuadernos americanos* 183 (1972): 124–39.

Bustamante, Carlos María de. *El indio mexicano o Avisos al rey Fernando Séptimo para la pacificación de la América septentrional* [The Mexican Indian, or Advice to King Fernando VII for the pacification of North America]. 1817–18. Study by Manuel Arellano Zavaleta. México: Instituto Mexicano del Seguro Social, 1981.

Cabañas, Pablo. "Las '*Noches tristes*' de Lizardi." *Cuadernos de literatura* 1 (1947): 425–41.

Cadalso, José. *Cartas marruecas.* 1789. Ed. Juan Tamayo y Rubio. Madrid: Espasa-Calpe, 1935.

———. *Cartas marruecas. Noches lúgubres.* Ed. Joaquín Arce. Madrid: Ediciones Cátedra, 1978.

———. *Noches lúgubres.* 1789–90. Ed. Edith F. Helman. Santander, Madrid: Ed. Antonio Zúñiga, 1951.

Cairns, David, and Shaun Richards. *Writing Ireland: Colonialism, Nationalism and Culture.* Manchester: Manchester University Press, 1988.

Calvet, Louis-Jean. *Linguistique et colonialisme.* Paris: Payot, 1974.

Camargo y Cavallero, Juan. "Report to the King: Camargo's Historical Account of New Spain, 1815." Trans. John Severn Leiby. Diss. Northern Arizona University, 1983.

Camp, Roderic A., Charles A. Hale, and Josefina Zoraida Vázquez, eds. *Los intelectuales y el poder en México.* Los Angeles: UCLA, El Colegio de México, 1991.

Cárdenas de la Peña, Enrique. *Historia marítima de México. Guerra de Independencia 1810–1821.* Vols. 1, 1a. Mexico City: Ed. Olimpia, 1973.

Carilla, Emilio. *La literatura de la independencia hispanoamericana (Neoclasicismo y prerromanticismo).* Buenos Aires: Ed. Universitaria, 1964.

Carrió de la Vandera, Alonso (Concolorcorvo). *El lazarillo de ciegos caminantes.* Ed. Emilio Carilla. Barcelona: Ed. Labor, 1973.

"Cartilla ó catecismo del ciudadano constitucional." Reimpreso en Méjico: Imprenta de Ontiveros, 1820.

Casas de Faunce, María. *La novela picaresca latinoamericana.* Madrid: Cupsa Editorial, 1977.

Castanien, Donald G. "The Mexican Inquisition Censors a Private Library." *Hispanic American Historical Review* 34 (1954): 374–92.

Castro Leal, Antonio, ed. *La novela del México colonial: Estudio preliminar, selección, biografías, notas preliminares, bibliografía general y lista de los principales acontecimientos de la Nueva España de 1517 a 1821.* 2 vols. Mexico City: Aguilar, 1964.

Catalogue of Mexican Pamphlets in the Sutro Collection, 1623–1888; With Supplements,

1605–1887. San Francisco: California State Library, Sutro Branch, 1939–41. Kraus Reprint, New York: 1971.

Catecismo de los Padres Ripalda y Astete. 4 vols. Madrid: Imprenta de la Administracion del Real Arbitrio de Beneficencia, 1800.

Certeau, Michel de, Dominique Julia, and Jacques Revel. *Une politique de la langue: La Révolution française et les patois*. Paris: Ed. Gallimard, 1975.

Césaire, Aimé. *Discourse on Colonialism*. 1955. Trans. Joan Pinkham. New York and London: Monthly Review Press, 1972.

Chadwick, Owen. *The Secularization of the European Mind in the Nineteenth Century*. Cambridge: Cambridge University Press, 1975.

Chatterjee, Partha. *Nationalist Thought and the Colonial World—A Derivative Discourse*. London: Zed, 1986.

Cicerón. *Los oficios de . . ., con los dialogos de la vejez, de la amistad, las paradoxas, y el sueño de Escipion*. Trans. Don Manuel de Valbuena. 2nd ed. Madrid: Imprenta Real, 1788.

Clavijero, Francisco Javier. *Historia antigua de México*. (The Ancient History of Mexico.) 1780. 7th ed. Prol. Mariano Cuevas. Mexico City: Ed. Porrúa, 1982.

Condillac, Etienne Bonnot de. *Lógica*. 1780. Put into dialogue form and trans. D. Valentin de Foronda. Madrid: Don Benito Cano, 1800.

Contreras García, Edna. *Los certámenes literarios en México en la época colonial*. Mexico City: UNAM, 1949 (Tesis profesional).

Cordero, Salvador. *La literatura durante la Guerra de Independencia*. 2nd ed. Paris: Vda. de C. Bouret, 1920.

Correo americano del Sur. 1813. Facsimile ed. Mexico City: PRI, 1976.

Cortázar, Julio. *Hopscotch*. 1963. Trans. Gregory Rabassa. New York: Avon, Random House, 1966.

Cotten, Emily. "Cadalso and His Foreign Sources." *Bulletin of Spanish Studies* 8 (1931): 5–18.

Cros, Edmond. "The Values of Liberalism in *El Periquillo Sarniento*." *Sociocriticism* 2 (1985): 85–109.

Cruz, Francisco Santiago. *La nao de China*. Mexico City: Ed. Jus, 1962.

Cruz, Salvador. "Feijoo y Lizardi." *Cuadernos del Congreso por la Libertad de la Cultura* 88: 91–93.

Cypess, Sandra Messinger. *La Malinche in Mexican Literature: From History to Myth*. Austin: University of Texas Press, 1991.

Darwin, John. *Britain and Decolonisation: The Retreat from Empire in the Post-War Period*. New York: St. Martin's Press, 1988.

Davidson, Cathy N., ed. *Reading in America: Literature and Social History*. Baltimore and London: Johns Hopkins University Press, 1989.

———. *Revolution and the Word: The Rise of the Novel in America*. New York and Oxford: Oxford University Press, 1986.

Davis, Jack Emory. "Algunos problemas lexicográficos en *El periquillo sarniento*." *Revista Iberoamericana* 23 (1968): 163–71.

———. "Picturesque 'Americanismos' in the Works of Fernández de Lizardi." *Hispania* 44 (1961): 74–81.

de Alba-Koch, Beatriz. "Ilustrando la Nueva España: Texto e imagen en 'El Periquillo Sarniento' de Fernández de Lizardi." Diss. Princeton University, 1997.

de Ercilla, Alonso. *La Araucana*. Madrid: Antonio de Sancha, 1776.

"Defensa del Pensador mexicano por su aprendiz." Mexico City: Imprenta Imperial, n.d.

Defoe, Daniel. *El nuevo Robinson*. Escrito en aleman por el señor Campe, traducido al castellano con varias correcciones por D. Tomas de Iriarte. Madrid: n.p., 1820.

Deforneaux, Marcelin. *Inquisición y censura de libros en la España del siglo XVIII*. Madrid: Taurus, 1973.

de la Torre Villar, Ernesto. *Los Guadalupes y la Independencia*. Mexico City: Ed. Jus, 1966.

de la Torre Villar, Ernesto, and Ramiro Navarro de Anda, eds. *Testimonios históricos guadalupanos*. Mexico City: Fondo de Cultura Económica, 1982.

Demos, John, and Virginia Demos. "History of the Family: Adolescence in Historical Perspective." *Journal of Marriage and the Family* 31 (1969): 632–38.

de Olaguibel, Manuel. "José Joaquín Fernández de Lizardi." In *Hombres ilustres mexicanos*, ed. Eduardo L. Gallo. Vol. 3. Mexico City: Imprenta de I. Cumplido, 1874.

El Despertador Americano. [Guadalaxara] Dec. 20, 1810–Jan. 17, 1811. Facsimile ed. Mexico City: Instituto Nacional de Antropología e Historia, 1964.

Dhareshwar, Vivek. "Toward a Narrative Epistemology of the Postcolonial Predicament." *Inscriptions. Traveling Theories, Traveling Theorists* 5 (1989): 135–57.

Diario de México. [México, D.F.] Vols. 1–17, Oct. 1805–Dec. 1812. New Series, vols. 1–8, Dec. 1813–Dec. 1816.

Diderot, Denis. *Encyclopédie, ou Dictionnaire raisonné des sciences, des arts et des métiers*. 17 vols. Paris: Chez Briassou et al., 1750–80. Stuttgart: Friedrich Frommann Verlag, 1966.

"Discurso dogmático sobre la jurisdicción eclesiástica." [Unsigned]. México: Imp. de D. Mariano Ontiveros, 1812, 23 pp.

Domínguez, Jorge I. *Insurrection or Loyalty: The Breakdown of the Spanish American Empire*. Cambridge: Harvard University Press, 1980.

Dorfman, Ariel. *Hacia la liberación del lector latinoamericano*. Hanover, N.H.: Ediciones del Norte, 1984.

Ducray-Duminil, François Guillaume. *Alejo ú La casita en los bosques, Manuscrito encontrado junto á las orillas del rio Isera*. Publicado en frances por M. Ducray-Duminil, y traducido por Don J. y Don T. M. L. (Barcelona: Imprenta de José Torner, 1821).

Erskine, Noel Leo. *Decolonizing Theology: A Caribbean Perspective*. Maryknoll, N.Y.: Orbis, 1981.

Fabbri, Maurizio. "La novela como cauce ideológico de la Ilustración: el influjo de Montengón en Fernández de Lizardi." *Homenaje a Noël Salomon*. Ed. Alberto Gil Novales. Barcelona: Universidad Autónoma de Barcelona, 1979. 31–37.

Fanon, Frantz. *A Dying Colonialism*. 1959. Trans. Haakon Chevalier. New York: Grove Press, 1967.

———. *The Wretched of the Earth.* 1961. Trans. Constance Farrington. New York: Grove, 1963.

Feijóo y Montenegro, Fray Benito Jerónimo. *Obras escogidas.* Vol. 56. Biblioteca de Autores Españoles. Madrid: Ed. Atlas, 1952.

———. *Teatro crítico universal.* 1727–39. Sel. de Agustín Millares Carlo. Vol. 1. Madrid: Espasa-Calpe, 1968. 3 vols.

———. *Theatro crítico universal, o Discursos varios en todo género de materias, para desengaño de errores comunes.* Vol. 5. Madrid: Imprenta Real de la Gazeta, 1773.

Fernández del Castillo, Francisco, comp. *Libros y libreros en el siglo XVI.* 1914. Facsimile ed. Mexico City: Archivo General de la Nacion, Fondo de Cultura Económica, 1982.

Fernández de Lizardi, José Joaquín. *Calendario histórico y pronóstico político. Para el año bisiesto de 1824.* Mexico City: Oficina del Autor, 1824.

———. *Calendario para el año de 1825. Dedicado a las señoritas americanas, especialmente a las patriotas.* Mexico City: Oficina de D. Mariano Ontiveros, 1825.

———. *Don Catrín.* Ed. Julio Caillet-Bois. Buenos Aires: Ed. Universitaria, 1967.

———. *Don Catrín de la Fachenda y Noches tristes y día alegre.* Ed. Jefferson Rea Spell. Mexico City: Ed. Porrúa, 1970.

———. *El Periquillo Sarniento.* Mexico City: Alejandro Valdés, 1816.

———. *The Itching Parrot.* Intro. Katherine Anne Porter. Trans. Eugene Pressly. Garden City, N.Y.: Doubleday, Doran, 1942.

———. *Noches tristes y día alegre.* Intro. Agustín Yáñez. Mexico City: Imprenta Universitaria, 1943.

———. *Obras.* Vol. 1, *Poesías y fábulas.* Research, compilation, and edition by Jacobo Chencinsky y Luis Mario Schneider. Preliminary study by Jacobo Chencinsky. Mexico City: UNAM, 1963.

———. *Obras.* Vol. 2, *Teatro.* Edition and nots by Jacobo Chencinsky. Prol. Ubaldo Vargas Martínez. Mexico City: UNAM, 1965.

———. *Obras.* Vol. 3, *Periódicos El Pensador Mexicano.* Compilation, edition, and notes by María Rosa Palazón y Jacobo Chencinsky. Intro. by Jacobo Chencinsky. Mexico City: UNAM, 1968.

———. *Obras.* Vol. 4, *Periódicos Alacena de frioleras/Cajoncitos de la alacena/Las sombras de Heráclito y Demócrito/El conductor eléctrico.* Compilation, edition, notes, and intro. by María Rosa Palazón M. Mexico City: UNAM, 1970.

———. *Obras.* Vol. 5, *Periódicos El amigo de la paz y de la patria/El payaso de los periódicos/El hermano del perico que cantaba la victoria/Conversaciones del payo y el sacristán.* Compilation, edition, notes, and preliminary study by María Rosa Palazón Mayoral. Mexico City: UNAM, 1973.

———. *Obras.* Vol. 6, *Periódicos Correo semanario de México.* Compilation, edition, notes, and intro. by María Rosa Palazón Mayoral. Mexico City: UNAM, 1975.

———. *Obras.* Vol. 7, *Novelas La educación de las mujeres o la Quijotita y su prima, Historia muy cierta con apariencia de novela; Vida y hechos del famoso caballero Don Catrín de la Fachenda.* Compilation, edition, notes, and preliminary study by María Rosa Palazón Mayoral. Mexico City: UNAM, 1980.

————. *Obras.* Vol. 8, *Novelas El Periquillo Sarniento* (Vols. 1 and 2). Prologue, edition, and notes by Felipe Reyes Palacios. Mexico City: UNAM, 1982.

————. *Obras.* Vol. 9, *Novelas El Periquillo Sarniento* (Vols. 3 and 4); *Noches tristes y día alegre.* Intro., edition, and notes by Felipe Reyes Palacios. Mexico City: UNAM, 1982.

————. *Obras.* Vol. 10, *Folletos* (1811–1820). Compilation, edition, and notes by María Rosa Palazón Mayoral and Irma Isabel Fernández Arias. Intro. by María Rosa Palazón Mayoral. Mexico City: UNAM, 1981.

————. *Obras.* Vol. 11, *Folletos* (1821–1822). Edition, notes, and intro. by Irma Isabel Fernández Arias. Mexico City: UNAM, 1991.

————. *Obras.* Vol. 12, *Folletos* (1822–1824). Compilation, edition, and notes by Irma Isabel Fernández Arias and María Rosa Palazón Mayoral. Prologue by María Rosa Palazón Mayoral. Mexico City: UNAM, 1991.

————. *Obras.* Vol. 13, *Folletos* (1824–1827). Compilation, edition, notes, and indexes by María Rosa Palazón and Irma Isabel Fernández Arias. Prologue by María Rosa Palazón Mayoral. Mexico City: UNAM, 1995.

————. *Obras.* Vol. 14, *Miscelánea, Bibliohemerografía, listados e índices.* Compilation by María Rosa Palazón Mayoral, Columba Camelia Galván Gaytán, and María Esther Guzmán Gutiérrez. Edition and notes by Irma Isabel Fernández Arias, Columba Camelia Galván Gaytán, and María Rosa Palazón Mayoral. Indexes by María Esther Guzmán Gutiérrez. Prologue by María Rosa Palazón Mayoral. Mexico City: UNAM, 1997.

————. *El Pensador Mexicano.* Intro. Agustín Yáñez. 3rd ed. Mexico City: UNAM, 1962.

————. *El Periquillo Sarniento, por El Pensador Mexicano.* 2 vols. (vols. 1–2 in vol.1; vols. 3–4 in vol. 2) 2nd ed. Mexico City: J. Valdés y Cueva, R. Araujo, 1885.

————. *El Periquillo, por el Pensador Mexicano.* Contains "Ligeros apuntes para la biografía del Pensador Mexicano." 4 ed. México: Librería de Galván, 1842.

————. *El Periquillo Sarniento, por El Pensador Mexicano.* 2 vols. Corrected editon. Barcelona: Editorial Sopena, 1901. Volume 1 has a prologue by Luis González Obregón, "Ligeros apuntes para la biografía del Pensador Mexicano," and "Apología del Pensador Mexicano." Volume 2 begins with "Copia de los documentos que manifiestan la arbitrariedad del gobierno español en esta América, relativos a este cuarto tomo . . . ."

————. *El Periquillo Sarniento.* Pref. Octavio N. Bustamante. Mexico City: Editorial Stylo, 1942.

————. *El Periquillo Sarniento.* Prol. Jefferson Rea Spell. 14th ed. Mexico City: Ed. Porrúa, 1974.

————. *La Quixotita y su prima, Historia muy cierta con apariencia de novela.* Intro. María del Carmen Ruíz Castañeda. Mexico City: Ed. Porrúa, 1967.

————. *Ratos entretenidos, o Miscelanea útil y curiosa, compuesta de varias piezas ya impresas.* 2 vols. Mexico City: D. Alexandro Valdés, 1819.

Fernández Retamar, Roberto. *Caliban. Apuntes sobre la cultura en nuestra América.* Mexico City: Editorial Diógenes, S.A., 1971.

———. *Algunos usos de civilización y barbarie.* Buenos Aires: Ed. Contrapunto, 1989.

Fernández-Santamaría, J. A. *The State, War and Peace: Spanish Political Thought in the Renaissance 1516–1559.* Cambridge: Cambridge University Press, 1977.

Fielding, Sarah. *La huerfanita inglesa ó Historia de Carlota Summers.* Imitada del inglés por Mr. de la Place, y traducida al castellano por D. E. A. D. 2nd ed. Madrid: Gomez Fuentenebro y Cia., 1804.

Fishman, Joshua, Charles A. Ferguson, and Jyotirindra Das Gupta, eds. *Language Problems of Developing Nations.* New York: John Wiley and Sons, 1968.

Flores Caballero, Romeo. *La contrarevolución en la Independencia. Los españoles en la vida política, social y económica de México (1804–1838).* 1969. Mexico City: El Colegio de México, 1973.

Forner, Juan Pablo. *Exequias de la lengua castellana.* 1782. Ed. Pedro Sáinz y Rodríguez. Madrid: Espasa-Calpe, 1967.

Foucault, Michel. *Discipline and Punish: The Birth of the Prison.* 1975. Trans. Alan Sheridan. New York: Pantheon, 1977.

Foz y Foz, Pilar. *La revolucion pedagógica en Nueva España: 1754–1820 (María Ignacia de Azlor y Echeverz y los colegios de la Enseñanza).* Madrid: CSIC, 1981. 2 vols.

Franco, Jean. "En espera de una burguesía: la formación de la intelligentsia mexicana en la época de la Independencia." *Actas del VIII Congreso de la Asociación Internacional de Hispanistas.* Ed. A. David Kossoff et al. Vol. 1. Madrid: Ediciones Istmo, 1986. 21–36. 2 vols.

———. "La heterogeneidad peligrosa: Escritura y control social en vísperas de la independencia mexicana." *Hispamérica* 12 (1983): 3–34.

———. *An Introduction to Spanish-American Literature.* London: Cambridge University Press, 1969.

———. "The Nation as Imagined Community." In *The New Historicism.* Ed. H. Aram Veeser. New York: Routledge, 1989.

———. *Plotting Women: Gender and Representation in Mexico.* New York: Columbia University Press, 1989.

———. "Women, Fashion and the Moralists in Early Nineteenth-Century Mexico." In *Homenaje a Ana María Barrenechea.* Ed. Lía Schwartz Lerner and Isaías Lerner. Madrid: Castalia, 1984. 421–30.

Freire, Paulo. *La importancia de leer y el proceso de liberación.* 1984. Trans. Stella Mastrangelo. 5th ed. Mexico City: Siglo XXI, 1987.

Freud, Sigmund. *The Standard Edition of the Complete Psychological Works of Sigmund Freud.* Trans. James Strachey. Vol. 19, *The Ego and the Id and Other Works.* London: Hogarth Press and the Institute of Psycho-analysis, 1961. 24 vols.

Fritz, Robert Karl. "The Attitude of José Joaquín Fernández de Lizardi (El Pensador Mexicano) Toward Mexican Independence from Spain." Diss. Indiana University 1975.

Frost, Elsa Cecilia. *Las categorías de la cultura mexicana.* Mexico City: UNAM, 1972.

Fuentes, Carlos. *La nueva novela hispanoamericana.* 1969. Mexico City: Editorial Joaquín Mortiz, S.A., 1972.

Fuero Juzgo en latín y castellano, cotejado con los mas antiguos y preciosos códices. La Real Academia Española. Madrid: Ibarra, Impresor de Cámara de S. M., 1815.

Gaceta del Gobierno de México. Vols. 1–12, 1810–21. Mexico City: D.F.

Gante, Fray Pedro de. *Doctrina cristiana en lengua mexicana.* Facsimile ed. of 1553 ed. Critical study of catechisms and *cartillas* as tools of evangelization and civilization by Ernesto de la Torre Villar. Mexico City: Ed. Jus, 1982.

García, Genaro, comp. *Documentos históricos mexicanos.* 1910. Vol. 6. Mexico City: Instituto Nacional de Estudios Históricos de la Revolución Mexicana, 1985.

García Cantú, Gastón. *Utopías mexicanas.* Mexico City: Fondo de Cultura Económica, 1978.

Gerbi, Antonello. *The Dispute of the New World: The History of a Polemic, 1750–1900.* 1955. Trans. Jeremy Moyle. Rev. ed. Pittsburgh: University of Pittsburgh Press, 1973.

Gifford, Prosser, and William Roger Louis, eds. *The Transfer of Power in Africa: Decolonization 1940–1960.* New Haven: Yale University Press, 1982.

Giffords, Gloria Kay. *Mexican Folk Retablos.* Tucson: University of Arizona Press, 1974.

Gil Novales, Alberto, ed. *Homenaje a Noël Salomon, Ilustración española e independencia de América.* Barcelona: Universidad Autónoma de Barcelona, 1979.

Girardi, Giulio. "Marxism Confronts the Revolutionary Religious Experience." Trans. Rosanna M. Giammanco. *Social Text* 19/20 (1988): 119–51.

Gleaves, Robert M. "La emancipación literaria de México." *Language Quarterly* 4 (1966): 35–40.

Godlewska, Anne, and Neil Smith, eds. *Geography and Empire.* Oxford: Blackwell, 1994.

Godoy, Bernabé. *Corrientes culturales que definen al "Periquillo."* Guadalajara: n.p., 1938.

Goic, Cedomil, et al. *La novela hispanoamericana: Descubrimiento e invención de América.* Valparaiso: Universidad Católica de Valparaiso, Chile, 1973.

Gómez Alvarez, Cristina, and Francisco Téllez Guerrero. *Una biblioteca obispal. Antonio Bergosa y Jordán, 1802.* Puebla: Instituto de Ciencias Sociales y Humanidades, 1997.

———. *Un hombre de estado y sus libros. El Obispo Campillo, 1740–1813.* Puebla: Instituto de Ciencias Sociales y Humanidades, 1997.

Gonzalbo Aizpuru, Pilar. *La educación popular de los jesuitas.* Mexico City: Universidad Iberoamericana, 1989.

———. "La lectura de evangelización en la Nueva España." In *Historia de la lectura en México.* Mexico City: El Colegio de México, 1988. 9–48.

———. *Historia de la educación en la época colonial. La educación de los criollos y la vida urbana.* Mexico City: El Colegio de México, 1990.

———. *Las mujeres en la Nueva España: Educación y vida cotidiana.* Mexico City: El Colegio de México, 1987.

González, Aníbal. "Periodismo y narrativa en la Hispanoamérica del siglo XIX: El caso de *El Periquillo Sarniento.*" In *Esplendores y miserias del siglo XIX. Cul-*

tura y sociedad en América Latina. Ed. Beatriz González Stephan, Javier Lasarte, Graciela Montaldo, and María Julia Daroqui. Caracas: Monte Avila, 1995. 331–53.

González Casanova, Pablo. *La literatura perseguida en la crisis de la colonia.* Mexico City: Colegio de México, 1958.

———. *El misoneísmo y la modernidad en el siglo XVIII.* Mexico City: Colegio de México, 1948.

González Casanova, Pablo, and José Miranda. *Sátira anónima del siglo XVIII.* Mexico City: Fondo de Cultura Económica, 1953.

González Echevarría, Roberto. *Isla a su vuelo fugitiva: Ensayos críticos sobre literatura hispanoamericana.* Madrid: Ed. José Porrúa Turranzas, S.A., 1983.

———. "The Law of the Letter: Garcilaso's *Commentaries* and the Origins of the Latin American Narrative." *The Yale Journal of Criticism* 1 (1987): 107–31.

———. *Myth and Archive: A Theory of Latin American Narrative.* New York and Cambridge: Cambridge University Press, 1990.

González de Mendoza, Juan. *Historia de las cosas más notables, ritos y costumbres del Gran Reino de la China.* 1585, Rome. Ed. P. Félix García. Madrid: M. Aguilar, 1944.

González Obregón, Luis. *Don José Joaquín Fernández de Lizardi (El Pensador Mexicano. Apuntes biográficos y bibliográficos).* Mexico City: Oficina Tip. de la Secretaría de Fomento, 1888.

———. *Novelistas mexicanos, Don José Joaquín Fernández de Lizardi (El Pensador Mexicano).* Mexico City: Ediciones Botas, 1938.

González Peña, Carlos. *Historia de la literatura mexicana desde los orígenes hasta nuestros días.* 1928. 9th ed. Mexico City: Ed. Porrúa, 1966.

———. "El Pensador Mexicano y su tiempo." In *Conferencias del Ateneo de la Juventud.* Ed. Antonio Caso. Mexico City: UNAM, 1962.

González Stephen, Beatriz, and Lúcia Helena Costigan, coord. *Crítica y descolonización: El sujeto colonial en la cultura latinoamericana.* Caracas: Universidad Simón Bolívar, 1992.

González Stephen, Beatriz, Javier Lasarte, Graciela Montaldo, and María Julia Daroqui. *Esplendores y miserias del siglo XIX. Cultura y sociedad en América Latina.* Caracas: Monte Avila, 1995.

Gramsci, Antonio. *The Modern Prince and Other Writings.* 1957. Trans. Louis Marks. New York: International Press, 1978.

Granada, Luis de. *Los seis libros de la rhetorica eclesiastica, o de la manera de predicar.* Barcelona: Imprenta de Juan Jolis y Bernardo Pla, 1772, 1775, 1778. Madrid: Plácido Barco, 1793.

Green, Stanley C. *The Mexican Republic: The First Decade 1823–1832.* Pittsburgh: University of Pittsburgh Press, 1987.

Greenblatt, Stephen J. "Learning to Curse: Aspects of Linguistic Colonialism in the Sixteenth Century." In *First Images of America: The Impact of the New World on the Old.* Ed. Fredi Chiappelli. Vol. 2. Berkeley, Los Angeles, and London: University of California Press, 1976, 561–80. 2 vols.

Gruzinski, Serge. *La colonisation de l'imaginaire. Sociétés indigènes et occidentalisation dans le Mexique espagnol. XVIe–XVIIIe siecle.* Paris: Editions Gallimard, 1988.

Guedea, Virginia. *En busca de un gobierno alterno: Los Guadalupes de México.* Mexico City: UNAM, 1992.

Guha, Ranajit. "The Prose of Counter-Insurgency." In *Selected Subaltern Studies.* Ed. Ranajit Guha and Gayatri Chakravorty Spivak. New York and Oxford: Oxford University Press, 1988, 45–86.

Guibert, Rita, ed. *Seven Voices.* 1972. Trans. Frances Partridge. New York: Knopf, 1973.

Guiton, Margaret. *La Fontaine: Poet and Counterpoet.* New Brunswick, N.J.: Rutgers University Press, 1961.

Guridi y Alcocer, José Miguel. "Apología de la aparición de nuestra Señora de Guadalupe." Mexico City: Alejandro Valdés, 1820.

Gutiérrez, Gustavo. *Dios o el oro en las Indias.* Salamanca: Ediciones Sígueme, 1990.

Hale, Charles A. *Mexican Liberalism in the Age of Mora, 1821–1853.* New Haven, London: Yale University Press, 1968.

Hamill, Hugh M., Jr. *The Hidalgo Revolt. Prelude to Mexican Independence.* Gainesville: University of Florida Press, 1966.

———. "The Rector to the Rescue: Royalist Pamphleteers in the Defense of Mexico, 1808–1821." In *Los intelectuales y el poder en México.* Ed. Roderic A. Camp, Charles A. Hale, and Josefina Zoraida Vázquez. Los Angeles: UCLA, El Colegio de México, 1991. 49–61.

Hamnett, Brian R. *Roots of Insurgency. Mexican Regions, 1750–1824.* Cambridge: Cambridge University Press, 1986.

Hanke, Lewis. *Aristotle and the American Indians.* 1959. Bloomington: Indiana University Press, 1971.

Harlow, Barbara. *Resistance Literature.* New York and London: Methuen, 1987.

Harrison, Regina. *Signs, Songs, and Memory in the Andes: Translating Quechua Language and Culture.* Austin: University of Texas Press, 1989.

Harss, Luis, and Barbara Dohmann, eds. *Into the Mainstream.* 1966. New York: Harper and Row, 1967.

Heath, Shirley Brice. *Telling Tongues: Language Policy in Mexico (Colony to Nation).* New York: Teachers College Press, Columbia University, 1972.

Hechter, Michael. *Internal Colonialism: The Celtic Fringe in British National Development, 1536–1966.* Berkeley and Los Angeles: University of California Press, 1975.

Herrejón, Carlos, ed. *Morelos, Antología documental.* Mexico City: SEP, 1985.

Hervás [y Panduro], Lorenzo. *Catalogo delle lingue.* 1789–99. Vol. 1. Study and selection by Antonio Tovar. Madrid: Sociedad General Española de Librería, 1986. (Spanish translation, *Catálogo de las Lenguas*; English, *Catalogue of Languages*).

———. *Historia de la vida del hombre.* Vols. 3, 4. Madrid: Imprenta Real, 1794.

Herzog, Kristin. *Finding Their Voice: Peruvian Women's Testimonies of War.* Valley Forge, Penn.: Trinity Press, 1993.

Hiner, N. Ray. "Adolescence in Eighteenth-Century America." *History of Childhood Quarterly: The Journal of Psychohistory* 3 (1975): 254–55.

Hobsbawm, Eric, and Terence Ranger, eds. *The Invention of Tradition.* Cambridge: Cambridge University Press, 1983.

Honour, Hugh. *The European Vision of America.* Cleveland: The Cleveland Museum of Art, 1975.

————, *The New Golden Land, European Images of America from the Discoveries to the Present Time.* New York: Pantheon, 1975.

Horkheimer, Max, and Theodor W. Adorno. *Dialectic of Enlightenment.* Trans. John Cumming. New York: Seabury Press, 1972.

Howitt, William. *Colonization and Christianity: A Popular History of the Treatment of the Natives by the Europeans in All Their Colonies.* 1838. New York: Negro University Press, 1969.

Ibarra de Anda, Fortino, and Manuel A. Casartelli. *El Periquillo Sarniento y Martín Fierro: Sendas semblanzas sociológicas de México y Argentina.* Puebla: Eds. del Grupo Literario "Bohemia Poblana," 1966.

Iguíniz, Juan B. *La imprenta en la Nueva España.* Mexico City: Ed. Porrúa, 1938.

Irwin, Robert. "El Periquillo Sarniento y sus cuates: el 'éxtasis misterioso' del ambiente homosocial en el siglo diecinueve." *Literatura mexicana* 9 (1998): 23–44.

Isla, José Francisco de. *Fray Gerundio de Campazas.* 1758. Ed. Russell P. Sebold. 4 vols. Madrid: Espasa-Calpe, 1969.

Iturbide, Agustín de. *El Libertador. Documentos Selectos de . . . .* Ed. P. Mariano Cuevas, S. J. Mexico City: Ed. Patria, 1947.

Jackson, Mary H. *The Portrayal of Women in the Novels of José Joaquín Fernández de Lizardi. The Northwest Missouri State College Studies* 32, no. 4. Maryville: Northwest Missouri State College, 1971.

Jameson, Fredric. "Third-World Literature in the Era of Multinational Capitalism." *Social Text* 15 (1966): 65–88.

Jamin, Nicolás. *Conversaciones entre Placido y Maclovia sobre los escrupulos.* Trans. Gabriel Quijano. Madrid: Imprenta de Joseph Herrera, 1787.

————. *Le fruit de mes lectures, ou, Pensées extraites des auteurs profanes, rélatives aux différents ordres de la société, accompagnées de quelques réflexions de l'auteur.* Paris: J.F. Bastien, 1776.

————. *Placido a Escolastica; sobre el modo de portarse en el mundo en lo perteneciente a la religion.* Trans. Gabriel Quijano. Madrid: Imprenta de Blas Roman, 1792.

————. *Verdadero antidoto contra los malos libros de estos tiempos ó Tratado de la Lectura Christiana; en el que no solo se propone el método que se debe observar en la lectura de los buenos libros, á fin de sacar utilidad de ellos, sino que al mismo tiempo se descubre el veneno que ocultan muchos de los Modernos, manifestando los artificios con que procuran con aparentes razones difundir sus errores, y atraer á las gentes sencillas á diversos vicios y disoluciones.* Trans. Don Gabriel Quijano. Madrid: Don Miguel Escribano, 1784.

JanMohamed, Abdul R., and David Lloyd, eds. "The Nature and Context of Minority Discourse." *Cultural Critique* special issues 6 and 7 (1987).

Jennings, Francis. *The Invasion of America: Indians, Colonialism, and the Cant of Conquest.* New York: W. W. Norton, 1975.

Jiménez Rueda, Julio. *Historia de la cultura en México: El Virreinato.* Mexico City: Editorial Cultura, 1950.

——. *Letras mexicanas en el siglo XIX.* Mexico City: Fondo de Cultura Económica, 1944.

Jitrik, Noe. *Cuando leer es hacer.* Santa Fe, Argentina: Cuadernos de extensión universitaria, 1987.

Johnson, Julie Greer. *Satire in Colonial Spanish America: Turning the New World Upside Down.* Austin: University of Texas Press, 1993.

Jones, Ricardo Rees. *El despotismo ilustrado y los intendentes de la Nueva España.* Mexico City: UNAM, 1979.

Kahn, Victoria. *Machiavellian Rhetoric: From the Counter-Reformation to Milton.* Princeton: Princeton University Press, 1994.

Katz, Friedrich, ed. *Riot, Rebellion, and Revolution: Rural Social Conflict in Mexico.* Princeton: Princeton University Press, 1988.

Keitner, Wendy. "Patterns of Decolonization in Contemporary Canadian Literature." In *Language and Literature. ACLALS Proceedings.* Ed. Satendra Nandan. Suva, Fiji: Fiji Times Herald, 1983. 202–13.

Kicza, John E. *Colonial Entrepreneurs: Families and Business in Bourbon Mexico City.* Albuquerque: University of New Mexico Press, 1983.

Kiell, Norman. *The Universal Experience of Adolescence.* Boston: Beacon, 1964.

Knowlton, Edgar C., Jr. "China and the Philippines in *El Periquillo Sarniento.*" *Hispanic Review* 31 (1963): 336–47.

L. M. "Solfeada y palo de ciego a todo autorcillo lego, ó Memorias para servir a la historia de la literatura de Nueva España, ó sea Examen critico-apologetico de los escritores del dia." Mexico City: Oficina de M. Ontiveros, 1820.

Labouret, Henri. *Colonisation, colonialisme, décolonisation.* Paris: Larose, 1952.

Ladd, Doris M. *The Mexican Nobility at Independence, 1780–1826.* Austin: University of Texas Press, 1976.

Lafaye, Jacques. *Quetzalcoatl and Guadalupe: The Formation of Mexican National Consciousness, 1531–1813.* 1974. Trans. Benjamin Keen. Chicago: University of Chicago Press, 1976.

Lanning, John Tate. *Academic Culture in the Spanish Colonies.* New York: Oxford University Press, 1940.

——. "The Church and the Enlightenment in the Universities." *The Americas* 15 (1959): 331–50.

Lardizábal y Uribe, Manuel de. *Discurso sobre las penas contrahidas a las leyes criminales de España.* Madrid: J. Ibarra, 1782.

Lasarte, Pedro. "*Don Catrín, Don Quijote,* y la picaresca." *Revista de Estudios Hispánicos* 23 (1989): 101–12.

Las Casas, Bartolomé. *Colección de las obras.* Ed. Juan Antonio Llorente. 2 vols. París: Casa de Rosa, 1822.

Lavrin, Asunción, ed. *Sexuality and Marriage in Colonial Latin America.* Lincoln and London: University of Nebraska Press, 1989.

Lawrence, Karen R., ed. *Decolonizing Tradition: New Views of Twentieth-Century*

"British" Literary Canons. Urbana and Chicago: University of Illinois Press, 1992.

Lazarus, Neil. *Resistance in Postcolonial African Fiction.* New Haven: Yale University Press, 1990.

Leal, Luis. *Aztlán y México: Perfiles literarios e históricos.* Binghamton, N.Y.: Bilingual P/Editorial Bilingüe, 1985.

———. "La literatura mexicana del diecinueve, en busca de una expresión." In *La literatura iberoamericana del siglo XIX.* Ed. Renato Rosaldo and Robert Anderson. Tucson: University of Arizona Press, 1974. 169–74.

———."Picaresca hispanoamericana: De Oquendo a Lizardi." In *Estudios de literatura hispanoamericana en honor a José Juan Arrom.* Ed. Andrew P. Debicki and Enrique Pupo-Walker. Chapel Hill: University of North Carolina Press, 1974. 47–58.

Leonard, Irving. *Baroque Times in Old Mexico.* 1959. Reprint. Westport: Greenwood Press, 1981.

———. *Books of the Brave.* 1949. Intro. Rolena Adorno. Berkeley: University of California Press, 1992.

León y Gama, Don Antonio de. *Descripción histórica y cronológica de las dos piedras que con ocasion del nuevo empedrado que se esta formando en la plaza principal de Mexico se hallaron en ella el año de 1790.* Ed. Carlos María Bustamante. 2nd ed. Mexico City: Imprenta del Ciudadano Alejandro Valdés, 1832.

Levene, Ricardo. *Las Indias no eran colonias.* 3rd ed. Madrid: Espasa-Calpe, S.A., 1973.

Liss, Peggy K. "Jesuit Contributions to the Ideology of Spanish Empire in Mexico." *The Americas* 29 (1972–73): 314–33, 449–70.

———. "Late Colonial Intellectuals and Imperial Defense." In *Los intelectuales y el poder en México.* Ed. Roderic A. Camp, Charles A. Hale, and Josefina Zoraida Vázquez. Los Angeles: UCLA, El Colegio de México, 1991. 31–47.

Locke, John. *On Politics and Education.* 1685. Intro. Howard R. Penniman. New York: Walter J. Black, 1947.

Longhurst, John E. "Fielding and Swift in Mexico." *Modern Language Journal* 36 (1952): 186–87.

López Cámara, Francisco. *La génesis de la conciencia liberal en México.* Mexico City: El Colegio de México, 1954.

Lozano, Carlos. "El *Periquillo Sarniento* y la *Histoire de Gil Blas de Santillane.*" *Revista Iberoamericana* 20 (1955): 263–74.

Macdonell, Diane. *Theories of Discourse: An Introduction.* New York and Oxford: Basil Blackwell, 1986.

MacLachlan, Colin M. *Spain's Empire in the New World. The Role of Ideas in Institutional and Social Change.* Berkeley: University of California Press, 1988.

MacLachlan, Colin M., and Jaime E. Rodríguez O. *The Forging of the Cosmic Race: A Reinterpretation of Colonial Mexico.* Berkeley and Los Angeles: University of California Press, 1980.

"La Malinche de la Constitucion. En los idiomas mejicanos y castellano." Mexico City: Oficina de D. Alejandro Valdés, 1820.

"La Malinche Noticiosa que vino con el exército trigarante. Diálogo entre una señora y una india." Mexico City: Imprenta Imperial de Don Alejandro Valdes, 1821.

Mannoni, O. *Prospero and Caliban: The Psychology of Colonization.* 1950. Trans. Pamela Powesland. New York: Praeger, 1964.

Manuel, Frank E. *The Eighteenth Century Confronts the Gods.* Cambridge: Harvard University Press, 1959.

Maravall, José Antonio. *Culture of the Baroque: Analysis of a Historical Structure.* 1975. Trans. Terry Cochran. Minneapolis: University of Minnesota Press, 1986.

Marin, Louis. *Portrait of the King.* 1981. Trans. Martha M. Houle. Minneapolis: University of Minnesota Press, 1988.

———. *Utópicas: Juegos de espacios.* 1973. Trans. Rene Palacios More. Madrid: Siglo Veintiuno, 1974.

Martínez, José Luis. *La emancipación literaria de México.* Mexico City: Antigua Librería Robredo, 1955.

Martínez Ocaranza, Ramón, ed. *Poesía insurgente.* Mexico City: UNAM, 1970.

Martínez Rosales, Alfonso, comp. *Francisco Xavier Clavigero en la Ilustración mexicana 1731–1787.* Mexico City: El Colegio de México, 1988.

Mateos, José María. *Historia de la masonería en México desde 1806 hasta 1884.* Mexico City: "La Tolerancia," 1884.

McClintock, Anne. "The Angel of Progress: Pitfalls of the Term "Post-Colonialism." *Social Text* 31/2 (1992): 84–98.

McKegney, James C. "Dos obras recien descubiertas de Lizardi." *Historiografía y bibliografía americanistas* 16 (1972): 193–220.

———. "El Payo del Rosario y la riña de Lizardi con José María Aza." In *Crítica Histórico-Literaria Hispanoamericana.* Vol. 3. Madrid: Ediciones Cultura Hispánica del Centro Iberoamericano de Cooperación, 1978. 1445–57.

———. "El Pensador Mexicano—Reactionary?" *Revista de Letras* 3 (1971): 61–67.

———. "Some Recently Discovered Pamphlets by Fernández de Lizardi." *Hispania* 54 (1971): 256–87.

McKeon, Michael. *The Origins of the English Novel, 1600–1740.* Baltimore and London: Johns Hopkins University Press, 1987.

McLuhan, Marshall. *The Gutenberg Galaxy: The Making of Typographic Man.* Toronto: University of Toronto Press, 1962.

Medina, José Toribio. *Historia del tribunal del Santo Oficio de la Inquisición en México.* 1905. Facsimile ed. Mexico City: UNAM, Miguel Angel Porrúa, 1987.

Mejía Duque, Jaime. *Narrativa y neocolonialismo en América Latina.* Medellín: Editorial La Oveja Negra, 1972.

Mejía Sánchez, Ernesto. *Las Casas en México, 1566–1966.* Mexico City: UNAM, 1967.

Memmi, Albert. *The Colonizer and the Colonized.* Trans. Howard Greenfield. Boston: Beacon, 1967.

———. *Dominated Man.* 1969. Boston: Beacon, 1968.

Méndez Plancarte, Gabriel. *Humanistas del siglo XVIII.* Mexico City: UNAM, 1941.

Meneses, Ernesto. *El código educativo de la Compañía de Jesús.* Mexico City: Universidad Iberoamericana, 1988.

El Mentor Mexicano. [México, D.F.] Vol. 1. 1811.

Merrim, Stephanie. "The Apprehension of the New in Nature and Culture: Fernández de Oviedo's *Sumario.*" *1492–1992: Re/Discovering Colonial Writing.* Ed. Rene Jara and Nicholas Spadaccini. *Hispanic Issues* 4 (1989): 165–99.

Mier Noriega y Guerra, Fray José Servando Teresa de. *Cartas de un americano 1811–1812.* Ed. Manuel Calvillo. Mexico City: SEP, 1987.

Mignolo, Walter. "Colonial Semiosis." Working Paper, Latin American Studies Association Meeting, Los Angeles, 1991.

Mintz, Sidney W., ed. *Slavery, Colonialism, and Racism.* New York: W. W. Norton, 1974.

Miquel i Verges, Josep María. *La independencia mexicana y la prensa insurgente.* Mexico City: Colegio de México, 1941.

Miranda, José. *Vida colonial y albores de la independencia.* Mexico City: Sep/Setentas, 1972.

Miscelanea instructiva, curiosa y agradable. 7 vols. Alcala: Oficina de la Real Universidad, 1796–98.

Monsivais, Carlos. *Nuevo catecismo para indios remisos.* 1982. Mexico City: Siglo XXI Editores, S.A., 1985.

Montesinos, José F. *Introducción a una historia de la novela en España en el siglo XIX, seguida del Esbozo de una bibliografía española de traducciones de novelas (1800–1850).* Madrid: Ed. Castalia, 1955.

Moore, Ernest R. "Una bibliografía descriptiva. El Periquillo Sarniento de J. J. Fernández de Lizardi." *Revista Iberoamericana* 10 (1946): 383–403.

———. "La desconocida segunda edición del Periquillo." *Revista de literatura* 1 (1940): 307–17.

———. "Un manuscrito inédito de Fernández Lizardi: El compendio del tomo cuarto de El Periquillo Sarniento." *Abside* 3, nos. 11, 12 (1939): 3–13, 3–30.

Moraña, Mabel. "*El Periquillo Sarniento* y *La ciudad letrada.*" *Revista de Estudios Hispánicos* 23 (1989): 113–26.

Moreno, Rafael. "La filosofía moderna en la Nueva España." *Estudios de historia de la filosofía en México.* Mexico City: UNAM, 1963. 145–202.

Morse, Richard M. "Language as a Key to Latin American Historiography." *The Americas* 11 (1955): 517–38.

———. *New World Soundings.* Baltimore and London: Johns Hopkins University Press, 1989.

Muñoz, Juan Bautista. *Las polémicas de . . . Cargos hechos por . . . contra el Abate Filibero de Parri Palma o sea el Abate D. Ramon Diosdado Caballero sobre la Historia antigua de México por el Abate D. Francisco Xavier Clavijero.* Ed. Carlos W. de Onís. Madrid: Ed. José Porrúa Turanzas, 1984.

El Museo Mexicano. [México, D.F.] Prospecto, Núm. 1. July 1, 1812.

Musgrove, F. *Youth and the Social Order.* Bloomington: Indiana University Press, 1965.

Mylne, Vivienne. *The Eighteenth-Century French Novel: Techniques of Illusion*. Manchester: Manchester University Press, 1965.

Nájera Corvera, René, comp. *La isla de Saucheofú, Fernández de Lizardi, Educador.* Mexico City: SEP, 1986.

Navarro B., Bernabé. *Cultura mexicana moderna en el siglo XVIII*. Mexico City: UNAM, 1964.

Neal, Clarice. "Freedom of the Press in New Spain, 1810–1820." In *Mexico and the Spanish Cortes, 1810–1822*. Ed. Nettie Lee Benson. Austin: University of Texas Press, 1966.

Ngugi wa Thiong'o. *Decolonising the Mind: The Politics of Language in African Literature*. 1986. Portsmouth, N.H.: Heinemann, 1988.

Niranjana, Tejaswini. *Siting Translation: History, Post-structuralism, and the Colonial Context*. Berkeley: University of California Press, 1992.

Noticioso General. [México, D.F.] July 24, 1815–Dec. 31, 1821.

O'Gorman, Edmundo. *La supervivencia política novo-hispana, Monarquía o república.* Mexico City: Universidad Iberoamericana, 1986.

O'Kane, Eleanor S. "El refrán en las novelas de Fernández de Lizardi." *Anuario de la Sociedad Folklórica de México* 6, pt. 2 (1945): 403–8.

Oliveira e Castro, Luís Filipe de. *Anticolonialismo e descolonização, Ensaios*. Lisboa: Agencia do Ultramar, 1963.

Ong, Walter J. *Orality and Literacy: The Technologizing of the Word*. London: Methuen, 1982.

———. *The Presence of the Word: Some Prolegomena for Cultural and Religious History*. Minneapolis: University of Minnesota Press, 1967.

Osorio Romero, Ignacio. *La enseñanza del latín a los indios*. Mexico City: UNAM, 1990.

Pagden, Anthony. *Spanish Imperialism and the Political Imagination: Studies in European and Spanish-American Social and Political Theory 1513–1830*. New Haven and London: Yale University Press, 1990.

Palazón, María Rosa. "La nobleza pícara o *Don Catrín de la Fachenda*." *Nuevo texto crítico* 4 (1991): 159–72.

Parker, Alexander A. *Literature and the Delinquent: The Picaresque Novel in Spain and Europe 1599–1753*. Edinburgh: The University Press, 1967.

Parkes, Henry Bamford. *A History of Mexico*. 1938. Boston: Houghton Mifflin, 1969.

Parry, Benita. "Problems in Current Theories of Colonial Discourse." *The Oxford Literary Review* 9 (1987): 27–58.

Pastoral Team of Bambamarca. *Vamos caminando: A Peruvian Catechism*. Trans. John Medcalf. Maryknoll: Orbis Books, 1985.

Pawlowski, John. "The Novels of Fernández de Lizardi." Diss. Northwestern University 1972.

———. "*Periquillo* and *Catrín*: Comparison and Contrast." *Hispania* 58 (1975): 830–42.

Paz, Octavio. *El laberinto de la soledad.* 1950. Mexico City: Fondo de Cultura Económica, 1972.

———. *Sor Juana Inés de la Cruz o Las trampas de la fe.* 1982. Mexico City: Fondo de Cultura Económica, 1985.

Pêcheux, Michel. *Language, Semantics and Ideology.* Trans. Harbans Nagpal. London: Macmillan Press, 1982.

Pechey, Graham. "On the Borders of Bakhtin: Dialogisation, Decolonisation." In *Bakhtin and Cultural Theory.* Ed. Ken Hirschkop and David Shepherd. Manchester: Manchester University Press, 1989. 39–67.

Peers, E. Allison. "The Influence of Young and Gray in Spain." *Modern Language Review* 21 (1926): 404–18.

Peña, Margarita. "Feminismo de Fernández de Lizardi?" *Fem* 1 (1977): 63–65.

Pérez Marchand, Monelisa Lina. *Dos etapas ideológicas del siglo XVIII en México a través de los papeles de la Inquisición.* Mexico City: El Colegio de México, 1945.

Pérez Memen, Fernando. *El episcopado y la Independencia de México (1810–1836).* Mexico City: Ed. Jus, 1977.

Phillips, Rachel. "Marina/Malinche: Masks and Shadows." In *Women in Hispanic Literature: Icons and Fallen Idols.* Ed. Beth Miller. Berkeley: University of California Press, 1983.

Piana, Francesca. "José Joaquín Fernández de Lizardi: The Mexican Thinker." M.A. thesis, University of San Francisco, 1973.

Pocock, J. G. A. *The Machiavellian Moment.* Princeton, N.J., and London: Princeton University Press, 1975.

Portuondo, José Antonio. *La emancipación literaria de Hispanoamérica.* La Habana: Casa de las Américas, 1975.

"Post/Colonial Conditions: Exiles, Migrations, and Nomadisms." *Yale French Studies*, nos. 82–83 (1993).

Pratt, Mary Louise. *Toward a Speech Act Theory of Literary Discourse.* Bloomington: Indiana University Press, 1977.

Pupo-Walker, Enrique. *La vocación literaria del pensamiento histórico en América.* Madrid: Ed. Gredos, 1968.

Radin, Paul, ed. *An Annotated Bibliography of the Poems and Pamphlets of J. J. Fernández de Lizardi: The First Period (1808–1819).* San Francisco: California State Library, 1940.

———. "An Annotated Bibliography of the Poems and Pamphlets of Fernández de Lizardi (1824–1827)." *Hispanic American Historical Review* 26 (1946): 284–91.

———. *The Opponents and Friends of Lizardi.* Mexican History Series, no. 2, part 2. San Francisco: California State Library, 1939.

———. *Some Newly Discovered Poems and Pamphlets of J. J. Fernández de Lizardi (El Pensador Mexicano).* Mexican History Series, no. 1. San Francisco: California State Library, n.d.

Rama, Angel. *La ciudad letrada.* Hanover, N.H.: Ediciones del Norte, 1984.

Rangel, Nicolás. "El Pensador Mexicano: Nuevos documentos y noticias bio-gráficas." *El libro y el pueblo* 4 (1914): 41–50.

Raymond, Kay E. "Women in the Works of José Joaquín Fernández de Lizardi." Diss. Indiana University 1983.

Raynal, Abbé Guillaume-Thomas. *A Philosophical and Political History of the Settlements and Trade of the Europeans in the East and West Indies.* 1770. Trans. J. O. Justamond. 2nd ed. London: A. Strahan, 1798. 6 vols.

El Redactor Mexicano [México, D.F.] Núm. 1–20. Sept. 7–Nov. 26, 1814.

Regueiro, Ovidio G. "Ilustración e intereses estamentales: La versión castellana de la 'Historia' de Raynal." In *Homenaje a Noël Salomon.* Ed. Alberto Gil Novales. Barcelona: Universidad Autónoma de Barcelona, 1979. 165–205.

Reissner, Raúl Alcides. *El indio en los diccionarios. Exégesis léxica de un estereotipo.* Mexico City: Instituto Nacional Indigenista, 1983.

Representacion que hizo Nuestro Soberano El Señor D. Fernando VII a su Padre el Señor D. Carlos IV. En octubre de 1807. Reimpreso en Cadiz, y por su original en la Oficina de Doña Maria Fernandez de Jauregui. Año de 1809. México.

Reyes, Alfonso. *La experiencia literaria.* 1942. Mexico City: Fondo de Cultura Económica, 1983.

———. "El 'Periquillo Sarniento' y la crítica mexicana." *Obras.* 1944–66. Vol. 4, 169–78. Mexico City: Fondo de Cultura Económica, 1956. 18 vols.

"¿Los reyes son puestos por Dios en la tierra?" [Unsigned]. Mexico City: Reimpreso en casa de D. José Maria de Benavente, 1814.

Reynolds, Winston A. "The Clergy in the Novels of Fernández de Lizardi." *Modern Language Forum* 40 (1955): 105–12.

Rodríguez O., Jaime E. "Down from Colonialism: Mexico's Nineteenth-Century Crisis." In *The Mexican and Mexican American Experience in the 19th Century.* Ed. Jaime E. Rodríguez O. Tempe: Bilingual P/Editorial Bilingüe, 1989. 7–23.

———. "La transición de colonia a nación: Nueva España, 1820–1821." *Historia mexicana* 43 (1993): 265–322.

———, ed. *The Independence of Mexico and the Creation of the New Nation.* Los Angeles and Irvine: UCLA Publications and Mexico/Chicano Program, 1989.

Rojas Garcidueñas, José. "La novela en la Nueva España." *Anales, Instituto de Investigaciones Estéticas* 8 (1962): 57–78.

Rousseau, Jean-Jacques. *Emile or On Education.* 1762. Intro., trans. Alan Bloom. New York: Basic Books, 1979.

———. *On the Origin of Languages.* With Johann Gottfried Herder, *Essay on the Origin of Language.* Trans. John H. Moran and Alexander Gode. Chicago: University of Chicago Press, 1966.

Ruffinelli, Jorge. *Poesía y descolonización.* Oaxaca: Editorial Oasis, Universidad Veracruzana, 1985.

Said, Edward W. *Culture and Imperialism.* New York: Vintage, 1994.

———. "Representing the Colonized: Anthropology's Interlocutors." *Critical Inquiry* 15 (1989): 205–25.

Salignac de la Mothe-Fénelon, F. *Aventures de Télémaque*. 2 vols. 1699. Paris: Libraire Victor Lecou, 1853.

Salomon, Noël. "La crítica del sistema colonial de la Nueva España en *El Periquillo Sarniento*." *Cuadernos americanos* 138 (1965): 166–79.

Sánchez, Luis Alberto. *Proceso y contenido de la novela hispano americana*. 1953. Madrid: Ed. Gredos, 1968.

Sarrailh, Jean. *La España Ilustrada de la segunda mitad del siglo XVIII*. 1954. Trans. Antonio Alatorre. México, Madrid, Buenos Aires: Fondo de Cultura Económica, 1974.

Sartre, Jean-Paul. *Colonialismo y neocolonialismo, Situations V.* Trans. Josefina Martínez Alinari. 1964. Buenos Aires: Ed. Losada, 1965.

Sebold, Russell P. *Cadalso: El primer romántico "europeo" de España*. Madrid: Ed. Gredos, 1974.

Seed, Patricia. "Colonial and Postcolonial Discourse." *Latin American Research Review* 26 (1991): 181–200.

———. "The Colonial Church as an Ideological State Apparatus." In *Los intelectuales y el poder en México*. Ed. Roderic A. Camp, Charles A. Hale, and Josefina Zoraida Vázquez. Los Angeles: UCLA, El Colegio de México, 1991. 397–415.

———. *To Love, Honor, and Obey in Colonial Mexico: Conflicts Over Marriage Choice, 1574–1821*. Stanford: Stanford University Press, 1988.

Sefchovich, Sara. *México: País de ideas, país de novelas. Una sociología de la literatura mexicana*. Mexico City: Ed. Grijalbo, 1987.

"Segunda Parte del Indio Constitucional, o Idioma de la sensibilidad." Mexico City: Oficina de D. Alejandro Valdés, 1820.

Seminario de Historia de la Educación en México. *Historia de la lectura en México*. Mexico City: El Colegio de México, 1988.

Shafer, Robert J. *The Economic Societies in the Spanish World (1763–1821)*. Syracuse: Syracuse University Press, 1958.

Shohat, Ella. "Notes on the Post-Colonial." *Social Text* 31/2 (1992): 99–113.

Sieber, Harry. *Language and Society in La vida de Lazarillo de Tormes*. Baltimore and London: Johns Hopkins University Press, 1978.

Sierra, Justo, ed. *Antología del Centenario: Estudio documentado de la literatura mexicana durante el primer siglo de Independencia*. Comp. Luis G. Urbina, Pedro Henríquez Ureña, and Nicolás Rangel. 2 vols. Mexico City: Imprenta de Manuel León Sánchez, 1910.

Sigüenza y Góngora, Carlos de. *Infortunios de Alonso Ramírez*. Ed. Lucrecio Pérez Blanco. Madrid: Historia 16, 1988.

Silva Gotay, Samuel. "El pensamiento religioso." In *América Latina en sus ideas*. Mexico City and Paris: Siglo XXI and UNESCO, 1986. 118–54.

Sims, Harold. *Descolonización en México. El conflicto entre mexicanos y españoles (1821–1831)*. Trans. Lillian D. Seddon. Mexico City: Fondo de Cultura Económica, 1982.

Slawek, Ewa, and Tadeusz Slawek. "A Trope of Desire: Geographical Implications of Voice." In *Europe and Its Others*. Ed. Francis Barker et al. Vol. 2. Colchester: University of Essex, 1985. 120–32.

Smith, Sidonie, and Julia Watson, eds. *De/Colonizing the Subject: The Politics of Gender in Women's Autobiography*. Minneapolis: University of Minnesota Press, 1992.

Social Text. Vol. 31/32 (1992). Issue devoted to postcolonialism and the Third World.

Solanas, Fernando E., and Octavio Getino. *Cine, cultura y descolonización*. Mexico City: Siglo XXI, 1978.

Solís y Valenzuela, Pedro de. *El desierto prodigioso y prodigio del desierto, Primera novela hispanoamericana*. 1650. Ed. Héctor H. Orjuela. Bogotá: Instituto Caro y Cuervo, 1984.

Sommer, Doris. "Irresistible Romance: The Foundational Fictions of Latin America." In *Nation and Narration*. Ed. Homi K. Bhabha. London and New York: Routledge, 1990. 71–98.

Spacks, Patricia Meyer. *The Adolescent Idea: Myths of Youth and the Adult Imagination*. New York: Basic Books, 1981.

Spell, Jefferson Rea. *Bridging the Gap: Articles on Mexican Literature*. Mexico City: Ed. Libros de México, 1971.

———. "Dos manuscritos inéditos de 'El Pensador.'" *Revista Iberoamericana* 13 (1947): 53–66.

———. "The Educational Views of Fernández de Lizardi." *Hispania* 9 (1926): 259–74.

———. "Fernández de Lizardi: A Bibliography." *Hispanic American Historical Review* 7 (1927): 490–507.

———. "Fernández de Lizardi and His Critics." *Hispania* 11 (1928): 233–45.

———. "Fernández de Lizardi: The Mexican Feijoo." *Romanic Review* 17 (1926): 338–48.

———. "The Genesis of the First Mexican Novel." *Hispania* 14 (1931): 53–58.

———. "The Historical and Social Background of *El Periquillo Sarniento*." *Hispanic American Historical Review* 36 (1956): 447–70.

———. "An Incident in the Life of Guridi y Alcocer and *La Quixotita*." *Hispanic American Historical Review* 25 (1945): 405–8.

———. "The Intellectual Background of Lizardi as Reflected in *El Periquillo Sarniento*." *PMLA* 71 (1956): 414–32.

———. "The Life and Works of José Joaquín Fernández de Lizardi." Diss. University of Pennsylvania, 1931.

———. "Lizardi and Taxco." *Library Chronicle of the University of Texas* 7, no. 4 (1964): 3–25.

———. "Mexican Society as Seen by Fernández de Lizardi." *Hispania* 8 (1925): 145–65.

———. "New Light on Fernández de Lizardi and His *El Periquillo Sarniento*." *Hispania* 46 (1963): 753–54.

———. *Rousseau in the Spanish World Before 1833: A Study in Franco-Spanish Literary Relations*. 1938. New York: Octagon Books, 1969.

———. "A Textual Comparison of the First Four Editions of *El Periquillo Sarniento*." *Hispanic Review* 31 (1963): 134–47.

Spivak, Gayatri Chakravorty. "Can the Subaltern Speak?" In *Colonial Discourse and Post-Colonial Theory: A Reader*. Ed. Patrick Williams and Laura Chrisman. New York: Columbia University Press, 1994. 66–111.

Staël Holstein, Anne Louise Germaine Necker, Baronne de. *Corina ó la Italia, sacada de lo que escribió en francés . . . por Don Pedro María de Olive*. Madrid: Ibarra, 1818.

Stafford, Barbara Maria. *Artful Science: Enlightenment Entertainment and the Eclipse of Visual Education*. Cambridge: MIT Press, 1994.

Staples, Anne. "El catecismo como libro de texto durante el siglo XIX." In *Los intelectuales y el poder en México*. Ed. Roderic A. Camp, Charles A. Hale, and Josefina Zoraida Vázquez. Los Angeles: UCLA, El Colegio de México, 1991.

———. "La lectura y los lectores en los primeros años de vida independiente." In *Historia de la lectura en México*. Mexico City: El Colegio de México, 1988. 94–126.

Stoetzer, O. Carlos. *El pensamiento político en la América española durante el periodo de la emancipación (1789–1825)*. 2 vols. Madrid: Instituto de Estudios Políticos, 1966.

———. *The Scholastic Roots of the Spanish American Revolution*. New York: Fordham University Press, 1979.

Stolley, Karen. "Lazos de familia: El problema de la genealogía en la obra de Lizardi." In *La imaginación histórica en el siglo XIX*. Ed. Lelia Area and Mabel Moraña. Rosario, Argentina: UNR Editora, 1994. 181–91.

Stubbs, Michael. *Discourse Analysis*. Chicago: University of Chicago Press, 1983.

Surtz, Edward, S. J., and J. H. Hexter, eds. *The Complete Works of St. Thomas More*. Vol. 4. New Haven: Yale University Press, 1965.

Taléns, Jenaro. *Novela picaresca y práctica de la transgresión*. Madrid: Ediciones Júcar, 1975.

Tanck Estrada, Dorothy. *La educación ilustrada (1786–1836), Educación primaria en la ciudad de México*. Mexico City: El Colegio de México, 1977.

———. "La enseñanza de la lectura y de la escritura en la Nueva España, 1700–1821." In *Historia de la lectura en México*. Mexico City: El Colegio de México, 1988. 49–93.

———. "Tensión en la torre de marfil. La educación en la segunda mitad del siglo XVIII mexicano." In *Ensayos sobre historia de la educación en México*. 1981. Ed. Josefina Zoraida Vázquez et al. Mexico City: El Colegio de México, 1995. 27–99.

Taylor, Patrick. *The Narrative of Liberation: Perspectives on Afro-Caribbean Literature, Popular Culture, and Politics*. Ithaca: Cornell University Press, 1989.

Taylor, William B. *Drinking, Homicide, and Rebellion in Colonial Mexican Villages*. Stanford: Stanford University Press, 1979.

———. *Magistrates of the Sacred: Priests and Parishioners in Eighteenth-Century Mexico*. Stanford: Stanford University Press, 1996.

Tena Ramírez, Felipe. *Vasco de Quiroga y sus pueblos de Santa Fe en los siglos XVIII y XIX*. Mexico City: Ed. Porrúa, 1977.

Terdiman, Richard. *Discourse/Counter-Discourse*. Ithaca and London: Cornell University Press, 1985.

"El Tocayo de Clarita," "El Gran Hospital del periodico titulado: La Canoa." Mexico City: Oficina de Juan Bautista de Arizpe, 1820.

Torres Quintero, Gregorio. *México hacia el fin del virreinato español*. Mexico City: Bouret, 1921.

Torres-Ríoseco, Arturo. *The Epic of Latin American Literature*. Berkeley: University of California Press, 1964.

Torres-Villarroel, Diego de. *Vida*. 1743–59. Madrid: Espasa-Calpe, 1941.

Trilling, Lionel. "Mexican Classic." *Nation* 54 (March 28, 1942): 373–74.

Turner, Victor. *Dramas, Fields and Metaphors: Symbolic Action in Human Society*. Ithaca: Cornell University Press, 1974.

Tutino, John. *From Insurrection to Revolution in Mexico: Social Bases of Agrarian Violence, 1750–1940*. Princeton: Princeton University Press, 1986.

Urbina, Luis G. *La vida literaria de México y la literatura mexicana durante la Guerra de Independencia*. 1917. Ed. Antonio Castro Leal. Mexico City: Ed. Porrúa, 1965.

Urquhart, Brian. *Decolonization and World Peace*. Austin: University of Texas Press, 1989.

Van Young, Eric. "Agustín Marroquín: The Sociopath as Rebel." In *The Human Tradition in Latin America: The Nineteenth Century*. Ed. Judith Ewell and William H. Beezley. Wilmington: Scholarly Resources, 1989. 17–38.

———. "Quetzalcóatl, King Ferdinand, and Ignacio Allende Go to the Seashore; or Messianism and Mystical Kingship in Mexico, 1800–1821." In *The Independence of Mexico and the Creation of the New Nation*. Ed. Jaime E. Rodríguez O. Los Angeles, Irvine: UCLA Latin American Center, 1989, 109–127.

———. "The Raw and the Cooked: Elite and Popular Ideology in Mexico, 1800–1821." In *The Middle Period in Latin America. Values and Attitudes in the 17th–19th Centuries*. Ed. Mark D. Szuchman. Boulder, Colo.: Lynne Rienner, 1989. 75–102.

Vaughan, Alden T. "Caliban in the 'Third World': Shakespeare's Savage as Sociopolitical Symbol." *The Massachusetts Review* 29 (1988): 289–313.

Vázquez, Josefina Zoraida. *Nacionalismo y educación en México*. 1970. Mexico City: El Colegio de México, 1975.

Vázquez, Josefina Zoraida, Dorothy Tanck de Estrada, Anne Staples, and Francisco Arce Gurza. *Ensayos sobre historia de la educación en México*. 1981. Mexico City: El Colegio de México, 1995.

Venturi, Franco. "Oriental Despotism." *Journal of the History of Ideas* 24 (1963): 133–42.

———. *Utopia and Reform in the Enlightenment*. Cambridge: Cambridge University Press, 1971.

El Verdadero Ilustrador Americano. [México, D.F.] Nos. 1–9, 1812.

Vidal, Hernán. *Socio-historia de la literatura colonial hispanoamericana: Tres lecturas orgánicas*. Minneapolis: Institute for the Study of Ideologies and Literature, 1985.

Villoro, Luis. *El proceso ideológico de la Revolución de Independencia.* 2nd ed. Mexico City: UNAM, 1977.

Vogeley, Nancy. "China and the American Indies: A Sixteenth-Century 'History.'" *CLAR* 6 (1997): 165–84.

———. "The Concept of 'the People' in *El Periquillo Sarniento.*" *Hispania* 70 (1987): 457–67.

———. "Defining the 'Colonial Reader': *El Periquillo Sarniento.*" *PMLA* 102 (1987): 784–800.

———. "The Discourse of Colonial Loyalty: Mexico, 1808." In *Macropolitics of Nineteenth-Century Literature: Nationalism, Exoticism, Imperialism.* Ed. Jonathan Arac and Harriet Ritvo. Philadelphia: University of Pennsylvania Press, 1991. 37–55. Rpt. Durham, N.C.: Duke University Press, 1995.

———. "El discurso colonial en un contexto post-colonial: Mexico, siglo XIX." *Crítica y descolonización: El sujeto colonial en la cultura latinoamericana.* Ed. Beatriz González Stephan and Lúcia Helena Costigan. Caracas: Universidad Simón Bolívar, Ohio State University, 1992. 607–24.

———. "Colonial Discourse in a Postcolonial Context: Nineteenth-Century Mexico." *CLAR* 2 (1993): 189–212.

———. "La figuración de la mujer: México en el momento de la independencia." *Mujer y cultura en la Colonia hispanoamericana.* Ed. Mabel Moraña. Pittsburgh: Biblioteca de América, Instituto Internacional de Literatura Iberoamericana, 1996. 307–26.

———. "Intertextuality Defined in Terms of Nineteenth-Century Nationalism: *Perucho, nieto de Periquillo.*" *Bulletin of Hispanic Studies* 71 (1994): 485–97.

———. "José Joaquín Fernández de Lizardi and the Inquisition." *Dieciocho* 3 (1980): 126–35.

———. *La literatura manuscrita en el México independentista: Poesía inédita de Lizardi.* Mexico City: UNAM, forthcoming.

———. "Mexican Newspaper Culture on the Eve of Mexican Independence." *Ideologies and Literature* 4, 2nd cycle (1983): 358–77.

———. "Mexican Readings of Hugh Blair's *Rhetoric.*" *Dieciocho* 21 (1998): 153–65.

———. "Updating the Picaresque Tradition: Alfonso Sastre's *lumpen, marginación y jerigonça.*" *Ideologies and Literature* 2, new series (1987): 25–42.

Volosinov, V. N. *Marxism and the Philosophy of Language.* 1929, 1973. Trans. Ladislav Matejka and I. R. Titunik. Cambridge, Mass., and London: Harvard University Press, 1986.

von Humboldt, Alexander. *Political Essay on the Kingdom of New Spain.* 1811. Ed. Mary Maples Dunn. New York: Alfred A. Knopf, 1972.

Warner, Ralph E. *Historia de la novela mexicana en el siglo XIX.* Mexico City: Robredo, 1953.

Watt, Ian. *The Rise of the Novel: Studies in Defoe, Richardson and Fielding.* Berkeley and Los Angeles: University of California Press, 1974.

Whitaker, Arthur P., ed. *Latin America and the Enlightenment.* 1942. Ithaca: Cornell University Press, 1961.

White, James Boyd. *When Words Lose Their Meaning: Constitutions and Reconstitutions of Language, Character, and Community.* Chicago and London: University of Chicago Press, 1984.

Wicks, Ulrich. "Pícaro, Picaresque: The Picaresque in Literary Scholarship." *Genre* 5 (1972): 153–216.

Williams, Patrick, and Laura Chrisman, eds. and intro. *Colonial Discourse and Post-Colonial Theory: A Reader.* New York: Columbia University Press, 1994.

Williams, Raymond. *Keywords.* 1976. Rev. ed. New York: Oxford University Press, 1983.

Williford, Miriam. *Jeremy Bentham on Spanish America: An Account of His Letters and Proposals to the New World.* Baton Rouge: Louisiana State University Press, 1980.

Wold, Ruth. *Diario de México: Primer Cotidiano de Nueva España.* Madrid: Ed. Gredos, 1970.

Yancey, Myra L. "Fernández de Lizardi and His Foreign Sources for *Las noches tristes.*" *Hispanic Review* 9 (1941): 394–97.

Zamora, Margarita. *Reading Columbus.* Berkeley: University of California Press, 1993.

Zavala, Iris. "Representing the Colonial Subject." *1492–1992: Re/Discovering Colonial Writing.* Ed. Rene Jara and Nicholas Spadaccini. *Hispanic Issues* 4 (1989): 323–48.

Zavala, Silvio. *La filosofía política en la Conquista de América.* 1947. Mexico City: Fondo de Cultura Económica, 1984.

Zea, Leopoldo. "Colonización y descolonización de la cultura latinoamericana." *Boletín, Comunidad Latinoamericana de Escritores* 9 (1970): 23–29.

Index

65, 247–48. *See also Egoísmo;* Slavery
Bustamante, Carlos María de, 35, 37, 115.
   See also Diario de México; El indio mexicano

Cabañas, Pablo, 216
Cabrera Infante, Guillermo, 277n.1
Cadalso, José, 212, 214–16, 218, 225, 227,
   231, 233, 290n.1, 291nn.7, 9, 10, 292nn.
   11, 12. *See also Cartas marruecas; Noches
   lúgubres*
Cafes, 40–43, 57, 255
Caillet-Bois, Julio, 293n.15
Calendarios, 274n.51
Caliban, 7, 251, 271n.22
Calleja, Félix María (viceroy), 281n.4
Calprenede, Gauthier de la. *See Casandra,
   La*
Calvet, Louis-Jean, 265
Calvillo, Manuel, 281n.21
Calvin, John, 88
Calzada, Bernardo María de, 289–90n.16.
   See also Lennox, Charlotte
Camargo y Cavallero, Juan, 280n.9
Camoens, Vaz de, 49
Campanella, Tommaso, 125–26
Campe, Joachim Henrich. *See* Defoe,
   Daniel; *Nuevo Robinson, El; Robinson
   Crusoe*
Campillo y Cosío, José del, 111, 126
Candide, 217. *See also* Voltaire, François
   Marie Arouet
Cárdenas de la Peña, Enrique, 124
Carlos III (king of Spain), 94, 115, 235
Carlos IV (king of Spain), 59, 95–96
Carnero, El (Rodríguez Freyle), 270n.9
Carolina de Lichtfield, 68. *See also* Bottens,
   Isabelle de
Carrió de la Vandera, Alonso. *See Lazarillo
   de ciegos caminantes*
Cartas de un americano, 281n.21. *See also*
   Mier, Fray Servando Teresa de
Cartas de Isabela Sofía de Valliere, 68
Cartas marruecas, 47, 216. *See also* Cadalso,
   José
Casandra, La (Calprenede), 66, 277n.9
Casas de Faunce, María, 278n.14
Castañeda, Mariana Osuna, 25
Castanien, Donald G., 276n.33

Catechism, 161, 178–79, 187, 189, 202–5,
   212–33, 256–58, 267–68, 292n.14,
   295n.2, 297n.21; Bambamarca, 222;
   "Cartilla o catecismo del ciudadano
   constitucional," 267; catechetical
   learning, 78, 202–3, 228–30; death of,
   256; *Nuevo catecismo,* 219–20. *See also*
   Monsivais, Carlos; Ripalda, Jerónimo
Censorship, 32, 37, 45–46, 59, 70, 72–73,
   102, 112, 120, 149, 183, 205, 213–16,
   223–24, 234. *See also* Inquisition
Certeau, Michel de, 296n.6
Cervantes, Miguel de, 63, 69, 73, 75, 153,
   204, 261. *See also Don Quijote*
Césaire, Aimé, 6, 19–20
Chadwick, Owen, 267
Chateaubriand, François René. *See Atala*
Chatterjee, Partha, 296–97n.20
Chencinsky, Jacobo, 25, 286n.14
Chilpancingo (congress of), 112
China: Chinese, 48, 99, 123–28, 283n.22;
   chino, 99, 108, 114–15, 122, 127, 144. *See
   also* González de Mendoza, Juan; Orient
Chrisman, Laura, 270n.13
Church (Roman Catholic), 7, 96–97, 122–
   25, 175, 189, 212–13, 244, 249, 257,
   291n.9, 295n.4, 297n.22; clergy, 89, 107,
   172, 218, 232, 295n.30; ecclesiastical
   privilege, 112, 213–14, 279n.7, 290n.2;
   missionaries, 124, 221, 246; pope, 94,
   126, 221–22, 264, 279n.6; priests, 16–17,
   38, 96, 98, 107, 113, 136, 210, 213–14,
   217–20, 241–43, 252, 296n.6
Cicero, 77, 166, 194, 287n.6
Cid, El, 55
Civility, 136, 168, 192, 195, 261–62. *See also*
   France
Civilization, 2, 42, 84–85, 90, 103–4, 109,
   128, 193, 208
Clara Harlowe, 66, 277n.9. *See also*
   Richardson, Samuel
Class, 40–42, 188; and economic status, 16;
   and place of birth, 16; and race, 16, 41.
   See also Blacks; China; Consciousness;
   Criollo; *Gachupín;* Indians; *Ladinos;
   Mestizo;* Race; White
Clavijero, Francisco Javier, 61–62, 129–30,
   271n.27

97n.20. *See also* Discourse; Language; Reading

Defoe, Daniel, 238. *See also Nuevo Robinson, El; Robinson Crusoe*

Deism, 142, 279n.7, 286n.18. *See also* Philosophy

"De la littérature" (Staël), 67

Demos, John and Virginia, 160

de Onís, Carlos, 290n.20

de Pauw, Cornelius, 90, 129

Dependency, 84, 93, 135, 172–74, 188, 199, 208, 294n.17

Descartes, René, 285–86n.13

Desengaño, 52–53, 141, 166–67

Desierto prodigioso y prodigio del desierto, El (Solís y Valenzuela), 270n.9

Desunión, 97–99

Development studies, 20

Dhareshwar, Vivek, 273n.44

Dialogue, 54, 103, 194, 203, 243, 249; of the dead, 32, 275n.9; as dialectic, 180, 190, 219, 222–24, 240; Socratic, 222

Diario de México (gazette), 24, 29, 34–45, 58–66, 70, 74, 84–85, 95–96, 117–20, 128–29, 136–37, 147, 151, 157, 165, 170–71, 173, 189, 191, 196, 251–52, 261–62, 266, 269n.6, 271nn.20, 27, 273n.43, 275nn.11–13, 15–23, 25–31, 34, 37–38, 276–77n.39, 277nn.40, 45, 2, 9, 278nn.11,21, 1, 279n.2, 280nn.10–13, 16, 17, 282nn.10, 14–16, 283nn.29, 31, 284nn.3, 5, 287nn.4, 5, 11–13, 288n.4, 289nn.6–8, 293n.8, 294nn.18, 23, 295n.3, 296nn.9–11, 13–16

Díaz, Porfirio, 22

Díaz de Castillo, Bernal, 55, 62

Diderot, Denis, 283n.24, 285–86n.13, 296n.8. *See also Encyclopédie*

Digressions (textual), 83–84, 113, 175–84, 235, 237, 288n.15, 292n.2. *See also* Reading

Discourse, 5, 9–10, 14, 182, 271n.19, 294n.27; colonial, 8–9, 13–15, 41, 76, 94–95, 134–38, 254, 272nn.34, 36; counter, 7–8, 13, 74, 167, 200, 231–32, 251–54, 257; decolonizing, 1–26, 41, 182–84, 200–201, 210–11, 251–52, 261–62; of doubt, 217–22, 239; minority, 13;

political, 70; postcolonial, 296nn.13, 20; religious, 10, 48, 57, 70, 212–33, 250, 257; space for, 36, 151, 206, 240, 254–55; third, 200; as a tool of analysis, 9–10

Discourse on the Arts and Sciences, 252. *See also* Rousseau, Jean-Jacques

Discurso sobre las penas, 115. *See also* Lardizábal, Manuel de

Disobedience, 88–89, 236, 250, 264; apostates, 88, 279n.7; heretics, 88–89, 230, 245, 279n.7. *See also* Obedience

Doctor Purgante, 99, 140–41, 286n.15

Dohmann, Barbara, 56, 277n.1

Domínguez, Jorge, 271n.28

Dominicans (religious order), 273n.41, 282n.118

Don Catrín (Lizardi), 25, 46, 59, 123, 167, 192, 234–55, 266; *catrín* as symbol, 231–32, 234–35, 242–43, 249–50, 293nn. 13–15; design of, 237–38; ending of, 237–38, 241; plot of, 241–43; 250; publication of, 33, 46, 214, 224, 234; reception of, 234, 246–47, 292n.2; style of, 227. *See also* Authority; Caliban; Criollo; Comedy, Irony; Enlightenment; Feijóo, Benito; Gramsci, Antonio; Machiavellianism; Masonry; Military

Don Quijote (Cervantes), 45, 61–63, 74–76, 111, 153, 201, 205, 241, 277n.16. *See also* Cervantes, Miguel de; Fernández de Avellaneda, Alonso

Dorfman, Ariel, 277n.1

Double voicing, 269n.2

Dress, 44, 95, 119, 168–69, 171, 242, 254, 289n.9

Ducray-Duminil, François Guillaume. *See Alejo u la casita en los bosques*

Eclecticism, 90. *See also* Philosophy

Ecole des Moeurs, 93, 139. *See also* Blanchard, Jean Baptiste

Economics, 3–4, 99, 104; city-centered, 119; poverty, 88, 114, 154, 215, 218; *real patronato*, 94, 114; societies for discussion of, 240; systems, 88, 114, 119, 121–22, 154, 164–65, 235, 247–48, 267–68; wealth, 88, 118, 121–22, 124, 207–28, 218. *See also* Colonialism; Mining

Education, 134–59, 284nn.1, 3–6, 285n.11; civilizing, 135–36, 208; colonial, 1, 76, 78, 85, 89–90, 134–35, 187–88, 208–11, 240, 288n.2, 293n.10; institutions of, 89–90, 209–10, 240; professions and, 89, 135, 143–44, 240; religious, 134–35, 174, 178, 249, 257, 295n.29, 296n.6; self-education, 139–40; training for manhood, 171; vocabulary of, 134–38; of women, 187–88, 192–97, 201–5, 288n.2. *See also* Blanchard, Jean Baptiste; Books; Civility; *Desengaño*; Empiricism; Fables; Family; Fénelon, François de Salignac de la Mothe; Ignorance; Imitation; Knowledge; Reading; Reason; Rousseau, Jean-Jacques; Tradition

Egoísmo (self-love, selfishness), 95–96, 98–99, 133, 167, 223, 242, 247–48, 294n.24; self-interest, 104, 164, 171, 173, 247; tolerable egoists, 165–66; well-ordered, 101, 104. *See also* Self

Emile, 136, 139, 147–49, 160, 166, 178. *See also* Rousseau, Jean-Jacques

Emotion, 1, 11, 69, 93, 106, 167, 188, 218, 221, 228

Empiricism, 138–41, 151

Encyclopédie (Diderot), 178

England, 7, 55, 95, 119–20, 129, 192, 221, 235–36, 242, 244; capitalism, 247; Protestantism of, 10, 236, 279n.7. *See also* Slavery

Enlightenment (European), 41, 64, 72, 84, 118, 138–39, 170, 183, 200, 202, 207, 224, 235–36, 242–44, 247, 250–52, 261, 268, 295n.30; Mexican version of, 41, 84–85, 250, 285–86n.13; philosophers of, 48, 130–1, 135, 148, 283n.24, 285–86n.13; post-Enlightenment society, 261

Erasmus, Desiderius, 139

Ercilla, Alonso de, 55, 61, 69, 123, 125. *See also* "Araucana, La"; Arms and letters

Erskine, Noel Leo, 7

Escarmiento, 117, 150–53

Escoiquiz, Juan de, 54. *See also* Young, Edward

Espíritu fuerte, 242, 279n.7

Eusebio, 279–80n.8

Excommunication, 33–34, 96, 213–14, 234, 249, 279n.7, 290n.2

Exequias de la lengua castellana (Forner), 47

Experience, 3, 126, 137, 139–41, 155, 159, 194, 217–18, 264

Exposé (narrative technique), 153–58, 193–94

Fabbrini, Juan Valentín Matías (Foronda), 111, 259, 295n.3. *See also* Condillac, Etienne Bonnot de

Fables, 49–50, 139, 151, 180, 219. *See also* Fernández de Lizardi, José Joaquín

Faith (religious), 10, 12, 15, 49–50, 193, 205, 212–33, 236–43, 257, 261, 293–94n.16; salvation, 2, 7, 103, 135, 212

Family, 2, 83–107, 117, 134–38, 163, 170, 173–74, 200–201, 263–64, 289n.9

Fanaticism, 138, 237–38, 242, 252, 256

Fanon, Frantz, 6, 18, 270n.11

Fatherhood, 94–102, 134, 142–43, 173, 175, 261, 264, 284nn.3, 7

Feijóo, Benito, 47, 73, 246, 291n.7, 293n.8

Female Quijote, The (Lennox), 289–90n.16

Fénelon, François de Salignac de la Mothe, 66, 139–40, 190. *See also Aventuras de Telémaco*

Fernández Arias, Irma Isabel, 25

Fernández de Avellaneda, Alonso, 63–63. *See also* Cervantes, Miguel de; *Don Quijote*

Fernández de Lizardi, José Joaquín, 30–34, 97, 122, 126, 218, 234, 263–64, 266–67, 273n.47, 273–74n.49, 274nn.51, 52, 274–75n.6, 275nn.7, 24, 284n.4, 285n.11, 286n.21; almanacs of, 206; *calendarios*, 296n.19; fables of, 32–33, 70, 84, 187; novels of, 33, 57–59; poetry of, 70; *Ratos entretenidos*, 33, 46, 70, 147–49, 212, 215, 230–31, 285n.12, 291n.5; theater of, 32, 206. *See also Don Catrín; Noches tristes; Periquillo; Quijotita, La*

—newspapers of: *Alacena de Frioleras*, 32, 73–74, 277n.5; *El Amigo de la Paz y de la Patria*, 33; *Cajoncitos de la Alacena*, 32, 293n.12; *Conductor Eléctrico, El*, 33; *Conversaciones del Payo y el Sacristán*, 33; *Correo de los Niños, El*, 32; *Correo Semanario de México*, 33, 126, 220, 283n.23; *Hermano de Perico que Cantaba la*

Victoria, El, 33; *Payaso de los Periódicos, El*, 33; *Pensador Mexicano, El*, 23–24, 32, 37, 76, 88, 93, 95, 97–99, 101–2, 106–7, 109–113, 115, 122, 130, 136, 140, 146–47, 173, 274n.52, 279–80n.8, 284n.6, 284–85n.8, 286nn.18, 25; *Sombras de Heráclito y Demócrito, Las*, 32, 223–24, 294n.24
—pamphlets of, 32–33, 46, 70; "Bula del Sto. Padre" (Bull of the Holy Father), 296n.18; "Breve sumaria" (Brief Summary), 274n.5; "Carta de los indios de Tontonapeque" (Letter from the Indians), 294n.19; "Carta primera de El Pensador al Papista" (First Letter from the Mexican Thinker), 280n.15; "Chamorro y Dominiquín" (Chamorro and Dominiquín), 33, 161–62, 295n.1; "Dentro de seis años o antes" (In Six Years or Even Before), 283n.23; "Dudas de El Pensador consultadas con doña Tecla" (The Mexican Thinker Consults with Doña Tecla), 220; "Hacen las cosas tan claras que hasta los ciegos las ven" (Things Are Made So Clear that Even the Blind See Them), 52; "Hemos dado en ser borricos" (We've Gone Crazy), 292n.1; "Impugnación que los gatos" (Challenge that the Cats Make), 283n.23; "El indio y la india del pueblo de Actopán" (The Indian and His Wife from the Village of Actopán), 206; "No es señor el que nace, sino el que lo sabe ser" (He Is Not a Gentleman Because of Birth), 52; "Pronóstico político" (Political Forecast), 33; "Quien llama al toro sufra la cornada" (He Who Provokes the Bull Gets Gored), 278n.12; "Respuesta del Pensador al defensor del Payo de Rosario" (The Mexican Thinker's Reply to the Defender of Payo de Rosario), 274n.4; "Segundo sueño" (Second Dream), 283n.23; "La verdad pelada" (The Naked Truth), 52; "Vida y entierro de D. Pendón" (Life and Burial of D. Pendón), 296n.17
Fernández Retamar, Roberto, 251, 270nn.14, 16, 271n.22
Fernando VII (king of Spain), 30, 37, 60,

94–96, 110, 218, 235–36, 263, 269n.1, 280n.14. *See also Representación que hizo . . . a su Padre*
Fielding, Henry, 64. *See also Historia de Amelia Booth; Tom Jones*
Fielding, Sarah. *See La Huerfanita inglesa ó historia de Carlota Summers*
Filangieri, Gaetano, 125
"Filósofo Incógnito, El," 190
Flores, Ignacia, 191
Flores, Jorge, 275n.8
Flores Caballero, Romeo, 271n.26
Fontenelle, Bernard Le Bovier de, 63–64
Ford, Ford Madox, 176
Forner, Juan Pablo. *See Exequias de la lengua castellana*
Fortune, 103, 241, 293n.12
Foucault, Michel, 118
France, 38, 44, 47, 55, 95–96, 98–99, 118–19, 137, 206, 216, 235, 242, 244, 262, 279n.7, 281n.21, 286n.20, 296n.6; civility, 44, 168, 195; mode, 38, 161, 242; irreligion, 88, 95, 244, 262. *See also Afrancesados*; Civility; Colonialism; Enlightenment
Franciscans (religious order), 213, 273n.41
Franco, Jean, 24, 281n.1, 289n.9, 11, 12, 296–97n.20
Franklin, Benjamin, 285–86n.13
Fraternity, 163
Fray Gerundio, 48. *See also* Isla, José Francisco de
Freedom, 15, 26, 253–55. *See also* Press
Freire, Paulo, 269n.8
Freud, Sigmund, 166, 265
Friendship, 158–59, 163–66; *malos amigos* 99, 158–59, 166–67
Fritz, Robert, 97
Frost, Elsa Cecilia, 294n.17
Fruits de mes lectures, 177–78. *See also* Jamin, Nicolás
Fuentes, Carlos 277n.1
Fuero Juzgo, 122–23, 169. *See also* Lardizábal, Manuel de

Gaceta (gazette), 2, 29, 274n.1
Gachupines, 13, 112, 204
Galería de mugeres fuertes (Lemoyne), 190

Galván Gaytán, Columba Camelia, 25
Galván Rivera, Mariano, 285n.11
Gante, Pedro de, 213
García, Félix, 283n.21. *See also* González de
  Mendoza, Juan
García de la Huerta, Vicente, 47
García Gutiérrez, Celedonio, 190
Garcilaso de la Vega, el Inca, 61. *See also*
  Comentarios reales de los Incas
Garza, David T. 282n.23
Gassendi, Pierre, 285–86n.13
Gavillas, 99–100, 112, 280n.20
Genovesi, Antonio, 125
Gerbi, Antonello, 90
Getino, Octavio, 7
Giannone, Pietro, 125
Gibbon, Edward. *See Decline and Fall of the
  Roman Empire*
Gifford, Prosser, 270n.11
Giffords, Gloria Kay, 276n.27
Gil Blas, 66–67, 73, 75, 141, 278n.14,
  286n.15. *See also* Isla, José Francisco de
Ginés de Sepúlveda, Juan, 102, 281n.21
Godlewska, Anne, 270n.17
Godoy, Bernabé, 106
Godoy, Manuel, 95–96
Gómez Alvarez, Cristina, 276n.33
Góngora, Luis de, 291n.7
Gonzalbo Aizpuru, Pilar, 78, 282n.19,
  288nn.1, 2
González Casanova, Pablo, 276n.32,
  278nn.13, 16, 282n.18, 293n.7
González de Mendoza, Juan. *See Historia de
  las cosas de la China*
González Echevarría, Roberto, 270n.10
González Obregón, Luis, 24, 31, 187,
  274nn.2, 6
González Peña, Carlos, 23, 291n.7
González Stephan, Beatriz, 272n.39
Government, 25, 50, 103–4, 108, 110, 116,
  119, 130–33, 280n.18
Goya, Francisco de, 199, 239
Gracián, Baltasar, 139
Gracias de la niñez, Las (Jauffret), 190
Gramsci, Antonio, 249
Granada, Luis de. *See Retórica eclesiástica*
Gratitude, 86–95, 112, 116, 120, 132, 167,
  171–73, 228, 287n.13; ingratitude, 96,

  106, 166, 171, 173–74, 287n.11
Green, Stanley C., 292n.17
Greenblatt, Stephen J., 271n.22
Grégoire, Henri (Abbé), 281n.21, 296n.6.
  See also Las Casas, Bartolomé de
Greuze, Jean Baptiste, 178, 239
Gruzinski, Serge, 293–94n.16
Guadalupe. *See* Virgen de Guadalupe
Guedea, Virginia, 276n.27
Guerras civiles de Granada (Pérez de Hita),
  71
Guerrero, Vicente, 53
Guibert, Rita, 277n.1
Guiton, Margaret, 286n.14
Gulliver's Travels (Swift), 54, 66
Guridi y Alcocer, José Miguel, 209, 290n.20
Gutiérrez, Gustavo, 10
Gutiérrez, José Marcos, 123
Guzmán de Alfarache, 21, 73, 286n.16.
Guzmán Gutiérrez, María Esther, 25

Hale, Charles A., 284n.32
Hamill, Hugh M., Jr. 37, 271n.26
Hamnett, Brian, 13
Hanke, Lewis, 102
Hapsburg (royal house of), 246
Harlow, Barbara, 271n.31, 296–97n.20
Harrison, Regina, 292n.14
Harss, Luis, 56, 277n.1
Heath, Shirley B., 16–17, 273n.41
Hechter, Michael, 273n.45
Heliodorus, 68
Helman, Edith, 290n.1, 291n.10
Herrejón, Carlos, 294n.26
Herrera, Antonio de, 62
Hersent, Louis, 287n.13
Hervás [y Panduro], Lorenzo, 47–48
Herzog, Kristin, 295–96n.5
Hexter, J. H., 282n.13
Hidalgo, Miguel, 13, 37, 96–97, 102, 114,
  214, 249, 263, 272n.34, 279n.7, 284–
  85n.8
Hiner, N. Ray, 287n.1
L'Histoire philosophique, 126–27. *See also*
  Raynal, Guillaume Thomas
Historia de Amelia Booth, 66. *See also*
  Fielding, Henry
Historia de Carlo Magno y doce pares, La, 71

Kiell, Norman, 286n.1
Kierkegaard, Søren, 272n.38
King (of Spain), 2, 59, 86–87, 94–96, 110–11, 116, 123, 130–33, 137–38, 173, 209–10, 243, 245–47, 262; divine right, 279n.6; *Reyes Católicos*, 246. *See also names of individual kings*
Klopstock, Friedrich Gottlieb, 39, 276n.38
Knowledge, 134–35, 141, 156–57, 168, 188, 203, 228–29, 251–53, 259, 284n.7; *ciencias*, 143, 252. *See also* Ocular learning; Woman
Knowlton, Edgar C., Jr. 123–24, 283n.20

Laberinto de la Soledad, El, 257, 277n.43. *See also* Paz, Octavio
Labouret, Henri, 270n.11
Ladd, Doris, 271n.26, 287n.8
Ladinos, 17
Lafaye, Jacques, 290n
La Fontaine, Jean de, 139.20
Landívar, Rafael, 271n.27
Language, 15, 67–68, 125, 134, 181–82, 200–201, 250–55, 257, 266–67, 296n.6; Baroque, 48, 272n.37; bookish/literary, 56, 69, 227–28; Christian definition of, 91, 260; colonized, 6–8, 10–11, 57, 83–86, 91–93, 230–32, 248–49, 260, 265, 269n.2, 271nn.22, 29; connections with thought, 1, 3, 67–68, 111, 155, 222, 250–51, 259–60, 265–66, 296n.6; expressive of feeling, 1–2, 68, 155; familiar, 92; inner speech, 265–66; mark of humanness, 11, 84–85; norms of (*buen tono*), 34–35, 91; pedantic, 157; scientific, 48, 155–58; sign system, 35, 44, 259; topic for political debate, 34–35, 86; varieties of: African, 17–18, 41, 251; American, 35, 48, 181–82; Castilian, 16, 18, 34, 47, 79, 91, 122, 134, 136, 266; Filipino, 123; German, 68; Greek, 34; Indian (Nahuatl, Otomí), 16, 34, 41, 48, 53, 91, 154–55, 206, 251, 266, 273n.41; Italian, 54, 67–68; Latin, 34, 38, 76, 122, 113, 140–41, 268; Mexican, 34–35, 91; Oriental, 276–77n.39; Peninsular, 34–35, 91, 230. *See also* Catechism; *Diario de México*; Discourse; Education; Literature; Naming; Style

Lanning, John Tate, 285–86n.13, 289n.14, 293n.7
Lardizábal, Manuel de, 115, 123, 150–51. *See also Discurso sobre las penas; Fuero Juzgo*
Larousse, Pierre, 288n.16
Las Casas, Bartolomé de, 10, 102, 173, 271n.20, 279n.7, 287n.13. *See also Breve relación de la destrucción de las Indias*
Law, 84, 103–4, 108–9, 113, 115–19, 126, 130–33, 162, 169–70, 195, 209, 241, 243, 245, 248, 253, 263, 282n.9, 290n.2; impersonality of, 108; lawyers, 89, 113; natural law, 10, 86, 93, 102, 130–31, 136, 162, 195, 245. *See also Código de Indias*; Crime/punishment; *Escarmiento*; Lardizábal, Manuel de; Tradition
Lawrence, Karen R., 7
Lazarillo, 73, 295n.31
Lazarillo de ciegos caminantes (Carrió de la Vandera), 270n.9, 272n.33
Lazarus, Neil, 271n.30
Leal, Luis, 277n.43
Le Barbier, Jean-Jacques-François, 287n.13
Lecciones sobre la retórica y las bellas letras, 51, 69. *See also* Blair, Hugh; Munárriz, José Luis
Leibnitz, Gottfried Wilhelm von, 287–88n.14
Lemoyne, Pierre. *See Galería de mugeres fuertes*
Lenin, N. V., 270n.14
Lennox, Charlotte. *See Female Quijote, The*
Leonard, Irving A. 45
Leonidas, 149
León y Gama, Antonio, 274n.1
LeSage, Alain René, 67, 238, 278n.14. *See also Gil Blas*
Lessing, G. E., 63
Liberalism, 94, 106, 115, 230, 235, 279n.7, 284n.32
Liberty, 131, 158, 242, 252
Librepensamiento, 250. *See also* Philosophy
Linnaeus, 48
Liss, Peggy, 274n.1, 279n.6, 293n.11, 294nn.20, 21, 295n.29
Literacy, 11, 15, 20–21, 269n.8
Literature, 23, 45, 56–57, 69, 147, 149–51,

Pamphlets—*continued*
It May Embitter), 53; "La verdad.
Cuento de la India" (Truth. The Account
of the Indian Woman), 52; "La verdad
triunfa de la superchería" (Truth
Triumphs Over Deceit), 52; "La verdadera
libertad, felicidad é independencia de las
naciones" (The True Liberty, Happiness
and Independence of Nations), 52;
"Verdadero patriotismo" (True Patriotism), 52; "Viaje de Fr. Gerundio a la
Nueva España" (Fray Gerundio's Trip to
New Spain), 48; "La visita de Chana á
Pepa" (The Visit of Chana to Pepa),
296n.12; "Voz imperiosa de la verdad y
desengaños políticos contra preocu-
paciones vulgares" (The Imperious Voice
of Truth), 52; "Ya no dá leche la vaca
¿qué tetas mamará el leon? (The cow no
longer gives milk. From what teats will
the lion nurse?) 207–8. *See also* Fernández
de Lizardi, José Joaquín—pamphlets of
Parker, A. A., 141, 238, 286n.16
Parkes, Henry Bamford, 112, 269n.1
Parnaso español 55
Passion, 116, 131, 135, 148, 167–68, 172,
175, 221, 261. *See also* Sexuality
Paternalism, 25, 86–88, 97–99, 132–33, 173,
264–65, 268, 289n.9
Patria, 12, 21, 34, 52, 98, 101, 110–13, 135,
149, 171, 173, 262–63, 266–67, 284n.32;
madre patria, 87–88, 171–72, 201
Patriotism, 12, 60, 86–87, 112,173, 262,
296n.16
Pawlowski, John, 106, 292n.2
Payo/paya, 35, 155, 196, 205, 207, 224. *See
also Quijotita, La*, Pascual
Paz, Octavio, 266. *See also Laberinto de la
soledad, El*
Pêcheux, Michel, 17, 272n.32, 294n.27
Peers, E. Allison, 216
Pelado (type), 23–24
Peña, Margarita, 193, 290n.19
People, 22, 50–52, 57, 130–32, 175, 225,
277n.42
Pérez Blanco, Lucrecio, 270n.9
Pérez de Hita, Ginés. *See Guerras civiles de
Granada*

Pérez Marchand, Monalisa Lina, 45, 277–
78n.10
Periquillo Sarniento, El (Lizardi), 25, 36, 46,
59, 102, 125, 187, 235–36, 240, 260,
264, 274n.53, 278n.14, 18, 279n.4,
281n.22, 7, 281–82n.8, 282n.9, 12, 17,
284n.32, 285n.10, 11, 286nn.15, 23, 25,
287n.10, 292n.2, 293n.10, 296n.9;
comparison with *Don Quijote*, 75–76;
design of, 57, 70–79, 93, 138, 145, 151–
59, 174, 177, 180–81, 226, 237; language
as topic in, 83–85, 91–92; publication,
4–6, 21–22, 33, 46, 70–71, 74, 102, 273–
74n.49, 279–80n.8; reception, 5, 21–24,
36, 71, 105–6, 133, 176–77, 182–83,
191, 232, 274nn.51, 53; style, 24, 71,
74–78, 86, 91, 181–84, 224, 226, 260;
textual digressions, 83–84, 175–84, 237;
title, 74–75, 83–84, 144, 279n.4. *See also*
Adolescence; Digressions; Education;
Jauja; Language; Picaresque; Satire;
Utopia; Voice
Perucho, nieto de Periquillo, 273–74n.49
Pestalozzi, Johann Henrich, 287–88n.14
Philippines, 99, 103, 108, 113, 120, 123–25,
127, 281n.4, 283n.20
Phillips, Rachel, 277n.43
Philosophy, 232, 236, 255; classical, 240;
modern, 90, 130, 247. *See also* Deism;
Eclecticism; Empiricism; Enlightenment;
Humanism; Idealism; Liberalism;
Machiavellianism; Materialism;
Sensationalism; Stoicism
Piana, Francesca, 286n.17
Picaresque, 89, 151–52, 176, 204; delin-
quency, 141, 151, 236, 293n.6; literary
tradition, 73–73, 89, 99, 140–41, 205,
238–39, 243, 274n.53, 278n.14, 286n.16,
292n.2, 293n.5; Mexican *picardía*, 89, 99,
112–13, 141–44, 167, 169, 173, 182, 204,
213, 231–32, 236–38, 243–44, 250–51,
254–55, 258–59. *See also* Satire
Plato, 111, 114, 147–48, 275n.9
Plautus, 282n.9
Pliny, 77
Pocock, J.G.A. *See Machiavellian Moment,
The*
Poetry, 7, 12, 15, 60, 65, 67, 70, 123, 200,

Revillagigedo, Conde de, 171
Revolution (of 1910), 23, 273–74n.49,
    293n.13
Reyes, Alfonso, 21–23, 182, 274n.50
Richardson, Samuel, 64–65. *See also Clara
    Harlowe; Historia del caballero Carlos
    Grandison; Pamela Andrews ó La virtud
    premiada*
Ripalda, Jerónimo, 220–22, 258, 295n.2
Robespierre, M.F.M. de, 238
Robinson Crusoe, 66, 277n.9. *See also* Defoe,
    Daniel; *El nuevo Robinson*
Roche, Regina-Maria. *See Oscar y Amanda*
Rodríguez Freile, Juan. *See Carnero, El*
Rodríguez O., Jaime, 269n.5, 296–97n.20
Romanticism, 216, 225, 231, 271n.23,
    292n.11
Rousseau, Jean-Jacques, 66, 128, 139, 190,
    238, 284n.4, 285–86n.13. *See also
    Discourse on the Arts and Sciences; Emile;
    On the Origin of Languages*
Ruffinelli, Jorge, 7
Ruíz Castañeda, María del Carmen, 288n.1,
    288–89n.5, 289–90n.16

Saavedra Fajardo, Diego de, 111
Said, Edward W., 7, 270n.13, 272n.36
Saint-Pierre, Bernardin de. *See Pablo y
    Virginia*
Salomon, Noël, 24
Samaniego, Félix María de, 139
Sánchez, Luis Alberto, 270n.10, 281n.1,
    286n.23, 291n.8
Santos, Francisco (?), 73
Santos Capuano, José and Santiago de. *See
    Zumbas*
Sarna, 83, 278n.1
Sartre, Jean-Paul, 270n.11
Sastre, Alfonso, 293n.5
Satire, 15, 32, 44, 93, 151, 261, 278n.16;
    Lizardi's use of, 5, 64, 71–74, 179, 204–5,
    225, 239–40
Saussure, Ferdinand de, 5, 212
Schneider, Luis Mario, 25
Scholasticism, 39, 94, 240
Sebold, Russell, 292n.12
Second Treatise of Government, 173. *See also*
    Locke, John

Secularization, 19, 25, 101, 135, 177, 203,
    213, 219, 256, 267–68
Seed, Patricia, 289n.15, 297n.22
Sefchovich, Sara, 265, 293n.13
Self, 3–6, 8, 11, 25, 63–64, 86–86, 103, 127–
    30, 136, 140, 160–62, 167, 188, 271n.22,
    272n.38; personal happiness, 114;
    relationship to society, 101–2, 114, 143,
    174–75. *See also Egoísmo;* Other
Sensationalism, 135, 177–78, 288n.X16X.
    See also Philosophy
Sentiment, 4, 105, 116, 188–89, 200–201,
    231; feelings, 1–2, 11, 165; *sanguinarios
    sentimientos* (revenge), 174; suffering, 1, 3,
    117, 142, 150, 233. *See also* Emotion;
    Passion; Sexuality
Seriman, Count Zaccharia. *See Viajes de
    Enrique Wanton*
Servilismo, 220, 250, 253
Sexuality, 134, 163, 165, 167–72, 188;
    effeminacy, 65, 89, 170–71. *See also*
    Emotion; Passion; Sentiment
Shafer, Robert J., 240
Shohat, Ella, 20
Sieber, Harry, 295n.31
Siete partidas, 123
Siglo de Oro (Golden Age), 55, 73, 89,
    282n.19
Sigüenza y Góngora, Carlos, 57, 270n.9,
    271n. 27, 281n.1, 293n.9. *See also
    Infortunios de Alonso Ramírez*
Silva Gotay, Samuel, 7, 295n.32
Sims, Harold, 270n.11, 292n.17, 296–
    97n.20
Siting, 8
Slavery, 1, 3, 102–7, 114, 126, 251, 281n.21
Smith, Neil, 270n.17
Smith, Sidonie, 7
Social contract, 105–6
Socrates, 147, 149, 222
Solanas, Fernando E., 7
Soledades de la vida, 71.
Solís, Antonio de, 55
Solís y Valenzuela, Pedro de. *See Desierto
    prodigioso y prodigio del desierto, El*
Sommer, Doris, 296–97n.20
Sonship, 2, 86–93, 175, 264; attitudes
    toward parents, 89–90

Sovereignty, 37, 131–32, 294n.26
Spacks, Patricia Meyer, 286n.1
Spain, 1, 46, 86–87, 91–92, 96–97, 116,
  119–20, 122, 129, 137, 174, 209, 221,
  236, 239, 262, 279n.7; literary tradition,
  51, 54–55, 68–69, 71, 74–75, 84, 122–24,
  139, 214–16, 292n.17. *See also* Colonial-
  ism; King (of Spain)
Speech-act, 15, 40, 57; theory, 272n.35
Spell, Jefferson Rea, 24, 31, 70, 122, 127,
  138–40, 176, 187, 215, 225–26, 232–34,
  246, 274nn.2, 3, 274–75n.6, 275n.7, 285–
  86n.13, 286n.23, 290–91n.4, 291n.9
Spivak, Gayatri, 271n.21
Staël, Madame de. *See Corinne;* "De la
  littérature"
Stafford, Barbara Maria, 286n.20
Staples, Anne, 297n.21
Sterne, Laurence, 64
Stoetzer, O. Carlos, 94, 102, 293n.7,
  294n.20
Stoicism, 282n.18. *See also* Philosophy
Stolley, Karen, 274n.53
Storia antica del Messico, 129. *See also*
  Clavijero Francisco Javier
Stubbs, Michael, 9
Sturm, H.S.S. *See Reflexiones sobre la
  naturaleza*
Style (literary), 35, 47, 56–57, 68–70, 76–78,
  182–83, 215; *casero,* 77, 181; diffuse, 182;
  elevated, 24, 77–78, 224–25, 227–28;
  emotional, 228, 231–32; light, 38–39;
  low, 24, 77–78, 181, 183; mixed, 24, 77,
  181, 260; philosophical, 48; plain, 24, 74,
  77–78; strained, 225–26. *See also* Baroque;
  *Don Catrín; Noches tristes; Periquillo;
  Quijotita, La*
Suárez, Francisco, 115, 245, 279n.6
Sueño alegórico por la mexicana (Nava), 190–01
Surtz, Edward, 282n.13
Swift, Jonathan. *See Gulliver's Travels*

Tacitus, 77
Taléns, Jenaro, 293n.6
Tanck de Estrada, Dorothy, 78, 278n.19
Taylor, Patrick, 272n.38
Taylor, William, 280n.20, 282n.11, 293–
  94n.16

Tellability, 40
Téllez Guerrero, Francisco, 276n.33
Tena Ramírez, Felipe, 282n.18
Terán, Manuel (Ranet), 71, 75–79, 182,
  278n.18
Terdiman, Richard, 13
Theology, 124–25, 141–42, 232, 240,
  282n.18; liberation, 7, 222, 295n.32;
  theologians, 113
Thomas Aquinas, Saint, 111, 285–86n.13
Tlaxcala, 61
Tobacco, 201–2
Tolsá, Manuel, 59
Tomás, Santo (Saint Thomas), 209
Tom Jones, 54. *See also* Fielding, Henry
Torquemada, Tomás de, 62
Torres-Ríoseco, Arturo, 291n.6
Torres Villarroel, Diego de, 22, 47, 73, 292–
  93n.4
Tradition, 118, 131, 136–37, 209, 240,
  284n.7, 284–85n.8
Translation, 17, 53–56, 65–70, 176–77,
  270n.17, 295n.3
Trilling, Lionel, 176–77, 181
Truth, 39–40, 52–54, 61–62, 88, 90, 136,
  148–49, 155, 177, 194, 240, 257, 259;
  Christian, 148; dispersal, 53 as invented
  error, 50–51. *See also* Debate; *Desengaño;*
  Realism, Verisimilitude; Scholasticism;
  Theology
Turner, Victor, 263, 272n.34
Tutún, 113, 116–17, 119–20, 127–28, 133,
  150. *See also* China
Tutino, John, 282n.11
Tyranny, 4, 103, 106, 133, 204, 246, 248–49,
  256

Urquhart, Brian, 274n.54
Utilitarianism, 104, 115, 164, 239, 248. *See
  also* Philosophy
Utopia, 109–23, 143, 150, 282n.13. *See also*
  Jauja; Quiroga, Vasco de

Valdés, Alejandro, 46
Valerio Maximo, 287n.13
Van Young, Eric, 94, 282n.11
Vargas Martínez, Ubaldo, 25
Vaughan, Alden T., 270n.16

Nancy Vogeley is professor emerita of Spanish at the University of San Francisco. Among her studies of early nineteenth-century Mexico is *La literatura manuscrita: Un manuscrito inédito de poesías de José Joaquín Fernández de Lizardi* (forthcoming).